ETHICS IN THE PUBLIC DOMAIN

ETHICS IN THE PUBLIC DOMAIN

Essays in the Morality of Law and Politics

JOSEPH RAZ

CLARENDON PRESS · OXFORD

Oxford University Press, Walton Street, Oxford OX2 6DP
Oxford New York
Athens Auckland Bangkok Bombay
Calcutta Cape Town Dar es Salaam Delhi
Florence Hong Kong Istanbul Karachi
Kuala Lumpur Madras Madrid Melbourne
Mexico City Nairobi Paris Singapore
Taipei Tokyo Toronto
and associated companies in
Berlin Ibadan

Oxford is a trade mark of Oxford University Press

Published in the United States
by Oxford University Press Inc., New York

First published 1994
First issued in paperback 1995

British Library Cataloguing in Publication Data
Data available

Library of Congress Cataloging in Publication Data
Raz, Joseph.
Ethics in the public domain : essays in the morality of law and
politics / Joseph Raz.
p. cm.
Includes index.
1. Political ethics. 2. Law and ethics. I. Title.
JA79.R39 1994 340'.112—dc20 93–42442
ISBN 0–19–825837–2
ISBN 0–19–826069–5 (Pbk)

Printed in Great Britain
on acid-free paper by
Biddles Ltd., Guildford and Kings Lynn

PREFACE

One is forever searching for understanding, and the further one travels the further off the goal appears. Most of the essays collected in this book were started with the intention to use them to illustrate the application to one or another political or jurisprudential problem of general views about morality and the law which I have argued for elsewhere. More often than not, in the course of writing I realized that the problems I was addressing gave rise to difficulties that I did not anticipate, and that I had not directly addressed before. Luckily (or was it a delusion?) I felt that the general approach I have been pursuing in previous writings was also suitable for dealing with these, to me new, difficulties. The result is—I hope—that the general position I espoused is enriched and strengthened by these new reflections.

I called the first part of the book 'The Ethics of Well-Being: Political Implications' to indicate that it follows the approach, endorsed by many writers on moral and political theory and adopted by me in *The Morality of Freedom*, according to which political morality is concerned primarily with protecting and promoting the well-being of people. The present volume continues (in essays 3–5) the attempt to defend this approach against some opposing arguments which restrict politics by imposing constraints of so-called 'neutrality among competing conceptions of the good', or which regard rights as constraints on political action whose force derives from considerations which are unrelated to individual well-being. But the emphasis of the book is constructive, rather than polemical. The opening essay explores the notion of well-being and the ways in which one's well-being can and cannot be served by others. The paperback reprint of the book includes an additional essay: "Liberating Duties", previously intended for use in a different—now abandoned—project. This complements the essays immediately preceding and following it in exploring the notion of individual well-being and the relations that has to rights and especially to duties. These essays prepare the ground for the exploration of two important aspects of well-being: the importance of membership in groups—the role of belonging in well-being—and the implication of the active character of well-being, of the fact that it largely consists in successful activities. Both aspects of well-being have far-reaching political implications.

The active aspect of well-being raises vital questions for policies designed to promote people's welfare. If people's well-being can only be achieved through their own activities, what can others do for them? Should people be left to their fate, to prove themselves by overcoming whatever difficulties it throws in their way? If we say that people's lives should be neither devoid of challenges nor full of awesome challenges, are we guided by any principled understanding of a *via media*, or merely by a wishy-washy desire to compromise? Or perhaps by a desire to have it both ways? The issue of belonging is of vital importance to questions of the limits of toleration, and to our attitudes to diversity and pluralism.

For me the essays of the first part have another crucial implication, which is never openly addressed in it. As I indicated, they explored some aspects of well-being and of its moral and political implications on the assumption that the promotion and protection of well-being is the central task of political action. The more I pursued the implications of this assumption the more I came to doubt whether well-being can play the central role in ethics sometimes assigned to it. It still seems to me that the promotion of well-being is the pivotal ethical precept of public action. But ethics in the wider sense cannot be accounted for in terms of concern for well-being alone. These doubts hover in the background in this book. It is, however, a background which I find full of puzzling issues leading beyond the concerns here discussed.

Another theme which underlies much of the discussion, but emerges into the open only in essays 5 and 14, is doubt about the ability of philosophy, or theory in some wider sense, to provide determinate answers to the questions we face in politics. In doubting whether any theory of justice can provide concrete guidance in the solution of all the problems which arise in politics I am not advocating a retreat from rational debate, or from political theory. But I believe that those often run out at the hardest stage, when we are faced with alternative decisions of which all are reasonable and none is supported by decisive or overriding considerations. In many cases substantive reasons and the theory of justice can rule out some wild non-starters, but can reach no further than establishing which of the possible decisions are reasonable. This conclusion raises a wealth of questions which are only lightly touched upon in this volume.

The essays of the second part contain some of the elements of an account of the nature of law. Essay 9 sets the scene, by sketching the view that law is best understood against a background of a political society which goes through various processes from public debate and factional pressures to concrete actions and decisions which are represented as authoritatively binding on that society. The law is simply the standards which reached a certain stage of maturation and endorsement in this process. This—or so I argue—is our own self-understanding of the law. Or rather, it is an account of it which fastens on the most significant and illuminating elements in our self-understanding and purges it of incoherences, and other extraneous elements.

The other essays in this part articulate some of the consequences of that understanding of the nature of law. Not surprisingly, the central concern is the relation between law and morality. Like other recent writers on jurisprudence, I try to steer clear of the all-or-nothing approach which characterized much of the debate of previous generations. There are inherent connections between legal concepts and moral concepts, and between law and morality. The question is what are they. Perhaps two of the themes examined in the book should be singled out for special mention. First, in essay 10 I offer an argument for the view that the content of the law is capable of being identified by reference to social facts only. The argument is not conclusive, and the issue requires further consideration. But it is to my mind an argument of crucial importance which has been ignored by both supporters and opponents of the thesis about the social identification of the law. The second theme is an attempt to explain the dynamic aspect of law. Those who regard the law as identifiable on the basis of social facts tend to view it as a set of standards for the guidance of conduct. There is no doubt that the law contains such standards, and in a way it can be said to consist of such standards. But the law also 'regulates its own creation', to use Kelsen's expression. This is often understood—as it was by Kelsen himself—to mean that the law endows people and institutions with powers to make new laws. Again, there is no doubt that the law does that. But it does more. It often sets objectives that future legislation should achieve, objectives which regulate not the procedure of law-making but its content. How can an existing law determine the content of a future law? This problem has been relatively neglected in the jurisprudential writings in English. I try to answer the question in essays 11 and 12 below.

The arguments of the book are tentative and incomplete. But I hope that they help clarify the nature of and the reasons for views which have often been misunderstood by supporters and opponents alike.

J. R.

Balliol College
Oxford
January 1994

CONTENTS

ABBREVIATIONS

The following books by Joseph Raz will be cited by title only:

The Authority of Law: Essays on Law and Morality (Oxford: Oxford University Press, 1979)
The Concept of a Legal System, 2nd edn. (Oxford: Oxford University Press, 1980)
The Morality of Freedom (Oxford: Clarendon Press, 1986)
Practical Reason and Norms (London: Hutchinson, 1979; 2nd edn., 1990)

PART I
THE ETHICS OF WELL-BEING
POLITICAL IMPLICATIONS

1

Duties of Well-Being

In this essay I explore some of the implications for the moral duties people owe each other of the fact that well-being has a strong active aspect. Part, but only part, of morality concerns duties to protect and promote the well-being of people. That is the only aspect of morality touched upon here. The discussion proceeds on the assumption that we all owe a duty to protect and promote the well-being of all people. You may say that it explores the nature of that duty on the assumption that morality, or at least this part of it, is universalist and agent-neutral. The conclusions reached do, however, apply—with obvious modifications—even if moral duties regarding people's well-being are not impartial, and if they are agent-relative.

The first section will outline the main ways in which well-being has an active aspect. Its aim is not to justify this view of well-being, but merely to sketch it as a basis for the discussion in the following sections concerning the duties of well-being we owe each other, that is, the duties to protect and promote people's well-being.

I. ASPECTS OF WELL-BEING

Well-being and personality or character are the two most basic (and deeply inter-connected) dimensions by which people understand and judge themselves and others. How good or successful we are depends on who we are (character) and what sort of life we have (well-being). Evaluation of people's well-being involves judgments about their lives, or periods of their lives, and the degree to which they do or did do well, were good or successful. In large measure our well-being consists in the (1) whole-hearted and (2) successful pursuit of (3) valuable (4) activities.[1] To flesh out this way of understanding well-being in two stages I will first sketch the basic idea, and then take up a couple of the many possible objections to it.

To start from the end: the definition of well-being sees life as active. While being alive does not literally imply activity, we recognize non-active life as vegetative. 'X is very much alive' cannot be said of the comatose; it implies being 'alive and kicking'. So the concentration on activity is meant to flow from the very notion of a life.[2] For this to be true of the relation

---

[1] This issue is discussed in some detail in *The Morality of Freedom*.

[2] I am not suggesting that this concept is scientific rather than normative and culturally dependent. I am only saying that it is the one we have from which we cannot escape. The concept of life which forms our self-consciousness is that of activity.

between life and activity, the latter notion has to be broadly construed. The definition of well-being as successful activity is no endorsement of a hyperactive conception of the good life, consisting of perpetual jogging, climbing, eating, making love, or winning tennis competitions. Activity is to be understood to include the pursuit of a career in medicine, the pursuit of a hobby like chess, attending to one's relations with friends, institutions, or communities, living as befits one's station in life (even if this consists largely in doing very little), relaxing in front of the television, and the like. Activity here is contrasted with passivity, and includes inaction motivated by attitudes and goals which one holds to, as in Christian retreats or Buddhist meditation. The core idea is controlling one's conduct, being in charge.

The definition of well-being itself, while it insists that activity is the key to well-being, does not discriminate between comprehensive activities, i.e. those which encompass many aspects of one's life for long stretches of time (a career in architecture, or parenting) and short-term activities (a holiday in Venice, watching a Louis Malle film). A good life need not be integrated through one or a small number of dominating goals. It can be episodic and varied. However, the nature of comprehensive activities means that their success and the success of activities which are undertaken as part of them are interdependent. Activities with an instrumental value differ from those with an independent intrinsic one. An activity undertaken for its intrinsic value, such as a casual tennis game, can have elements which are independently intrinsically rewarding, e.g., the sense of well-being in physical exercise, or the skillful execution of a particular stroke. Those same elements, and others which are not independently valuable, can also derive value from their contribution to making the game as a whole a good game, assessed by the intrinsic standard of tennis games, but the value of the game as a whole depends of course on its constitution, on its parts even if they are not independently valuable. Things are simpler with instrumentally valuable activities. The instrumental purpose determines whether the comprehensive activity or its component activities set the standard for success. In part (a large part) success as a doctor is success in treating one's patients, and nursing them back to health. To this extent success as a doctor is a function of success—independently defined—in treating patients. On the other hand, treating a patient (an activity which may last a long time) is an activity each element of which is successful if it contributes to the success of the activity, the treatment, as a whole. Here, success in the larger activity is independently defined, and success in its component activities follows from it. Success in such activities often acquires additional intrinsic value for the life of the agent, the value of which derives from doing well something which is (instrumentally or intrinsically) valuable.

Only valuable activities contribute to our well-being. A life is not a good life for being spent in petty vindictive pursuits, or in self-debasing ones, etc. These make it a lousy, despicable, pitiable life—not a good one. Though they are included under this element of the definition, one need not think primarily of moral highs and lows—of the life of the villain or of the moral hero or saint—nor should one think primarily of great creative talents or, on the other hand, the great debasers of culture. For most people the valuable and that which is devoid of value take more ordinary forms of insensitivity to the feelings of one's loved ones, neglect, and many forms of blinkered obsession. Contrasted with those are the ordinary cases of valuable activities which may be devotion to one's family, conscientious performance of a job, good neighbourliness, weekends spent bird-watching, volunteer work for social or political causes, etc. The value of activities—in which the value of the manner of their pursuit is included—is not exclusively their moral value. Nor is it value which can be judged or elucidated independently of an understanding of the good life, which reveals what forms of life are valuable and what activities contribute to them. Yet again, there is here an interdependence of different elements of the picture: the goodness of a life depends on the value of the activities it comprises, and their value is revealed through understanding what a good life consists of.

Needless to say, failure detracts from and success adds to one's well-being. A person who has set his heart on being a painter, and turns out to be a lousy one has, other things being equal, a lousy life. In this case, perhaps his failure may be due to lack of talent. In others it will be attributable to lack of judgment, mismanaging one's career, weakness of resolve, and other failings of character or action, or to bad luck, which in this context encompasses all factors beyond one's control. A failed speculator or politician may have never put a foot wrong; nevertheless his failure casts a deep shadow on his life. A promising academic may find that a budgetary crisis in the universities forces him out of his chosen career, a blow to his life from which, depending on age and circumstances, it may be impossible for him to recover. Many questions arise as to what counts as success in the present context. Does the fact that a brilliant plan by an architect was abandoned for lack of finance mean that he failed? Or is it the failure of whoever commissioned the plan? All these and others have to remain unexplored here.

Finally, to contribute to one's well-being one's engagement in one's activities has to be whole-hearted. Many activities require certain attitudes, commitment, pure motives, etc., for successful engagement in them. But not all do. All or most allow various forms of estrangement and alienation consistent with success. A brilliant chess-player may hate himself for being a chess-player, or may just hate playing chess. A good and dedicated teacher may hold himself in low esteem for being a teacher. The condition of whole-hearted engagement with one's life is meant to exclude self-hatred, pathological self-doubt, and alienation from one's life as they undermine well-being. It is not meant to exclude rational self-examination, and the attitudes which go with it.

The wholehearted requirement provides the main subjective element in this account of well-being. Some subjective accounts insist on a condition of transparency: they hold that a person cannot have a good life unless he is aware of the fact that he has a good life.[3] Some (relatively extreme) subjectivists would insist that the transparency condition is both necessary and sufficient. The view that the good life consists of the successful pursuit of worthwhile activities rejects both versions of the transparency condition. It is an objectivist account of well-being, but it includes a strong subjectivist component. A life can prosper only through the successful pursuit of activities, and these must be prosecuted willingly, and with the spirit suitable to the activity.[4]

The condition of whole-hearted pursuit presupposes that even where the activity, commitment, or relationship is not one which the agent chose, or could abandon by choice, he is in control of the manner of his engagement in it. He has to direct his conduct in the light of his objectives and commitments, to guide himself towards his goal. Given this, the question can always arise whether the agent is pursuing whatever activity he is engaged in willingly or unwillingly, whole-heartedly or half-heartedly, resentfully or not. But one should not be misled by the parallelism of positive and negative phrases here. In the main, the notions involved are negative; they exclude resentment, pathological self-doubt, lack of self-esteem, self-hate, etc. One is acting whole-heartedly if one is not prey to one of these attitudes. Nothing else is required: no reflective endorsement of one's activity, no second-order desire to continue with it, etc. Such endorsement and desires sometimes exist, and where it is appropriate, or even required, that one should be reflective about one's activities they are important. But there is no general need to be reflective, and in some matters reflection can be inappropriate. The fact that certain alternatives never cross one's mind may be a condition of having an appropriate attitude to people or activities.[5]

---

[3] Notice that this is weaker than insisting that he must be content or happy with his life. A person may think that he had a good life while feeling unhappy or discontented on the ground, e.g., that he does not deserve his good fortune, that he should have dedicated his life to a moral cause, even though this would have brought much suffering to him. Some people think that such discontent undermines the view that the person had a good life. One cannot believe that one has had a good life if one is discontented with it. I see no reason to accept this position. Similarly a person may believe that he had a good life, even though it was full of suffering, if, for example, he thinks that his life was well spent in the steadfast pursuit of a valuable goal.

[4] With some activities, engaging in them in the spirit they require for success includes enjoying the activity while it lasts. But this is not always the case. On the other, objective, hand, they all tend to include welcoming events which do not originate with the agent (gifts, affection bestowed by friends, etc.). Success may be foiled not only by failure of one's own action but also by the absence of appropriate response from others.

[5] These remarks may contradict the understanding of identification with one's actions and tastes powerfully, and influentially, argued for by H. Frankfurt (see e.g., chs. 5, 7, and 12 of *The Importance of What We Care About* (Cambridge: Cambridge Univ. Press, 1988)). Another

Does this account ignore the value of passive pleasures, such as lying on the beach in the sun? It does not, for a reason which is often overlooked. Not all pleasures contribute to one's well-being. The thought that they do is a result of a belief that, if pleasures are intrinsically good, valuable, *qua* pleasures, then they must contribute, however minutely, to one's well-being. In its simplest form this reflects a simple aggregative view of well-being, made popular by crude versions of utilitarianism. More sophisticated versions will avoid simple aggregation, but will insist that anything good which happens to a person must contribute to that person's well-being. I doubt that that is so. I stretch myself on the beach and enjoy the warmth of the sun, I see a pretty rose, and enjoy the sight. My life is not better or more successful as a result. It is different if I am a beach bum, or a rose-grower (or just a rose- or flower-lover). But in that case the passive pleasure fits in with my activities, I am the sort of person who will make sure that there is room in his life for these pleasures. In that case the occasional pleasure contributes (if it does) to my well-being because it contributes (a tiny bit) towards the success of activities I am set upon. If I have no interest in sun on the beach or in flowers, these pleasures, while being real enough and while being valuable as pleasures, do not contribute to my well-being. They have no bearing on my life as a whole.[6] But is not the smell of a rose the same for a flower lover and for one who takes pleasure in it but is not a flower lover? It is and it is not. The olfactory bodily sensation which is pleasurable is the same, but the pleasure is different for it has a meaning in the life of the flower lover which differs from its meaning in the life of the one who is not. That difference makes it reasonable to regard the pleasure as active in one case and passive in the other. It is active where it meshes with one's general orientation in life.

We need, I am suggesting, a way of relating pleasurable episodes to life as a whole, or else, good as they are, they do not affect people's well-being, which is a matter of how they fared in their life as a whole. Not everything which happens in the course of one's life, not even every good thing,[7] is relevantly connected to how one's life goes. I am not sure how the required connection should be stated. It is reasonable to suppose that the connection obtains if an event temporally dominates one's life, as in the case of a chronic and painful illness. Another connection is when an episode fits in

---

respect in which the above seems at odds with his view is that I am not assuming that whole-heartedness has one manifestation, say in the form of a second-order desire to have certain tastes or projects. Resentment, self-hate, pathological self-doubt are all different psychological phenomena, any one of which negates whole-heartedness. Moreover, there is no finite and informative list of such phenomena. More can emerge with the development of human pathology.

[6] This does not betray my refusal to endorse the superior value of comprehensive activities as such.

[7] Or bad. I continue to refer exclusively to goods only for reasons of convenient exposition.

with a larger activity which does have a dominant role in one's life. The remarks above assume that that is the normal connection. If so, episodes of passive pleasures normally matter only if they fit in with one's active concerns and plans.[8]

Do we not need certain things—food, warmth, health, absence of pain, etc.—for our survival and physical comfort, and is not the provision of those goods a contribution to our well-being independent of its contribution to any activity we engage in? I think not. The provision of the goods necessary for survival and physical comfort is good instrumentally, in that their absence has a disabling effect. In extremes it makes valuable activities impossible altogether, leaving the possibility of vegetative existence only. In less extreme cases it merely restricts the range of activities one is capable of, perhaps forcing the struggle against one's illness or pain to be one of one's dominant activities. For these reasons these goods are instrumentally invaluable. But are they intrinsically valuable? The answer seems to depend on whether there is value in vegetative existence. I believe that there is none.

Are there any requirements regarding the range, nature, and distribution of the activities which constitute people's lives, beyond the requirement that they be valuable? Should they tax the potential of the person to the limit? Should they balance between the physical, imaginative, and intellectual aspects of life? As will emerge in the sequel, we need not debate these matters here, as they do not affect the argument of this essay. One important point they remind us of: there are more valuable activities than any person can engage in in a lifetime. This means that very often a person can and must choose which of a range of valuable activities to engage in, and that a part of people's life is devoted to such choices, and the preparations for them. People learn what some of the options are, and what they really amount to, and how to choose between them. It also means that sometimes, if people are frustrated in their activities, they can change and try something else. We put it down to experience, we say as we turn our back on our failures, and try again somewhere else. The boundaries between learning experiences and failures are not sharp ones.

II. DUTIES OF WELL-BEING: THREE BASIC FACTS

One obvious consequence of the fact that well-being consists to a considerable degree of successful activities is that no one can make a success of another person's life. Our duty to protect and promote the well-being of all

---

[8] Though some exceptions to my statement of the connection between episodes and a life as a whole come readily to mind: consider dissipation through frequently succumbing to episodic pleasures and neglecting what one really cares about. On the other hand, what was said in the text about passive pleasures may be true of some cases of sporadic active pleasure.

people falls short of a duty to make them flourish, to make their life a success. The discharge of this task is logically impossible, and I take it that, even though we are subject to duties we are unable to discharge, it makes no sense to suppose that we are subject to duties which it is logically impossible to discharge.

People's well-being is—ultimately—up to them and to them alone. Nobody can take over their life and make it prosper for them. No one but I can make me a good teacher, a good parent or friend. To me there is a great comfort in this fact. In practice it may not mean much. Every moral theory, even those which do not concur with this view of well-being, will find some reason why in practice we should not do more than (broadly speaking) facilitate the well-being of people. People, they will say, are the best judges of what is best for them. Trying to interfere too closely in their lives is not an efficient way of using one's efforts; it is too labour-intensive. If we concentrate instead on raising people's standards of living, we will be able to do more to promote their well-being than if we dedicate our efforts to making them prosper in more intimate aspects of their lives, etc. All this is wrong-headed—not because such considerations do not have a role, but because they are allowed to disguise the essential fact. At bottom, the question is not one of economy of effort or conflict of duties. It is one of the basic nature of well-being, and the impossibility of one person making another person prosper.

Nor is this basic fact without moral consequences, as its logical nature may suggest. While it is logically impossible to make other people's lives go well, it is possible to try to do so, and such attempts are often disastrous. If the attempt is thorough it is liable to stifle and destroy the victim's chances of having a good life. There are easier ways in which we can spoil other people's chances of having a good life, or even eliminate all such possibilities. We can kill, maim, torture, disable people, or render them unemployed, terrorized, or intimidated for life, to mention but few of the many ways of harming people's well-being, sometimes irreparably. The plain fact is that in principle our ability to harm others is more far-reaching than our ability to help them. I say 'in principle' for, as a matter of fact, it may be easier to help than to hinder. It may, for example, be easier to behave in a courteous manner to a neighbour than to be discourteous. For well-mannered people it is no more than doing what comes naturally. But in principle it is possible to render a good life impossible for another person, while it is impossible to make it inevitable.

I do not know whether this asymmetry contributes to the appeal of the belief that our duties of well-being are confined to not harming other people's chances of a good life. But if it does, it is a flawed reason for that belief. If the question is of our ability to protect and promote people's well-being, then its scope is enormous and far-reaching. We can do more than protect people against harm to their prospects of a good life by other people—which can be regarded as part of the 'do not harm' attitude to the duties of well-being—and by nature—which clearly transcends the scope of the 'no harm' duty. We can also promote people's chances of a good life not only by helping them acquire the skills they need and develop the motivation and the strength of will which will stand them in good stead (all of which we regularly do, and not only with regard to children) but also by providing them with the material resources, and with the natural, social, cultural and economic environments, which facilitate a good life.

It is difficult to articulate a boundary to one person's ability to promote the well-being of another. One may say: 'People's actions can be an intrinsic contribution to the quality of their own lives but can only contribute instrumentally to the quality of other's lives.' This is not so. The fact that others act with one or hire one to act in the theatre is constitutive of an actor's career. Without at least occasional collaboration with other actors, with directors and producers, one is not an actor. To the extent that one's well-being consists in being a successful actor, others contribute to it intrinsically. Such contributions can reach to the very heart of one's being. Being loved by another person can be as significant a contribution to one's well-being as anything one can do for oneself. Perhaps there is little one can say other than that others cannot do for one what one must do for oneself. That little must in any case include three basic facts. First, that if one is to have a good life there are some activities—and I do not mean some specific ones—that one must engage in oneself. Second, that other people can contribute to one's well-being intrinsically only if they fit into one's life in the right way, for example, by reciprocating one's love. One way or another, the love has to mesh with and to contribute to people's hopes, goals, relationships, and commitments. And those hopes, goals, commitments, and relationships are those which one develops, endorses, or otherwise generates oneself. By doing so one determines how others can, and how they cannot, advance one's well-being. Third, that while one may conceivably prosper without deliberate help from others, i.e. without people doing anything with the purpose of advancing or protecting one's well-being, one cannot prosper without others. It is not merely that companionship and friendship are among the most important goods one can realise in one's life, but that all the others, careers, leisure activities, cultural interests, and the rest, are the products of people interacting with each other, against the background of existing social practices, ever in a state of flux.

III. A LIMIT ON DUTY

People's well-being depends not only on themselves (to repeat the truism); it requires that conditions which make their activities possible, and give them their meaning, obtain. The question arises of how far the duties of well-being reach. I said that they are duties to protect and promote the well-being of all people. Does it mean that I have a duty to love someone who loves me because reciprocating his love would boost his well-being tremendously?

Some people deny that the question arises, since they believe that there cannot be a duty to love someone. The common reason for this supposed impossibility is that love is an emotion and the emotions cannot be commanded. This is a misguided view of both love and the emotions. Love is an attitude, not an emotion (though 'being filled with love', feeling 'love swelling in one's bosom', and their like are—diverse—emotions). Parents have a duty to love their children, and that duty, as much as the shared experiences they have with their children, accounts for the fact that many parents love their children, and for the character of their love. Proper consideration of these matters falls outside the ambit of this essay. So let us return to the question: when loved, do we have a duty to reciprocate and to love those who love us?

It is no good to say that, as we will suffer by loving someone we do not like, and do not wish to be attached to,[9] this will, in the balance, defeat any duty we may have to love such people. It is no good because we really do not believe that there is such a duty in the first place. There is nothing to defeat. Nor can one say that there is no such duty because people may find it too difficult to comply with it, or because belief in its existence is counterproductive. These may be good reasons for holding that certain reasons do or do not exist. But in this case they do not get to the root of the matter. In particular, it is wrong to hold that the duty does not exist because morality cannot impose duties which touch the core of our existence. The duty to love our children does just that, and we may be in circumstances in which sacrificing our life, or acting in a way which will incur a debilitating injury, is our moral duty. So if there is not even a prima-facie duty to reciprocate love, why is this?

Some activities and relationships require for their success that they be undertaken for certain reasons, or in a certain spirit, with a certain attitude. Most—though not all—loves are supposed to grow out of a liking for the other person. We see this clearly when we consider both normal and exceptional cases. It taints love of the kind that may lead to stable partnership to discover that it is the result of a wager with a friend, or induced by the prospect of marrying into wealth, or into a prestigious family. I do not wish to suggest that love cannot survive a tainted origin. Sometimes it can, with effort and with time which change the character of the love, erasing

---

[9] It is possible to love someone we do not like. It is even possible to be *in love* with someone we despise. People's lives are torn and ruined by such loves.

the traces of its origin in so far as is possible. That does not diminish the fact that an inappropriate motive flaws the love it leads to. Therefore there cannot be a moral obligation to fall in love as an act of generosity, or as a duty of well-being, since this would be an inappropriate motive.

This reply will took suspiciously complacent to many. True, it will be said, given the role and meaning of love in our culture, a moral duty to reciprocate love is not accepted as a proper motive for love ('you never really loved me, you just pitied me' would be the expected and appropriate response, given our practices and conventions), but that does not mean that there is no moral duty to reciprocate love. It only shows that its implementation is impossible given our shared meanings, our conventions, which thereby stand condemned as falling short of the morally desirable shape they should take. After all, having admitted a parental duty to love one's children, there cannot be a principled obstacle to changing our practices so that one has a duty to reciprocate love.

The objection is commonly based on a misguided understanding of the relationship between abstract moral principles and concrete (and contingent) moral practices. It is a common implicit, sometimes explicit, assumption that abstract, universal principles are external to and independent of our practices, which are to be judged by their conformity with them. If the practices fail the test of universal principles, they should be modified to conform to them. There is no denying that our practices have to account to universal principles, and that they may fail the test. But it is wrong to think of universal moral principles as altogether external to our practices and independent of them, and, more directly relevant to our concern, the common picture disregards the internal logic of practices, which cannot be moulded to fit any alleged ideal. In the case we are considering, the hoped-for ideal is of extending love to all those who 'need' to be loved by (for example) holding that there is a duty to reciprocate love. This assumes that the duty could make love more widely available, or available where 'needed', without of course changing it. In fact, were there to be such a duty it would do the opposite. It will transform what we think of as love out of recognition, thus denying it—that is what we know as love—to those who have it, while at the same time failing to extend it to the intended beneficiaries.

Once a duty to reciprocate love is recognized love turns into something by which one is put under the power of others: by loving us they force themselves upon us. We have no choice but to love them in return. Outside the family our love, love as we know it in our culture, is an expression of our 'spontaneity'; that is why it is important that we should love because we like a person. The rest, the circumstances which turn a liking into a love, may relate to needs of various kinds, and may even include an element of deliberate inducement. But at its core love speaks of a spontaneous, unplanned response to another, expressed in liking him and being attracted to him.[10] That is the love which the advocates of a duty of reciprocation want to spread around. But a duty of reciprocity destroys the very attitude it seeks to extend. The fact that most kinds of love require a proper mode of origination is essential to them. If it turns out that all love is immoral, which is of course absurd, it will be forbidden. But it cannot be tinkered with in the way imagined by our imaginary objector.

These considerations apply not only to love but to all deep personal relations. They set an outer limit to duties of welfare. They cannot affect in this way our innermost relationships. This does not mean that our deepest relationships are immune from moral duties leading to their sacrifice. Morality may require people to abandon their loved ones to fight in just wars, or to save the whale, or to feed the poor. But, subject to some exceptions like that of parental love, it cannot impose a duty to love or to befriend.[11] This is so even though we can affect other people's well-being by becoming deeply involved with their lives, fulfilling a role in them which they happen to desire. Nothing in the above denies that. Nor does it deny that some people may be moved to reciprocate love, and perhaps even to do so because of their realization of the good they can thus bring. There need be nothing wrong with this if it is a thought which accompanies a liking of the other. Even where it is a misguided motive, the flaw it introduces can, as I remarked above, sometimes be remedied. All I argued for is that there cannot be moral duties such as a duty to reciprocate love. This means that the duties of well-being must be confined to providing people with the conditions which facilitate their well-being, rather than demanding that we play a role in their emotional life which they assigned to us.

IV. THE QUESTION OF THE BASELINE

To be a teacher is possible only if there are schools in the neighbourhood, and if one has the possibility of acquiring the required qualifications, etc. While only the agent can make himself a successful teacher, others can help secure the conditions which facilitate such success. How far should they go? Clearly, the existence of teacher-training schemes is helpful, and the existence of schools in which to teach is essential. But should we create special training schemes tailor-made for each candidate? Should we reduce the number of students per class to enable anyone who desires to and has

---

[10] The love one owes to one's children or parents is different. It is demanded of us by moral duties. But while it is not spontaneous, neither is it planned. It is meant to grow with the joint life of parents and children (and perhaps siblings as well), directed or helped by awareness of the duty. Nor are the duties involved ones which put us at the mercy of anyone who happens to come to love us. While it is plausible to think that they are conditioned by reciprocity, they are limited to one's parents and one's children.

[11] Nothing here said excludes the possibility that costs and sacrifices should be valued independently of their impact on one's well-being, and that they matter even when they have no such impact.

appropriate qualifications to get a teaching job? It is tempting to say that such measures would be desirable and should be pursued to the degree that they do not conflict with other goals (e.g. the interests of students, or other needs of the economy reflected in the cost of the proposed measures). But popular though such replies are, they are mistaken.

No one would suggest that the way to ensure success for aspiring mountaineers is to flatten mountains, so that the tallest will be only 1,000 ft. high, with gentle slopes. Clearly, the accomplishment of being a good mountaineer will not be what it is if the skills it requires are those needed to climb a molehill. In many enterprises, the value of success to those engaged in them is in their success in skilful, taxing, challenging activities. The same goes for the musical, artistic, or intellectual achievements of the conductor, painter, novelist, historian, bank manager, barrister, accountant, or surgeon. And so is it with keeping a stiff upper lip, being a good friend, behaving according to one's station, and other less achievement-oriented activities.

Of course, we welcome any advance in medical technology which, by making surgery less skilful, makes it safer. We welcome any advance in educational methods which enables less skilled teachers to achieve good educational results with their students, etc. But in all these cases the benefit to consumers, as it were, is purchased at the cost of reducing the appeal of the job for producers.[12] Given how plentiful are the opportunities for the producers, and how great the needs of the consumers, we quite rightly do not think of such changes as involving any loss. But once the process goes too far, and methods of production generate mechanical, mind-numbing production lines, we do not take comfort in the fact that no one can fail in such a job. Once success is that easy it loses its value. Its value for the agent depends on the exercise of skill, judgment, self-discipline, physical prowess, ingenuity, etc. The value of success for the agent depends on its being success in non-trivial goals which the agent has set himself and which he achieved. To allow for the possibility of success one must allow for the possibility of failure. If people were always completely protected from failure, no one would have a good and successful life (at least not if the existence of the protection were known). One way of caring for the well-being of others is to allow them the opportunity to fail, for therein lies the opportunity to succeed.

Where does this reflection leave our concern for the success of others? To have a successful life they must succeed in worthwhile activities. We cannot do this for them, but we can help them in creating the conditions for success. Now it appears that, by creating the conditions for success we change the task they set out to succeed in. We reduce the difficulties they

---

[12] This point has to be clarified. Making the job less skilful brings it within the realistic aspiration of some for whom it might have been beyond contemplation before. It may therefore make it more valuable overall, even from the point of view of producers. My point was merely that a certain value of achieving great and difficult skills is lost.

face, and the skills they require, thereby diluting the value of their success. Does this mean that all we can do for others is to let them fail without let or hindrance? This might suggest an agent-neutral endorsement of the agent-relativity of one kind of moral egoism.[13] Or, more cogently, it might suggest a morality one of whose supreme injunctions is that, in deciding what to do, people should disregard any concern for the well-being of others. But this advice is one of despair. It does not deny that we should protect and promote people's well-being if we can. It simply concludes that we cannot. As this conclusion is clearly premature, we can dismiss it and turn to an examination of a few ideas about what we may be able to do.[14]

It may be thought that the right way to behave towards others is to create the conditions which, given their individual abilities, will on the one hand be challenging and on the other hand assure that they need not fail in any project they set their heart on if they do their reasonable best. I will call this the Both-Ways Principle. Legal education should stretch the student, but should not be beyond his reach. Of course, we will not allow totally incompetent lawyers to qualify (if we can help it) just because they could not be stretched any further. But such considerations stem from concern for third parties who will be or may be affected by the agent. Our discussion deals only with the agent's own well-being. The Both-Ways Principle may be unworkable in practice. We do not have the information required, and never will have it. Practicalities force us to devise uniform procedures for all, or at least for broad categories of people. We cannot tailor the environment to suit each individual. Such reservations limit the possibility of applying the principle in practice. But do we approve of it theoretically? Can we use it as a benchmark against which to compare less than perfect but practical measures? I do not think so. It is not a universally valid or even desirable principle.

At least in liberal modern societies, there are recognized second-order personal pursuits of finding out what 'one is cut out for', what 'would be right for one'. We train people to be able to change career in mid-life because of economic forces, or technological advances which make their previous occupations obsolete. In the same spirit we train them, or at least should do so, to be able to try something (a career or a relationship, or some other activity) and change if it turns out to be unrewarding for them. In a society built on social, occupational, and geographical mobility, failure is regarded as itself potentially rewarding and enriching. It is part of the process of maturation, growing self-awareness and self-control.

[13] I have in mind that version of moral egoism which says 'it would be best if everyone looked after his own interest exclusively'. This presupposes that there are some other, non-egoistic standards by which it is judged that this would be best (in my discussion, the well-being of all), and also a non-egoistic goal, i.e. the achievement of a state of affairs in which everyone looks after himself exclusively. See. B. Williams, *Ethics and the Limits of Philosophy* (London: Fontana, 1985), 12–13.

[14] Though I shall not explicitly return to this point, the conclusions of this essay amount to a refutation of the suggestion that there cannot be duties of well-being.

This is sufficient to reject the Both-Ways Principle, but there are further reasons to do so. Its appeal is in directing our efforts to create the circumstances in which well-being is independent of luck. Where the Both-Ways Principle is fully realized, whenever people's lives go badly they are to blame. Many moral philosophers, throughout history, were motivated to devise conceptions either of well-being which make them luck-proof or of moral duty to minimise the role of luck, or conceptions of moral responsibility and desert, of character and virtue, which expunge any influence of luck. In their main thrust all these efforts are misguided. Luck does play a meaningful role in our lives. The delight in a piece of good fortune, even in fine weather, is very different from the delight in success through our own efforts, and our lives would be severely impoverished if we missed the delight in good luck. The same is true of the thrill provided by uncertainty, and by risk-taking.

Furthermore, notoriously, bad luck is sometimes a relief, a welcome excuse from having to carry on with an undertaking which has become oppressive, dull, etc. The frequent uncertainly or ambiguity as to whether failure (complete or partial) is due to fault or to luck is a relief from what may otherwise be a relentless critical self-gaze. On these occasions, admittedly, bad luck, if it indeed caused the failure, is not welcome. But were we never to suffer it we would not have the benefits of uncertainty and ambiguity as to whether failure is due to fault.

I fear that some will take these last remarks as extremely fatalistic. They will insist that, rather than attempting to provide this justification for regrettable features of reality, we should try to eliminate them as best we can. But this misconstrues my remarks. They neither justify luck nor condemn it as regrettable. They accept it as inevitable, and offer a beginning towards an explanation of its role in our life and thought. Given its inevitability and the fact that it can on occasion play a positive role in our lives, it would be a mistake to make its imagined complete disappearance a bench-mark for progress, as the Both-Ways Principle does. For doing that, i.e. condemning the inevitable, is playing utopian moral philosophy, which is worse than pointless, for it disregards the actual meaning luck has in our life.

V. THE BASIC-CAPACITIES PRINCIPLE AND THE QUESTION OF SUFFERING

Rejecting the Both-Ways Principle[15] reinstates the question of the way promoting others' well-being should figure in determining right action. One principle which suggests itself is the Basic-Capacities Principle. It requires

---

[15] The rejection is not total. The principle may be suited to some limited educational contexts. As Drucilla Cornell has suggested to me, it may be the appropriate principle in raising young children.

us to promote conditions in which people have the basic capacities for pursuit of goals and relationships of sufficient range to make for a rewarding and fulfilling life. Even to benefit from failure one needs to have the basic capacities for acquiring skills required for pursuing projects and relationships in the society in which one lives. Not all capacities are required. I have never suffered by not having the capacity to acquire the skills of an airline pilot. But I had enough other capacities.[16] We should help everyone to acquire the (nearly) universal capacities, i.e. those necessary for all or almost all valuable pursuits. These include the basic physical and mental abilities of controlled movement and, where disability deprives one of them, appropriate substitutes. They also include the mental abilities to form, pursue, and judge goals and relationships. We should also help people acquire and retain enough other basic capacities, or the opportunities to acquire them, to enable them to pursue an adequate range of projects and goals.

The Basic-Capacities Principle may sound like a second-order Both-Ways Principle, which says that we should have the capacities which will enable us successfully to choose all goals which we could successfully pursue, i.e. the capacities which enable us to choose correctly goals that we will attain if we pursue them with the right spirit. Such a principle does not require that goals be shaped so that we can successfully pursue all of them. There will be goals, possibly many, which are beyond our reach. But it requires that we should be able to recognize which goals are within our reach, and that we should be able to choose them. Failure at that level will be—if the principle is fully implemented—not subject to luck. If we fail at that level it will be our fault. But it would be wrong to understand the Basic-Capacities Principle in this way. It is an interpretation unduly preoccupied with the fear of failure, and the avoidance of luck. As we saw, luck, uncertainty, bad luck, and even failure can have positive value in our lives. Failure need not undermine well-being so long as there is enough success in the life concerned. The point of the Basic-Capacities Principle is to assure one of the possibility of success, not of the possibility of avoiding all failure.

It may be objected that the Basic-Capacities Principle does not solve the problem of how difficult goals should be allowed to be. Saying that one needs the basic capacities for successful pursuit of goals sounds like saying that they should not be too hard, given people's capacities. But that merely fudges the issue. Think of it in this way. Imagine the heroic Soviet pilot, who lost his legs and learnt how to fly fighter planes with his artificial legs. Given that one can become a fighter pilot without limbs, does it matter if people are so disabled? It makes their task harder, but it also makes success more rewarding.

Can one refer the answer to this question to the theory of well-being? Can one say that once we know what counts as a good life we will know

---

[16] So the principle is not an egalitarian one. It does not require that everyone should have the same capacities, so long as each person has adequate capacities.

what are the basic capacities needed to be able to have a good life? In a way this is, of course, true. But we cannot resort to it as a way of postponing the question. The problem is that there are many ways of having a good life. Some find it through marriage, others by avoiding all long-term (voluntary) commitments. Some find it through regularity and routine, others through danger and adventures. Some seek fulfilment through self-expression and creativity, others through caring for other people. In a way, it is the fact that there are so many ways of having a good life which poses the question. The disabled pilot has a good life, which is not a bit worse than the life of a prosperous and ingenious managing director of a software company. Does it mean that we have no duty of well-being to the disabled person who wishes to regain his skill as a pilot?

Ultimately there is no universally valid answer to the question of how hard or easy life should be. In principle, as I have been emphasizing, valuable options impose difficulties and, while we may well wish to reduce the worthless options available in society, that is not to be equated with making life easier. It has nothing to do with making life easier, only with making it more valuable. A lot depends on the social conventions of the time and place: there are various ways of drawing the required line which are acceptable in principle. In the absence of a reason to prefer less arduous to more arduous activities and pursuits, we seem to be driven towards a conservative conclusion. We must say that, so long as a society offers an adequate range of options which enable its members, assuming that they have the basic capacities to take advantage of them, to have good lives, there is no reason to change the character of the options available in that society to make them any easier and less arduous to accomplish. The Basic-Capacities Principle takes its baseline from the social practices of the society in question, provided only that it meets the condition of offering an adequate range of activities and pursuits.[17] Our duties of well-being are to provide the condition in which people will enjoy the basic capacities to take advantage of the opportunities available in their society.

I will return to the suspicion that this is an excessively conservative principle. First we must observe that there are two points of general relevance which make clear two ways in which degree of difficulty in attaining success in a pursuit or activity may be unacceptably high. First, certain achievements in the face of great handicaps are admirable, and reflect favourably on the character of the agent, without showing that his life was successful. Secondly, sometimes success in one dimension of life is gained, because of the handicap, at the cost of sacrificing much else. Women may become top

---

[17] This paragraph relies heavily on the argument in *The Morality of Freedom*, and 'Mixing Values' (*Proceedings of the Aristotelian Society*, supplementary vol., 1991), for its two presuppositions: (1) that valuable activities and pursuits depend on social practices for their availability and, to a degree, even for their existence, and (2) that a controlling principle applies to practices by which one can determine whether they provide an adequate range of options.

executives, but only if they do not marry, etc. A limbless person may become a pilot, but only if he continues to exercise at the expense of any possible relaxation on holidays, etc. We can admire one aspect in the life of the person without judging his well-being to be very high. One way of judging this is to compare it with our response to people who by choice, and without a handicap, amputate their life in such ways (i.e. when they cut themselves off from certain dimensions of life because this is necessary to try and achieve more in some other dimension). If we fault them for doing so, we should regard handicaps which force such sacrifices on people as undesirable, and strive to avoid them, or compensate for their occurrence.

Still, many would feel uncomfortable with at least one aspect of the view I have been exploring. They will be suspicious of the degree to which it is indifferent to, even approves of, pain and suffering. There is a genuine difficulty here. I have insisted that anguish, frustration, and even suffering are often part and parcel of rewarding activities and experiences, which depend on the suffering, etc., for their meaning, and therefore for their value as well. The same can be said, to a more limited extent, of pain. While frustration and anxiety, or at least the ever-present risk of them, are common elements in most of the relationships, activities, and undertakings of human life, pain and the risk of it are an inherent element only of certain specialized activities, some forms of sex, of sports, etc. Pain is therefore rather different from the various forms of suffering, anxiety, etc. In all cases anxiety, frustration, fear, and suffering, while being inseparable from valuable activities, are there to be avoided or overcome. This is the puzzle: they are valuable while we still wish to avoid them. The fact that we wish to avoid them has led to the view that they are always bad. This has had the undesirable result that some contemporary cultures dedicate much effort to the elimination or minimization of pain and suffering. This has a devastatingly flattening effect on human life, not only eliminating much which is of value in our culture, but also making the generation of deeply rewarding forms of life, relationships, and activities impossible. It is to be hoped that the trend will be reversed.[18]

This should not be taken as expressing indifference to pain and suffering where their prevention does not enhance people's well-being. They are, we should not forget, undesirable in themselves.[19] They are valuable only when they are a constructive element of a valuable activity, pursuit, or relationship. None of this can minimize the need to solve the problems of illness, poverty, and deprivation when they are stultifying and make a good life impossible for an individual. At that point they run against our duties of well-being. Where pain and suffering become persistent and intrusive, they

[18] Perhaps the (modest) trend towards natural birth, or natural agriculture, is a sign of a reversal occurring, though it would be a pity if it remains confined to romantic, partly anti-high culture strands in our society.

[19] In some cases pain is an exception to this.

dominate one's life and prevent one from engaging in rewarding and valuable activities. In those cases the Basic-Capacities Principle requires their
elimination. But, and most importantly, I do not wish to deny that there may
be genuine moral concern especially for the minimization of pain, even
where it can form a meaningful challenge, or an element in a rewarding
activity. Clearly, we feel that pain due to illness or injury should be alleviated
even if, were it not, coping with it would become a positive experience in
one's life. All I wanted to deny was that our concern for the minimization
of pain, when justified, can be exhaustively explained as arising out of
concern for the well-being of the sufferers. On the contrary, it is one of a
variety of reasons for thinking that alleviation of pain is a moral requirement
whose source is independent.[20]

VI. A DEFENSIVE DETOUR: COMPREHENSIVE AND LOCAL GOODS

A powerful objection to my whole argument runs as follows. Suppose I am
in a position to help another person (call him Adam) in his pursuit. He
wants to get to the mountains this weekend but his car has broken down.
I will not require my car. Is it not the case that a greater good will be done
by lending Adam my car, and therefore that I am morally required to do so?
How can my argument avoid this conclusion? It does because my car is not
necessary for his well-being. Neither giving it to him nor denying him its
use will affect the success of his life one way or another (if it does, if it is
his one chance . . . I should give it to him). Giving it to him will be a gesture
of friendliness, and I should do it if I owe him friendliness, or wish to be
friendly to him, or towards neighbours of whom he is one, etc.

This, the objection runs, is inconsistent. How can one reconcile the following statements to which I am committed. (1) It makes no difference to
Adam's well-being whether he gets to the mountains. (2) He has reason to
take the car there, and if he doesn't this will adversely reflect on his well-
being, for it will show that his commitment to mountaineering is not as
solid as he thinks it is, or that he is weak-willed, etc. (3) It will cause
him pleasure and avoid frustration if I give him the car. (4) It is a friendly
gesture to do so. (5) I am not morally required to give him the car (even
though I do not need it, he is a reliable driver, etc.).

I think all these statements are reconcilable as follows. Suppose at the
end of his life Adam, or someone else, surveys his life. Surely his getting to
the mountains, or his failure to do so because his car broke down, will have
no significance in judging his well-being. It is an insignificant failure due to
reasons beyond his control (therefore statement 1 is true). This, however,
does not mean that failure of nerve or of will to go to the mountains, if his

---

[20] See *The Morality of Freedom*, 413.

car is in good order, is equally insignificant. Each small failure of this kind is evidence of weakness of resolve, of ambivalence in one's commitment, etc. A single failure of the kind envisioned has but little significance to one's overall judgment of a life. But it has some significance (therefore statement 2 is true as well). That it will give him pleasure to be able to go to the mountains, and cause frustration if, because of his car's failure, he is prevented from doing so, can be taken for granted.[21] It is this which makes my lending him the car a friendly gesture, even though I am not improving his general well-being (see statement 1). But denying him that pleasure, and failing to save him the frustration, is not to be thought of as harming him, or doing him any disservice. He will be able to find other meaningful or enjoyable things to occupy himself with that day; and while he will not manage to avoid the frustration, it is a normal kind of frustration, I am tempted to say a meaningful frustration, for it is part of the normal course of pursuing a goal that one has to prepare, to cope with difficulties, and to contend with the unexpected. My frustration in trying, and failing, to explain the consistency of this view is another example of a meaningful frustration. (It is also an example of a case in which someone else coming and sorting me out is not necessarily a help. I want to do it myself, though this is not likely to be a significant consideration in the case of Adam.) One need not say that such frustrations are good in order not to be too impressed by them.[22]

VII. ACCENTUATING ACCESS

Does the Basic-Capacities Principle exhaust our duties of well-being? Probably not. As explained at the outset, I am proceeding on the assumption that we have duties of well-being which cover everything we can do to protect and promote people's well-being. Is there anything we can do beyond protecting and promoting people's basic capacities? The Basic-Capacities Principle covers much ground. In particular, it is important to realize that the duties it imposes are not discharged once and for all by making sure that young people have a good starting-point in life, that they are well socialized, and trained, and that they are emotionally balanced, etc., at the age of, say, 20. The principle also requires protecting people from injuries which disable or significantly harm their basic capacities, and to make sure that they acquire new basic capacities if they suffer loss through accident or misfortune, be it physical, economic, social, or emotional. Furthermore,

---

[21] Things would be otherwise if his dedication to mountaineering were in fact ambivalent. I am assuming that it is not.

[22] I believe that the above shows that there is a sense in which I can agree that the car will do more good to him than its denial will harm me, while maintaining that I am not morally required to give it to him. The previous considerations show how his commitment to mountaineering makes successful mountaineering expeditions good for him, without making them into a cumulative good, which would lead to moral requirements on grounds of maximization.

with ageing the capacities one needs change. Acquiring and preserving basic capacities is a continuous process.

Even so, the principle does not cover everything; in particular, it does not cover the extent to which people enjoy opportunities to take advantage of their abilities. Access to various activities and pursuits is often denied to people. Intuitively we divide limitations of access into those based on relevant qualifications—you need some knowledge of programming to be a computer programmer, etc.—and those which are external to the activity concerned—one must be of the right gender, or religion, to become a programmer. It is tempting to supplement the Basic-Capacities Principle with a no-extraneous-limitations-on-access-to-opportunities principle. But this is to require too much and too little at the same time. On the one hand, extraneous limitations on access need not affect one's opportunities to engage in valuable activities and relationships. If the golf club in my city decides to exclude Jews from membership, this will have no bearing at all on my access to valuable opportunities. At my age my tastes are formed and golf is not one of them, and when I was young such an exclusion would have been a much smaller bar to opportunities than my bad eyesight was. All one requires is access to an adequate range of options; extraneous limitations to some options can leave everyone with more than adequate access.

On the other hand, even limits of access that are integral to the activity or relationship they control may lead to people being denied adequate access to valuable options. For example, there can be, may be there are, countries in which parent–child relations are exclusive to biological parents. Such countries would deny that one can acquire parents or become a parent by adoption. This denies access to parenthood to barren people. Assuming for the sake of argument[23] that being a parent is such a central component of well-being that one's prospect of having a good life is severely restricted without it, we will have to judge a society which does not recognize adoptions as one which does not provide an adequate range of options. But the non-recognition of adoptions is not an external restriction on access to parenthood. It is integral to that society's practice of parenting. The parent–child relationship sustained by our societies is different in its meaning and implications from that of my imaginary society. Admitting adoption transforms it from a blood relationship into one based on care and fostering. It affects not only access but the nature of the good one has access to.[24]

---

[23] This is not an assumption I would want seriously to uphold. What is true is that a society is deficient if it does not allow adequate opportunities for adults to relate to children, and vice versa. But those can be provided in other ways, e.g. in child-minding, teaching, being a close uncle or aunt, a godfather. I am making the simplifying assumption that an opportunity to parent must be made available to all to simplify the exposition of the general point the example is meant to serve.

[24] M. Walzer, in *Spheres of Justice* (New York: Basic Books, 1983) has done much to draw attention to the fact that principles of access (or distribution) affect the goods they provide access to.

This, it seems to me, is the main theoretical objection to a No-Extraneous-Limitations-to-Access principle. The distinction between external and intrinsic limitations on access, while serviceable for many purposes, is theoretically inadequate to our task.[25]

The principle we should uphold is simply that every person should have access to an adequate range of options to enable him to have a successful life. Satisfaction of this principle does not recognize the distinction between inherent and external limitation of access, and is not limited to eliminating external limitations. While, as noted, it is not hostile to all external limitations, it may require a change in inherent limitations, i.e. transformation of the goods one has access to. Just as the Basic-Capacities Principle, i.e. the principle about the capacities necessary for one to have a successful life, is part and parcel of a consideration of the nature of the valuable options which should be available for people in a society, so the Principle of Adequate Access is not independent of but is inseparable from an argument about which valuable options should be available in a society. When people demand recognition of gay marriages, they usually mean to demand access to an existing good. In fact they also ask for the transformation of that good. For there can be no doubt that the recognition of gay marriages will effect as great a transformation in the nature of marriage as that from polygamous to monogamous or from arranged to unarranged marriage.

The case of gay marriages differs from the example considered above (section 3) of the impossibility of a duty to reciprocate love. For whereas those who desire that their love be reciprocated desire a spontaneous love based on liking and not on duty, those who ask for gay marriages to be recognised ask that committed unions of gay men or of lesbians be legally and socially recognised on the same footing as committed unions of people of differing genders. That goal is not at all impossible. It merely requires the passing away of the current type of marriage, which is exclusive to people of differing genders.

Here we can see the degree to which the approach I am advocating is conservative, and the limits on that conservatism. In the background is the thought that there are many valuable options, many routes to a good life. The fact that any one society makes realization of only a small fraction of them possible is inevitable. The fact that other societies have options not sustainable in ours is no cause for moral concern. Likewise, the fact that people living in one country at the same time do not have all the same options available to them is no cause for moral concern. The only thing

---

[25] How can one draw a principled divide between inherent and extrinsic limitations on an activity? Should steroids be banned from athletics? It depends on what sort of competition the branch of the entertainment industry known as athletics is thought to be. The question is the same as the problem whether dance with speaking dancers is still dance, or theatre, or some unholy hybrid. Tradition and people's desires for the future development of such activities are the only relevant factors. No conceptual distinction between what is inherent to the activity and what is extrinsic to it will solve the problem.

which matters, in so far as ours is a moral concern with the well-being of others, is that everyone will have an adequate range of options realistically available to him. To that extent the outlook is conservative. But while it is reasonable to surmise that just about all societies have an adequate range of acceptable options available in them, many of them bar sections of their populations—foreigners, the poor, people of colour, people with a disapproved-of sexual orientation—from access to an adequate range of valuable options. The main cause for social reform, and for moral action based on concern for others' well-being, is to secure adequate access. But, as I have emphasized, securing access, even when it requires no more than providing better educational facilities, or redistributing material resources, usually involves a change in the value of the goods to which access is being secured. Sometimes the change is external;[26] often it is also internal, changing the very character of the good affected. The very abundance of possible avenues to a good life which made my approach conservative, inasmuch as it denied a moral reason to make options particularly easy to succeed in and denied that we have reason to make the same options available to everyone and to every society, makes it, when it comes to the issue of access, radical. The need to secure adequate access, like the need to provide basic capacities, overrides any fondness for existing forms of activity and relationship. If access to some requires a change in options to all, so be it. No one should be denied adequate access to valuable options on the ground that to allow access would lead to the transformation or the disappearance of a much-cherished existing form of a valuable activity or relationship.

VIII. SELF-RESPECT

Throughout this discussion I have ignored one central range of issues, those which arise out of the relation between ideals of life and of character and personality, between ideals of doing and of being. Let me give one example of their connection. Well-being consists in successful activities. Failure, as was remarked above, can be constructive, but only if it helps one to succeed. But cannot continuous failure in all one's goals still be consistent with a successful life? There are various aspects to this problem. The only one I touch upon raises the question of the relations between character and life. Failure can be character-forming. If a successful life is one which makes one an admirable person, perhaps there could be success in continuous failure.

There is another way success in life could be related to character and personality. A successful life could perhaps be defined as the life that an admirable person would have, thus assuming—as does the formulation in the preceding paragraph—an independent identification of and case for the

---

[26] Consider the impact of income redistribution on positional goods, or of the spread of education on the 'élitist' aspects of high culture.

doctrine of the ideal person. But should we say that a person's life is good or successful if it is of the sort that an admirable, good, exemplary person would lead, or should we say that a character is good or admirable if it is one which is likely to lead to a good life? The issue is complex, and we cannot deal with it here. There are two interdependent processes. On the one hand, our character has a great influence on the course of our life, especially on those aspects which determine its success. On the other hand, the course of our lives affects our character. There are also conceptual connections between the two. One who has never faced danger can be neither courageous nor cowardly. Conversely, the meaning of certain events depends on the character of the person in whose life they figure. If that person is ambitious, they manifest ambition; if not, not. The two are closely interwoven factors, while being at the same time relatively independent. An admirable person can have a miserable life, in which his promise was not fulfilled, while a less than totally admirable person may, by good fortune, enjoy a great success and have a very fulfilling and rewarding life.

By and large, of the two notions, that of a good life dominates. One's character consists of (some of) one's abilities and dispositions. These are judged by the activities they tend to support or undermine, by the life that they tend towards. Yet it is possible to make the fashioning of one's character one of one's life's projects. And it is possible to judge a life by the character it fashioned, even when this was not the agent's supreme goal in life. To the extent that the formation of character is at least allowed to serve as the measure of the success of the life, in some instances a life of failures in projects and goals can still succeed at least in making the agent an admirable person.

One central aspect of well-being that inescapably brings the good life and the good person together is that of dignity and self-respect. We noted that well-being consists of the whole-hearted pursuit of valuable activities. Those who whole-heartedly engage in relationships and pursue goals feel dedicated to their projects and relationships, and are aware of their value. They can feel pride in what they do; they find nothing to be ashamed of, nothing to hate or to demean themselves for. They enjoy self-respect. But self-respect requires the absence of shame, self-hate, etc., not only in one's activities but in one's being. The self-respect of those who are ashamed of their nationality, gender, sexual preference, or race, for example, is damaged. Self-respect involves accepting oneself for what one is without shame, self-hate, or feeling that one is not worthy, not good enough, that one is inferior or second-rate.

That does not mean that self-respect is inconsistent with a realistic assessment of one's abilities or accomplishment. People who are aware that their talents are limited, that their life has not been very successful, that their character is flawed can have self-respect. Indeed, their self-awareness, their pitiless self-knowledge can be a source of a sense of their inner worth, in spite of their flaws or misfortunes. Self-respect concerns one's ability to accept without alienation one's core being, one's core pursuits and relationships and those aspects of one's character and circumstances that one identifies with most deeply. We tend to think that every person should possess self-respect. I would prefer to say that every person who earned the right to self-respect should possess it. People can forfeit that right. So self-respect, just like other aspects of well-being, manifests the active nature of the good life.

The clarification of the notion of self-respect cannot be undertaken here.[27] Our concern is merely to note the vital role it plays in people's well-being. As with other elements of well-being, so with self-respect: the agent has to earn it in order to have it, but others can help and they can hinder. It is futile to try to enumerate all the ways in which our actions affect other people's ability to have (well-deserved) self-respect. They range from conditions which are necessary for mental health, and the provision of mental-health care for those who need it, to the eradication of racism and other forms of bigotry. The latter constitutes the major part of the politics of identity. It concerns the fact that people born into societies which denigrate aspects of their being central to their own sense of who they are cannot but be affected by those attitudes. They may come to share them, sometimes even while they openly reject them as unfounded, and be tormented by self-hatred and self-doubt. Or they may reject them and pay the price of defying their society. The price is expressed in alienation from the society, difficulty in engaging in pursuits which because of their social profile involve close integration in the society, and in many other ways. The current emphasis on the politics of identity in some countries may be a passing phase. But the pivotal importance of self-respect to the well-being of people is enduring and fundamental. The crucial importance of the fight against racism, homophobia, sexism, chauvinism, and the like, is a central element of the duties of well-being, even if its moral relevance may not be exhausted by its relevance to well-being.[28]

IX. CONCLUSIONS

Clearly, a person's well-being depends not only on himself. It also requires that the conditions which make his pursuits possible, and give them their

---

[27] See, among much else on self-respect, Thomas Hill, *Autonomy and Self-Respect* (Cambridge: Cambridge Univ. Press, 1991), essays 1 and 2; also my 'Liberating Duties', ch. 2 below.

[28] The importance of self-respect is often emphasized by deontic ethical theories as belonging to the non-consequentialist aspect of morality. My aim in the brief discussion above was to show that self-respect has implications for duties of well-being. But this does not mean that the importance of self-respect depends entirely on those implications. It is a focus of moral concern in its own right. Some of the political implications of the politics of identity are considered in chs. 5–7 below.

meaning, obtain. To be a teacher is possible only if there are schools in the neighbourhood, and if one has the possibility of acquiring the required qualifications, etc. While only the agent can make himself a successful teacher, others can help secure the conditions which facilitate such success. How far should they go?

The aim of the argument has been to show that in an important sense the question of the relation between the agent's self-interest and moral requirements is often not a matter of assigning more or less weight to one's own interest, because it is not a matter of comparing like with like. There is a difference in kind between the way we promote our own self-interest and the way we discharge our duties to others which are based on concern for their well-being.[29] We do the first by furthering our project and the second by enabling others to further theirs.

If, recognizing my duties to others, I abandon my current goal in order to discharge my duties to them, I am not necessarily sacrificing my well-being to promote or protect theirs. All I am doing is replacing one goal with another. I may, for example, be abandoning my job as a crane-operator for a job as a hospital nurse. But there is no reason to think that that will be a less satisfying way of life than that of a crane-operator. There is no difference between this case and swapping one's job as a crane-operator for a career as a landscape-designer because one feels attracted to the latter career. The motivation is different, and it tells us that the new landscape-designer is taking up his new career willingly. The new nurse may be doing it reluctantly, out of a sense of duty. If he becomes resentful and for ever regrets his bad luck which forced him to change career, then his well-being will be adversely affected. The main difficulty in facing up to the demands of morality, I would suggest, is the difficulty of disruption. A doctor suffers no ill from the fact that volunteers are needed in time of medical emergency. He is already there. If I have to leave the university for the hospital, I will find this much more difficult, and the impact on my life can be disastrous unless I manage to adjust to the new circumstances without resentment and deep regrets. It is primarily in terms of disruption that we should weigh the cost to individuals of moral duties to the well-being of others.[30]

Of course, it may be the case that our duties to others cannot be discharged without sacrificing our own opportunities to have a good and successful

[29] Are there not many occasions in which an agent acts merely to create conditions which would enable him to pursue his goals and commitments? Are they not the common case, and is not the comparison in such cases of like with like? I believe not. Arguably, whatever an agent does, his success is rewarding not only by its result (which may be the creation of conditions enabling him to do something else) but also by the fact that he succeeded in something he set out to do (though sometimes, e.g. scratching one's head, it is not success which is rewarding but failure which is frustrating).

[30] Nothing here said excludes the possibility that costs and sacrifices should be understood and measured independently of their impact on one's well-being, and that they matter even when they have no such impact. That case has not yet been made by those who raise arguments based on the demandingness of morality.

life. Since, other than examining the implication for such duties of the active character of well-being, nothing here said enables us to conclude what our duties to the well-being of others actually are, it is impossible for me to say anything here about how often such conflicts arise and how they should be resolved. But the discussion in this essay leads to one or two helpful conclusions: first, that having to give money to others is comparable with having to volunteer to work as a nurse. Reasonably affluent people can give up quite a lot with no cost at all to their well-being. If the giving has implications for their well-being (e.g. having to forgo a foreign holiday for several years), it is similar to taking on nursing as an evening job, i.e. it is a case of moral concerns leading one to change one's goals and pursuits. Instead of foreign holidays one goes walking in the mountains near one's home, or something like that. Again, if the transition is successful there need be no sacrifice involved.

Furthermore, these considerations also show that the duty to ameliorate the material conditions of others may not be as extensive as is sometimes supposed. Admittedly, in a world in which millions of people suffer starvation and acute deprivation this point offers little comfort. But when we think about the principles involved, it is relevant to reflect that, just as a reduction in the standard of living of the affluent need not mean any sacrifice, since it merely makes them change from one rewarding pursuit to another, with no loss to the quality of their life if they adjust to their new circumstances, so too for the less affluent. For those who do not actually suffer real deprivation (and I am not implying either a rigid or a universal test for this condition), the improvement of their material conditions means the availability of additional opportunities which enable them to change their pursuits, and more often than not is accompanied by pressure (social, economic, or psychological) to do so. Their change may not involve an improvement in the quality of their life, and they too will face the dangers of disruption, which can be great. While normally we expect adjustment to greater affluence to be easier than adjustment to less affluence, that is not always the case, and it is not normally the case when the greater affluence involves serious dislocation, as has often happened when rehousing breaks down neighbourhoods and communities of work.

The previous paragraph may sound incredibly complacent. It should not be read this way. It does, it is true, reflect an emphasis on the eradication of serious deprivation and on the politics of identity, as opposed to some conventional wisdom about the benefits of continuous improvement of one's material conditions. In the order of argument, that paragraph is merely the reverse side of the preceding paragraphs with their potentially radical implications, namely that, contrary to much popular opinion, we have only limited escape from observing our moral duties to the well-being of others on grounds that they are too demanding.

2

Liberating Duties

There is much that the political culture of the West, especially of the English-speaking countries, owes to John Locke. He crystalised and gave shape to ideas about natural rights, private property, toleration, the general duties and powers of government, the organs of government and their interrelations, the theoretical foundations of democracy, and the theoretical justification of revolutions, which for good or ill have left an indelible mark on our political culture. With politics' importance having grown in the modern world, and with its ever increasing impingement on people's lives, it is not surprising that Locke's influence has reached beyond the political issues which concerned him into our general moral outlook and has contributed to the formation of the contemporary liberal moral outlook in general. In this his ideas were mixed with and helped by the doctrines of the Utilitarians and the Marxists who reversed the Aristotelian precept that politics is an extension of ethics and have come to regard morality from a perspective dominated by concern with public life and with politics.

The contemporary perception of the centrality of rights exemplifies both the influence of Locke and the way our moral ideas have been affected by our political principles. Locke is a key figure in the rise of rights to a place of pre-eminence in liberal culture.[1] Natural law, having been traditionally understood as the doctrine of people's duties and obligations, has become the doctrine of the natural rights of people. In Locke's work natural rights explain both the need for government (the efficient protection of people's natural rights), the justification of government (through the contractual transfer of the natural right to punish to the civil authority), and the limits of government (by the inviolability of the natural rights). His doctrines were not accepted by all without change or challenge. But ever since Locke's day the institution and implementation of bills of fundamental rights has become a foundation stone of the doctrines of limited government and of the liberty of the individual.

Rights have come into prominence as a notion crucial to an understanding of the relationship between people and their government. But

First published in *Law and Philosophy* VIII (1989) 3–21. Reprinted here by permission of Klewer Academic Publishers. © 1989 Kluwer Academic Publishers. Presented at the Cassassa Conference, at Loyola-Marymount University in Los Angeles, and at a conference on Rights and the Philosophy of Law, at the University of Miami, Corol Gables, Florida, both in March 1988.

[1] Recent scholarship has shown that Locke's own views were more in line with the traditional emphasis on the importance of law and duties than the perspective ascribed to him here, and which represents his main influence today. But ambiguities within his own writings provided the seeds for his successors to see him as a crucial figure in the rise of rights-oriented liberalism.

gradually the political centrality of the notion has affected common perceptions of its role in individual morality. Of course, the concept of rights had
its ups and downs. Neither Utilitarians nor Marxists found it particularly
useful in formulating their political ideals.[2] The new Liberal and, in a different version, Marxist, science of economics, which played a formative role
in shaping modern politics, has never learned how to cope with rights.
Nevertheless, ever since the Second World War, the march of rights has
seemed unstoppable and recent years in particular saw Utilitarianism, in all
its versions, replaced by various rights-oriented theories as the leading con-
tender for the status of the moral and political orthodoxy of today.

The purpose of this article is to contribute a challenge to this orthodoxy
by pointing out inherent limitations of rights-oriented doctrines, and to the
need to regard rights as subsumable under and derived from a more fundamental doctrine of well-being on the one hand, and a complementary
need to give duties a central role in our understanding of moral and political
life, which is independent of their role in protecting and promoting rights,
on the other hand. Finally, I will argue that the common, and in my view
distorted, perception of duties which is supposed to make plain their
subordination to rights, in fact leads to a belittling of the role of rights. My
aim is to outline some of the shortcomings of the concentration on rights,
rather than to defend in detail the case against rights. That case, it should
be remembered, is not that rights do not have an important role to play in
our moral and political thinking, but that their role is subordinate, that they
are to be understood from a wider and a more fundamental perspective, in
which they are no more than the equal of duties.

1. ORTHODOXY

Often in practical philosophy the dominance of one view is the result of its
rivals ceasing to make sense. It seems difficult to argue for the orthodox
view, and impossible to argue against it. Its correctness is manifest. Rival
heterodox views are not there to be refuted. They are condemned through
their own unintelligibility. We can just understand what their supporters are
saying, but it seems so pointless. It is mysterious how anyone might maintain such a view, unless they are blind to simple conceptual connections.
To argue for the orthodox view can amount to no more than pointing out
those connections.

Such is the case with the relations of rights and duties. For many members of our culture it has become plain that duties derive from rights, and

<hr />

[2] See Waldron, *Nonsense On Stilts* for a collection of Utilitarian and Marxist writings criticis-
ing doctrines of natural rights.

that there can be no duty except to serve and protect someone's right. Sometimes this is taken to be such an obvious truth that it hardly needs to be argued. Its truth is manifest because a right is always to a benefit. Therefore rights can stand on their own feet. They secure benefits to people, and that can be instrinsically good. They are the sort of thing which is capable of being of ultimate, rock-bottom moral value.

Duties, on the other hand, necessarily apply regardless of whether or not one desires to do that which one has a duty to do. Their point is precisely that. If one has a duty to perform an act then one should do so regardless of whether one wants to or not. Even if one does not want to do that which is one's duty, one should do it nevertheless, because it is one's duty. The independence of duties of their subjects' will is even more far-reaching. Duties are categorical reasons, i.e., they are binding independent of the will or goals of their subjects. There cannot be a duty, the reason for which is that its performance would facilitate the realization of one's goals.[3] Therefore duties are fetters and restrict people's ability to do as they wish. Restrictions cannot be good in themselves. They are good only if they serve a good purpose, and their value derives from the value of the purpose they serve. Hence duties cannot have intrinsic or ultimate value.

From here it is but a short step to the desired conclusion. Justifying a claim that a duty is incumbent on one requires showing what good it does, what purpose it serves. That purpose must be that doing that which one has a duty to do serves the interest of someone: that it either renders a benefit to someone or makes it more likely that his interest will be protected or promoted.[4] But whenever the interest of a person is sufficient to hold another under a duty that person has a right. To have a right is just that. A person has a right if, and only if, his interest is sufficient to hold another duty bound to do something on the ground that that action respects or promotes that interest.[5] It follows that all duties derive from rights. Rights are primary, their value is that they render benefits. Their value to their subject can justify their existence and they can have intrinsic value. Duties being fetters cannot be justified by their value to their subjects and they cannot have intrinsic value. Where one is under a duty its value derives from the fact that it serves someone else's interest, that its performance benefits someone else, that is, that someone has a right to the benefit the duty protects or promotes.

[3] See my 'Promises and Obligations', in *Law, Morality, and Society*, essays in honour of H. L. A. Hart, edited by P. M. S. Hacker and J. Raz (Oxford, 1977) for some suggestions towards an analysis of duties.

[4] Sometimes the point of a duty might be in the very being under a duty. But such cases are slightly paradoxical and parasitic on the normal case in which the justification of the duty is in the value of its observance.

[5] See my *The Morality of Freedom* (Oxford, 1986), ch. 7, for a defence of this general view of rights.

Despite its flaws this argument is to be taken seriously. It reveals important features of many contemporary approaches to rights and duties, and can be regarded as the canonical argument concerning the relations of rights and duties. One obvious gap in the argument helps in bringing out the two main features of the orthodoxy which raise doubts as to its cogency. Can there not be duties to oneself? The canonical argument moves from the assertion that duties do not carry their point on their face, that since they impose fetters they are in need of justification, to the conclusion that their justification must be in rendering benefits to others. But it may be possible to explain a person having duties on the ground that they serve his very own interest. One could have a duty not to smoke based on reasons of one's own health, for example. If there are duties towards oneself, then not all duties arise out of rights since clearly one cannot have rights against oneself.

Current conceptions of individual well-being find difficultly with the idea of duties towards oneself, or of owing duties to oneself. The reason is the one mentioned above. Duties can only be based on categorical reasons. One cannot have a duty to perform an act simply because one wants to perform it, nor because one ought to perform it for its performance will serve one's goals. So even though I wish to remain in good health, and putting on an overcoat is the way to remain in good health, I do not have a duty to put on an overcoat, at least not for that reason. The most popular conception of individual well-being in our culture, and in its philosophy, regards it as consisting in the satisfaction of one's desires, or preferences, or of some subclass of them, e.g., those which are rational, or self-regarding, or those that one would still endorse if one were well informed. Given this understanding of well-being there can be no duties to oneself. For oneself one can only do what one wants to do anyway, if only one were rational, or strong-willed, or well informed, etc., and one can have no duty to do that.

That there are, to use the current jargon, no prudential duties is sometimes overlooked because of the attention paid to paternalistic duties and their possible justification. Paternalistic duties are those imposed by authority, e.g. by law, for the protection of their subjects. These, like all rights and duties which are the product of authority, give rise to special considerations. Whatever their justification they do not create a real difficulty to the canonical argument as they are not duties to oneself, but duties owed to the authority (e.g., to the State) which arise out of its right to rule. Where the imposition of paternalistic duties is justified this is often accounted for because individuals have a right against the authority (e.g., the State) that it shall protect them against their own folly, neglect, or ignorance, e.g., by placing them under duties to wear car seat belts, to refrain from using various drugs, and so on.

It is interesting that there is an asymmetry between rights and duties which is made apparent in the explanation of the impossibility of duties and rights to oneself. The very idea of a right to oneself is absurd. Not so the notion of a duty to oneself. The non-existence of such duties results not from the very notion of duty itself but from the orthodox understanding of individual well-being. Later on I will suggest that individual well-being should not be regarded as a function of one's desires. This mistaken view of individual well-being is among the main contributors to the orthodox view of duties; its correction is the major step towards their liberation from that blinkered view of their role and nature. Once one is equipped with a sound view of individual well-being the way is open to admitting the importance of duties towards oneself.

Nothing, however, can legitimize the notion of rights against oneself. The very idea is self-contradictory, for rights are essentially interpersonal. Their existence entails consequences to others. The contemporary orthodoxy has a simple explanation of the relational character of rights. According to it rights are essentially confrontational. To assert a right is, as we know, to assert that the right-holder's interest is sufficient reason to hold another subject to a duty. The duty's purpose is to protect the interest of the right-holder. The protection of that interest is its *raison d'être*. The person subject to the duty is encumbered in the interest of the right-holder. Their relationship need not be adversarial in fact. One may be, for example, the child of the other, who very much wants to help his parent in the prescribed way. But the relationship is confrontational in principle. The duty does not depend on any harmony of interests between the right-holder and the person subject to the duty. It exists regardless of the existence or absence of such harmony. This essential confrontational aspect of rights explains, according to the current orthodoxy, the impossibility, even in principle, of there being rights against oneself.

This common belief in the confrontational nature of rights is the second element on which I will focus attention. It derives directly from the conception of duties as fetters. Since rights justify duties, and duties are to the disadvantage of their bearers, rights are confrontational. If duties are not essentially fetters detrimental to their subject, then rights need not be considered as essentially confrontational.

3. THE EMBEDDEDNESS OF RIGHTS AND DUTIES

I would like to sketch briefly three arguments whose purpose is, first, to illustrate the view that both rights and duties should be understood as embedded within a wider theory of individual well-being; second, to show how such a theory gives duties a role independent of the support of rights; and, finally, to demonstrate how the confrontational conception of rights diminishes their status.

Philosophical discussion of morality and politics is sometimes dominated by our perception of widespread endemic conflict among people. One cause of disagreement is conflict of interest. Resources are limited and people compete for them. Both private and political morality are, to a degree, concerned with adjudicating in this kind of competition. But not all conflict is of that kind. Much of it expresses disagreement over common goods, regarding which people's interests do not conflict but over which there is room for honest disagreement. Common goods can be material, e.g., the hisotric buildings, or the public parks of a city, or they can be patterns of human activity, e.g., the general atmosphere of toleration and kindness that prevail in human relations among the inhabitants of a city. They are public goods in that first, the benefits of each public good are available to all, and no member of the community can be excluded from them without denying the good to all others. And, second, their enjoyment is shared by all in a non-competitive way. That is, the enjoyment of one person does not detract from that of others.[6]

Typically individuals do not have rights to common goods. This is not really surprising. Typically the continued existence of common goods depends on co-operative behaviour of many individuals. A right protects the interests of the right-holder, but that interest, the stake that any one individual has in the existence or preservation of a common good, does not normally justify holding so many people to a duty to behave in the way which is required for its production or preservation. The value of common goods to each individual can be great. It is often greater than the value of any individual good to a person who has a right to it. But their value depends on the cumulative contribution of many, sometimes most, members of the community. However great their value to a single individual, it does not justify the imposition of a duty on the many.

The non-existence of individual rights to common goods is, of course, compatible with the existence of duties to provide and preserve them. Typically governments and other public authorities have duties to protect the common goods of a community, because such duties derive from the basic function of governments to serve their subjects. Their duties are to the community as a whole rather than to any individual right-holder.[7] Similarly,

---

[6] This characterisation requires refinement and qualifications. For example, non-competetiveness may exist within certain boundaries only. If too many people go to the public parks on weekends the enjoyment of everyone is diminished.

[7] Here I am disregarding the question whether there can be collective rights to common goods. In *The Morality of Freedom* (Oxford, 1986) ch. 8, I agrued that this is sometimes, but not always, the case.

individuals may well have a duty to bear their share in providing and protecting common goods, a duty which is also based on the interest of members of the community generally in their existence.

Thus, common goods are one particularly prominent case in which duties exist even when they do not serve anyone's rights, and where we can clearly see that any justification of rights and duties is nested in a wider theory of the good. This conclusion is strengthened by the second of the three arguments, at least if one is under the influence of the confrontational view of rights. For it is, perhaps, surprising that the contemporary orthodoxy, which gives rights pride of place over duties, also endorses the confrontational view of rights which itself provides sufficient grounds for denying them foundational status in morality. Consider one important point ovelooked in my statement of the canonical argument. While all rights are to benefits, it does not follow that it is always a benefit to have a right. Sometimes it may be better for a person not to have a right to a benefit. It may make it easier, e.g., for the benefit to be given to him out of the giver's free will because the receiver is liked, etc., and not because he has a right to it. This possibility indicates the importance of the influence of the confrontational view of rights, and the limitation it imposes on them. Where a confrontational relationship, in the sense explained, is to be avoided rights have no place. Rights are results oriented. They are suited to contexts in which what primarily matters is how one person's action affects the interests of another. If, on the other hand, what matters is that one should respect, help, etc. another out of friendship, or love or some other special motive, rights are out of place.[8]

Finally, let it be noticed that the interpersonal aspect of rights is a major barrier to any attempt to regard them as foundational. Rights serve the interests of the right-holders. But not everything a person has an interest in having does he have a right to. I may have an interest in having this house. It does not follow that I have a right to it. To give rise to a right an interest must be sufficient to justify the existence of a duty on another person to behave in a way which serves the interest of the right-holder. Whether or not such a duty is justified depends not only on the interest of the right-holder but, at the very least, also on that of the person who is to be subject to that duty. Some people would say that the existence of a right calls for weighing the service compliance with the duty will render to the right-holder with the detriment that it will, or that it may, bring to the person subject to the duty. Only if the service is greater than the (possible) detriment does the right exist. I think myself that this way of putting the matter is unsatisfactory for various reasons, one of which will emerge below. But the grain of truth in it is that rights are based on evaluating the interests not only

---

[8] Difficulties leading to complicated solutions arise when, while it is best that an act should be done out of the right motive, it is better that it should be performed than not. There is no need to examine such cases here.

of their beneficiaries, but also of others who may be affected by respect for them.

Thus, the interpersonal aspect of rights shows them to be the result of an evaluation of the well-being of people affected. They belong to the middle level of morality, to the level of rules, principles, and institutions recognized in the circumstances of life of certain groups or individuals to work best from the point of view of those considerations which are of ultimate concern.[9] They do not themselves belong with the considerations which are of ultimate concern.

4. WELL-BEING AND THE WILL

To understand rights and duties we have to gain a proper perspective of their nestedness in individual well-being. This will enable us to understand how duties, no less than rights, can be of intrinsic value to their subject. The well-being of an individual comprises everything which is good for him. This can be divided into two complementary aspects: that which makes an individual into a better person, and that which makes his life better or more successful. It is important to remember that when talking of a life as being better we mean, in the present context, the ways in which it is better for the person whose life it is. It may also be judged as better for his children, for his country, for humanity, or for culture. But while one's paternal, patriotic, cultural, etc. success may make one's life more successful for oneself, it need not do so. It is important to keep apart the different dimensions in which the goodness of a life can be judged, and to keep open the possibility that success in one dimension is purchased at the expense of success in some others. Of these, our concern is with what makes a life better for the person whose life it is, what makes it successful for him.

Individual well-being consists in the successful pursuit of worthwhile activities. This traditional view of well-being reflects the fact that human beings are conscious agents, and that we regard that as central to their own perception of themselves. For we are not merely creatures who, like plants, can prosper or wither, we are also creatures who are aware of ourselves as people capable of prospering or withering. Everyone is concerned (and I do not mean 'exclusively concerned') with his own well-being. This is not a fundamental brute fact about human motivation. Rather, it is a feature of our concepts, which shapes the nature of our self-awareness. It is logically possible for creatures, indeed for human beings, to exist while lacking this dimension of evaluation, that is, lacking a notion of their own prosperity

---

[9] This point is very effectively made by R. M. Dworkin regarding concrete rights (*Taking Rights Seriously*, ch. 4) and constitutional rights (*Ibid.*, ch. 9). The same considerations apply, however, to all rights, subject to the qualifications to be introduced below.

and that of other human beings as a major element in their conception of themselves and of others. But as it is, our conceptions of ourselves as humans, as persons, as rational agents, are all bound up with and reflected in our notion of personal well-being, of being successful as human persons. That is why our notion of well-being is of success over a lifetime, and that is why it is one of success in one's doings. These derive from and are intertwined with the very basic features of being a person.

Finally, and most important, that the notion of well-being is part of the way we conceive of our life from the inside explains why it cannot be just a matter of gaining what one wants. Such a conception of well-being is essentially an external one. An external observer may be impressed by everybody's life being one of strivings and of doings. Success can therefore appear to be just a matter of getting what one desires, or at least of achieving what one is striving for. But this takes our desires for granted. They are just there as brute ultimate facts. This is not how things appear to people from the inside, to the people whose desires these are.

To start with, everyone regards his desires as part of a larger pattern, and subject to evaluation. There may even be desires which we hate having and which we reject as not really ours, desires which we want neither to have nor to see fulfilled.[10] We judge our desires, goals, and aspirations as rotational, well-founded, sound, etc. Our well-being consists partly in having the right desires. In brief what is good for us may be so because we desire it, but only if that desire is one which passes the appropriate test.

Futhermore, and this is the crux of the matter, our desires do not spring into being from nowhere, or from unintelligible aspects of our personality. They are not brute facts which we encounter about ourselves, like our height, or hair colour. Except in pathological cases, they are intelligible and subject to partial volitional control. At the very least we can guide our desires as we can guide our beliefs, witholding assent when the evidence is insufficient, granting it when it is prudent to do so, etc. This semi-voluntary control is possible precisely because our desires are part of the intelligible aspect of our life. Like beliefs, desires are guided by reasons. What we want, we want for reasons, which, up to a point, we understand. When there is reason to desire something we do desire it, and when there is inadequate reason to desire it we do not.[11] To be sure we are liable to have

---

[10] H. Frankfurt has done much to draw attention to that fact and to its significance. See his *The Importance of What We Care About* (Cambridge: Cambridge University Press, 1988).

[11] With both beliefs and desires many cases fall into an intermediate area where reason is indeterminate, where neither assent nor denial are irrational. In these cases the explanation of why some endorse the belief or desire while others do not transcends the realm of the intelligible. We simply know that some are more credulous than others, some more susceptible to the pleasures of music than others. There may be some physical or evolutionary explanations of these tendencies, but no rational ones. Some aspects of the relation between reason and desires are explained with greater care in my *The Morality of Freedom* (Oxford, 1986).

irrational desires, just as we are liable to have irrational beliefs. But, by and large, desires, like beliefs, belong to the realm of the intelligible, and, therefore, to what is partly controlled by us. That is why, on the whole, we identify with our desires and beliefs: what we are is partly determined by what they are.

Since our well-being depends in part on having appropriate goals, it cannot be merely a matter of satisfying all or some of the desires we have. It consists, it is true, in success in the aspects of our lives we care about. But we care not merely about having our wants satisfied, but about having reasonable wants. We value our lives, judge them to be successful, in proportion to their being occupied with worthwhile pursuits, and, of course, successfully so. This is why the notion of a person's well-being is sufficiently independent of that person's wants and desires to leave room for the notion of duties to oneself.[12]

5. SELF-RESPECT AND DUTIES TO ONESELF

Once this obstacle to the view that people have duties to themselves is removed it is hard to avoid the conclusion that such duties exist. To take one example, consider the notion of self-respect. At the core of this complex notion lies a simple belief. To have self-respect is to believe that there are things one should do and others one should not, and that the value there is in one's life depends on conducting oneself appropriately. This core belief commits the self-respecting person to the further belief that he should be treated in certain ways by himself and by others. In particular to have self-respect is to believe that one should discharge one's responsibilities oneself, and not expect others to bail one out every time. Correspondingly, the self-respecting person holds that others should treat one as someone who is capable of rational responsible agency, and should not treat one as a child or a mere object. Thus self-respect implies a belief that one's capacity for rational action, and one's endeavours to conduct one's life through the responsible exercise of that capacity, give value to one's life. That value is not, as we have seen, merely a guide to others, a constraint on other people's behaviour towards one. First and foremost, it guides the agent's own endeavours, one's conception of how to lead one's own life. When self-respect is justified this is because these beliefs are well-founded. That is, people should respect themselves because they are rational agents and

---

[12] This cannot be explained as satisfying certain second order desires, e.g., that one's goals will be well informed, consistent, rational, and in harmony with the good of humankind etc., as Blackburn might suggest (Cf. his *Spreading The Word*). We are talking of being open to judgment, of seeing one's life as subject to a certain evaluation, whether or not one wishes this to be so.

to the extent that they endeavour to behave responsibly as such, to the extent, in other words, that they are responsible agents.

Two ranges of self-regarding reasons emerge. First, all who can should meet the conditions which entitle them to self-respect. They should respect their own capacity for rational agency, and should endeavour to exercise it responsibly, they should be responsible agents. Second, those who are responsible agents and are therefore entitled to respect themselves should do so. These complementary reasons arise from and reflect the value of self-respect as the condition which all persons should be entitled to and should enjoy. Important to my argument is the fact that these reasons are independent of our will. To say that one has reason to seek the conditions which entitle one to self-respect if that is what one happens to want is to misunderstand the situation. We cannot help wishing to have self-respect, feeling demeaned and denuded of value when we feel that we've compromised our self-respect, etc. We have no choice in the matter. There is no other way for us to live.

I think this claim that all persons should deserve and should have self-respect is intuitively very appealing. It enjoys the sort of obviousness I remarked upon above, which suggests it is deeply embedded in the concepts through which we understand ourselves, concepts such as those of personhood, agency, and well-being. Why this is so is not far to seek. The notion of discharging one's responsibility, of responsible agency, which is crucial to this account of self-respect, is a formal notion. It does not specify what our responsibilities are. It merely identifies us as rational beings who are guided by reason. The explanation of the entitlement to self-respect in terms of responsible agency employs concepts which were also used to explain individual well-being. A person's well-being is the successful pursuit of worthwhile goals. Self-respect is earned by the endeavour to live a life of such pursuits. Self-respect is, therefore, a condition of individual well-being. Only those who deservedly respect themselves can have a successful life. Failing to respect oneself, or to be entitled to such respect, is perhaps the most fundamental way of failing in one's life.[13]

The reasons everyone has to earn and to possess self-respect imply, *inter alia*, that they have duties to treat themselves in the ways appropriate to

---

[13] Two caveats must be entered here in lieu of a more careful and extended discussion of the subject which will take us beyond the ambit of the present essay.

First, nothing follows from the above as to any reason people have or may fail to have to continue with their lives. The only implications are concerning appropriate ways of life, while one is alive, if I may be excused this pleonasm.

Second, further steps are required to establish that people should not merely meet the conditions which entitle them to self-respect but should also respect themselves when they are entitled to. This follows partly because the absence of self-respect tends to be destructive of the entitlement to it (one neglects one's rational capacity and its responsible exercise) and largely from the essential contribution of having a sound self-image for the quality of people's lives.

responsible agents. Duties are but a special kind of categorical reasons, they are peremptory reasons, reasons which exclude consideration of and prevail over certain categories of reasons. Given the importance of self-respect, one's concern for one's own self-respect is sufficient to establish self-regarding duties. In particular, there is every justification to regard each person as having a duty to preserve the conditions necessary for his own self-respect. We have little hesitation in holding that people are under a duty to honour the self-respect of others, when it is deserved, and to treat them accordingly. The very same considerations establish that each person has a duty to respect and protect the conditions which entitle him to self-respect.

What kind of duty is this? Is it a moral duty? It does not arise out of concern for others. It is a duty derived from considerations of each individual's own well-being. It is, therefore, a self-regarding duty, a duty each person owes to himself. Traditional morality regards such duties as moral. If morality encompasses all categorical reasons, that is, all the reasons whose validity does not derive from the contingent desires of the people to whom they apply, then we should classify the duty to meet the conditions of one's self-respect as a moral duty. In modern philosophical, and, to an extent, popular parlance, 'morality' has acquired a different sense. It has come to designate those reasons whose validity derives from considerations which relate to the welfare of others (i.e., people other than those to whom the reason applies). In that sense the duty to respect the conditions of one's own self-respect is not a moral duty.

I do not wish to suggest that this issue is without importance. But it is secondary to the basic lessons of this argument, namely, that given a proper understanding of individual well-being there are strong arguments for recognizing the existence of self-regarding duties, and that at least some of these are of great importance.

6. DUTIES AS CONSTITUTIVE OF GOODS

The previous section completes the main part of my argument. It establishes the existence of duties which do not derive from rights. It does so through explicitly challenging some conceptions of well-being and implicitly questioning common notions of the relationship between the so-called prudential and the so-called moral reasons. So far, however, the argument for the existence of duties we relied upon was the customary one. It is built around the claim that there is a good which the existence of the duty or the carrying out of the duty will serve. The relation between the duty thus established and the justifying good is external in that the good can be completely specified in a way which does not involve reference to the duty.[14] The good justifying the duty to see to the education of one's children, for example, is that they will receive an education, and that good is completely specifiable without referring to the duty.

One reason for the widespread misunderstanding of the role of duties is the assumption that all duties are justified by an external relation to a justifying good. Some deontological views reject that assumption and go to the opposite extreme. They deny that the justification of duties can depend or need depend on their relation to justifying goods. I will conclude this paper by arguing for a different point, namely that duties may be internally related to their justifying goods.

In its essentials the case is simple. There are many activities, relationships, etc., which are intrinsically good. Listening to good music is an example. It is good in being a worthwhile, enjoyable activity in itself, regardless of its consequences. Having a loving relationship with another human being is another example. Some activities and relationships cannot be specified except by reference to duties (or rights). Paying a debt might serve as an example. It is the paying of money one had a duty to repay. It is an activity internally related to a duty. It is not, however, an intrinsically valuable activity. The justifying good of this duty is in its contribution to welfare and that can be specified without reference to the duty. Some activities and relationships which cannot be specified except by reference to duties are intrinsically good. Friendship is such a case in which the two properties coincide. Friendships ought to be cultivated for their own sake. They are intrinsically valuable. At the same time the relations between friends, the relationship which constitutes friendship, cannot be specified except by reference to the duties of friendship. When this is the case the justifying good is internally related to the duty. The duty is (an element of) a good in itself.

Let us examine the implications of this case. Friends owe duties to each other, duties which arise out of the friendship. For example, there are duties of aid and support which friends owe each other, and which go beyond the general duty to aid people in need. These and similar duties are part of what makes friendship into what it is. They are constitutive of the relationship. A relationship between people who enjoy amusing themselves in each other's company but do not owe each other any special duties is not friendship. To become friends with another is to enter a relation of a known and predefined kind, one consisting, alongside patterns of attitudes and expectations, of rights and duties. It is not a rigid framework. Within its established contours there is much scope for individuals to define the nature of their friendship. But a framework there must be and it includes the normative components of friendship, its constitutive rights and duties. An essential element of this

---

[14] This distinction between an external and an internal relation should not be confused with the intrinsic/instrumental distinction. An external relation can be either intrinsic or instrumental, an internal relation is necessarily intrinsic.

argument is that for friendship to be possible it must be predefined. It is predefined by social practices which establish and mark out patterns of interaction between people. The ability of people to have a particular relationship depends on its being established by social practices known to them, and which they share, at least to some degree. People nowadays cannot establish the relations between master and apprentice which existed in mediaeval society. They are not part of our culture and cannot be authentically resurrected. The dependence of forms of valuable activities and relationships on social practices arises out of three factors.

First, intrinsic goods have a normative aspect. They are not patterns of action and interaction which we stray into accidentally (this may happen, but it is very unlikely, and in any case is not typical). We aim at them because they are good. They must, therefore, be known so that one could aim at them, so that one could direct oneself in the relationship in a way which is consistent with its continuation and prosperity, when that is desirable. Second, relations and activities (e.g. practising medicine) are thick with details which make it impossible for people to engage in them except through internalizing through socialization the forms of conduct which constitute them, which make for the successful pursuit of such activities and relations. Hence the need for a social practice which will make the acquisition of the required implicit knowledge possible. Third, and finally, in most valuable activities and relations the participants' perception of their own situation is an integral part. In particular, there is a big difference between an exploratory, innovative, perhaps iconoclastic or rebellious activity and relationship, and a normal one. Consciousness of normality or its absence has deep ramifications for the nature of the relationship. Hence the importance of a background of established practices against which both normality and innovative deviation can be measured.

This dependence of intrinsically valuable activities and relationships on social practices helps explain how they can be partly defined by a structure of rights and duties. Social practices are an important means of establishing rights and duties. They are a familiar means for defining and circumscribing patterns of action and interaction. When engaging in such patterns is intrinsically valuable we have the internal relationship between duties and their justifying goods.

The justification of the duties of friendship is that they make, or are part of, a relationship which is intrinsically valuable. This is an internal justification since it justifies the duty by reference to a good which is itself made in part by that duty. This does not lead to circularity in the justification. It merely means that the justification of the duty is by placing it in a wider context to which it contributes and which is good in itself. Some duties are constitutive of the good. They make activities and relationships such as friendship into the goods they are.

7. LIBERATING DUTIES

Everything which was said of duties in the preceding argument applies with equal force to rights. But it is not surprising that it applies to rights. Rights are, we are all used to thinking, always goods. There is little resistance to the idea that they are sometimes intrinsically good. Not so with duties. They are fetters, they always, or so we are accustomed to thinking, are established for the interest of others and are liable to be against the interest of those subject to them. This is not thought to be an accident. The very role of duties in practical reasoning is seen to be to subject the actions of one person to the will or the interests of another. I have argued that this picture is fundamentally mistaken; that there are self-regarding duties, duties which arise out of their subjects' own well-being. Furthermore, duties may be intrinsically good, and their existence may be essential to the existence of valuable activities and relationships. Their existence creates valuable op-portunities, constitutes valuabe options. Without them we would not merely be less restrained by concern for the interest of others. But for their presence our own lives would be considerably impoverished.

3

Rights and Individual Well-Being

Groups and corporations can and do have rights. Nations have a right to self-determination; Woolworth owns stores and has rights against its employees, etc. Yet there is a sense in which individual rights are the central case of rights. Corporate and collective rights are in that sense extensions of the institution beyond its primary terrain. When ascribing rights to groups and corporations, just as when holding them to be subject to duties, to be responsible, guilty, etc., one is treating them as individuals, applying to them concepts whose direct and primary application is to individuals, concepts which are comprehensible in these further applications only by extending to them features of their primary domain.

The primacy of individual rights is therefore not so much a special feature of rights as a fact about groups and corporations. They are individuals by extension, on sufferance only. Nevertheless, many have seized on the primacy of individual rights as one sign that the special role of rights, their special function or significance in moral and political thought, is that they represent the individual's perspective or interest against the general or public good or against the claims, demands, needs, or requirements of others generally. Challenging this view is the purpose of this essay. It has no specific target. It will not consider any of the many yet diverse writings which embraced the idea that in some such conflict between concern for the individual rightholder and the general good lies the key to the special role of rights in moral and political discourse. My target is rather a pervasive feeling, a generalized view of this nature which permeates much philosophical and some popular thought on the subject.

This being so, it may be surprising that I claim to be merely explicating the underlying features of our common culture. My contention is that the view that conflict between the individual and the general good is central to the understanding of rights misinterprets surface features of rights. The correction of such distortion will retain enough of the sources of the distortion to explain how it arises, and yet will avoid its misleading conclusions.

To the extent that the views to be outlined below can be here defended, the argument is phenomenological in style: it points to fundamental features of our common culture. No more than a gesture towards such an argument is possible here. But a word must be said in defence of relying on such an argument. Is it based on the complacent assumption that our

First published in *Ratio Juris*, 5/2 (July 1992).

moral beliefs and political arrangements are all right as they are? Not in the least. Though the conclusions are normative, they can and should be based on our common culture, for they do not defend a particular view about the proper distribution of rights or the specific grounds for the possession of rights. Such conclusions cannot rest on an examination of the status quo. What can be based on existing culture are conclusions about the nature of our concepts, their structure and general features, and about their role and function in moral and political thought. The question of the relation between concern for the right-holder and for the public good, and its significance to an understanding of the foundations of rights, belongs to this structural or conceptual level, hence the phenomenological approach.[1]

I. A PROBLEM TO START FROM

There is a puzzle about rights which, even if not deep, is revealing of the motives for many of the common views about them. On the one hand, typically rights are to what is, or is thought to be, of value to the right-holder. On the other hand, quite commonly the value of a right, the weight it is to be given, or the stringency with which it is to be observed do not correspond to its value to the right-holder. Since rights are, generally speaking, to benefits, to what is in the interest of or is valuable for the right-holder, it is plausible to suppose that that interest is the basis of the right, i.e. that the reason for the right, its justification, is the fact that it serves the right-holder's interest. But in that case we would also expect the weight or importance of the right to correspond to the weight or importance of the interest it serves. Since this is clearly not the case, since the weight of rights diverges from the weight of the interests they serve, one would expect that the reasons for or justification of rights relate to considerations other than those interests. But if so, why do rights dovetail with interests? Why do we generally have rights only to what is in our interest? Can this be a mere coincidence?

The suggestion that no more than a coincidence is involved may be thought to be sustained by the cautious generalization stated that it is only generally the case that what one has a right to is in one's interest. But the possible exceptions to this rule are not ones which undermine the thought that there is a strong conceptual connection between a right and the interest of the right-holder. Most have to do with disputes about the nature of individual interest. Consider the view that offenders have a right to be punished.

---

[1] I do not mean to deny that a radical critique of our culture and its very concepts can sometimes be successful and play a legitimate role.

We find it odd precisely because being punished is not commonly thought to be in the interest of the punished. The defence of the right invariably includes showing that in fact it is, that it is not merely good that offenders are punished but that it is good to them to be punished. A person's interest will be understood to mean that which is good for him, i.e. that which makes his life intrinsically a better life, better not for others or for a cause but in itself as a human life. This familiar notion of personal well-being is the one that people use in deliberating about their own life, or aspects of it. The notion of the good life for a person is closely connected to the notion of the life that a person would (logically) desire for himself, be proud of or content with, etc. By and large it consists of the successful pursuit of and engagement in worthwhile pursuits, activities, and relationships, and in the absence of factors which impede such success. Once the notion of individual well-being is so understood we can remove the qualification and assert that rights are always to what is in the interest of the right-holder.[2]

It is, therefore, not accidental that rights are to what is in the interest of the owner, and it is implausible that that fact does not affect the reasons justifying the existence of rights. But saying this only restates the puzzle. For it seems equally clear that the importance of a person's right often bears little relation to the importance of his interest. One type of example is often produced to illustrate the point. I may own something which is of little value to me, say, an old shirt. Since it is my shirt, others have a duty to respect my right to it. Rights always justify the existence of duties on (some) others. This in itself shows that the right exceeds in importance the interest which it protects, since had I no right to it my interest in having the shirt would not have justified holding others to be duty-bound to let me have it.

The same conclusion can be reached by a different route. Imagine two people with an equal interest in having the shirt. It is clear that the one who owns it should have it. But as their interest gives them equal claim to it, this can only be because the right-holder's right to the shirt is a reason for giving it to him which is greater than his interest. His right does not merely reflect his interest, it adds to it an additional, independent reason.

[2] Several additional clarifications are called for but cannot be explored in detail here. One of them, the care one has to take in explaining the various common ways of stating what one has a right to, will be mentioned below. Another important clarification is obvious: what one can have a right to may be in one's interest to have in some respect but not in others. One may have a right to some valuable property which may make one a target for criminals or for temptation. It may be in one's overall interest not to have it, but as having the property is in one's interest in some respect one can have a right to it. Finally, sometimes the right-holder's interest, which is the reason or justification for his having the right, is not in what he has a right to but in the having of a right. Trivially, rights are assets. But only exceptionally is the fact that if I have a right to something I'll have an asset the justifying reason for my having that right. See *The Morality of Freedom* for a more thorough exploration of this as well as other aspects of the views expressed here.

II. SEIZING THE SECOND HORN: SEN'S GOAL-RIGHTS

Faced with our mini-dilemma, Sen embraces the second horn with some gusto.[3] Pointing to the apparent lack of correspondence between the weight of rights and the weight of the interest in the object of the right, he concludes that rights are separate from a person's interests. In moral thought they represent independent moral goals with their own distinct weight. In considering what is to be done, we should act on the balance of reasons, which is based in part on a comparison of people's conflicting interests and in part on the additional, independent factor that some of them have rights.

Had morality been a hypothetical-deductive system designed to generate people's moral judgments, Sen's view might possibly be acceptable. It is possible that most of the moral judgments common in our society can be derived from an axiomatic system consisting of separate interest-promoting and rights-protecting principles. But morality resembles much more a system of reasoning or a network of intelligible connections between interconnected ideas. Moral theory is not committed to reproducing or vindicating common moral beliefs. It aims at displaying the connections between moral ideas and principles in ways which manifest their intelligibility. Sen's position leaves the puzzle we started from as perplexing as it was. It does not explain why rights are to benefits. This remains a mysterious coincidence, made even more mysterious by being a conceptually necessary coincidence. Sen cannot say that the point of rights is to protect and promote people's interests. According to him, while rights always serve the right-holder's interests, they do so by endowing the protection of these interests with importance greater than their intrinsic importance warrants. This mystery left unexplained raises the suspicion that if this is what rights are then no rights are ever justified.

I think that there is a second snag in Sen's account. It assumes that in reasoning what to do we normally add the weight of rights to the reasons arising from the interests those rights serve. When considering whether to take my friend's book without his consent, I am supposed to weigh as two separate and independent factors the value of the book to him and his right to the book. In fact, while the two factors figure in our reasoning, they figure as interdependent considerations. I will not take the book because it belongs to him and because it is important to respect this particular right more than (for instance) his right to the old shirt, because the book is of great value to him. The value of the book, in other words, figures in assessing the importance of the right, and is not an independent separate consideration.

[3] A. Sen, 'Agency and Rights', *Philosophy and Public Affairs*, 11 (1982).

III. EMBRACING THE FIRST HORN: FINESSING THE
INTEREST THEORY

The relevance of the interest promoted or protected by the right to the
assessment of its importance is just what one would expect, given the close
connection between rights and right-holders' interests. The trouble is that
this merely returns us to the dilemma: if the two are that closely connected,
why does the importance of rights so often fail to match the value of the
interests of the right-holder that they are meant to protect? One response is
to claim that in fact the alleged mismatch is merely illusory. A fuller, subtler
understanding of the right-holders' interests will eliminate the worrying
apparent discrepancy.

This response deserves to be taken seriously. Even if it fails to close the
gap and to solve the puzzle, it may narrow the gap, instructing us in the
process about the complex relationship between interests and values and
the institutions which serve them. I refer to institutions deliberately, for one
of the common arguments used to bridge the apparent gap between the
weight of interests and that of rights is to the effect that rights belong to
the ground level of practical thought in which we use simple-to-apply rules,
whereas the interests protected by the rights are referred to at the more
fundamental level of thought at which the justification for the ground-level
rules are established. The need for ground-level rules to be simple to learn
and apply is invoked to explain why they deviate from the accurate measure of the interest they are there to serve. This, however, does not after all
show that there is a gap between the weights of rights and the right-holders'
interests that they serve. The gap appears only if one has a blinkered view
of the right-holders' interests that rights serve, a view which is blind to the
interest in being able to guide one's action on the basis of simple and
manageable rules.[4]

There is a second way in which the gulf between right-holders' interests
and their rights may be claimed to be distorted by some superficial accounts
of the question. They disregard people's interest in freedom, in being able
to control a segment of their environment according to their will. Consider
my interest in an old shirt or in a book. The previous remarks on such cases
disregarded the fact that I have not only an interest in having the shirt or

---

[4] That interest is itself partly a derivative one. It is the interest in having one's other interests
reliably served, which cannot be done except by relying in most circumstances on simple
rules. In part, however, it is a distinctive separate interest in having a life in which calculations
and complicated evaluations play only a minor role. My remarks in the text above are consistent with the previous observation that the interests rights serve are used to determine
the importance of rights. It is merely that only on relatively rare occasions would one avoid
the general rule relating the average importance of an interest to the weight of the protecting
right, and proceed to examine its importance to the individual concerned at the time in
question.

the book but also in being the one who decides whether I shall have them or destroy them.

The right-holder's interest in freedom is part of the justification of most rights and is the central element in the justification of some. It is, of course, particularly prominent in the justification of the great civil liberties. Freedom of religion, freedom of speech, freedom of association, of occupation, of movement, of marriage, and the like, are all important not because it is important that people should speak, should engage in religious worship, should marry or travel, etc., but because it is important that they should decide for themselves whether to do so or not.

While this point is obvious when we refer to these rights as 'freedom of such and such', or as civil liberties, it is less obvious when they are referred to as the right to marry, to travel, etc. Then we are liable to confuse the fact that the importance of the matters the rights deal with (speech, marriage, occupation) accounts for the importance of individual freedom in these matters with the different (and often much exaggerated) claim that individuals have an interest in exercising these rights in certain ways (getting married, speaking out, etc.). The confusion is all the more common in the case of some other rights. It is easy to overlook the role of the interest in freedom in the justification of property rights, and this accounts for much of the impression that there is a big gulf between the importance of the right-holder's interest and the importance of the right.

These remarks move us some way from our original puzzle. They lead to the rejection of the view that the interest of the right-holder in what he has a right to can be expected to be the reason for the right. While it is true that rights are to benefits, the justifying benefit need not be the benefit one has a right to. It is often the freedom to control the fate of that benefit. What the right is a right to, as the expression is here understood, depends on how the right is described, and often there are different ways of describing it, so that the same right can be said to be a right to marry and a right to have the freedom to marry, etc. What puzzles us, however, cannot be eliminated by verbal reformulations. It is the putative gap between the value of right-holders' interests on which a right is supposed to be based and the value of that right itself. The remarks above show that this gap is much smaller than often appears.

IV. THE INTEREST OF OTHERS

While the gap may be narrower than it appears once the relations between rights and ground-level rules, and the importance of our interest in freedom, are taken into account, these considerations fail to bridge it. There are still the cases where you know not only that I do not need the book but that I do not mind and have no reason to mind your taking it without permission, i.e. that my interest in freedom is not at stake either. On such occasions, when all the facts are known and known to be known, there is no reason to follow a generalized simple rule. Rather, one would do better by acting on the basis of a more thorough and sensitive evaluation of the considerations underlying the rule.

Single-minded rights-holder interest theorists may not be deterred by the remaining mismatch between common evaluations of the importance of rights and their importance when judged according to their account of them. They may remind us that the appeal to common judgments concerning rights was not an end in itself. We were never set on vindicating common morality. Rather, we were looking for a better understanding of the concept of rights and its role in moral thought. The mismatch between common views about rights and the judgments generated by a theory was mere evidence that the theory missed some of the central features of the concept. If it did not, then the discrepancy in judgment is mere evidence of common fallacies about rights. Given that the remaining mismatch is not much, and is relatively sporadic and unsystematic, it seems consistent with the view that rights are indeed based exclusively on the interests of the right-holders, and that the notion is sometimes misapplied in practice.

In fact—and that is the snag in this argument—the remaining mismatch between the theoretical account we are examining and common judgments does include a systematic distortion of the role of rights in practical thought, and cannot be completely accounted for as a result of misapplying the concept. Though unusual, the right of a condemned pregnant woman not to be executed until after her child is delivered can serve as a point of departure. The right protects an interest of the woman, but the respect with which it is treated in some of the countries which maintain capital punishment is due to concern not for the woman but for her child. It is the child's interest which is the justifying reason for the woman's right. It is the woman's right none the less, for the child does not yet exist and has no rights, and because his interest in this respect is served by serving the interest of the woman.

Welfare law provides many similar examples. I, as a parent, have, in English law, a right to a periodic payment known as child benefit, which I receive because I am a parent and because benefiting me is a good way of benefiting my child. People who support invalid parents or spouses have similar rights to reductions in their tax liability, and there are many other examples. In all of them the weight of the right does not match the right-holder's interest which it serves, because in all of them the right is justified by the fact that by serving the interest of the right-holder it serves the interest of some others, and their interest contributes to determining the weight due to the right.

These examples indicate the road the argument should follow to solve the initial puzzle. How can rights both be based on the right-holders' interests and fail to match the weight and importance of these interests? They can since the right-holders' interests are only part of the justifying reason for many rights. The interests of others matter too. They matter, however, only when they are served by serving the right-holders' interests, only when helping the right-holder is the proper way to help others.

The examples mentioned have another common feature which is, I suspect, of general significance. They are cases in which, so far as the rights in question extend, the interests of the right-holders and those of the others whose benefit is part of the justifying reason are doubly harmonious. Not only do the others benefit through the benefit to the right-holders but the right-holders themselves benefit from the service their rights do to those others.

All the examples have concerned benefits to dependent relations. People's success in pursuing worthwhile relationships contributes to their own well-being. Having rights which are designed to benefit one's children, spouse, or parents helps one in the conduct of one's relations with these people. Hence, by having rights for the benefit of others one does, in the cases we discuss, benefit oneself through benefiting others just as much as those others benefit from one's (financial) benefit secured by these rights.

Two clarificatory comments may help at this point. First, it is clear that the examples under discussion concern cases in which one is duty-bound to look after one's children, spouse, or parents. The right helps one in discharging one's duty, and it may be tempting to think that this shows that there is here a conflict between the right-holder's interest and that of his dependent relations. This would be to fall into the mistake of regarding a person's duties as essentially curtailing his freedom to pursue his own interest, and therefore as always in conflict with his interest. Far from this being so, duties often define avenues through which one's well-being can be promoted. The duties of friendship, for example, are part of what defines friendship and makes it a valuable option for people.[5] Second, two complementary points have been emphasized. On the one hand, rights are sometimes justified by the service they secure for people other than the right-holder. On the other, other people's interests count for the justification of the right only when they are harmoniously interwoven with those of the right-holder, i.e. only when benefiting him is a way of benefiting them, and where by benefiting them the right-holder's interest is served. But this harmonious relation should not be thought to reduce the justification of the right to the interest of the right-holder alone. Though he gains from the

---

[5] On friendship, see Raz *The Authority of Law*, ch. 15. There is no denying, of course, that commitments to friends and relations may well call for action contrary to self-interest on occasion.

benefit the right secures to others, the weight and importance of the right depends on its value to those others, and not on the benefit that this in turn secures to the right-holder. The dilemma of the relations between the right-holder's well-being and the right it justifies is solved by escaping between its horns, not by embracing one of them.

V. RIGHTS AND THE COMMON GOOD

The examples we have considered are special, but they exemplify only one type of a general category, the most important and common type of which are rights which are based on the general interest, as well as on the interest of the right-holder. I shall refer variably to the 'general, or common good or interest' in its traditional sense, in which it refers not to the sum of the good of individuals but to those goods which, in a certain community, serve the interest of people generally in a conflict-free, non-exclusive, and non-excludable way.[6]

Oxford is even today a beautiful city. For the people of Oxford, its beauty is a common good in this sense, and so is the existence of those of its buildings, streets, town-planning regulations, etc., which lend it its beauty and preserve it. Living in a beautiful city, I am of course assuming, is in one's interest. It may conflict with some other aspects of one's interest. Some people leave beautiful cities to take a job, to look after their parents, to get married, etc. One may have conflicting interests, and one's interest in living in a beautiful city may not be one's greatest interest. So a person may have interests which conflict with his interest to live in a beautiful city. But even though not necessarily in their best interest all things considered, living in a beautiful city serves an aspect of everyone's interest, and there-fore the beauty of a city is a good to its people. And it is a common good, for its enjoyment by one person does not detract from its enjoyment by others, and because none of its inhabitants can be denied that good. It is what I have called elsewhere a collective good, i.e. it is a conceptual truth that it is a public good in the currently common sense of the term among economists.

The protection of many of the most cherished civil and political rights in liberal democracies is justified by the fact that they serve the common or general good.[7] Their importance to the common good, rather than their contribution to the well-being of the right-holder, justifies the high regard in which such rights are held and the fact that their defence may involve a

---

[6] For a particularly clear explanation of the notion see J. M. Finnis, *Natural Law and Natural Rights* (Oxford: Oxford Univ. Press, 1980), ch. 6.

[7] Arguably the same is true of all rights, though the importance to the common good of protecting them varies from case to case.

considerable cost to the welfare of many people. When people are called upon to make substantial sacrifices in the name of one of the fundamental civil and political rights of an individual, this is not because in some matters the interest of the individual or the respect due to the individual prevails over the interest of the collectivity or of the majority. It is because by protecting the right of that individual one protects the common good and is thus serving the interest of the majority.

The defence of this claim may start by observing that the common good often meets the condition of dual harmony with individual interest. Consider Juliet, an architect who is hired by Oxford City Council to devise a preservation scheme for central Oxford. She has a personal interest in being able to carry out the task. However, in doing her job she is serving the common good as well as her personal interest. If the public rises in uproar when property speculators scheme for her unjust dismissal, this is likely to reflect more than the public concern that an individual shall not be unjustly treated. It will also reflect the public interest in the beauty of the city. The evil is seen to be doubly great in being aimed against the common good as well as being an injustice to an individual. In this case Juliet's interest displays the doubly harmonious relation to the public good. In protecting her interest one protects the common good, and, as always, the protection of the common good serves her interest since she is a member of the community.

Juliet's right is protected with particular vigour because of its importance to the common good. But hers is a special case. By dint of a combination of circumstances her interest in her contract of employment serves, for a time at least, the common good. The claim staked above is that a combination of private interest and the public good characterizes many of the fundamental civil and political rights and accounts for their centrality in our public culture.

The argument has two stages. The first establishes that the protection of individual civil and political rights serves the common good. The second shows that the common good served by those rights is, in the majority of cases, more important to individuals than the enjoyment of their own civil and political rights, and therefore that the status the rights enjoy in the liberal democracies is due to their contribution to the common good.

Consider freedom of contract. It is a vital means for assuring people a measure of control over the conduct of their affairs. Its value to individuals depends on protection from duress, deceit, misrepresentation, restraint of trade, etc. Hence individuals have rights securing them from such abuses. These rights also contribute greatly to the existence of an open market, i.e. an environment in which people can compete and make agreements free from the abuses we mentioned. The existence of such an environment is a common good. It serves not only those who make contracts. If you doubt this, think of young children. They do not make contracts, but they benefit from the fact that they live in a free society in which people generally have power to control the conduct of their own affairs, to the extent that that is guaranteed by freedom of contract and the existence of a free market. Furthermore, the existence of a free market and the institutions protecting it is a common good to all those who are thereby made able to make contracts, for our contractual relations are what they are because of the market and would have been very different but for it.

Here is a typical case of individual rights playing a major part in securing the existence of a common good. Similar relations between rights and the common good recur across a whole array of civil and political rights. Rights such as freedom of marriage and freedom of occupation are most like free-dom of contract. They create an environment in which careers are freely chosen and family ties freely undertaken. In so doing they contribute to determining the character of marriage, and the significance of careers in the lives of individuals. For arranged marriages are, for the majority, a different kind of relationship from freely contracted ones, and the meaning for a skilled jeweller of his career differs depending on whether he engages in it out of his own free choice or because his father was a jeweller and he had virtually no choice but to follow in his footsteps. Freedom of contract, freedom of occupation, and freedom of marriage, by affecting the mode of entry into various relationships and enterprises, affect the nature, content, and significance of those enterprises. And their impact is not confined to those who make use of them. They affect everyone in the community where they prevail.

One last example will have to do here. Freedom of expression is among the foundation-stones of all political democracies. The right of free expression serves to protect the interest of those who have it and who may wish to use it to express their views. It also serves the interest of all those who have an interest in acquiring information from others. But here again the right serves the interests of those who are neither speakers nor listeners. Everyone who lives in a democracy is affected by the fact that this is a society enjoying a free exchange of information. One may go one step further. If I were to choose between living in a society which enjoys freedom of expression, but not having the right myself, or enjoying the right in a society which does not have it, I would have no hesitation in judging that my own personal interest is better served by the first option. I think that the same is true for most people. Politicians, journalists, writers, etc., excepted, their right of free expression means little in the life of most people. It rightly means less to them than their success in their chosen occupation, the fortunes of their marriages, or the state of repair of their homes.

This explains why civil and political rights which are the prize of the official culture of liberal democracies do not enjoy a similar place in the estimation of most ordinary people. Many people judge them by their contribution to their well-being, and it is not much. Their real value is in their contribution to a common liberal culture. That culture serves the interests of members of the community. Given the great contribution that observance of the civil and political rights of individuals makes to the preservation of the common good, it would be irrational not to let that fact be reflected in the value of the rights. Given the doubly harmonious relation between the individual interest served by these rights and the public good they contribute to, and given that this mutually reinforcing relation is stable and secure, rather than coincidental, there is every reason to regard the value of the rights to the common good as part of their justification. That makes it also a factor in determining the weight of the rights. Here, then, we have arrived at the core of the explanation of our initial puzzle: in the case of the central civil and political rights of liberal societies, the main reason for the mismatch between the importance of the right and its contribution to the right-holder's well-being is the fact that part of the justifying reason for the right is its contribution to the common good.[8]

VI. THE CASE FOR CONSTITUTIONAL JUDICIAL REVIEW

Most of the liberal democracies have developed political systems which endow the courts with special responsibility for the protection of the fundamental civil and political life of the individual. Sometimes this is done through an attachment to a constitutional document with officially declared superior standing in which the fundamental rights are enshrined (as in the USA). Alternatively this is done in the name of fundamental doctrines of a common law; though formally the legislature can override such a law, the official assumption is that it will not intend to do so, and therefore legislative acts can be 'interpreted' beyond recognition to conform with the fundamental rights (as in the UK).[9] The question of the suitability of the courts to the task they are expected to perform raises many issues concerning the history of the countries concerned and their political culture and institutions, the exploration of which extends well beyond the province of political theory. The preceding reflections on the nature of rights do, however, throw some light on the question.

---

[8] I wish to claim that this is the only valid explanation of the puzzle, but this claim requires an extensive examination of alternative accounts of rights which cannot be undertaken here.

[9] Far be it from me to suggest that the two types of protection of fundamental rights yield the same results. My only point is that the difference between them is often exaggerated, especially by those who overlook the degree to which the USA Supreme Court compromises with the legislative trends of the day. The difference in the practice of judicial review between the American court 100 years ago and the court today may well be greater than the difference between it and the British courts.

One of the ancient disputes concerning the role of constitutional review concerns the question of the relations between the courts and politics. Are the courts, in their constitutional adjudication, in charge of the creation and development of the law of the constitution in the light of political considerations of the kind which figure in ordinary and in constitutional law-making? Or are they to remain outside politics altogether? It is ancient wisdom that when both answers are repeatedly put to the critical test and are found, time and again, wanting, the fault lies with the question. Recent years have seen a new wave of attempts to escape the stifling barrenness of the question, and the preceding remarks point in the same direction.

Litigation concerning fundamental civil and political rights brings before the courts issues which inextricably combine issues of individual rights and issues of public policy concerning the common good. Any thought that the fact that the issues raised are matters of individual right keeps politics at bay is based on a profound misunderstanding of the nature of rights generally and of civil and political rights in particular.[10] Responsibility for fundamental rights brings the courts into the centre of the political arena, and makes their political involvement essential to their ability to discharge their functions.

Constitutional review is to be understood in relation to a model of a division of power between the different organs of government. But it is a division of political power—not a separation of powers which keeps the courts out of politics. It does not follow, however, that the courts merely duplicate the role of democratic or administrative law-making. There are many different kinds of political consideration, and constitutional review requires the courts to concentrate on one range of such considerations, while striving to steer clear of others.[11]

The politics of the common good, questions regarding what is and what is not in the public interest, are as controversial as other political issues. But

---

[10] The comments in the text inevitably skirt round many issues. One of them is this: assume that the courts have to decide matters which concern the common good. It does not follow that it is for them to settle substantive questions concerning what is required by the common good. All they have to do is give effect to the legislator's understanding of what is required by the common good. This view is based on a misunderstanding of the nature of the law. While legislators have power to turn their views into binding law, they have to do so before their views become binding. Just entertaining certain thoughts, or even expressing them at cocktail parties, public lectures, or in newspaper articles does not make them into law. They have to be properly enacted. Legislators can and do bind the courts to give effect to their (the legislators') views on the common law when they enact them. But when they enact laws or bills of rights requiring the courts to give effect to people's right of free expression, or privacy, etc., what they enact is the duty of the court to ascertain what are the proper limits of such rights and enforce them. In doing so the legislators direct the courts to consider substantive issues concerning the common good, for the determination of the rights is impossible without this. For a similar argument see R. M. Dworkin, *Taking Rights Seriously*, 2nd edn. (London: Duckworth, 1977).

[11] Note that this is a matter of degree. In the practical world of politics no clean division of labour is possible.

they are relatively free from conflict. By and large they concern the question of what is in the interest of all. The controversy involved is that of people who share a common interest but disagree on the best way to pursue it. It is not unreasonable to develop a different political mechanism for handling controversies of this kind from that for controversies which fundamentally reflect conflicts of interests. In particular, there is more room for procedures which rely on open argument and less reason to rely on democratic procedures. To the extent that the democratic process is meant to establish what is in people's individual interests, and to encourage them to engage in trading some of their interests with others in return for reciprocal agreement, such procedures are particularly apt for the politics of conflicting interests. The reasons to use the same procedures in the politics of the common good are less compelling.

The fact that the politics of the common good differ from the politics of conflicting interests manifests itself in the fact that beliefs about the general principles defining the common good of a society constitute much of the common political culture of that society. Much as the details of the common good, including important details, are subject to controversy, its general principles are agreed upon at least by central sections of the population. This is no accident. A good cannot be a common good in a society, however much it deserves to be so, unless it is enshrined in its general practices and respected by its political culture.

The tie between the political traditions of a country and its common good provides the answer to one crucial objection to the preceding argument. It may be objected that I have exaggerated the degree to which controversies about the common good are free from conflict. They involve balancing the common good against other interests from individuals, and to that extent they too are affected by conflicts of interests. The point is valid. The actual degree of conflict involved depends to a considerable extent on the strength and limits of the common tradition underpinning belief in the common good.

We now have an outline of an account of the proper role of constitutional review in most liberal democracies, in matters of fundamental civil and political rights. Since these fundamental rights inextricably combine issues of individual interest with questions of the public interest, they can and should, like other issues of individual rights, be dealt with by the courts. But at the same time they inevitably involve the courts in politics, since they cannot be settled except by deciding questions concerning the public interest. Since, controversial though these issues are, they are relatively free from conflict of interests and are to be settled on the basis of the central tenets of the political tradition of the country concerned, it is fitting that they should be removed from the ordinary democratic process and be assigned to a separate political process.

This means that the courts are political, but the political issues they deal with in constitutional review of fundamental rights differ for the most part in kind from the stuff that democratic politics is mostly concerned with. This does not mean, of course, that the job of the courts is to arrest the march of time and freeze the process of change which affects a country's political culture, and its common good, just as it affects everything else. All that is meant is that, in responding to change and in encouraging change, the courts should be attuned to the community's political traditions and to changes, which are normally continuous and gradual, in its common good, and not to short-term swings, however violent, in democratic politics.

The existence of a strong and independent judiciary and a legal profession imbued with the values of the liberal political culture of the country are necessary for the courts to be able to fulfil adequately this political role. When these and other necessary conditions obtain, one finds the familiar view of a judiciary which appears conservative and radical at the same time. It is conservative in its adherence to the persisting, only slowly changing tenets of a country's political culture. And yet it is radical in its willingness to ride political storms, to court unpopularity and the hostility of powerful groups in being loyal to those central traditions even in times when the tidal waves of politics make the majority or the powers that be blind to their value.

VII. CONCLUSION

A major theme of this essay is that the image of right as a bulwark of the right-holder's interest against the claim of others distorts the nature of the concept and its role in our thought. Little has been said to challenge directly theories such as Nozick's,[12] which start from first principles to derive propositions sustaining a view of rights in which their conflict with the interests and moral claims of others are central. But enough has been said to suggest that such views are radically revisionary. They gain no support from a balanced understanding of our concept of rights, nor from the role of rights in our moral and political culture.

The rejection of the picture of the fundamental conflict between the right-holder and the rest is premised on the rejection of another dichotomy, the dichotomy between self-interest and the moral claims of others, and alongside it the dichotomy between egoism and altruism. The traditional notion of the common good marks one crucial location where these distinctions fail. Instead of essentially competing with the well-being of the individual, the common good is presupposed by it. The range and nature of common

---

[12] R. Nozick, *Anarchy, State and Utopia* (New York: Basic Books, 1974).

goods determine the options available to individuals in their lives; they determine the channels which define the well-being of individuals. This leaves ample room for occasional conflict between individual well-being and the common good. But it marks the essential supportive connection between them.

Liberal political thought has often been guilty of overemphasizing the degree to which politics is a process of reconciling conflicting interests. The politics of the common good differs from the politics of conflict. The fact that it leads to heated public controversy should not obscure the difference, for we should not equate controversy with conflict of interests. This point is evident to academics, who naturally assume that no conflict of interest is essentially involved in the many academic controversies they engage in. The same is true of conflicts concerning the common good.

It is no accident that in the politics of the common good conflicting interests play a less important role than in other areas of politics. The existence of common goods depends on wide-ranging consensus. The relative absence of conflict of interests and the background of a common tradition makes the courts a suitable forum for the conduct of this branch of politics. Here, rights have a crucial role to play. Civil and political rights enjoy their centrality in our culture because they are effective means of protecting our liberal-democratic culture. The protection of rights is traditionally one of the central tasks entrusted to the courts. It is not surprising, therefore, that the courts have a central role to play in the politics of the common good. By serving individual rights they serve their community, in contributing to the protection and the development of its common culture.

4

Facing Diversity: The Case of Epistemic Abstinence

Both friends and foes often emphasize the way liberal thought is concerned primarily with individuals. The pursuit of freedom is often pictured as the protection of the individual from the tyranny of the majority. All too often this concern with individuals is taken to show liberalism's neglect of the importance of communities. Whatever truth this accusation may have when levelled at the way some writers have understood the liberal ideal, it is misguided when aimed at the ideal of individual freedom itself. People's individuality expresses itself in ways fashioned by social practices, and through their ability and inclination to engage in socially formed relations and pursuits. Concern for individual freedom requires recognition that an important aspect of that ideal is the freedom of people to belong to distinctive groups, with their own beliefs and practices, and the ability of such groups to prosper.

In recent years several liberal writers have made the response to pluralism —the response to the fact that our societies consist of groups and communities with diverse practices and beliefs, including groups whose beliefs are inconsistent with each other—central to their concern. In their work the connection between individual freedom and group prosperity becomes particularly evident.

This essay examines the contemporary philosophical responses of John Rawls and Thomas Nagel to the diversity of opinions, customs, and ideologies prevalent in our societies. While these responses differ in many important respects, they share a common core; they manifest, and try to defend, a common attitude marked by three features. First, the response of both thinkers to diversity is basically tolerant. They allow, to use Rawls's words, 'for a plurality of conflicting, and indeed incommensurable, conceptions of the meaning, value and purpose of human life'.[1] Second, the justification of tolerance is based not on the positive value of diversity, nor on the dangers of entrusting governments with the power to suppress it, but on considerations of fairness.[2] Third, these considerations lead them to draw boundaries, based on epistemic distinctions, to the reasons on which governments may

First published in *Philosophy and Public Affairs*, 19/1 (winter 1990). I am grateful to G. A. Cohen, Simon Coval, Gerald Dworkin, S. White, and the Editors of *Philosophy and Public Affairs* for helpful comments.

[1] 'Justice as Fairness: Political not Metaphysical', *Philosophy and Public Affairs*, 14/3 (summer 1985), 225 (hereafter referred to as 'Political not Metaphysical').

[2] I take it that Nagel's concern with impartiality is a concern with one aspect of fairness.

act. They advocate an epistemic withdrawal from the fray. Governments, like everyone else, should of course act for good reasons. This would seem to require governments to ascertain which reasons for action are valid and which are not. But, says Rawls, governments should not be concerned with the truth or falsity of the doctrine of justice which guides them. Nagel, following a slightly different line of reasoning, suggests that the reasons for certain views are so personal that a (true) doctrine of justice must disqualify such views, even if true, from serving as reasons for governmental action.

At least since Mill propounded the harm principle, liberal political thought has been familiar with arguments that certain true beliefs that individuals are justified in relying upon in the conduct of their private affairs may not be relied upon by governments. The arguments put forward by Rawls and Nagel are, however, novel. For never before has it been suggested that governments should be unconcerned with the truth of the very views (the doctrine of justice) which inform their policies and actions, and never before has it been argued that certain truths should not be taken into account because, though true, they are of an epistemic class unsuited for public life.[3] The purpose of this essay is limited and purely critical: it is to challenge the cogency of the reasons offered by both writers for epistemic abstinence.

I. EPISTEMIC ABSTINENCE

Some of Rawls's recent writings are concerned to explain and defend the foundations of his enterprise. When *A Theory of Justice* first appeared it impressed people not only by the scope of its conclusions, by the body of theory which seemed derivable from its principles of justice, but also by the depth of its foundations. In an age where there seemed little to choose between the intellectually barren battle of dogmatic ideologies (capitalist and Marxist in particular), on the one hand, and the narrow, uninspiring, pragmatic squabbling over details within each camp, on the other hand, *A Theory of Justice* demonstrated that there is room for rational theory-building on a grand scale.

The scale was impressive partly because it rejected the hand-to-mouth, piecemeal intuitionism of the many articles on 'relevant' topics such as racism, conscientious objection, and abortion, and showed how such diverse problems can be treated systematically as part of a unified theory based on a few leading ideas. Moreover, it was a theory which addressed the central aspects of our society, the fundamental issues of the distribution of power, status, and resources, and not merely peripheral areas of discontent such as

---

[3] Notice that the novelty in Nagel's position is in disqualifying certain true beliefs from providing justification for governmental action without showing that the beliefs are suspect and unreliable.

conscientious objection and civil disobedience, or particularly topical and urgent problems such as racism.

But the scale was equally impressive because, in its advocacy and use of the method of reflective equilibrium and of contractarian arguments, the theory revived Aristotelian and Kantian themes, and promised a method of resolving by rational argument the ancient disputes of political morality, and, as the more daring souls hoped, of morality generally. This revival of theoretical interest in the foundations of morality is the target of much of Rawls's recent writing, which is designed to disavow any such claims or aspirations. Instead, Rawls claims that the road to a theory of justice of an unmistakably liberal cast is through a good deal of epistemic abstinence.

Justice for Our Times

Epistemic abstinence is only one aspect of Rawls's modest conception of political theory. Four themes have to be distinguished, all of which are captured by the slogan 'Justice as Fairness: Political not Metaphysical'. First, it is a theory of *limited applicability*; second, it has *shallow foundations*; third, it is *autonomous*; finally, it is based on *epistemic abstinence*. I will explain these features one at a time, starting with the first.

Rawls's theory has limited applicability. We know that it is not a comprehensive theory of justice; it is a theory of the justice of the basic structure of society only.[4] What I have in mind here is the theoretically more startling fact that the theory does not apply to the basic structure of all societies: 'Justice as fairness is framed to apply to what I have called "the basic structure" of a modern constitutional democracy.'[5] This must have surprised the many early readers of Rawls who remember him limiting the application of his theory in a different way, to the description of perfectly just societies only, leaving out all the principles which apply only in societies which fall short of this ideal. Many readers saw this as making the theory irrelevant to our countries.[6] The new limitation on the applicability of the theory is designed not only to make it political and not metaphysical, but also to render it realistically relevant to contemporary circumstances, and to remove any trace of utopianism.

Rawls has never attempted a precise or exhaustive analysis of the features of modern constitutional democracies which make his theory suited to them.

[4] See *A Theory of Justice* (Cambridge, Mass.: Harvard Univ. Press, 1971), sec. 2, and 'The Basic Structure as Subject', in A. Goldman and J. Kim (eds.), *Values and Morals* (Dordrecht: Reidel, 1978), 47.

[5] 'Political not Metaphysical', 224.

[6] It would seem that Rawls, as many suspected, thinks that the USA and other modern Western democracies are basically just societies. This, as we will see, is a necessary, indeed a crucial, assumption if his theory is to be applicable to the contemporary societies it is meant for. On the limited applicability of the original theory, see *A Theory of Justice*, 245–6.

To my mind this is one of the very attractive features of his position. It is not merely the result of a desire to avoid pedantry; it should be seen as fundamental to the nature of Rawls's whole enterprise. The firm starting-point is the society of the here and now, and every society sufficiently like it. Generalizations regarding the basic features of the society of the here and now are not definitive of the boundaries of the enterprise. They are but (empirical) assumptions or conclusions which can be re-examined and revised. The only definitive foundation is the rootedness in the here and now.[7] This feature goes very deep. It affects not only the conditions of applicability of Rawls's theory but also the very aim of political philosophy. 'The aims of political philosophy depend on the society it addresses.'[8] Only because we live in societies of this kind is the construction of a theory of justice along Rawls's lines, a theory which has the aims he set it, a proper task for political philosophy. In parallel, these conditions of contemporary democracies determine not only the content but the very function and role of a doctrine of justice.

While Rawls gives no precise and exclusive enumeration of the contemporary conditions which make us subject to his theory of justice, two factors or clusters of factors figure prominently in his argument. First and foremost is *the fact of pluralism*. There is 'a diversity of general and comprehensive doctrines' and a 'plurality of conflicting and indeed incommensurable conceptions of the meaning, value and purpose of human life' which are 'affirmed by the citizens of democratic societies'. 'This diversity of doctrines —the fact of pluralism—is not a mere empirical condition that will soon pass away; it is . . . a permanent feature of the public culture of modern democracies.'[9] Second, our societies share a rich enough *common culture*

---

[7] To ask what is the scope of the indexical is to misunderstand its function. It is ineliminable. The writer's theory must, to be successful, apply to his society at the time of writing, but there is no general answer as to which other societies and what other times it applies to. The applicability of the theory to different societies must be examined on a case-by-case basis. General guidelines can be useful, but they should never be understood as exhausting the range of relevant considerations. The reflections here and in the text above go beyond anything Rawls can be regarded as committed to. They explain some of the background which makes me assent to his claim of limited applicability.

[8] 'The Idea of an Overlapping Consensus', *Oxford Journal of Legal Studies*, 7, (1987), 1. This is the opening sentence of the article.

[9] Ibid. 4. Altogether Rawls lists 7 features: '(1) the fact of pluralism; (2) the fact of the permanence of pluralism, given democratic institutions; (3) the fact that agreement on a single comprehensive doctrine presupposes the oppressive use of state power . . . ; (4) the fact that an enduring and stable democratic regime, one not divided into contending factions and hostile classes, must be willingly and freely supported by a substantial majority of at least its politically active citizens; (5) the fact that a comprehensive doctrine, whenever widely, if not universally, shared in society, tends to become oppressive and stifling; (6) the fact that reasonably favourable conditions . . . which make democracy possible exist; and finally, (7) the fact that the political culture of a society with a democratic tradition implicitly contains certain fundamental intuitive ideas from which it is possible to work up a political conception of justice suitable for a constitutional regime.'

consisting in principles accepted by all as valid. We have a public culture and a public reason which can be appealed to as standards whose validity is, in spite of the fact of pluralism, beyond dispute.

This delicate balance between diversity and agreement sets the task of political philosophy in constructing a theory of justice and identifies the presupposition of both its success and its applicability.

'Conditions for justifying a conception of justice hold only when a basis is established for political reasoning and understanding within a public culture. The social role of a conception of justice is to enable all members of society to make mutually acceptable to one another their shared institutions and basic arrangements, by citing what are publicly recognized as sufficient reasons, as identified by that conception.'[10]

This task of a political philosophy for our time—to construct a conception of justice out of the beliefs and principles which are part of our common culture, the beliefs which transcend the diversity endemic to our culture—brings us to the second sense in which the theory is political and not metaphysical. A theory of justice for our time has *shallow foundations*. Its justification starts with the fact that certain beliefs form the common currency of our public culture. It does not seek deep foundations for these beliefs; it concerns itself neither with their justification nor with its absence. A theory of justice 'tries to draw solely upon basic intuitive ideas that are embedded in the political institutions of a constitutional democratic regime and the public traditions of their interpretation. . . . it starts from within a certain political tradition.'[11]

The shallowness of the foundations is not forced on Rawls by the limited applicability of his theory. It is, in his mind, a result of its other two features, its autonomy and its epistemic abstinence. The *autonomy* of the theory of justice is its autonomy from general moral theory. As Rawls explains, his theory 'is not to be understood as a general and comprehensive moral conception that applies to the political order',[12] or to our concrete historical circumstances. Naturally, a theory can have limited applicability simply through including the conclusion that a universal theory bears on a particular subject or in particular circumstances. But Rawls's theory is no application of any more general moral doctrine. It is a self-standing political theory, which is not to be justified by its relations to a wider moral doctrine. This is one explanation of its shallow foundations: it starts not with general moral truths but with the givens of our common culture, which it takes as facts, irrespective of their validity or truth. And that is as far as it goes.

---

[10] 'Kantian Constructivism in Moral Theory', *Journal of Philosophy*, 77 (1980), 517 (hereafter referred to as 'Kantian Constructivism').

[11] 'Political not Metaphysical', 225. See also 228, and 'Overlapping Consensus', 6.

[12] Ibid. 3.

Embracing autonomy and shallow foundations is Rawls's response to the fact of pluralism. We should reconcile ourselves to pluralism. It should be accepted not merely as a permanent fact, but as one which shapes the doctrine of justice. That doctrine must derive from the elements in our culture which transcend pluralism, which form its common public culture. The beliefs, attitudes, and institutions which constitute that public culture may well have a sound foundation in some comprehensive, possibly universal, moral theory. Alternatively, they may lack sound foundations. Neither matters. The common culture matters to Rawls as a fact, regardless of truth. That is the meaning of the shallow foundations. They, and the autonomy of the doctrine of justice, allow the generation of a theory of justice which can form the basis of a consensus in the face of pluralism.

While Rawls regards the limited applicability and shallow foundations of his theory as independent though complementary aspects, he thinks that together, and combined with his doctrine of the social role of justice which informs them, they force on him the fourth measure of modesty we referred to above. The doctrine of justice must adopt a posture of epistemic abstinence. Rawls's *epistemic abstinence* lies in the fact that he refrains from claiming that his doctrine of justice is true. The reason is that its truth, if it is true, must derive from deep, and possibly non-autonomous, foundations, from some sound, comprehensive moral doctrine. Asserting the truth of the doctrine of justice, or rather claiming that its truth is the reason for accepting it, would negate the very spirit of Rawls's enterprise.[13] It would present the doctrine of justice as one of many competing comprehensive moralities current in our society, and this would disqualify it from fulfilling its role of transcending the disagreement among these many incompatible moralities.

To fulfill its social role of forming a basis for a consensus on the fundamental structure of society—thus enabling the citizens of a pluralistic society to discuss the constitutional principles of their society, and the implications of these principles, by reference to reasons which are acceptable to all regardless of their political, moral, and religious views—a doctrine of justice must be advocated on the ground that it commands or is capable of gaining a consensus of opinion, and not on the ground that it is true.

'Questions of political justice can be discussed on the same basis by all citizens, whatever their social position, or more particular aims and interests, or their religious, philosophical or moral views. Justification in matters of political justice is addressed to others who disagree with us, and therefore it proceeds from some consensus': "Overlapping Consensus", 6.' 'By avoiding comprehensive doctrines we

---

[13] As G. A. Cohen observed to me, this conclusion does not follow if all members of the community regard the doctrine of justice as self-evident. Then they could all agree to its truth without getting involved in any disagreements arising out of their comprehensive ethical and political views. Rawls has, of course, sufficient empirical evidence to know that his theory of justice is not accepted as self-evident by all in our society.

try to bypass religion and philosophy's profoundest controversies so as to have some hope of uncovering a basis of a stable overlapping consensus.'[14]

'Some might say', adds Rawls, 'that reaching this reflective agreement is itself sufficient grounds for regarding that conception as true, or at any rate highly probable. But we refrain from this further step: it is unnecessary and may interfere with the practical aim of finding an agreed public basis of justification.'[15] The social role of justice can be purchased only at the price of epistemic distance.

Justice in Our Time, or Has Rawls Become a Politician?

Having concluded this preliminary examination of Rawls's conception of his enterprise, let us turn to some interpretative and critical questions. The last quotation, which is of crucial importance, provides a point of departure. It emphasizes the practical aim of the doctrine of justice. This seems to be the natural concomitant of epistemic abstinence. The aim is not to direct us towards true, valuable ideals, but to achieve certain practical political goals— to 'help ensure stability from one generation to the next'[16] to secure stability and social unity,[17] and to achieve this through bringing about a consensus on certain constitutional principles. 'The aim of justice as fairness as a political conception is practical. . . . it presents itself not as a conception of justice that is true, but one that can serve as a basis of informed and willing political agreement.'[18] A society that has achieved consensual unity and stability by endorsing a common doctrine of justice is called by Rawls 'a well-ordered society':

To say a society is well ordered by a conception of justice means three things: (1) that it is a society in which all citizens accept, and acknowledge before one another that they accept, the same principles of justice; (2) that its basic structure—its main political and social institutions and the way they hang together as one system of cooperation—is publicly known, or with good reason believed, to satisfy those principles, and (3) that citizens have a normally effective sense of justice, that is, one that enables them to understand and to apply the principles of justice, and for the most part to act from them as their circumstances require. *I believe that social unity so understood is the most desirable conception of unity available to us; it is the limit of the practical best.*[19]

---

[14] 'Overlapping Consensus', 14.   [15] Ibid. 15.   [16] Ibid. 1.

[17] 'Political not Metaphysical', 251; see also 249–50.   [18] Ibid. 230.

[19] 'The Priority of Right and Ideas of the Good', *Philosophy and Public Affairs*, 17/4 (fall 1988), 269, italics added (hereafter referred to as 'The Priority of Right'). The language and emphasis of this article, seen here in the use of the expression 'the practical best', while not explicitly withdrawing from epistemic abstinence, is inconsistent with it. I will return to this point below.

This is, of course, the stuff of all democratic politics. It is concerned with give and take, with exploring a common ground for agreement on common policies and principles. When politics is concerned with fashioning a constitution, it requires near-unanimity, and, of course, it deals with principles which will provide the framework within which all other political issues will be resolved. It sounds as if Rawls's practical aim is to engage in practical constitutional politics, with one difference: whereas politicians, at least sometimes, try to secure agreement by convincing people that the principles underlying their proposals are true, Rawls abjures this argument, and seeks to secure agreement simply by pointing out that certain principles are already implicitly agreed to, or nearly so.[20]

There is nothing wrong with engaging in politics, though some may doubt whether this is really what political philosophy is about. The suggestion that political philosophy should be no more than the sort of politics where the only thing that counts is success in commanding general agreement, the kind of politics where any principle, whatever its content, will be accepted provided it commands general assent, and where every principle will be compromised or rejected if it fails to gain universal approval, is objectionable. But is this really what Rawls has in mind?

Rawls assures us that 'political philosophy is not mere politics'. But he simply points out that it takes a longer view.[21] It is essentially constitutional politics. It would be wrong, however (though, given much of what he says, entirely understandable), to regard the politics Rawls advocates as an unprincipled search for consensus at all costs. Two crucial elements in his thought rebut this misinterpretation. First, his aim is to reach 'a consensus that includes all the opposing philosophical and religious doctrines likely to persist and to gain adherents in a more or less just constitutional democratic society'.[22] In other words, only because our societies are nearly just societies can it be right for political philosophy to regard the pursuit of consensus as its overriding goal; and the consensus need not encompass every passing fashion, but only those comprehensive outlooks which are likely to persist in nearly just societies.

There is a problem here. The doctrine of justice itself reflects the consensus of our societies. Is it not inevitable that they will live up to their own standards? Rawls unflinchingly recognizes the self-referential nature of the condition. The consensus to be sought, he says, is one between the opposing

---

[20] Rawls is aware that there may not be enough common ground in a society actually to reach an overlapping consensuses on a doctrine of justice. Narrowing down apparent differences is all that can be aspired to. Alternatively, the desire to reach agreement may lead people to modify those of their views which stand in the way of a consensus, thus making it possible after all. See 'Political not Metaphysical', 228, and 'Overlapping Consensus', 7, 16, 19.

[21] 'Overlapping Consensus', 24.

[22] 'Political not Metaphysical', 225–6; see also 246–7, 249, and 'Overlapping Consensus', 1, 9.

doctrines likely to thrive 'over generations in a more or less just constitu-tional democracy *where the criterion of justice is that political conception itself*'.[23] Of course, a society may avow principles which it does not live up to. There is no reason to refuse to pursue consensus in such a society. The consensus sought is among the competing moral, religious, or philosophical theories. The fact that the practice of that society does not conform to them is not reflected in the consensus view of justice which emerges, and does nothing to discredit it. So perhaps the condition of near justice imposed by Rawls is vacuous, and does little to qualify the unqualified pursuit of consensus at any price.[24] Though I do not know what non-self-fulfilling condition Rawls may have in mind, it is clear that he means this condition, or something like it, to have substantial bite and to place the pursuit of consensus in a context which makes it an appropriate aim.

That consensus is the goal only in nearly just societies is an external condition on Rawls's methodological conception. It limits its applicability. The second corrective to the 'consensus at any price' understanding of Rawls is the internal condition built into the special meaning he gives the expression 'an overlapping consensus'. He discusses this as part of his explanation of why an overlapping consensus is to be distinguished from a mere *modus vivendi*. Of the various marks of that distinction two are relevant here.[25]

First, and this factor explains all the others, a *modus vivendi* is a com-promise based on self- or group interests; it reflects no principles other than the fact that it is an acceptable compromise.[26] A theory like Rawls's is genuinely a theory of justice. Not every consensus can be presented as a theory of justice. To be that, it must be a moral conception (though of course neither a comprehensive nor a deep one). It must possess internal coherence in expressing 'conceptions of person and society, and concepts of right and fairness, as well as principles of justice with their complement of the virtues'.[27] Second, the theory of justice is one which each of the many incompatible comprehensive moral, religious, and philosophical views can accept from its own standpoint. It is not, or not merely, based on a con-sensus among members of a society; it is primarily a consensus among the different conceptions of the good in that society: 'We hope to make it

[23] 'Overlapping Consensus', 1.

[24] A similar problem applies to a second, related condition imposed by Rawls. The consen-sus is between conceptions of the good which are 'each compatible with the full rationality of human persons' ('Political not Metaphysical', 248). But Rawls suggests that the concept of the person he is employing is itself simply the one current in our culture. I will return to this text, and discuss the related statement on p. 9 of 'Overlapping Consensus', below.

[25] It is worth remembering that the distinction is introduced for a different purpose—to show that the doctrine of justice is not advocated on purely prudential grounds. See 'Political not Metaphysical', 247.

[26] See e.g. 'Overlapping Consensus', 1, 2, 10, 11.

[27] 'Political not Metaphysical', 247.

possible for all to accept the political conception as true, or as reasonable, from the standpoint of their own comprehensive view, whatever it may be.'[28]

These internal conditions on a doctrine of justice make it much harder to achieve. A prudential give-and-take among relatively rational individuals may well lead to a compromise, but it is likely to lack the complexity and the structure of internal justification required by Rawls. Rawls's aim is a genuinely philosophical conception of justice, not merely a political expediency. It is not surprising that he is not particularly optimistic about the chances of actually achieving consensus on a theory which meets these conditions. 'All this is highly speculative and raises questions which are little understood.' All we can do is hope that a basis for such a consensus may be found, and that a consensus may emerge on that basis.[29]

Can There Be Justice Without Truth?

These comments help to explain in what sense Rawls's theory is both philosophical and practical. It is philosophical in that it calls for a complex moral doctrine of justice. Yet it is practical, for the one and only reason Rawls mentions for the desirability of setting political philosophy this task is that it is necessary to ensure consensus-based social stability and unity. These practical goals explain the desirability of a doctrine of justice based on overlapping consensus, and one which is internally coherent and complex, that is, which constitutes a moral doctrine.[30] The fact that political philosophy can only assure us of the possibility of consensus and that its actuality is merely speculative does not make the philosophical enterprise any less practical.[31] The only reason for philosophy to establish the possibility of stability is, presumably, that that is the only way philosophy can contribute towards achieving non-coerced social unity and stability.

But why should philosophy contribute to these goals rather than to others? Presumably because they are worthwhile goals. So it would appear that while the goal of political philosophy is purely practical—while it is not concerned to establish any evaluative truths—it accepts some such truths as the presuppositions which make its enterprise intelligible. It recognizes that social unity and stability based on a consensus—that is, achieved without excessive resort to force—are valuable goals of sufficient importance to make them and them alone the foundations of a theory of justice for our societies. Without this assumption it would be unwarranted to regard the theory as a theory of *justice*, rather than a theory of social stability. In an

[28] 'Overlapping Consensus', 13.

[29] 'Political not Metaphysical', 250; 'Overlapping Consensus', 25.

[30] Political not Metaphysical', 250–1; 'Overlapping Consensus', 1, 11–12.

[31] Naturally, the theory, if successful, establishes the truth of instrumental judgements to the effect that certain policies make stability and unity possible, or likely. Every practical inquiry does that. I take Rawls's point to be merely that the theory need not go into moral issues.

uplifting conclusion, Rawls declares that political philosophy aims at 'the defence of reasonable faith in the real possibility of a just constitutional regime'[32]—by which he surely means that the real possibility, which he has argued for, of achieving consensus and securing stability is reason for faith in the possibility of a truly just regime, not merely the possibility of a regime which is called just by its members.

My argument is simple. A theory of justice can deserve that name simply because it deals with these matters, i.e. matters that a true theory of justice deals with. In this sense there are many theories of justice, and they are all acceptable to the same degree as theories of justice. To recommend one as a theory of justice for our societies is to recommend it as a just theory of justice, i.e. as a true, or reasonable, or valid theory of justice. If it is argued that what makes it *the* theory of justice for us is that it is built on an over-lapping consensus and therefore secures stability and unity, then consensus-based stability and unity are the values that a theory of justice, for our society, is assumed to depend on. Their achievement—the fact that endorsing the theory leads to their achievement—makes the theory true, sound, valid, and so forth. This at least is what such a theory is committed to. There can be no justice without truth.[33]

II. POLITICAL INDEPENDENCE

Justice as Fairness: Practical or Theoretical?

The previous section concludes my main argument, which is directed against the epistemic abstinence that is one of the four features central to Rawls's recent writings on the justification and standing of his theory. In the present section I will discuss the remaining features—the autonomy of the theory

---

[32] 'Overlapping Consensus', 25.

[33] I have been equating 'true', 'sound', 'valid', and so on. Could it be that Rawls merely refuses to endorse truth, while being willing to apply one of the other adjectives? I think that the text suggests otherwise. The important point, however, is that he is committed to applying to the theory of justice whichever adjective is appropriately applied to moral propositions. There is no room for epistemic distance. Non-cognitivists and some others will find the reference to the possible truth of a theory of justice unintelligible. Theories of justice, in their view, are not the sort of things which can be either true or false. I am not taking sides in this debate here. My argument is purely *ad hominem*. Rawls is happy to contemplate the possibility that theories of justice are bearers of truth values, and that at least one is true. His argument is that the truth or falsity of a theory of justice does not matter to its acceptability. His is the theory of justice for us even if it is false. Therefore, his epistemic abstinence gives no support to non-cognitivists or others who find the application of 'truth' to theories of justice objectionable. He cannot and does not wish to rely on arguments from that source. Neither does he claim that it is unknowable whether a theory of justice is true or false. He is willing to contemplate the possibility that there are some who know what the true theory of justice is, and that it is incompatible with his. He is, in effect, arguing that such persons should nevertheless support his theory rather than the incompatible true theory, for his theory is the theory for us. My argument above is not so much that such a claim is not morally justified as that it is incoherent, for in claiming that this is the theory of justice for us for such-and-such reasons, one is claiming that those reasons show (or make) this the true theory of justice (if truth applies to theories of justice).

of justice and its shallow foundations. I will conclude that Rawls's theory is strengthened if the thesis of the shallow foundations is jettisoned, and the idea of an overlapping consensus, to which it led, radically reinterpreted. Furthermore, a weak thesis of the autonomy of the theory of justice, which is completely independent of the discarded theses of epistemic abstinence and shallow foundations, should replace Rawls's strong autonomy. First, however, let us note the consequences of reuniting the practical and theoretical aspects of the theory of justice.

In his attempt to sustain his epistemic abstinence Rawls claims, as we saw above, that the theory of justice should be judged by its success in performing a practical task. It should not be regarded as a theory claiming truth for itself. Even if it is false it is still successful, it is still the theory we should accept, if it fulfills its practical role. My reply above was that if fulfilling the practical role assigned it by Rawls vindicates the theory of justice, then it shows it to be true (assuming *ad arguendum*, as Rawls does, that it can be true or false). Once epistemic abstinence is avoided, we recognize that the practical role of the principles of justice in achieving consensus-based unity and stability is a theoretical consideration bearing on the truth (or validity) of the principles. We reject the dichotomy between the practical and the theoretical, and we are able to see how they are interrelated.

As a result, we no longer need to see, nor can we see, in the achievement of consensual unity and stability the be-all and end-all of the theory of justice. It becomes one among many considerations bearing on the truth of the theory. In 'The Priority of Right and Ideas of the Good', for example, Rawls follows his positing of the well-ordered society as the practical goal of a theory of justice with a passage pointing to the two ways in which a well-ordered society is good for people individually.[34] In 'Justice as Fairness: Political not Metaphysical' he says that

'the overarching fundamental intuitive idea, within which other basic intuitive ideas are systematically connected, is that of society as a fair system of cooperation between free and equal persons. Justice as fairness starts from this idea as one of the basic intuitive ideas which we take to be implicit in the public culture of a democratic society.'[35]

Later he observes that

'since the question of which conception of political justice is most appropriate for realizing in basic institutions the values of liberty and equality has long been deeply controversial within the very democratic tradition in which citizens are regarded as

[34] 'The Priority of Right', 270. As Rawls points out, the goal is also a social goal achieved only through social co-operation. This is one aspect of his theory which may disprove the criticism that it is individualistic. Much depends on whether Rawls's theory yields the conclusion that a well-ordered society is intrinsically good, or whether it is good only instrumentally in enabling individuals to achieve their individual aims. If it is intrinsically good, then Rawls's theory is not individualistic, as it recognizes an essentially social goal as intrinsically good.
[35] 'Political not Metaphysical', 231.

free and equal persons, the aim of justice as fairness is to try to resolve this question by starting from the basic intuitive idea of society as a fair system of social co-operation in which the fair terms of cooperation are agreed upon by citizens themselves so conceived.'[36]

These passages can be read as providing arguments to show that Rawls's doctrine of justice is true. They are all points which speak in its favour.[37] It is true, we can understand these passages as saying, because it represents a correct balance between freedom and equality, the balance which is required by a doctrine which is to be, as any doctrine of justice must be, a fair system of co-operation between free and equal people, Rawls's epistemic abstinence stops us from reading them in this way. His epistemic abstinence means that his doctrine of justice should be accepted even if false. To be consistent with epistemic abstinence these passages must be understood as pointing simply to beliefs which command general consent in our culture. Even that fact is not used to show that the principles are true. It merely shows that they can form part of a doctrine of justice which fulfills the practical role assigned to it by Rawls—that is, securing consensual unity and stability.

Once we are rid of the epistemic abstinence, however, we can reverse the connection between the goal of consensual stability and unity and that of achieving a fair system of co-operation between free and equal people. Being epistemically unshackled, we can conclude that the achievement of consensual unity and stability is worthwhile because (at least in part) without them there can be no fair co-operation between *free* and equal people.[38]

Digging Deeper

If the fact that the principles of justice enable us to establish a fair system of co-operation between free and equal people counts in their favour, what is the relevance of the popularity of the ideal of a fair system of co-operation in modern constitutional democracies? Would it not have been an argument for Rawls's doctrine of justice that it secures such co-operation had we lived in a society in which its value is not generally appreciated? Rawls thinks it important to start from the common beliefs of our culture. We called this feature of his theory its shallow foundations. But what purpose does it serve? Possibly he feels committed to it by his epistemic abstinence. If we shun the question whether the theory is true, we must instead make sure that it is

[36] Ibid. 244. See also 'The Priority of Right', 253.
[37] As do other passages, esp. the long discussion in 'The Priority of Right' of the goodness of justice as fairness.
[38] Many of Rawls's readers have understood him in this way all along. They fail to realize that this reading is inconsistent both with his epistemic abstinence and with his shallow foundations, on which more below.

acceptable to people, given their current beliefs. Can the shallow founda-tions survive the rejection of epistemic abstinence?[39]

Several possible reasons for assigning weight to the general belief in the desirability of a fair system of co-operation between free and equal people ought to be mentioned only to be rejected. First, it may be said that if a doctrine of justice is to fulfill its social role, it must rest on wide social support, which will enable it to form the common background of political debate.[40] To understand the ideal of a fair system of co-operation in this way is to revert to the view which denies it primary justificatory force. If Rawls's understanding of our common culture is correct, this point shows that his doctrine of justice may come to be accepted by people in our countries. But while acceptability may indeed be an important condition for any sat-isfactory theory of justice, it cannot be its main virtue. That has to involve considerations which bear directly on the justice of its recommendations. Not every feasible doctrine is a valid one. Feasibility or workability can only be a small part of such an argument. Second, some readers have understood Rawls's shallow foundations as having evolved from, and having inherited the status of, his doctrine of reflective equilibrium. According to this reading of his recent work, the social acceptability of certain beliefs shows them to be true, for it shows them to be held in reflective equilibrium. Reflective equilibrium is interpreted by such readers as requiring social convergence, rather than merely a certain mode of individual endorsement. I see no rea-son to accept this understanding of the point. It is true that it has the merit of reconciling relying on the desirability of a fair system of co-operation with relying on its popularity in our culture. Its popularity, on this interpre-tation, establishes its desirability. But this interpretation does violence to the essential features of Rawls's position. For him, reflective equilibrium is the fundamental method of justification; it is an epistemic doctrine of universal application. His advocacy of shallow foundations, on the other hand, is limited to a theory of justice for our society. In fact the correctness of shallow foundations is itself to be judged in reflective equilibrium. The two cannot be identified.

Is it possible, however, that shallow foundations are truth-making in our culture? Is it possible that Rawls believes that a fair system of co-operation among free and equal people is a valid ideal for us because it is generally acceptable in our culture? It is difficult to see how the popularity of a (putative) ideal bears on its validity except insofar as it reflects on the feas-ibility of its implementation. One possibility is that Rawls starts from the pre-supposition that our countries are just. We do not know what makes them just, as there are many incompatible opinions and arguments regarding

---

[39] My argument in the previous section amounts to showing that shallow foundations are in any case inconsistent with epistemic abstinence.
[40] See e.g. Rawls, *A Theory of Justice*, 454–5.

their justification. So we jettison any deep theory, which would have to adjudicate between the competing views, and embrace shallow foundations. For we know that, since our countries are just, the views which are common ground must be sound. This presupposition makes the theory essentially complacent. Any moral and political theory must be open to the possibility that the societies to which it applies are fundamentally defective. Radical criticism of common institutions and common beliefs is, at least in principle, part of the function of such theories.[41]

Another suggestion might be that commonly endorsed beliefs enjoy the consent of (just about) everyone, and that consent is the foundation of moral or political validity, or at least an overriding consideration, validating principles however objectionable they are on other grounds. But there is nothing in Rawls's account to show that the common acceptance of such principles is achieved under conditions which amount to a free and informed consent to them;[42] and it is doubtful whether consent which is not free and informed is binding in the required way. It would seem, therefore, that if the desirability of a fair system of co-operation should count in favour of Rawls's principles of justice, then it is the validity of this ideal, and not its popularity, which is required to support the argument. Shallow foundations have to be abandoned along with epistemic abstinence.

What Sort of Autonomy?

I suggested earlier that Rawls sees epistemic abstinence, the shallow foundations of his doctrine of justice, and its autonomy as closely connected and mutually supportive. Must his view of the autonomy of the doctrine of justice suffer the fate of the other two facets of his recent writings? Not necessarily. An autonomous political theory is a theory which argues for the truth of propositions about specifically political values, virtues, and so on. Being autonomous, it is not concerned with non-political moral truths.[43] But its whole purpose and function is to argue for political moral truths. Rawls's argument leads from the political values of consensus-based social stability and unity, or of a fair system of co-operation, to the political doctrine of justice. All these are autonomous political values, for (*a*) 'social unity and stability' and 'a fair system of co-operation' are social predicates which only indirectly bear on individual behaviour, and (*b*) the justification of the value

---

[41] Nor does Rawls claim otherwise, for he is willing to consider, in conformity with his epistemic abstinence, the possibility that such ideals are invalid but should be accepted none the less. Notice that my point in the text above is consistent with the view that every criticism must, in some sense, be rooted in the culture and the tradition it addresses. Those who believe that this is so can admit the possibility of radical criticism, rooted, for example, in a sociologically deviant strand of the culture.

[42] Needless to say, Rawls does not rely on this argument, at least not explicitly.

[43] I distinguish below 2 senses in which a political theory may be called 'autonomous'.

of stability and unity is independent of other moral values. Politics is not morality applied to a special subject.

Can Rawls's conception of the autonomy of political morality, of its independence from all comprehensive moral doctrines, be sustained? The key to the problem is the role of overlapping consensus. So far we have seen one way, and I take it to be the main way, in which that idea figures in the argument. It plays a crucial instrumental role. Principles which command an overlapping consensus fulfill the social role of justice: they help secure consensual social stability and unity. They do so in a special way which suggests that overlapping consensus may play a second, justificatory role. Consensual stability and unity are, as we saw, achieved through the fact that everyone (or almost everyone) agrees with the theory of justice for his own reasons. Starting from different standpoints, all end up endorsing the same principles.[44]

This seems to suggest that the people who are governed by the principles of justice accept them each from the point of view of his or her own comprehensive conception of the good. For them, political philosophy does not appear to have shallow foundations. They regard it as an application of their comprehensive morality to the special problems of politics. In what sense is it then autonomous? For whom is it autonomous? Recall the passage we examined before: 'Some might say that reaching this reflective agreement is itself sufficient grounds for regarding that conception as true, or at any rate highly probable. But we refrain from this further step: it is unnecessary and may interfere with the practical aim of finding an agreed public basis of justification.'[45] Why might the fact of a reflective agreement indicate that the conception of justice agreed on is (probably) true? One reason might be that it is unlikely that all reasonable conceptions of the good are false. Therefore whatever they all agree on is probably true. A second reason, which seems closer to the spirit of Rawls's argument, is that achieving reflective agreement secures the social role of justice (helping to ensure consensus-based stability and unity), and this shows that the conception of justice agreed on is true.

It seems that Rawls concurs but fears that saying so would interfere with securing an agreed public basis for justification. Naturally it is not the fact of the agreement which interferes with finding agreement. Rather what is suspect is the claim that its fulfilling the social role of justice, securing a consensus-based stability and continuity, shows that a theory of justice is true. This claim may not command agreement, and if put forward as part of the theory of justice will make it controversial and jeopardize its ability to fulfill its role. It would appear that the theory is supported by arguments whose advocacy would be self-defeating. What Rawls needs is not epistemic abstinence so much as an esoteric doctrine.

---

[44] See e.g. 'Overlapping Consensus', 9, 13.   [45] Ibid. 15.

What about us, Rawls's readers? How are we to treat his arguments? Are we to accept his theory of justice as an autonomous political doctrine for the reasons he explains, or should each of us accept it as part of his or her comprehensive conception of the good? How does Rawls himself view his theory? Is it, in his eyes, part of an autonomous political theory with shallow foundations? Or is it part of his comprehensive conception of the good? One cannot have it both ways.

A distinction between two ways in which a political theory can be autonomous will help here. It is weakly autonomous if it is part of a pluralistic comprehensive conception of the good. A pluralistic conception of the good recognizes the existence of irreducibly many intrinsic goods, virtues, and values. Some independent goods are essentially political. Distributive justice may be such a value. It manifests itself politically, in the constitutional structure of society, and in its observance. The personal virtues which are associated with distributive justice are political virtues. They mark the quality of people as citizens. They are forms of individual excellence which are manifested in public attitudes and actions. Political theory understood as dealing (at least in part) with irreducibly political values can nevertheless be part of a comprehensive moral view. It is justified by establishing how its values fit and make sense together with the other values embraced in the comprehensive conception. By contrast, a strongly autonomous political theory is a theory whose validity or truth does not depend on non-political considerations.

Which is Rawls's own view ? His is a theory which makes no claim to truth or validity, and is thus independent of any moral foundations. It is strongly autonomous. Which view should be attributed to Rawls once his theory is freed from its stance of epistemic self-denial? It seems clear that even then Rawls should be understood to endorse strong autonomy. Weak autonomy would make the theory part of particular comprehensive conceptions of the good, and it is the thrust of Rawls's whole argument to deny this, to suggest that a theory of justice for our times should not be part of a comprehensive conception of the good.[46]

There are at least two decisive objections to viewing political philosophy as strongly autonomous.[47] First, justification of moral and political values depends in part on the way they can be integrated into a comprehensive

[46] This is confirmed by 'The Priority of Right', 252–3, where Rawls draws a similar distinction between two conditions of autonomy (the first corresponding to my weak autonomy) and asserts that both obtain. The discussion on pp. 261–2 of the same article may, however, suggest that all that is required is weak autonomy within an overlapping consensus of comprehensive, and otherwise divergent, moral theories.

[47] My characterization of strong autonomy is too vague to allow conclusive discussion. E.g. if autonomy is infringed by justifying political values by reference to individual well-being, then on the humanistic assumption that what matters in the end is the well-being of people, valid political theory cannot be strongly autonomous. I will, however, understand strong autonomy

view of human well-being.[48] Moral and political justification is in part holistic. Second, the practical implications of any value depend on whether it conflicts with other values, and if so, which of the conflicting values prevails in particular circumstances of various kinds. Since a strongly autonomous political theory prevents us from considering its political values in the comprehensive context of a complete moral theory, it cannot yield practical conclusions. It can neither assure us that conflicts do not arise nor adjudicate when they do arise.

The question of possible conflicts between his doctrine of justice and other values is specifically addressed by Rawls: 'How can a political conception of justice express values that, under the reasonably favourable conditions that make democracy possible, normally outweigh whatever other values conflict with them?' His answer, in brief, is that 'the values which conflict with the political conception of justice and its sustaining virtues may be normally outweighed because they come into conflict with the very conditions that make fair social cooperation possible on a footing of mutual respect'.[49] One might quarrel with this answer in various ways. One is to face Rawls with a dilemma. If what he means is that general compliance with the principles of justice is necessary to achieve the goal stated, it does not follow that absolute compliance in each case is necessary. So particular conflicts require examination of their particular circumstances. If, on the other hand, what Rawls means is that one person or institution can be just to another in the individual case only if he deals with him in conformity with the principles of justice, this leaves open the question whether being absolutely just to another is always more important than all other possible moral considerations.

Whatever one's response to this objection, the important point is that Rawls agrees that a doctrine of justice yields practical conclusions only if its requirements are compared with and assessed in relation to other values. This amounts to the (inevitable) abandonment of strong autonomy, and to an acceptance of weak autonomy instead.

---

as allowing appeal to individual well-being in justification of political values and institutions. What is not allowed is appeal to other concrete virtues and values which are not themselves political.

[48] Goods and values are often said to be interdependent in another sense as well: they are said to depend on each other in their operation, in that they are merely conditionally good. They are good in a normal context. Trust is good in most circumstances, but there will always be circumstances in which any good turns bad and any virtue loses its value. This argument convinced Kant that only the good will is unconditionally good (*Groundwork of the Metaphysics of Morals*, ch. 1). I do not wish to endorse this thesis of interdependence.

[49] 'Overlapping Consensus', 17. Rawls makes other comments in this context. But they seem to be addressed to a conflict between his doctrine of justice and comprehensive moralities which are fundamentally hostile to it. My argument assumes that one accepts Rawls's doctrine of justice in its own right and is merely worried about conflicts between it and other morale values.

Political Theory as Morality's Foreign Office

In a way, only now, having rejected Rawls's epistemic abstinence, his shallow foundations, and his thesis of the strong autonomy of his theory, are we able to do full justice to the idea of an overlapping consensus. Our recent reflections started with a quandary: does the theory of justice rest on the need to secure a consensus-based social unity and stability, or is it nested in a sound, comprehensive conception of the good? The specific purpose of Rawls's recent writing is to deny that his theory of justice is to be accepted because it is part of a true comprehensive moral theory. At the same time he maintains (or rather would maintain if he were to abandon his epistemic self-denial) that it is true or valid (in part) because everyone who accepts it accepts it as part of his comprehensive moral theory. Does this mean that all who so accept it are mistaken in doing so,[50] but the fact that we are all mistaken makes the theory true?

This is the only possible interpretation on the assumption that Rawls's theory is strongly autonomous.[51] But having rejected the strong autonomy thesis, we can explore the possibility that the theory of justice is defended by Rawls—or rather by some of his arguments—as part of a comprehensive moral theory. That defence is best reconstructed as resting on four limbs:

1. *The embeddedness of the justification*: The doctrine of justice is part of a true comprehensive moral theory.
2. *The ad hominem element*: Those who do not accept the true comprehensive moral theory are nevertheless committed to its doctrine of justice, for it is consonant with their comprehensive views as well.
3. *The interdependence of arguments*: The *ad hominem* element is essential to the justification of the doctrine as part of the sound and comprehensive moral theory.
4. *The similarity of the arguments*: The reason the doctrine of justice can be argued for *ad hominem* is the extensive similarities among the diverse moral theories in our societies.

The special character of the defence lies not in its being independent of the true, comprehensive moral theory, but in the fact that (*a*) the doctrine of justice is embedded in both true and false moral theories in a similar way, and (*b*) that way includes cross-reference in each theory to the fact that it is so embedded in the others. An outline of Rawls's reconstructed argument will show how these features figure in it.

[50] I.e. everyone has the wrong reasons for accepting it.

[51] It is true that Rawls refuses to judge whether the various comprehensive moral theories are true or false. But he is committed to condemning them all as falsely endorsing a non-autonomous theory of justice, or else he must abandon his claim that the theory is autonomous.

First, every (comprehensive) moral theory must address the question: How are those who disbelieve it to be judged and treated? It may declare that their disbelief is irrelevant. Moral principles apply to all regardless of their beliefs, and everyone is judged by them in the same way. Many theories do not take this line. They may, for example, regard responsibility as dependent, at least to a degree, on people's frame of mind when they engaged in the activities on which they are being judged. Some religions distinguish between universal principles that bind all, and principles that bind only believers in the right faith. Such theories have a special doctrine regarding the way one should behave towards non-believers. One's duties and responsibilities towards them and their duties and responsibilities may differ from those which bind the religiously or morally faithful.

Second, the true moral theory for our societies recognizes that there is special value in people freely developing their own understanding of the meaning of life and the ways one can flourish, and also in people living in accord with their own freely developed conception of the good. This means that those whose lives are not guided by such freely chosen conceptions of the good are diminished and that those who are so guided are better off for being so guided, even if their particular conceptions of the good are mistaken.

This is a very crude version of the sort of belief in the value of autonomy that Rawls attributes to Kant and Mill—that is, a belief in the value of autonomy as part of a comprehensive theory of the good and of the meaning of life. Rawls, of course, abstains from expressing judgment on it,[52] though it seems to me that his claim that we have a higher-order interest, which dominates all other interests,[53] in 'realiz[ing] and exercis[ing]' our 'capacity to form, to revise, and rationally to pursue a conception of the good'[54] commits him to nothing less. In any case, the preceding argument suggests that the idea of an overlapping consensus must make each of us situate the doctrine of justice within *some* comprehensive conception of the good. It is reasonable to attribute this kind of liberalism to Rawls. But this conception can be seen as an example only. If not this, then his liberalism must rest on some other conception of the good, which needs spelling out.

Third, it follows that while one may try to convince others of the error of their ways, one should not force or manipulate them to live in ways other than those they accept. They should be given opportunities freely to develop their own conceptions of the good. It is vital to the validity of the argument that this point is self-referential. Only if people agree that giving them opportunities to develop their own conceptions of the good is valuable do they develop their ideas and conceptions of the good in the spirit

[52] See 'Political not Metaphysical', 245–6; 'Overlapping Consensus', 5, 9.
[53] Except the other higher-order interest in living in a just society.
[54] 'Kantian Constructivism', 525.

required according to the above claim about people' higher interests. Their higher interests, that is, are understood to include self-recognition, recognition that these are people's higher interests. This fact applies to my concern for my own life too. While I am concerned to lead the life that I now believe to be the right one, I am even more concerned to be able to lead the life that conforms to my freely developed conception of the good as it may be from time to time. Hence the way to relate to others who do not share our conception of the good is to establish a scheme of co-operation, to which all could agree, and which would enable all to pursue their own conceptions of the good within fair terms of co-operation.

Fourth, as a matter of fact the conclusions reached in the previous point (everyone should be allowed to pursue his own conception of the good, within a framework which commands general consent), though not the grounds for them, are part of the common culture of modern constitutional democracies. We therefore know that other people freely accept them as true, though not necessarily for the reasons that we do. This means that there is reason to hope that an agreement on principles of justice based on these two requirements may be forthcoming.

Fifth, the last point shows how our own endorsement of a doctrine of justice from the point of view of our own conception of the good (as explained in the second point above) depends on that doctrine's acceptability to other people in our society, who do not share our conception of the good. Hence there is here a possibility of give-and-take. We are willing, upon reflection, to modify our own interpretation of the common culture, and those aspects of our conception of the good on which it depends, in order to reach the kind of agreement that our conception of the good recommends, that is, in order to overcome some differences of opinion between us and others. The fact that an agreement is demanded of us by our own conception of the good renders that conception open to revision in order to secure that agreement.

As is clear, this is not Rawls's own argument. It is a reconstruction to which we have been driven in view of the difficulties we found in sustaining Rawls's espousal of epistemic self-denial and shallow foundations, and the strong autonomy of his theory of justice. The reconstructed argument preserves the limited applicability of the theory, the doctrine of a higher-order interest in autonomy, and the central role of the idea of an overlapping consensus. It does not make much of Rawls's insistence on the importance of social unity and stability. These can lead to an alternative reconstruction, which relegates Rawls's statements about higher-order interests to the body of the doctrine of justice rather than to its deep justification. This second reconstruction simply says that the true moral theory for our society regards consensus-based social unity and stability as of paramount importance. Therefore, since only principles which command general consensus among all viable comprehensive moralities current in our society can secure stability and unity, the doctrine of justice should rest on an overlapping consensus. And Rawls's theory of justice happens to command, or nearly to command, such a consensus. This reconstruction is closer to the view that the theory of justice is weakly autonomous.

Consensus and Stability

Rawls's response to pluralism has two aspects; he attempts to avoid taking sides in the argument among conflicting conceptions of the good in two ways. First, by opting for shallow foundations and epistemic abstinence, he seeks to avoid basing his doctrine of justice on controversial grounds. Second, the practical implications of his doctrine of justice are meant to avoid favouring one conception of the good over any other. Within the framework set by the principle of justice, each is allowed to pursue his conception of the good, in his own way. As regards the first aspect of Rawls's response to pluralism, we have seen that his own arguments can sustain neither epistemic abstinence nor shallow foundations. Our reconstructed argument based on the idea of an overlapping consensus makes the doctrine of justice morality's department of foreign affairs. It is a special part of a comprehensive conception of the good, but it is a part of it all the same. The reconstruction was designed to guarantee the non-controversiality of the doctrine of justice which emerges (where non-controversiality means a *potential* overlapping consensus, one which can be reached by people motivated to seek consensus who rationally explore the implications and the flexibility of their comprehensive conceptions of the good). Whether such a non-controversial doctrine of justice can in fact be justified depends on the success one may have in filling in the bare outlines of the reconstructed argument offered here. The difficulty is that we have moved a long way from Rawls' original intentions. The evaluation of the principles of justice depends, according to the reconstructed argument, on the soundness of a comprehensive moral theory which yields them. For it was that comprehensive moral theory which through its own internal logic came to regard overlapping consensus as necessary to secure justice. If the sound conception of the good does not contain the reconstructed argument, then the doctrine of justice falls with it. So we have to await a statement of Rawls's general moral theory to answer the question. It would not do to take too seriously the reconstructed argument above. It is too sketchy, and it is not Rawls's.

This is not the place to discuss the other aspect of Rawls's response to the fact of pluralism. I would like, however, to remark here that the success of his principles of justice in being at least roughly neutral between different conceptions of the good (meaning here 'that the state is to ensure for all citizens equal opportunity', that is, equal chances of success, 'to advance any conception of the good they freely affirm')[55] seems to me essential to their persuasiveness. It is true that the neutrality of the principles of justice is subject to several exceptions, the most important being that conceptions of the good inconsistent with the principles of justice are likely to be at a disadvantage. In reiterating this second point in 'The Priority of Right', Rawls has expressed himself in a way which may suggest to the incautious reader that his theory does not aspire to (rough) neutrality (in this sense of the term).[56] His words there, however, should not be so understood. If one reason supporting his doctrine of justice is that it is roughly neutral, then this exception can be easily accommodated. It does no more than admit that, given the denial by some conceptions of the good of an equal opportunity to those who pursue other conceptions, neutrality can be achieved only by disadvantaging the intolerant conceptions. It follows, of course, that the feasible neutrality is not complete. But this is consistent with arguing that Rawls's theory is as neutral as any can be.

Why does the case for Rawls's doctrine of justice rest on the (rough) neutrality of his principles? Rawls's general argument rests on the assumption that in the original position people would opt for the principles of justice because they insure themselves against the worst eventualities. For this reason they would opt for a distribution of primary goods as equal as is consistent with making the lot of the worst off as good as possible. This conclusion follows only if the distribution of primary goods correlates fairly accurately with what people care most about. Only if it does will insuring themselves against the worst allocation of primary goods amount to insuring themselves against the worst eventualities. According to Rawls, people care most about their ability to realize their own conceptions of the good.[57] So the success of his argument for the principles of justices depends on the claim that primary goods provide an equal chance of advancing any conception of the good a person may have (excluding those inconsistent with the principles of justice). If they do, then the principles of justice are as neutral as possible in ensuring to all people the same chance of realizing their conceptions of the good regardless of what those conceptions are.[58] Elsewhere I, like many other writers, have criticized Rawls's principles of justice for failing to be neutral in this sense; I will not return to this issue here.[59]

There is, however, one more aspect of Rawls's argument which should be considered here: the argument for overlapping consensus from the need

---

[55] 'The Priority of Right', 262.

[56] See ibid.: 'The priority of right excludes the first meaning of neutrality of aim, for it allows only permissible conceptions (those that respect the principles of justice) to be pursued.'

[57] I am inclined to say that they care most about realizing the sound conception of the good.

[58] In 'The Priority of Right', 275–6, Rawls seems to display an indifference to the considerations adumbrated above which appears to me to undermine his own theory.

[59] See Raz, *The Morality of Freedom*, ch. 5.

for social stability and unity. That need can be taken for granted.[60] Does it vindicate the idea of an overlapping consensus? This requires three restrictive elements: first, social unity and stability are to be secured through agreement on principles; second, the whole community, or at least all those who adhere to conceptions of the good which are likely to survive within it, will agree on the same set of principles of constitutional government; third, the principles agreed upon form a coherent and complex body of theory with its own internal structure of justification—that is, they are mutually supportive.

The third element is, as was mentioned above,[61] the only one explicitly justified by Rawls. He regards it as necessary to guarantee stability. Without such deep agreement, shifting power relations, or temporary changes in alliances within the community, may undermine the consensus, and with it social stability. If this argument holds, then it will also justify the other restrictive requirements. I doubt, however, whether any of them plays the central role in securing social unity and stability assigned to them by Rawls. Rather, affective and symbolic elements may well be the crucial cement of society, and to these one has only to add the little power individuals have to affect societal affairs.

Stable societies are marked by a high degree of identification of individuals with their society. People are proud members of their nation. The identification is marked by attachment to national symbols, cultural and conventional as well as legal (language, literature, foods, flag, and anthem). These evoke emotion, and create common bonds among those who share these attitudes. They are important elements in shaping one's imagination, and in defining one's historical horizon. People share a common pride in a shared historical experience. Such identification normally includes attachment to certain values. But these are normally expressed at a high level of abstraction (liberty, equality, fraternity) which is compatible with complete disagreement about constitutional principles (e.g. between royalists and republicans, or between fascists, democrats, and revolutionary communists).

Obviously there may also be agreement on some constitutional principles. But there need not be complete agreement. There may, for example, be an overlapping agreement in a sense different from Rawls's—that is, agreement between any two people about some of the prevailing constitutional principles, so that each principle enjoys a measure of support, although no one agrees to them all. Or there may be other forms of overlap.

Symbolic and affective identification and a partial cognitive overlap may be a very firm foundation for social unity and stability, especially when we remember that individuals find it both prudentially and morally undesirable

---

[60] Though only in the sense of assigning it some importance. There is no reason I know of for assigning it absolute importance.

[61] See Sec. I above.

to undermine the status quo, or even to try to evade its consequences, given the small chances of success. Of course, many factors contribute to the stability of a country's political system: the nature of its culture, its history of past conflicts, the depth of feeling concerning current rivalries, and so on. The point is that they are only partially sensitive to the existence of anything remotely like Rawls's overlapping consensus. The latter is neither necessary nor sufficient, and even were it to exist it would play only a partial, perhaps even a merely subsidiary, role in securing unity and stability. None of this denies that common agreement to a theory of justice will contribute to such goals. But given the way the world actually works, the modesty of that contribution raises doubts as to whether Rawls has identified the concerns which should dominate political philosophy today. No reason seems to have been given for political philosophy to abandon its traditional goals of understanding the moral presuppositions of existing institutions and criticizing them and advocating better ones—in the full light of reason and truth.

III. IMPARTIALITY AGAINST TRUTH

Thomas Nagel has offered an ingenious argument which he presents as an attempt to capture the sound intuitions behind the position advocated by Rawls, among others, Like Rawls's own arguments, it rests on the advocacy of epistemic abstinence. Does it fare any better? Its examination occupies the rest of this essay.

The Role and Limits of Justification

Traditionally, normative political theory sought to determine and to explain the truth of value judgments concerning political authority and its actions. One wonders whether this goal is shared by Nagel. 'Political stability', he remarks, 'is helped by wide agreement to the principles underlying a political order. But that is not all: for some, the possibility of justifying the system to as many participants as possible is of independent moral impor- tance.'[62] Justification, he explains, is a normative concept, which may faciliate agreement, but is neither necessary nor sufficient to that end. Justification,

---

[62] 'Moral Conflict and Political Legitmacy', *Philosophy and Public Affairs*, 16/3 (summer 1987), 218 (hereafter referred to as 'Conflict and Legitimacy'). Much of the time Nagel appears not to express his own views but rather those of 'some', as here, or of 'liberals' or 'liberal theory'. I will assume that normally Nagel agrees, at least tentatively, with these views. Nagel does not share the sensitivity displayed by Rawls to the range and variety of liberal views. The idea that liberalism can be identified with some political theory put forward by one or more writers over the last few years shows little respect for the history of the subject, or for the vitality and richness of the liberal tradition.

as I understand it, is the explanation of the truth of a value judgment—in this case concerning the scope and limits of legitimate authority. It seems, therefore, that Nagel's object is to argue for the truth or validity of certain principles of governmental action. But things are not so simple.

The goal of justification, says, Nagel, is 'to persuade the reasonable'. The attempt to justify has a practical point. Its point is not, or not only, to discover under what conditions governments have a right to rule. It is not, or not only, to learn the truth. Rather it is to secure the independent practical value of convincing the reasonable. That is why Nagel can conclude that 'given the actual range of values, interests, and motives in a society, and depending on one's standards of justification, there may not be a legitimate solution [that is, a valid justification], and then one will have to choose between illegitimate government and no government'.[63] But if government lacks justification, is it rational to choose it none the less? If it is rational, that must be because having a government is desirable in that it serves some values. But then that fact would provide the sought-for justification.[64] If justification is simply the explanation of the truth of a value judgment, then the choice that Nagel refers to can never be a rational one. Justification for Nagel, it would therefore seem, must be something different. Rather than being the road to normative truth in general, it seems to be but one practical value among many. If no justification is available, it may still be worth having an unjustified—that is, illegitimate—government for the sake of other values that this may serve. As we shall see, the gap between truth and justification is both the source of the appeal of Nagel's proposal and the root of its weakness.

Convincing the reasonable is valuable in itself. It is, one might say, always nice to have everyone agree that one's actions are sensible and just. But there can be no doubt that this is at best a luxury.[65] The matter acquires urgency, according to Nagel, when the action concerned is that of a political authority. The reason is that political authorities exercise coercion over their subjects. That is why their actions should enjoy the consent of their subjects: 'This question is part of the wider issue of political legitimacy . . . of justifying coercively imposed political and social institutions to the people who have to live under them.'[66]

Several of the points I have attributed to Nagel now have to be unpacked. First, convincing those subject to governmental power, securing their actual

---

[63] Ibid.

[64] Remember that the issue is not whether one is justified in obeying the government. One may be justified in obeying an illegitimate government. The question is whether the government is legitimate or justified.

[65] The luxury is in the desire to secure actual agreement. Possibly, whenever we act, the reasons for our actions, the maxim of our action, should be objectively valid. This may be enough to secure the agreement of the reasonable under ideal conditions.

[66] Nagel, 'Conflict and Legitimacy', 218.

agreement, is ultimately what is desired. One's duty to others, however, is confined to acting on grounds which are known and which will convince if reasonably attended to. If they fail to convince, that is not one's fault. Hence the objective of one's action is convincing the reasonable. The basic motivation is to secure consent, but it is hedged by a certain understanding of the limits of one's responsibilities towards others. Responsibility lapses if its failure to achieve its object is due to other people's unreasonableness.

Second, the special need to base political action on consent arises from its coercive character. 'This element of coercion imposes an especially stringent requirement of objectivity in justification.'[67] The result is that only the consent of those who are coerced by a political act (or against whom it would be coercively enforced) need be secured. This may narrow the scope of the constraints of impartiality that Nagel is seeking to justify more than he intends. Those constraints will not apply to non-coercive action like declaring a certain religion the state religion, or to the granting of other (inexpensive) public honours and privileges to that religion or to its practitioners. But these are marginal matters. Once the core of Nagel's contention is established, there may well be ways of extending it to certain peripheral regions.

Rational Consent

Justified coercion is based on consent. This is Nagel's first principle. I will call it the principle of consent. The consent he requires is individual consent to every single measure. His object is to set a limit to the measures governments may adopt. Any measure of which a citizen would reasonably say 'I withhold my consent to that' is ruled out. This requirement goes well beyond such consent as is secured by the existence of a democratic government.[68] Nagel's interpretation of the principle, however, involves strands of thoughts which some who are attracted by its basic idea may not wish to follow. His is a rationalist notion of consent: the reasonable consent when reason indicates that consent is due. Reason always indicates that consent is, other things being equal, due when the proposed action confers a clear advantage, or is part of a scheme which is imposed on a group, compliance with which secures advantages for all.[69] Refusal to consent to such measures as the compulsory wearing of car seat-belts, compulsory vaccination whose benefits are clear, and so on is not protected by Nagel's principle as he understands it. Others have distinguished between theories based on benefit to the governed and those based on their consent. Nagel elides the two.

[67] Ibid. 223; cf. also 238.
[68] I discuss below the way in which Nagel attempts to incorporate democratic principles into his theory.
[69] 'Conflict and Legitmacy', 224.

It may be suggested that Nagel feels forced into this position by a mis-understanding of the limits he sets to justification. The principle that we need justify our actions only to the reasonable seems to leave no room for a gap between reason and consent. If an action is to my benefit, then by reason I ought to consent to it. No one has to justify it to me if I unreason-ably fail to consent. So far this seems plausible enough. Other people's actions should not be restricted by my unreasonableness. But Nagel is using the principle to set the limit to the justification of coercion, and this puts a completely different complexion on the problem. I am the one to be coerced. It is not so much a matter of whether others are limited by my unreasonableness, though it is that as well. It is primarily a question of whether whenever I act unreasonably I am liable to be coerced, whether my reasonableness sets the limits of my freedom. Is there no right to err freely, to act unreasonably against one's own interests?

One way to argue for such a right is to show that it is sometimes more important for a person to choose freely than to choose correctly, that acting freely is itself an important ingredient of individual well-being. Nagel, like Rawls, shuns such arguments as being sectarian—as dependent on accept-ing a particular conception of the meaning and value of life rather than remaining neutral. Others have strongly argued that respecting persons is an imperative binding on us independently of any conception of the good, an imperative that enjoins us to respect the will of others, rather than their intellect.[70] Nagel is not prevented from accepting such views by his prin-ciple of the limits of justification. Even those who act unreasonably need to be reasonably convinced that curtailing their freedom when they act unrea-sonably is justified. That one person's conduct in acting against his own best interests is unreasonable does not mean that the act of another in coercing him can be justified to the reasonable. Nagel's rationalistic version of the contractarian argument is independent of his view on the limits of justification.

It would be a mistake to conclude that Nagel's principle applies only to the measures and to all the measures restricting one person for the benefit of others. This is the line adopted by what I shall call 'moral contractarians', those who wish to derive all of morality from the agreement of individuals with non-moral motivations and principles only. This is not Nagel's road. His contractarianism is political only.[71] People have, right or wrong, moral beliefs. These are to be justified by other means. People's

---

[70] In *The Morality of Freedom*, 57, I have followed the first route mentioned here. The justification of authority must take into account that often it is better for people that they control their own lives than that their actions be to their own advantage. Robert Nozick's *Anarchy, State, and Utopia* (New York: Basic Books, 1974) is a most powerful argument for the second line of argument.

[71] This is what Nagel calls the 'mixed' theory, which he thinks is characteristic of contem-porary liberalism. See 'Conflict and Legitimacy', 219.

political morality is special. Given that it sanctions coercion, it must rest on agreement. That agreement is forthcoming not only to very basic paternalistic measures but also to the prevention of harm to others, since such measures are based on values that are generally shared and therefore agreed to.

The problem of legitimacy is that of justifying governmental action which rests on values not generally shared. But why should their being commonly shared or not matter? All that Nagel's principle of consent requires is appeal to principles which are true and which can be shown to be true to the reasonable. Given Nagel's rationalistic political contractarianism, he can object neither to the exclusive reliance on reason (rather than the will) nor to the reliance on moral principles. They can be established independently of consent, and he specifically eschews reliance on scepticism concerning moral values.[72] In other words, given the acceptance of the rationality of moral beliefs, and a rationalistic interpretation of consent, Nagel's first principle lacks any bite. It adds nothing to the demand that coercive political action should be based on well-reasoned principles. If it is so based, it can also meet the test of convincing the resonable.[73]

Impartiality and Belief

Nagel is, of course, aware of this. His principle of consent acquires its practical significance from its combination with a second principle: the principle of impartiality. The theory which Nagel explores, which he once refers to as 'true liberalism', requires that consent shall be secured not through any rational reasons, not through successful appeal to the truth or rationality of the relevant moral principles, but through appeal to impartial grounds only. 'The defense of liberalism requires that a limit somehow be drawn to appeals to *the truth* in political argument.'[74] That limit is in the idea of impartiality, understood not only in the sense of giving equal weight to the interests of all: 'Liberal impartiality goes beyond this, by trying to make the epistemological standpoint of morality impersonal as well.'[75] This

---

[72] Ibid. 228–9.

[73] But does Nagel, in the passages discussed above, do more than predict the likelihood of consent in cases of clear self-interest (and clear potential harm to others)? I think he does. Nagel has distanced himself from the need to rely on actual consent by relying on the consent of the reasonable. This requires a test of reasonableness which goes beyond saying that the reasonable consent when there is good reasons to consent. Nagel provides no such test, and the discussion referred to above suggests that he regards consent of the reasonable to follow good reason. In the absence of such a test, the principle that the reasonable consent when there is good reason to consent is a logical truth, not a prediction or a moral principle. This shows that consent has lost its moral force; it necessarily trails clear good reason.

[74] 'Conflict and Legitimacy', 229.

[75] Ibid. 230. Nagel embeds this discussion in his familiar view about points of view that vary in 'objectivity': 'On the view I would defend, there is a highest-order framework of moral reasoning . . . which takes us outside ourselves to a standpoint that is independent of who we are. It cannot derive its basic premises from aspects of our particular and contingent starting

means, as we will see in a moment, that the reasons, or the method of reasoning, used to justify the different principles must be acceptable to all. But Nagel approaches this idea obliquely.

[1] The idea is that when we look at certain of our convictions from outside, however justified they may be from within, the appeal to their truth must be seen merely as an appeal to our beliefs, and should be treated as such unless those beliefs can be shown to be justifiable from a more impersonal standpoint. . . . This does not mean we have to stop believing them—that is, believing them to be *true*. Considered as individual beliefs they may be adequately grounded . . . the standards of individual rationality are different from the standards of epistemological ethics.[76]

One aspect of this passage seems to me puzzling, yet Nagel regards it as crucial to his argument. If we rely on beliefs which are, for us, 'from within' well grounded, how can we be deemed to be appealing merely to the fact that we have certain beliefs rather than acknowledged for what we are actually doing—that is, appealing to their truth? 'The reason is', says Nagel,

[2] that unless there is some way of applying from an impersonal standpoint the distinction between my believing something and its being true, an appeal to its truth is equivalent to an appeal to my belief in its truth. . . . I have to be able to admit that I might turn out to be wrong, by some standards that those who disagree with me but are also committed to the impersonal standpoint can also acknowledge. The appeal to truth as opposed to belief . . . must imply the possibility of some standard to which an impersonal appeal can be made, even if it cannot settle our disagreement at the moment.[77]

This, especially the last sentence, which seems to make the point most succinctly, must be right. But is it compatible with the drift of the previous quotation? As Nagel reminds us, to believe in a proposition is to believe it to be true. That belief is not, and cannot be (very special cases, which I will disregard, excepted), the believer's reason for thinking that the proposition is true. My belief in a proposition is, *a fortiori*, no reason for others to accept it.[78] When a person relies on a proposition, his belief in the proposition merely shows that he has confidence in its truth. It does nothing to justify that confidence or to point to its sources. I believe that it is dark outside not because I believe that it is dark outside, but because there is no light

points within the world, though it may authorize reliance on such specialized points of view if this is justified from the more universal perspective' (ibid. 229). I shall not consider the significance of this way of considering the issue. To my mind it is inessential and distracting. As we saw, the substantive issue, according to Nagel, is whether there is ever justification for 'a kind of epistemological restraint' (ibid.), i.e. not acting for valid reasons. This issue does not depend on the metaphor of 'points of view'.

[76] Ibid. 230.   [77] Ibid. 231.

[78] Though, of course, if I witnessed the events I believe in, or have special competence to judge such matters, or have access to adequate evidence, then my belief, together with such facts, is reason supporting a similar belief.

showing through my window. If I act relying on my belief, my reason for the action is not the fact that I hold the belief but, as Nagel puts it, its truth.

Notice that in all this the position of the believer is the same as that of the observer. Neither would accept the fact that the believer believes in a proposition as a ground for action. Both will accept the truth of the proposition as a ground for action. Moreover, and this is the crucial point, both know that only if the believer is capable of distinguishing between believing a proposition and its truth as grounds for accepting it, for acting on it, and so on can he have beliefs at all. For the points just made are at the core of the notion of believing, and while persons need not be able to articulate them to have beliefs, they must recognize them, and apply them correctly, to be capable of having beliefs. The logical prerequisites of the capacity to believe include recognition of the possibility of error and of an impartial or objective recognition of such an error. Nothing less is required by the fact that to believe a proposition is to believe it to be true, and by the distinction between the fact of believing a proposition and its being true.

But if all this is so—and this I take to be the burden of passage 2 above— Nagel's earlier statement (in passage 1) must be false. There is, as we saw, complete symmetry in the matter between the believer and the spectator. It therefore cannot be 'that when we look at certain of our convictions from outside, however justified they may be from within, the appeal to their truth must be seen merely as an appeal to our beliefs'. If it is an appeal to their truth, rather than merely to their existence, from the inside, it must be recognized as such from the outside as well. The conditions separating appeal to truth and appeal to mere belief are one and the same from all perspectives. In particular, from within as well one can sustain the view that one is relying on the truth of a belief only if one recognizes that one may be wrong by objective and impartial standards.[79]

Impartiality and Acceptable Reasons

Perhaps, however, none of this touches the heart of Nagel's point. Clearly nothing in the above denies one contention in passage 1, that one should not rely in justifying coercive political actions on principles the reasons for which are not acceptable to all those subject to the authority. I referred rather vaguely to the acceptability of reasons, meaning something like: If p is an acceptable reason for a certain action, or for the adoption of a certain principle or the institution of certain political arrangements, then while

---

[79] Indeed, as we saw, the very possibility of belief depends on that recognition. Those who lack it cannot be said to be relying on their beliefs either. Nagel's suggestion of a contrast between those who rely on their believing and those who rely on the truth of their beliefs is chimerical; it is logically impossible to do the first.

there may be disagreement over whether *p* is the case, whether it is not overridden or defeated by other reasons, and so on, it is nevertheless agreed that *p*, if true, is a reason for the claimed conclusion. When the reasons proposed for coercive political actions meet this test they are acceptable reasons, they are what Nagel calls 'a common ground of justification', though evidently their acceptability is far from guaranteeing actual agreement.

Nagel's own explanation of his requirement of the common ground of justification is different. For him it requires

first, preparedness to submit one's reasons to the criticism of others, and to find that the exercise of a common critical rationality and consideration of evidence that can be shared will reveal that one is mistaken. This means that it must be possible to present to others the basis of your own beliefs, so that once you have done so, *they have what you have*. . . . Public justification requires, second, an expectation that if others who do not share your belief are wrong, there is probably an explanation of their error which is not circular. That is, the explanation should not come down to the mere assertion that they do not believe the truth.[80]

While I agree with the second requirement, the core of the first is so stringent that it rules out reliance on common everyday observations of fact, as well as much scientific knowledge. We often rely on sense perception and on memory as important reasons for our beliefs. Similarly we rely on our situation (right next to the accident, in the bright light of day, and so on) as reasons to trust our sense perceptions or our memories. All these are acceptable reasons in the sense I explained. Others may doubt whether the Centurion saw Jesus rise from his grave. But they agree that if he did, it is evidence, even though perhaps not conclusive evidence, of the Resurrection.

This point is of crucial importance to Nagel's argument. If he relaxes the test to allow for the acceptability of ordinary reasons (for example, by admitting counterfactuals such as 'had they been in your situation they would have shared what you have'), then many religious doctrines he is particularly eager to exclude[81] are admitted with them. In fact, many Roman Catholic, Anglican, and other Christian and Jewish theologians rely on nothing but acceptable reasons, such as eyewitness evidence to historical events, often of a public nature, and ordinary methods of reasoning, such as are invoked in the ontological or other arguments for the existence of God.

But have I not missed the point? Is it not obvious that Nagel's aim is to exclude revelation and the judgment that certain beliefs are self-evident from public reliance? Perhaps, but does he provide any reason for doing so? He could have argued that revelation is unreliable and self-evidence an incoherent (or perhaps merely an unreliable) ground for belief. But he does not. To do so would undermine the justification for accepting the beliefs

---

[80] 'Conflict and Legitimacy', 232.   [81] Cf. ibid. 229, 232.

based on revelation or self-evidence by the people who hold them. Nagel's strategy depends on accepting that the people who hold certain beliefs are justified in doing so, and yet asserting that for epistemic reasons those beliefs may not be relied upon in supporting public policies.

Perhaps one should distinguish between private and public revelation. But why should the number of people actually present matter? A more promising distinction is between revelation which relies on sense perception and is admissible, and that which does not rely on a familiar and trusted mode of acquiring knowledge and so is suspect. Again, this argument fails to draw the line between what is rational for the private believer and what is rational for the polity. Notice that the second kind of revelation may be public. Thousands may testify that they felt in some mysterious way the presence of a mysterious and wonderful being, and heard, in their mind's ear, his message, even though the place was completely quiet. The identify of the reports of many people of what they felt at the same time and place makes this revelation public. One may think that the fact that many had the same experience at the same time lends credence to the report of each one of them. But it does not differ in principle from the report of a single person of the same experience, even when it was not witnessed by others. Either such reports are acceptable by all, or they are not to be trusted even by the person who had the experience.

We do in fact hold ourselves open to accept reports of extra-sensory perceptions, as in the case of diviners. Our grounds for either confidence in or mistrust of their ability to identify the presence of water underground are inductive: their past successes or failures. But so is their own reason for confidence in their own ability. If I suddenly feel that there is water under the ground I am standing on at the moment, I will not, nor should I, have any confidence that water is to be found there.[82] Once my ability is empirically proven I will acquire confidence in it, and so should other people. It is true that the level of evidence which makes it rational for a person to come to hold a certain belief is not the same as that which makes it rational for a public authority to come to adopt a policy based on such a belief. It may be rational for people to come to believe that certain drugs are safe, or that they are dangerous, by evidence which falls short of the level required to justify the Food and Drug Administration in licensing or banning them. But that is a common phenomenon which seems to have no bearing on the issues discussed by Nagel.

Nagel gives us little indication of what sort of grounds are cogent enough to justify one in accepting certain beliefs as true, and yet not acceptable as grounds for coercive political action. Oddly enough, he mentions just about

---

[82] Does the fact that having the feeling means having the thought that there is water there gives me confidence? I do not think so. I would feel assaulted by the thought. It is there for reasons beyond my comprehension. Even though I have it, I know that I cannot trust it.

any kind of public issue as falling, at least prima facie, within that category 'in the present state of moral debate'. The enforcement of religious views, abortion, sexual conduct, and the killing of animals for food are examples of matters all current beliefs on which fail the impartiality test. So do issues concerning the morality of nuclear deterrence, the death penalty, and the fundamental problems of economic and social policy governed by different conceptions of social justice.[83] That he does not wish to exclude the last three from coercive political action is due not to the impartiality test but to other considerations.[84]

These reflections demonstrate that Nagel's principle of impartiality in itself does little to justify the 'true liberal' policies which he invokes it to justify. But the doubts that Nagel's list of cases raises go to the very heart of his understanding of his principle. He seems to regard any widespread disagreement over policies as indicating a failure to meet the condition of epistemic impartiality, and provides no independent analysis of the grounds resorted to in such debates. But, as Nagel himself says, the existence of a common ground of justification is far from guaranteeing agreement, 'nor does it mean that only one belief is reasonable on the evidence. I may hold a belief on grounds that I am willing to offer in objective justification, suitable for the public domain, while acknowledging that others who consider that justification and yet reject the belief are not being irrational or unreasonable, though I think they are wrong.'[85] 'Reasonable belief is partly a matter of judgment, and is not uniquely determined by the publicly available arguments.'[86]

If the existence of a common ground does not guarantee actual agreement even when the evidence is shared—let alone when it is not, as of course in reality it rarely is—how can disagreement be a reliable indicator of the absence of a common ground of justification? We require a direct analysis of the way such arguments are conducted, of the reasons actually advanced for different policies. None is offered. Nagel, when addressing the difficulty of applying his impartiality test, refers back to his distinction between appeal to the fact that one holds a belief and appeal to the truth of that belief as providing the touchstone;[87] but since that distinction is incoherent it does not advance matters.

[83] See ibid. 233–4.

[84] Nagel regards these matters as essentially public in nature, so that the government must adopt some position on them, or at least as matters which are accepted by all as matters of public concern (see ibid.). These are especially weak arguments. Issues of social justice are accepted as matters of public concern in precisely the way that abortion is. And while the morality of *state*-wielded nuclear deterrence or capital punishment is inevitably a matter on which the state must take a view, the state's relation to nuclear weapons owned by private individuals or to capital punishment meted out by them is on a par with its relation to private abortions. Is it reasonable to hold that considerations which determine the morality of nuclear threats and of the death penalty should determine public policy regarding their use by the state, but should be excluded from affecting public policy regarding their use by individuals?

[85] Ibid. 234.   [86] Ibid. 235.   [87] See esp. ibid. 236.

We are left in a frustrating position. We know that the test of 'sharing all the evidence' must be relaxed. But nothing in the rest of Nagel's discussion suggests how to relax it. I suspect that the principle of impartiality, when relaxed to admit all acceptable reasons, fails in the task that Nagel assigns it. Like Nagel's principle of consent, it is a toothless tiger. It can rule out only blatantly irrational beliefs. It does not rule out as grounds for coercive political action any beliefs that individuals are justified in holding to be true. No one is justified in holding beliefs that are not based on acceptable reasons. But the heart and soul of Nagel's argument is for epistemic restraint in appealing to truth, for the contention that some truths which individuals are justified in believing, they are not justified in relying on politically. This seems an impossible task, given that to be personally justified in believing a proposition one must accept that one's belief is in principle subject to impersonal, impartial standards of correctness. Those who comply with this condition do subject their beliefs to valid impersonal tests. It may be that others do not see it that way, and deny the validity of those tests. But given that the tests are both valid and publicly, objectively, and impartially available, it seems impossible that others can *reasonably* deny the validity of those tests, unless they lack information. And that lack can be remedied, and so cannot serve as the basis of Nagel's theory. Ultimately Nagel's principle is bound to fail because it depends on driving a wedge between appeal to truth and acceptance of objective standards of justification; and that wedge comes unstuck.

Impartiality and Respect

Nothing in the above undermines a cluster of related valid points. First, within certain limits, people may seek to promote their personal preferences for a certain worthwhile environment and style of life by political action. But in doing so each person's preferences are to count equally. Such cases are part of the case for a democratic constitution.[88] They do not involve any epistemic restraint, for there is no suggestion that there is any truth withheld. I simply believe that plenty of music opportunities are valuable. You believe that open spaces are important. We are both right. But scarcity of resources imposes a need to choose. That is why numbers count.

Nagel notices correctly that a 'large range of legislative and communal issues . . . are put under the control of the preferences of the majority, or of coalitions among minorities'.[89] He does not justify this practice by reference to his condition of impartiality, and it seems doubtful whether it can so be justified. This practice is an expression of a democratic outlook which, in matters of the consent of the governed, is much less demanding than Nagel's

---

[88] See ch. 4 below.   [89] 'Conflict and Legitimacy', 239.

contractarian view. The problem is not that democratic governments decide many issues on the basis of nothing better than the subjective preference of their subjects. Rather, it is that the principle decreeing that matters should be so resolved does not seem to meet the condition of impartiality. There is little consensus, and not much argument in the public arena, on when people should vote simply to express their personal preferences, and when they should vote in support of valid general principles. I can think of no reason why this issue should be more immune to Nagel's impartiality test than issues of economic and social justice, and so on. It is possible that this part of Nagel's argument is out of line with its main thrust.

Second, there are reasons, not based on preferences, which apply to one individual but not to others. These arise out of commitments and undertakings, status, and office, as well as through the fundamental fact that every person is a different person. Needless to say, such reasons should not be imposed on people to whom they do not apply. But neither they nor individual preferences involve any epistemic restraint. Both the agent and others agree that those preferences and reasons exist, and that they apply only to the agent.

Third, there are principles and ideals which apply to all, but which call for no political enforcement or support. They may be inimical in nature to any political intervention, being based on strong voluntaristic principles. Or they may be concerned with dimensions of human life to which politics can make no difference. Obviously, such ideals should not be, cannot be, pursued politically. Equally obviously, no measure of epistemic restraint is exercised in reaching this conclusion.

Finally, principles calling for coercive action may indeed require justification of a special kind, with the result that measures which are admirable if undertaken voluntarily may not be coercively imposed. Again, this view requires no epistemic restraint. It calls for no holding back on the truth, but rather for a recognition that different measures require different justifications, that different propositions are true only if justified by different arguments.

My criticism of Nagel turns on the cogency of his analysis, rather than on the attractiveness of his vision. There is a deep appeal in the idea that coercive measures are justified only if based on the consent of those subject to them. It seems to solve at a stroke the problem of justifying coercion. According to Nagel, it expresses Kant's categorical imperative that one should treat humanity never merely as a means but always also as an end.[90] Ultimately we have to account for the importance of both coercion and consent in our political outlook. For the present, suffice it to point to the dilemma facing contractarian theories of politics (i.e. those which allow that moral principles other than political ones are to be justified on other grounds,

---

[90] Ibid. 223, 238.

and form the basis on which consent to political principles is sought). They may, with Rawls, attempt to base political principles on an overlapping consensus. That is, they may seek principles to which all viable ideologies in the relevant political morality implicitly agree, or are committed to agreeing, or nearly so. Or they may, with Nagel, look for principles based on reasons which are generally acceptable in the relevant society.

Rawls's route seems barren in pluralistic societies, such as ours. The degree of existing diversity is just too great. Furthermore, as argued above, there seems little reason to reject valid or true principles, the implementation of which may actually be of benefit to all, just because a small sector of the population cannot be convinced of this fact. Nagel's alternative relies on the dubious epistemological claim that there can be reasons for belief and for action which are *quite reasonably* not recognized as such by people generally but which are valid nevertheless. If one rejects this possibility, then it is tempting to say that our duty to act only on political principles to which the reasonable consent is simply the duty to act on well-founded, valid principles. For that is what the reasonable consent to. This eliminates the independent role of consent.

The problem is not why one should assign consent any role. It is more fundamental. The puzzle is how one can give consent a viable role, without saying that only principles already agreed to by all can be relied upon. One must find a reasonable interpretation of the intuitively appealing idea that political principles must be accessible to people as they are. It is not enough, according to this intuition, that those who are totally rational and open to rational conversion will be persuaded, and be radically changed. Politics must take people as they come and be accessible to them, capable of commanding their consent without expecting them to change in any radical way. But at the same time, justified political principles may be controversial, and may fail to command actual consent. Nagel and Rawls offer interpretations of this intuition which aim to be both coherent and attractive. Their failure suggests that the underlying idea may be at bottom unstable and incoherent. There may be no middle way between actual (including implied) agreement and rational justification.

5

Liberalism, Scepticism, and Democracy

Our culture combines a dedication to individual freedom with bitter disagreements about its limits. In a way the disagreements tell of the strength of the commitment to freedom. They result from controversies concerning the reasons for that commitment, which lead to differences in our understanding of its meaning and limits. The fact that individual freedom is supported by so many currents of thought, by so many religious and philosophical tendencies in our society, is evidence of the strength of our commitment to this ideal and of its centrality to our culture.

Nor should the alternative ways of understanding the value of individual freedom be thought of as necessarily incompatible. There are indeed many powerful arguments in support of this ideal, and they are largely mutually reinforcing, although they differ in detail, and therefore, part company round the edges. All this means is that in some instances the case for freedom is supported by only some of the myriad reasons which bolster it in the majority of cases.

Some of the best arguments for individual freedom are of a practical, or pragmatic, cast. One points to the success, cultural and economic, that the free play of ideas and the spirit of enterprise have brought to the countries which encouraged them.[1] Another argument points to the contribution of respect for individual freedom to social stability, and individual prosperity, in a world riven by fundamental moral and religious disagreements. Respect for individual liberties provides the *modus vivendi* necessary for the stability of pluralistic societies. It also ensures that not only members of ideological groups which are temporarily in the ascendancy, but the bulk of the population, can enjoy relative prosperity. A third argument rests on the principled limitations on the ability of any government or any large bureaucracy to achieve complex moral goals, and on the inevitable undesirable by-products of bureaucratic interventions.

This essay is an expanded version of an Ida Beam lecture given at the University of Iowa College of Law in Oct. 1988. The lecture was funded in part by grants from the Iowa Humanities Board and the National Endowment for the Humanities. It was first published in the *Iowa Law Review*, 74 (1989). I am grateful to members of the law school and the philosophy department at the University of Iowa for their kind hospitality and lively discussion and comments. I owe a special debt of gratitude to Gerald Dworkin, Peter Hacker, and Peter Jones, and especially to G. A. Cohen and Steven Burton for invaluable criticism and comments on an earlier draft of the lecture.

[1] Of course, this argument is partially self-fulfilling. Free cultures tend to define cultural flourishing in terms of those values and ways of life that they tend to produce. In other words, freedom is not external to their culture but an integral part of it. They also tend to emphasize, perhaps even overemphasize, the importance of economic prosperity to individual well-being.

I mention these powerful pragmatic arguments only in order to say that the fact that I am not going to consider them does not mean that I underestimate their importance. But my concern here is with some moral arguments for respecting individual freedom. In certain quarters there is in the air an atmosphere of moral privatization, of a tendency to separate morality from the state. According to these trends, morality is a matter of which we know little, something on which objective judgment is impossible, something which should be left to the individual. The state should keep out of morality. At most it should merely hold the ring, providing impartial adjudication among private opinions.

People who hold such views often regard them as supporting individual freedom. By excluding the state from the moral realm, or from all but procedural morality, they seek to leave individuals free to pursue their hearts' content. I think that in the main such views are misguided and dangerous. They are based on confused reasoning, and they give freedom a bad name. They present a morally anaemic argument for freedom. The case for individual liberty is alleged to rest on the weakness of morality, or on our inability to understand moral issues. Partly because of this, such arguments tend to encourage toleration bred by indifference to others, toleration which is excessively individualistic in spirit. I begin by criticizing the view that moral scepticism or moral fallibility provides an important moral foundation for respecting individual liberty. I then criticize a certain conception of democracy which, though based on neither scepticism nor fallibility, has some intellectual affinities with the previously considered views. I conclude with a brief summary of an alternative view defending individual liberty as a positive value, as an element in the moral ideal of the free person.[2] It will become clear that this view of freedom is not infected by the individualism of which liberals are often accused.

I. SCEPTICAL THEMES

Sceptical Liberality

As a teacher I am constantly surprised at the deep roots of value scepticism among the better-educated in our society. Every year, when the new students arrive, I am reminded that while very few people are thorough sceptics, many are half-sceptics. That is, while people do have their views and their principles, they often combine them with general scepticism and agnosticism about values. They hold that there is no way of 'objectively' establishing or justifying any value judgements. Every person's view is just his view. Somebody else will have a conflicting view, and there is little

---

[2] It hardly needs saying that there are many other principled, moral arguments in support of individual freedom which I neither examine nor mention here.

more to be said on the matter. As I have said, this attitude is generally part of an outlook which is vaguely supportive of individual freedom. Since no one can really show that his view is better than that of the next person, everyone should tolerate the view of the next person. Sociologically, scepticism tends to be connected with weak respect for freedom. It leads to toleration based not on valuing the freedom of others, but on distance, sometimes on mutual incomprehension. Freedom is protected not because it is valuable, but because there is no moral sanction for anything, not even for the suppression of freedom.[3]

I am not concerned with the familiar and vexing question of the coherence of various forms of scepticism. Rather, our interest is confined to the relation between scepticism and toleration. Global value scepticism, i.e. the claim that no knowledge can be gained on any moral issue and, more broadly, on any question involving values, not only cannot serve as a basis for belief in toleration but is inconsistent with it. It denies that we can have any reason to believe in toleration. It is true that global scepticism also rules out intolerant attitudes and policies which are rooted in principles and in values. This, however, merely leaves people free to pursue actions and policies which do not depend on any belief in the validity of any principles or values. It is doubtful whether people, liberated from the constraining influence of their value beliefs, are more likely to follow tolerant policies rather than intolerant ones or any arbitrary mix of actions.

Such global value scepticism leaves little room for any justification of general policies. It normally is thought that it leaves open the possibility of self-interested justifications, but their relevance, and therefore their availability, are doubtful. On appropriate occasions, self-interest can in some sense justify, or at any rate explain, why certain people support a policy. It is to their advantage, or so they believe. But that does not show that the policy is justified and is normally irrelevant to its justification. Furthermore, theories which aim to show that morality rests on enlightened self-interest, along Hobbesian lines, are not sceptical theories. Hence those who believe that under fairly common conditions tolerant policies are in every person's long-term interests, whatever their plausibility, are not advancing sceptical arguments. When self-interest can justify general policies of toleration, scepticism is at an end. The impossibility of showing that global scepticism paves the road to toleration is conceptual.

Global scepticism is to be distinguished from local scepticism, i.e. the view that we cannot obtain knowledge on certain particular issues. For

---

[3] Such arguments do not find much favour with philosophers, though they are not altogether without supporters. See B. A. Ackerman, *Social Justice in the Liberal State* (New Haven Conn: Yale Univ. Press, 1980), 365–9; and Peter Jones, 'Liberalism, Belief and Doubt', *Archiv für Rechts und Soziale Philosophie*, 36 (1989), reflection on which triggered much of this section.

example, some people claim that no one can know the answers to questions such as whether punishment deters, whether foetuses are human beings, or whether solitary confinement is a form of torture. Local scepticism is no more successful in supporting a general policy of tolerance. It all depends on what we are ignorant about. Sometimes ignorance would lead to what may be regarded as a more tolerant attitude. Ignorance about the value of capital punishment may, when combined with other suitable premisses, support its abolition. In other cases, however, the rational outcome is likely to be nontolerant. Ignorance about the status of foetuses may well justify criminal prosecution of anyone who is an accomplice to an abortion.

Corrigibility and Tolerance

Scepticism, whether local or global, holds little promise for any political theorist. The realization that our beliefs may be mistaken should not, however, be confused with scepticism. Does our fallibility provide an argument for toleration? It is certainly often thought to do so, but is the argument cogent?

The connection is in the common belief that realization of our fallibility justifies reducing our confidence in our own beliefs. If they may be right and I may be wrong, does it not follow that I am not entitled to be confident that I am right, and should not that lead me to adopt a tolerant attitude toward their views? Should realization of my fallibility undermine my confidence in my beliefs? Should I be less than certain that I am sitting in my room writing this simply because it is possible, as it surely is, that in fact I am lying in bed dreaming, or with my brain stimulated to produce delusions and false beliefs? This familiar chain of thought reflects deep confusions about the reasons for certainty or for doubt.

Justified certainty rests not on a belief in infallibility but on a belief that one is not in fact mistaken, that there is no reason to suspect a mistake, and every reason, based on evidence and on one's situation, to trust one's beliefs. I am absolutely certain that George Bush is today [i.e., 1988] President of the United States, that Australia is in the southern hemisphere, that the British Parliament sits in London, etc. Although I may be wrong each time, I am absolutely certain of these beliefs, and rightly so.

The point is that uncertainty is an awareness of a flaw ('the document appears to have been interfered with'), inadequate evidence, or an inferior situation one is in ('I'm too far away to tell', 'the light is misleadingly bright'). Mere realization of fallibility is not a discovery of a flaw, but an awareness of the conditions of knowledge. The possession of knowledge depends on the exercise of skills and judgment. They are capabilities which can be used and abused, whose use can be successful or may misfire. Becoming aware of our fallibility can amount to no more than realization of this fact.

The fact that to realize that we may be wrong is merely to realize something about the conditions of knowledge may be obscured by the view that sometimes we have infallible beliefs. Mathematics is often thought to be an example. It is then felt that fallible beliefs are flawed, that they lack whatever it is which gives infallible beliefs that quality. The simple fact is that, in general, mathematical beliefs are as fallible as any others, and the many mistakes committed by everyone, from a young pupil to an expert mathematician, demonstrate this. It is true that there are propositions, such as that I have a body, and including some simple mathematical propositions, such as that $2 + 2 = 4$, acceptance of which is not revisable. These are propositions which fix the use of our basic concepts and determine our fundamental orientation in the world. Even to doubt them is incoherent. Rejecting them is a sign of conceptual confusion or ignorance. Severe cases mark cognitive collapse, or even insanity. But such beliefs, far from being the standard and norm of all rational beliefs, are exceptional and in many ways unlike normal beliefs. For example, while we can have evidence for these basic beliefs, our confidence in them does not depend on such evidence. These are highly difficult and contentious issues which we cannot explore here. The crucial point is that ordinary knowledge is fallible.

Recognition that fallibility is part of the conditions of ordinary knowledge underpins the attitude of critical rationality. It includes realization of the corrigibility and revisability of all ordinary beliefs, precisely because of our fallibility, and a readiness to re-examine our beliefs as necessary. Critical rationality has political implications. Its desirability argues for political institutions which adopt that attitude, and which allow adequate opportunities for periodic re-evaluation of public policies. What counts as adequate is a difficult question which need not detain us here. Suffice it to say that there is no general answer suitable to all cases. The same is true of ordinary personal beliefs. Some of our beliefs should be re-examined periodically, whereas others, while open to revision if contrary evidence is forthcoming, need not be subject to routine re-evaluation. Sometimes it is appropriate to embrace certain beliefs on fairly slender evidence, while at others an assurance that the matter was thoroughly investigated is a condition of rationality.

The requirements of critical rationality affect the structures of institutions and the processes of decision-making more than they affect the substance of policies. Still, these requirements yield a powerful constraint on substantive policies. Other things being equal, policies which are incompatible with the existence and proper functioning of political institutions whose actions and policies are open to re-evaluation and revision should be avoided. Certain ways of running the secret service, for example, which may have various advantages, should none the less be avoided because they presuppose the absence of the kind of accountability that critical rationality

requires. As a consequence, the realization of the possibility of error suggests that, other things being equal, one should prefer policies which provide for reversible measures over those which rely on irreversible ones.[4]
This is one of the traditional arguments against capital punishment. Clearly,
liberal thinkers traditionally have paid much attention to the implications of
the requirements of critical rationality. Equally clearly, these arguments do
not support as great a degree of toleration and pluralism as advocated by
traditional liberal theories.

So far we have considered only the principled, global belief in the possibility of error. Error is more likely in some areas than others. Thus, realization that our knowledge of nuclear technology and its implications is
very incomplete, and therefore, that our beliefs in issues of nuclear safety
are particularly vulnerable to doubt, is a reason against the use of nuclear
power. This caution may be reinforced by the fact that the results of accid-
ents or of long-term contamination through the proliferation of radioactive
material can be catastrophic, so that even a small risk of error may be sufficient to inhibit action.

The special danger of error in particular areas has, therefore, further
political implications which go beyond the general adoption of an attitude
of critical rationality and apply even to those who do not wish to adopt it
as a matter of general principle. These implications, just like those of local
scepticism, bear no special relation to liberal theories and do not in general
lend support to tolerant rather than to intolerant policies. I suspect that if
a general trend can be discerned in the way in which local doubts operate,
it is in favour of a cautious and conservative attitude. In general, such
doubts tend to affect new, or relatively recent, policies more than long-
established ones, as the consequences of the latter are better known. Of
new policies, radical departures and far-reaching innovations do more often
give rise to doubts than small-scale amendments to existing policies. Cautious conservatism is sometimes perceived as supporting toleration. In fact
it merely favours the status quo. It supports toleration only if you already
practise it.

The Vulnerability of Values

It is sometimes thought that we are particularly prone to error on questions
of value, or, alternatively, that bureaucracies are particularly vulnerable to
error in such matters. It is of great importance to realize that even if this is
so, advocates of toleration can find little comfort in this fact. When debating
the use of nuclear energy we have a choice between its use and its rejection.

---

[4] But the fact that it is not a strong argument against allowing houses to be demolished by
their owners shows that this preference is not in general a very strong one.

Our ignorance of the hazards of the nuclear industry does not infect our actions if we avoid developing that industry.[5] If you do not use radioactive material you avoid the hazards of radioactivity. Is there anything comparable regarding the hazards of morality and of value? There can be only if some of our actions carry moral significance whereas their omission does not. I suspect that this is not the case. In particular it seems plausible that if any action carries moral significance, so does its omission. The very fact that an action is morally significant confers significance on its omission. If there is a duty to perform an act then it is wrong not to perform it. The same seems to be true in all matters of value.[6]

Whatever the truth of this matter, it is itself a moral issue. If I am wrong, then I made a wrong moral judgment. In other words, the proposition that we can avoid moral mistakes and errors by avoiding actions which are morally significant is a moral proposition which, if all moral propositions are particularly vulnerable to error, is itself particularly vulnerable. It follows that even if morality is particularly vulnerable there is no way to avoid the risk of error. If there is a range of actions whose performance escapes moral significance, then this is itself a matter of moral judgement which is liable to the enhanced risk of error of all moral propositions.

It may be worth adding that, despite the popularity of the view that all value judgments are particularly vulnerable to error, this is not a view which can survive even the most cursory examination. Are we really more liable to error when we hold that torturing the innocent is wrong than when we think that the nuclear-energy industry is safer than coalmining (as the chairman of the former (British) Central Electricity Generating Board assured us)? There are no general theoretical reasons to think so.[7]

One natural line of retreat from the view that all value judgments are suspect is to the contention that, whatever the general vulnerability to mistake of value judgments, those made by public authorities are particularly vulnerable. The reasons given above concerning the general argument from vulnerability apply to and defeat this contention as well. A more modest

---

[5] Though there are, of course, opportunity costs to such decisions.

[6] It does not follow that their significance is the same. One important terminological clarification is necessary here. To simplify, I will use 'moral' to encompass all matters of value. Although I sometimes distinguish between morality, general issues of value, religion, etc., it is often convenient to refer to all of them by one short phrase. I usually use 'moral' to refer to any matter of value.

[7] Sceptical arguments about the possibility of moral knowledge are the only ones which help here. If one believes that moral propositions are either true or false, but that we can never have reason to ascertain their truth, and if one believes that there is no 'unconscious moral sense' which guides our moral judgements, it is quite likely that we are much more liable to moral error than to error in matters over which we can form rational judgments. Such sceptical arguments, however, are unstable, and liable to collapse into an argument that moral judgments are neither true nor false. Cf. S. Blackburn, Errors and the Phenomenology of Value', in T. Honderich (ed.), *Morality and Objectivity: A Tribute to J. L. Mackie* (New York: Routledge Chapman and Hall, 1985), 223.

version of it is, however, the most important argument for limited government. It tries to isolate certain ranges of issues regarding which public authorities are particularly prone to error. Various such areas can be identified. To an extent, they depend on the structure and constitution of particular authorities. One familiar general observation, however, seems appropriate. In mass, highly mobile societies, public authorities are particularly ill-adapted to judge matters in which having the right moral feelings, the proper moral sensibilities, is of particular importance. They are more suited to dealing with abstract principles, with general rights and duties than with matters of moral character, personal relations, etc. Such matters are better kept, as far as possible, within the private sphere and out of the public domain.[8]

Reasonable Disagreement

Another common theme in this context is that disagreement over value judgments is often reasonable disagreement. Questions of the good, of the meaning of life, and of right action are ones over which reasonable people disagree and which admit of reasonable doubt and reasonable disagreement.

Should the fact that someone reasonably disagrees with me weaken the trust I have in my view? A simple example shows that in general it should not do so. If I am found guilty of a crime I may agree that the case against me was proved beyond reasonable doubt. I may agree, in other words, that the jury not only reasonably doubted my protestations of innocence but was rationally compelled by the evidence to convict me, without in the least losing faith in my own innocence.

This case has the following special feature. The jury is likely to believe that I know whether I am guilty or not. When it finds me guilty it also comes to the conclusion that I probably am lying about my innocence. When I find them reasonable, I find reasonable their belief that I am lying. Most cases are not like that. In most cases one party has no reason to think that the other has special access to the truth. On the contrary, the typical case is one in which one person finds another's conflicting belief reasonable, given the evidence available to the other person, his experience in the matters concerned, etc., but believes that his own experience or evidence are superior. That is why his confidence is not shaken by the reasonable disagreement.

If others doubt my true and reasonable belief or disagree with it, their doubt and disagreement are reasonable when, through no fault of their own, they do not have evidence of the same quality that I have, but their evidence

---

[8] The difficulties in following this advice are vividly illustrated by the standing of women within the family. On the one hand, one wishes to keep such personal matters out of the political domain. On the other hand, the abuse of women by their husbands in some contemporary cultures makes this unacceptable.

is sufficient for them, given their degree of understanding and expertise in the matter, to base a judgment on, or else when the evaluation of the evidence is sufficiently difficult to make error not really surprising, given normal human capacities. Thus T. Nagel points out that, even when people share the same evidence, they may reasonably disagree due to differences in judgment understood as differences in the assessment of the evidence.

> I may think that it would be reasonable for someone else either to believe or not to believe *p* on the evidence available to me . . . yet find that I do believe it. Perhaps in that case I must also judge that it would not be reasonable for *me*, as I am, not to believe it on that evidence. . . .[9]

Evidently, such divergence of evidence or its evaluation can easily arise in circumstances which cast no doubt on the solidity of my beliefs. Knowing this, I may be rational to remain unmoved in the face of reasonable disagreement. Naturally, the fact that someone reasonably disagrees with me may, in appropriate circumstances, call into action my attitude of critical rationality. I will want to reassess my belief in order to be satisfied that I am right and the other person is wrong. But I may do so, reinforcing my original conviction, without denying that the other person's disagreement was and remains reasonable.

While not necessarily spreading doubt, the existence of a reasonable disagreement has moral implications. Those who act wrongly because of a reasonable mistake should be excused (though they may still have to make amends). Similarly, the fact that wrongdoing was based on a reasonable mistake affects our judgment of the character and virtue of the offenders. But none of this should induce one to desist from acting on beliefs with which others reasonably disagree. That seems to indicate that reasonable disagreement provides a limited basis for toleration. It may appear to support moderation in penal policies. One should not criminalize actions undertaken because of a reasonable belief that they are right. But this exaggerates the true significance of this consideration. The very fact that an act is prohibited by law may affect the reasonableness of a belief that it is an innocent act.

To take account of this, the degree of toleration based on reasonable disagreement is limited to the following: One should not criminalize actions undertaken because of a reasonable belief that they are right, if that belief will remain reasonable even if they are prohibited by law. Given this qualification, and given that reasonable disagreement bars neither public policies nor legislation based on the beliefs disagreed with, other than direct criminal prohibitions, it is evident that only a very limited measure of toleration can be derived from this consideration.

[9] 'Moral Conflict and Political Legitimacy', *Philosophy and Public Affairs*, 16 (1987), 235.

The emphasis in the previous remarks is on the reasonableness of a person's beliefs. It is interesting that the very fact that someone holds certain beliefs is an argument for toleration, regardless of their reasonableness. Think of a person who has a distorted view of the significance of sex in life. Assume that he neither harms nor affects others in any unfair way. His interest only is at stake. Can we make him better by making him conform to some other sets of beliefs, even though he continues to reject them? In such matters the only way to help him is to bring about a change of belief in him. We must act through his own attitudes and beliefs or not act at all. This is a powerful consideration in favour of toleration on many matters, which does not depend on any belief being reasonable. It supports tolerating the unreasonable as well. But it is an argument of limited scope. It is an argument for tolerating the conduct of those who have certain beliefs. It is no argument for letting them have a free hand in developing, retaining, or propagating any beliefs, however wrong.

Semi-Scepticism and Neutrality

Some people have in mind a more radical epistemic attitude when they talk of reasonable disagreement. Consider an example. John believes in a life of change, variety, and free experimentation. Joanna disagrees. She believes that people should be loyal to the traditions, tastes, and practices they were brought up on. But Joanna regards John's view as a reasonable one. To be precise, she thinks that these are matters over which it is impossible to find conclusive arguments either way.[10] John has strong arguments to support his view. Though she disagrees with him, she thinks that he is as likely to be right as she is.[11] She does not think that anything follows from that by itself. But she also believes that all people are entitled to be respected. The combination of people's right to respect with the fact that their views on the meaning of life, even those she believes to be wrong, are equally likely to be right, implies that they should be left to conduct their lives each by his or her own light.

Normally the proper reaction to such a situation is to suspend belief. If two mutually exclusive views are equally likely to be right, then we do not have adequate reason to accept either of them. One may argue, however, that given that one has to carry on with the business of life (we assume that suicide is not an acceptable option), one is more likely to have a good life if guided by some conception of the good than by none. Since one has no reason to change from the conception one has, it is best to remain faithful

[10] Most of my comments in this case apply also to cases in which Joanna simply believes that her evidence and ability to judge it are, as a matter of fact, no better than those of John.

[11] This epistemic attitude and something like its alleged implications considered here are considered by Jones, 'Liberalism, Belief and Doubt'.

to it, even while realizing that it is not more likely to be correct than the next person's.

Is this cognitive attitude logically possible? The difficulty is that having a certain belief commits one to disbelieving its contradictory. Joanna is supposed to believe in a certain conception of the good but also to believe that its contradictory is as likely to be true as it is. To assume that one believes a proposition (i.e. believes it to be true) while one regards it as no more likely to be true than its contradictory is to allow a radical rupture between belief and belief that one's belief is justified. This may be logically impossible.[12] The best way to understand Joanna's attitude is to say that she acts as if a certain conception of the good is correct, but without believing it to be correct.

This is an unstable state of mind, full of internal tensions. It seems an unpromising foundation for any far-reaching political principle. Does it in fact lend support for toleration? We should ask whether Joanna has any reason to believe that others will be better off if they live by their own conceptions of the good rather than by hers? By hypothesis the answer is no. She believes that her conception of the good is as likely to be right as any of its competitors and, therefore, has no reason deriving from considerations of the good of others to think that they are better off living in the ways they believe to be best than if they follow her ideals. It is true that she does not think that they will be better off following her ideals. She cannot endorse a policy favouring her ideals as against theirs for the good it will do them. But she may have plenty of other reasons to wish for such a policy, most notably that it may help her in pursuit of her ideals. If she has any reason to adopt a tolerant policy, this must derive from other considerations. One such consideration, already noted, is the restriction on the imposition of practices not believed in.

The tenuousness of one's beliefs, even if less than in the extreme case of Joanna, may provide an additional reason against interference with others, though it is not one based on their interests. Joanna may rightly feel reluctant to take the responsibility for other people's affairs which her interference will bring with it. The chances that she will be doing them harm rather than good are too great. But this is an argument about what is the right action for her, not about what is best for them. If they carry on their lives as they wish, then their success or failure is their responsibility. If Joanna makes them follow her ideals, their fortune is, at least in part, her responsibility. She may find a reason for non-interference in a principle that people should

---

[12] I am assuming that, since she believes that a view which is a contrary of her own is as likely to be true as hers, she is committed to the view that the contradictory of her belief (which is entailed by that contrary) is equally likely to be true. I do not assume, however, that believing a proposition commits one to holding that the available evidence for it is better than the evidence for its contradictory.

not assume responsibility for others' lives unless they have a clear and substantial reason to do so.

This weak principle of non-interference is both important practically and interesting theoretically. Its theoretical interest is in that it is not a logical principle (as e.g. 'intentional action is justified only if based on a valid reason'), for it imposes a 'burden of proof' heavier than is required by logic. On the other hand, as was remarked above, it is not based on simple concern for the well-being of others. It is a principle governing each person's own proper attitude toward others, as an element of an articulation of the doctrine of the good life. It establishes a presumption against interference, a weak 'mind your own business' presumption, as governing the proper attitude toward others. It is part of an attempt to strike a balance between concern for the good of all and a more self-directed attitude as the proper attitude for people to adopt. The practical importance of the principle is great, though dispersed. Even though there is no reason to believe that Joanna's attitude is a justified universal one, it is beyond doubt the proper attitude on numerous diverse occasions. On all such occasions the principle 'do not interfere except for a clear and substantial reason' comes into its own and forms a powerful force for toleration.[13]

So far we have been examining the implications, if any, of individual disagreement, that is, of the fact that this or that person disagrees with us. Suppose, however, that disagreement is general in our society. Does that make a difference? Some people regard the general controversiality of many value judgments as the foundation of a policy of toleration. This view seems much more plausible. If a view is controverted by many, then it is likely to be controverted by some who have the evidence and the sense to evaluate it. They may be mistaken but, on the other hand, they may be right, and the mistake may be mine. An attitude of critical rationality suggests that error is quite likely in such cases. Though, of course, re-examining the evidence and finding an explanation suggesting that the others, and not I, are in error will allay these doubts to a considerable extent.

Although these considerations apply to all controversial beliefs, there are special reasons to regard controversy as a mark of error in matters of value. First, there are no moral experts. There is no moral science, no hidden, yet-to-be-discovered bits of moral evidence. There is a sense, though it is not easy to explain, in which morality is entirely on the surface, and the basic moral factors are available for all to see. Controversy, therefore, does acquire special significance. Second, it is arguable that values are, at least partly, constituted by social practices. This would explain the absence of

---

[13] It remains to be argued whether the principle applies only to relations between individuals or also to the relations between governments and their subjects. I tend to believe that it applies there as well, for governments act in lieu of their subjects, and reasons which apply to their subjects carry over to them. See *The Morality of Freedom*, ch. 3.

moral experts and the fact that the moral facts necessary to establish moral principles are available for all to see. It also would reinforce the suspicion that moral controversy is a sign that something is wrong.[14] If practices play a constitutive role in establishing values, then controversy may show a defect in the constitution of the relevant value, not merely in its recognition. We shall return briefly to these matters. For present purposes, suffice it to note that these last ruminations took us a long way beyond scepticism towards a partially societal-based account of morality.

II. DWORKIN ON POLITICAL INDEPENDENCE

I have tried to describe some of the confusions which motivate the attempt to base freedom and toleration on scepticism and related attitudes. But the confusions were in the reasons, not in the conclusion. The sceptical and semi-sceptical arguments are thought to buttress, among other things, the conclusion that, while we may guide our own lives by our beliefs about the nature of the good life, we should refrain from relying on these beliefs when we act politically. The same view appears to be supported by a powerful argument which is based on an important understanding of the rationale for democratic decision-making. I will criticize this argument by criticizing the understanding of democracy which it presupposes. One way of seeing the force of this argument is to examine how it emerges out of a series of considerations presented by R. M. Dworkin.

Like some previous writers, Dworkin distinguishes between personal preferences (i.e. preferences for one's 'own enjoyment of some goods or opportunities')[15] and external preferences (i.e. preferences 'for the assignment of goods and opportunities to others').[16] The latter should not be given

---

[14] I have tried elsewhere to contribute a little to the explanation of the dependence of value on social practices. See ibid. ch. 10.

[15] *Taking Rights Seriously* (London: Duckworth, 1977), 234.

[16] Ibid. Dworkin's views are to be distinguished from those of the anti-perfectionist writers, such as Rawls, Nozick, and Ackerman, who deny that political decisions may be based on conceptions of the good life. On occasion Dworkin indicates support for that position. In a chapter titled 'Liberalism' in *A Matter of Principle* (Cambridge, Mass: Harvard Univ. Press, 1985), political morality is said to rest on the principle that governments ought to treat one with equal concern and respect (p. 191). The liberal theory of equality is said to suppose 'that political decisions must be, so far as is possible, independent of any particular conception of the good life, or of what gives value to life'. But this anti-perfectionism is withdrawn in the very next sentence, which clarifies Dworkin's real target: 'Since the citizens of a society differ in their conceptions, the government does not treat them as equals if it prefers one conception to another, either because the officials believe that one is intrinsically superior, or because one is held by the more numerous or more powerful group.' The government does not treat them as equals whenever a political decision is reached because, e.g. 'a majority decides to make criminal some act (like speaking in favour of an unpopular political position, or participating in eccentric sexual practices) . . . because the majority disapproves of those views or that sexual morality. The political decision, in other words, reflects . . . the domination of one set of

any weight in political decisions. Constitutional rights, according to Dworkin, are justified if they manage to exclude from the democratic process decisions which people are likely to take because of their external rather than personal preferences.[17] In discussing this principle Dworkin does not consider the status of people's political beliefs. They are clearly meant to be governed by the preferences which they entail. That is, any value judgment entails a preference for a state in which the value is realized. If that preference is external, the value judgment is not allowed to justify any public policy.

It is curious that when arguing in defence of this view Dworkin relies on an argument which does not support it at all. His argument supports, not the banishment of external preferences from the grounds of political decisions, but the exclusion of those preferences which deny that other people's preferences count, or that they count equally. The task he sets himself is to show what is wrong with basing political decisions on the fact that individuals prefer some other individuals to be given certain rewards or to be denied certain goods. An example would be the wish of many in the community that Sarah should be given a swimming-pool at public expense. But instead of arguing about cases of this kind, Dworkin deals exclusively with cases in which people's preferences relate, not to what others get, but to how much their preferences count, e.g. people's preferences that Sarah's preferences should count for twice as much in the day-to-day political decisions or that the preferences of blacks or Jews should be discounted.[18]

There is a good deal to be said for Dworkin's actual argument, and it may be worth our while to deviate from the main claim to examine the force of the argument concerning this special case. Dworkin distinguishes between decisions concerning the issue whether each should count for one and other decisions.[19] A political system which is committed to the principle that each should count as one has no business heeding anyone's desire to deviate from that principle except possibly, as Dworkin allows, on those occasions when the acceptability of that principle itself is under consideration.

This is really a logical point. The issue simply does not arise when ordinary decisions are taken within the political system as it is. It arises only

---

external preferences, that is, preferences people have about what others shall do or have' (p. 196).

[17] Ibid. ch. 17.

[18] See 'A Reply', in M. Cohen (ed.), *Ronald Dworkin and Contemporary Jurisprudence*, (London: Duckworth, 1983), 282–6, for Dworkin's response to Hart's criticism of his views on the exclusion of external preferences from political decisionmaking in Hart, 'Between Utility and Rights', in *Ronald Dworkin and Contemporary Jurisprudence*, 219–24. This is Dworkin's most recent and most complete attempted defence of the exclusion of external preferences. See also Raz, 'Professor Dworkin's Theory of Rights', *Political Studies*, 26 (1978), 131.

[19] 'A Reply', 284.

when the justification of the political system itself is in question. A decision whether to give Sarah a swimming-pool does not raise the issue of how people's preferences are to be taken into account. It is presented within a system where that issue is settled. Therefore, people's preferences on how many votes, if any, they or others should have are not involved. They are simply irrelevant. When the issue to be decided is the nature of the political system itself, when it is whether people's preferences should count equally, then it is far from obvious that any of their preferences, external or internal, matter. Whether they do is precisely the issue. It is arguable that the principle that people should have an equal right to political participation is to be justified independently of whether or not it is the view of the majority. If so, then the preferences some people may have regarding such issues never count directly. That is, they are never reasons to give effect to the policy thus preferred.

A utilitarian (who qualifies his utilitarianism to agree with me so far) may, however, wish to claim that the preference that other people's preferences should not count should be taken account of indirectly. While not satisfied, their frustration should be ameliorated. Frustrated Nazis should be given compensating goods to lessen the misery caused by the fact that they live in a society in which Jews count equally. Dworkin's position may be understood as leading to the rejection of this claim. It may be thought inconsistent with giving any weight at all to the frustrated Sarah-lovers' preferences that Sarah should have double the votes that other people have. He regards any political action based on that preference as inconsistent with the foundation of the political system, and therefore, unsustainable.[20] I cannot see that compensation for frustration is inconsistent with the foundation of the system. Would it not be humane and moral to alleviate the suffering that the frustration of various immoral drives (say, to murder or have sex with infants) may cause? The mistake in some crude utilitarian positions is that they assume that the frustration of preferences always causes suffering. They accept a craving picture of preferences. In fact, judgmental preferences, i.e. those that people have because they believe them to be right, are only rarely of this kind. Most of us accept that the world falls short of the ideal with considerable personal equanimity.

Let us return to Dworkin's main claim: that external preferences should not serve to justify any political decision. The trouble with the preferences ruled out by Dworkin's argument which we have just examined is not that they are external, but that they are allegedly inconsistent with the political system that he imagines to be in force, which is a utilitarian one committed

---

[20] It is possible, however, to read Dworkin as excluding counting external preferences directly, i.e. with a view to their satisfaction only. When it is a matter of alleviating the pain of their frustration, what counts is the legitimate concern with avoidance of pain and frustration, and not the source of that pain as such.

to weighing every preference just in virtue of its being a preference. Some personal preferences (such as that I should be given the opportunity to decide by myself all matters affecting me[21]) fall foul of the argument and are ruled out by it, whereas many external preferences (such as that Sarah be given a swimming-pool at public expense) are not.

Given that Dworkin's argument fails to support his exclusion of external preferences, is there any other reason to exclude them? Their exclusion appeals to a widespread feeling against people meddling in the affairs of others. It echoes the sentiment of the saying 'live and let live'. People may not be able to help having preferences concerning other people's lives, but these are essentially interfering, offensive preferences, and should not be the basis of decisions which affect the fate of people other than those who have them, i.e. they should not form the basis of political action. This position does not regard each person as an island. People are affected by their neighbors. A person's taste for rock-climbing, opera, or football will be taken account of by his community. In appropriate cases restraints will be imposed on others to enable him to satisfy his preferences. The basic utilitarian complexion of the position, with its willingness to compare and to trade off costs and benefits among people, remains intact. Only the meddling, offensive external preferences are banned. The trouble is that it is far from clear whether external preferences are indeed all of the offensive, interfering kind.[22]

Utilitarians and others who make much turn on people's preferences as such leave out of their reckoning much essential information. They regard people's desires as opaque natural events, whereas in fact they are, in most cases, active attitudes which people hold for reasons. They have an internal aspect, an internal structure. They are intelligible to the people whose preferences they are, and that makes them potentially intelligible to others. One preference is for an apple because it is sweet, another for a career in law because it is challenging, serves the community, etc. It is only by examining preferences as reason-based that we can judge which of them matter more to the agent. Only by considering the agent's beliefs in reasons do we realize that preferences are not so many atomized, discrete events, but that the more important of them (other than the biologically determined needs for food, sex, warmth, etc.) tend to form nested structures. One's desire to go to law school and to spend the summer in a law firm are part of one

---

[21] Some may say that the preference for deciding all matters affecting me by myself is an external preference, for it entails a preference for not being governed by others. But if so, then the preference to own the Taj Mahal is also external, as it entails a preference that it not be owned by others.

[22] Dworkin has another argument which applies to all external preferences. He claims that giving them weight is double-counting. But as has been pointed out before, this is mistaken. See Hart, 'Between Utility and Rights', 220–4; Raz, *Professor Dworkin's Theory of Rights*, 131. For Dworkin's reply, see 'Liberalism', 365–6.

project, to which the desire to spend time in Spain does not belong. An appreciation of these complex interrelations is a prerequisite for determining any intelligent attitude toward another person's preferences.

Examination of external preferences as reason-based reveals their enormous variety and their complex structure. They are very diverse. Some are principled preferences, such as the preference reflecting the judgment that murderers should be punished. Other external preferences arise out of our personal likes and dislikes, loves and hates, such as my preference that my friend be helped in a difficult task. It seems that there is little point in considering external preferences as such . We need an appreciation of the reasons on which they are based. That alone can tell us whether external preferences should or should not count as reasons for political decisions.

While not abandoning his rejection of all external preferences as such, Dworkin concentrates in most of his more recent articles on a narrower front, characterized from the internal, reason-oriented perspective. He advocates a right to moral independence which is typically characterized as follows: 'People have the right not to suffer disadvantage in the distribution of social goods and opportunities . . . just on the ground that their officials or fellow-citizens think that their opinions about the right way for them to lead their own lives are ignoble or wrong.'[23] This right does not exclude all external preferences. It does not even exclude all the preferences inconsistent with counting equally each person's preferences. It affects only decisions which disadvantage certain people, and only preferences which reflect a belief that the persons to be disadvantaged hold ignoble or wrong beliefs about how to lead their own lives.

On other occasions Dworkin extends the scope of the right to embrace the banning (from being the ground of any political decision) of the fact that anyone believes that people's lives (and not merely their opinions about their lives) are morally wrong or ignoble. One may say that Dworkin's right to political and moral independence excludes principled external preferences, i.e. those reflecting moral views, while not touching personal external preferences, i.e. those reflecting personal tastes, likes, and dislikes.

III. DEMOCRACY AND PREFERENCE

There can be little doubt that it is wrong to disadvantage one person because another person *believes* that the first has mistaken views or leads a misguided life.[24] That a person has certain beliefs is rarely a reason for treating anyone one way or another. It is important here to emphasize that

---

[23] Ibid. 353.

[24] Though there is no point in regarding this as anyone's right. As explained below, in its general form this is no more than an observation on the logic of practical reasoning.

this is in agreement with the way people perceive their own deliberations. Consider a person, call her Jane, who may be an official or an ordinary citizen about to vote on the allocation of a benefit to or its withdrawal from another, call him James, who applied for it. Imagine that Jane believes that James is cruel to his parents and that in accordance with this belief she intends to vote against him. She would be irrational to think that her belief that he is cruel to his parents is a reason for denying James his request. She believes that James's cruelty to his parents, not her belief that he is cruel, is a valid reason for denying him the benefit. This is seen most clearly if we imagine that the decision is not hers, but that she argues for denying James the benefit before the appointed tribunal. She will rely on James's cruelty. But she will not say, indeed, it makes no sense for her to say, 'I believe that he is cruel. Therefore, regardless of whether he really is, there is reason to deny him the benefit he has applied for.' The same is true in general of all agents. They believe in the existence of facts which they take to be reasons for certain actions. But they do not take the fact that they hold these beliefs, as distinguished from the truth of these beliefs, as such reasons.[25]

It is possible, of course, that while Jane does not and should not regard the fact of her having certain beliefs as a reason, others should so regard it. In particular, it is possible that the political system, being a democratic one, regards, not the truth of Jane's belief, but the fact that she has it, and that because of it she has formed a certain preference, as the reason for accepting her vote as influencing the outcome of political decisions. This conclusion seems forced on us by the very logic of democratic government. It appears to be based on the principle that people should use their votes to express their preferences, and that people's preferences should count as such, just because they are people's preferences, regardless of whether they are good or bad, true i.e. reflecting true beliefs) or false. The rationale for democratic political decisions, according to this view, disregards the internal aspects of people's votes. It disregards the fact that people view their votes as justified only if they are based on true beliefs. Democratic theory regards the vote itself, the bare expression of a belief, as the justification of political decisions.[26]

[25] But do we not refer to beliefs as reasons when we say, e.g. 'I did it because I believed that . . .'? We need to distinguish between explanatory and guiding reasons. Guiding reasons are reasons for taking actions. Explanatory reasons are beliefs in (guiding) reasons used to explain why actions were taken. Our concern is with guiding reasons, for it is a normative concern in what is regarded and what is to be regarded as a valid ground for action. Cf. Introduction to J. Raz (ed.), *Practical Reasoning* (Oxford: Oxford Univ. Press, 1978), 2–4.

[26] This argument has the consequence that tactical voting, in which a person votes in a way that does not express his preference on the main issue of the vote in order to prevent an outcome he fears, or for any other reason, is condemned as contrary to the democratic principle. To simplify the argument I will not raise this objection to the understanding of democracy discussed in the text. On my own understanding of democracy, tactical voting is often legitimate.

Now we finally have the argument about democracy I mentioned at the beginning of Section II. If that is the foundation of democracy, there is a powerful argument for suppressing some of our beliefs when we come to vote. The principle that one should not disadvantage other people because one *believes* them to be wrong, or their preferred style of life to be worthless or demeaning, is, on this view, consistently violated by democratic regimes that give effect to votes which reflect beliefs concerning the morality or value of other people's characters, actions, or styles of life. Hence this understanding of democracy leads once more to the familiar conclusion that one should lead one's own life by one's beliefs, and let others lead their lives by theirs. One should refrain from relying on one's beliefs about the value of different styles of life, etc., when voting or deciding public policies.

Yet there is a puzzle in this view of democracy. According to it, the reason a vote counts is different from the reason for which it is cast. My reason for voting to abolish capital punishment is that it is morally wrong. But the 'system's' reason for counting my vote is that I cast it. The system is alleged to be indifferent to my reason, indifferent to the true moral merit of capital punishment and concerned only with counting heads. There seems to be both something right and something wrong here. On the one hand, my vote counts even if it is based on a false belief. So it seems that my belief, rather than the fact which is my reason for it, matters. On the other hand, if my subjective belief is all that matters, why should I, in forming it, agonize about the rights and wrongs of the issues concerned? Why shouldn't I just express any belief or preference that comes first to mind? Why should I, as we all believe I should, try to form an informed judgment, i.e. one responsive to the truth?

We begin to see the way through this puzzle when we realize that it is not limited to democracy. It has wider ramifications, for it is tied up with the very structure of authority, democratic or otherwise. Take a typical case. The authority with power to license drugs for public use approves of drugs on the ground that they are safe. It regards the safety of the drugs, and not its own beliefs about their safety, as proper ground for its action. It investigates each case in order to reach a conclusion which conforms to the facts, and is willing to change its belief when it turns out to be at odds with the facts. At the same time, it is inevitably the case that its decision is binding because it represents its bona fide belief, not because it is a sound decision. Mistaken decisions are equally binding. It would not be an authority if it did not have the power to err.

It is therefore tempting to say that the reason for the authority's action is that it *believes* its action to be justified. That, and not the actual justification of its action, assures it of its binding force. Yet at the same time the reason for this is that acknowledging the validity of an authority's decision whatever its soundness, i.e. without making its soundness a condition of its validity, is deemed to be more likely to lead to action supported by sound reason than any alternative method of deciding what to do. In the terminology of two-level, rule-based justifications, the authority's belief in the soundness of the decision brings the decision under a rule which is itself justified because it is likely to lead to action in accord with sound reason, and not because it leads to action conforming to the authority's preferences.

In other words, it is the truth or soundness of the decisions which counts ultimately. Truth and soundness provide the argument for the legitimacy of the authority. Honest belief is merely a necessary means to the goal. An authority is legitimate only if its honest belief is, at least in the long run, a reliable indicator of the correct course of action to take.[27]

One appealing misconception needs to be sorted out. There is a view of democracy which suggests that, while the previous remarks are true of authority in general, things are otherwise with democratic authority. It is best understood as premissed on the belief that the good for people is to have their preferences satisfied. Its purpose is simply to assure each person that his preferences will count together with those of all others. This attempt to view utilitarianism as the necessary underpinning of democracy fails, like all versions of preference-satisfaction utilitarianism, because it misconceives individual well-being. People flourish and their lives are fulfilled and successful to the extent that they successfully engage in worthwhile activities, pursuits, and relationships. Success in the sense of preference satisfaction is only part of this story. To contribute to a person's well-being, the success has to be in a worthwhile, valuable activity, pursuit, or relationship. This is attested to by the fact that preferences are reason-based, and are held and valued by those who have them because they believe that they are preferences for what is valuable and worthwhile.

We can distinguish various kinds of political issue. Some have to do with deciding between right and wrong. Some concern the setting up of frameworks for individual lives, and for individual choices, to enable people to live in a decent, worthwhile environment and to have valuable choices. In these and many similar decisions, the value or merit of various choices is the primary ground of political action. Reliance on belief in that value is the way one aims at the value within structures of authority. Of course, some decisions are different. Some decisions concern a choice among goods, where there is no reason, independent of the subjective tastes and inclinations of the population, to prefer one to the others. In such cases it is proper to choose in accordance with people's tastes. If everyone prefers baseball to football, then all resources should go to baseball. If some prefer the one game and some the other, a just distribution should be achieved, and it may well be sensitive to the numbers who share the different tastes. But even

---

[27] See *The Morality of Freedom*, 158–60.

here we do not expect the electorate simply to vote for their own preference, but rather to vote for a package of measures which represents a just
distribution of the goods concerned, given their own and other people's
preferences.

This brief discussion, which is meant to be no more than a reply to one
important way of justifying democratic institutions, is incomplete in various
ways. One is in not discussing the intrinsic desirability of democracy as
offering means of participating in the public life of one's community. The
argument is not meant to deny or to minimize the importance of that fact.
But it is meant to suggest that democracy can be justifiably used to this end
only if it meets the instrumentalist condition explained above i.e. only if it
leads, by and large, to good government. The interrelations between the
instrumental and the participatory elements of democracy become complicated in two ways. First, because participation is valuable in itself, providing
opportunities for it through democratic constitutional arrangements is a
value which may justify putting up with some shortfall in other dimensions
of performance. This does not compromise the central role of the instrumental
aspect of democratic governments, as of any government. It merely allows
its partial compromise if necessary to secure the goal of participation. Second,
within a certain range, valuable goals are those endorsed by society collectively.[28] In such matters participation, assuming that it is the proper way
to determine social goals, is necessary for the system of government to discharge its instrumentalist goal.

Democracy is best understood as a political system allowing individuals
opportunities for informed participation in the political process whose
purpose is the promotion of sound decisions. Democracy is justified inasmuch as it is necessary to serve the well-being of people. It shares the
general structure of authority and relies, for its legitimacy, on its ability to
deliver sound decisions.

IV. LIBERALISM AND AUTONOMY

Autonomy and Value Pluralism

If what we have said so far is right, then beliefs about the value of people's
lives, while never being themselves the grounds of political decisions, have
their role in the process of political deliberation about the true grounds of
decisions. These grounds are considerations of what does and what does
not contribute to people's well-being, which options and what aspects of

---

[28] While this notion, which I cannot explore here, is sensitive to individual beliefs and
choices, it is not a simple aggregative function of them.

the common culture are valuable and to be encouraged and which are ignoble and to be discouraged. No value judgments are discounted. In voting for political measures one gives full weight to all one's beliefs. The idea that I should apply my beliefs about the good life to the conduct of my own life, but not to public policies which affect the fortunes of others, does not find any support in the arguments we have canvassed.

But this is precisely the view that many liberal thinkers have been shrinking from. It entrusts governments with the job of deciding what is good for people. What happens to the cause of freedom now? The fear that all liberals face is twofold. First, is the fear of a bureaucratic, dogmatic, insensitive, and inefficient big brother trying to lead our lives for us. Second, is the fear of a government fired by ideals trying to reshape people for their own good and imposing a uniform pattern of life on all. The first fear concerns the competence of governments in pursuing ideals of the good. The second rejects uniformity and insists on individual autonomy.

As I said at the outset, the response to the worry about competence will not concern us today. It is in essence a pragmatic rather than a principled response. There is no reason to think that governmental ignorance, incompetence, and insensitivity affect uniformly and overwhelmingly all the issues involved. It is likely to manifest itself more in some areas than in others, and the best response to it seems to vary from country to country and from issue to issue. It is the fear of uniformity and the insistence on the value of autonomy, of self-definition, that is the most immediate source of our moral fears. Can that concern be reconciled with the view that governments are to protect and promote, inasmuch as it is within their competence to do so, the well-being of individuals?

Fear of uniformity and of the denial of individual autonomy has led many liberal writers to insist that the state should have nothing to do with the promotion of ideals of the good life. This in turn has led to the impoverishment of their understanding of human flourishing and of the relations between individual well-being and a common culture. Instead, one should denounce the rejection of autonomy and the embracing of uniformity as misguided conceptions of individual well-being. Only through a conception of well-being based on autonomy and value pluralism can we restore the true perspective of the role of morality in politics. Let me explain.

'Pluralism' is often used to indicate a position according to which different ways of life and different conceptions of the good should be tolerated regardless of their moral value. 'Value pluralism' as used here marks a different and competing idea. It represents the view that there are many different and incompatible valuable ways of life. Different occupations (the physician, the politician, the miner, the police officer, the artist, the athlete, the academic) and different styles of life (that of the single person, of a member of a large family, of the lover of the open country or of metropolitan

cities) call forth different qualities, develop different aspects of people's per-
sonalities and suppress others. Some people have such distinctive abilities
and disabilities that they can find fulfillment in one way only. But most of
us have it in us, at least when we are still young, to develop in different
directions, to become different persons. The point I am anxious to stress is
one which I hope is implicitly generally recognized. It is that many of the
routes open to us in our lives are both incompatible and valuable. They are
valuable in that each style of life, each pursuit is good and contributes to
the well-being of the persons engaged in it. They are incompatible in
that no person can combine all of them in one single life, as they call on
different qualities and require the relative neglect or even suppression of
other qualities which are good in themselves. It is this value multiplicity,
this incompatibility of much that is valuable, that I mean by value pluralism.

Value pluralism is intimately associated with autonomy. The latter has
two major aspects. The first is that of self-definition. It is the thought that
what we are is, in significant respects, what we become through successive
choices during our lives, that our lives are a continuous process of self-
creation. This is not the rather repugnant thought of people having and
pursuing life-plans. It does not presuppose, though it is compatible with, a
reflective attitude to one's life as a whole, or the setting to oneself of life-
long targets, or of considering and evaluating one's course in life in a very
reflective, intellectual way. Some people are like that. Most are not. The
idea of self-definition is none the less crucial in understanding their lives
and its meaning. They make themselves into what they finally turn out to
be through successive small and medium-size decisions, through drifting as
much as through steering a course for themselves. Self-definition tells of a
view of individual well-being which emphasizes the importance of activity
in judging the success of a life, and rejects a sharp separation of the goodness of a person and the goodness of that person's life. One is what one
is making oneself into through the conduct of one's life. Or, at least, this is
so to a significant degree.

The second aspect of the idea of autonomy goes well beyond self-
definition. It is that autonomy is valuable only if one steers a course for
one's life through significant choices among diverse and valuable options.
The underlying idea is that autonomous people had a variety of incompatible
opportunities available to them which would have enabled them to develop
their lives in different directions. Their lives are what they are because of
the choices made in situations where they were free to go various different
ways. The emphasis here is on the range of options available to the agent.
This points to a connection between autonomy and pluralism. A pluralistic
society, we may say, not only recognizes the existence of a multiplicity of
values but also makes their pursuit a real option available to its members.
But it is not merely that autonomy and pluralism require the availability

of a wide range of options. They are also at one in requiring that those be valuable options.

We value autonomy to the extent that it adds to the well-being of the autonomous person. We regard the fact that a life was autonomous as adding value to it. We think of our own lives and the lives of others as better for having been developed autonomously. But we value autonomous choices only if they are choices of what is valuable and worthy of choice. Those who freely choose the immoral, ignoble, or worthless we judge more harshly precisely because their choice was free. If a person drifts into a wasteful, self-degrading way of life because he knows no better, because he never had the chance to develop differently, we judge his life for what it is worth, but mitigate our judgment of him because he had no choice. No such mitigation is available to those who freely and deliberately choose the same immoral, ignoble, or worthless life, having had opportunities to choose otherwise. This shows that autonomy does not always lead to the well-being of the autonomous person. It can make his life worse if it leads him to embrace immoral or ignoble pursuits. Autonomy contributes to one's well-being only if it leads one to engage in valuable activities and pursuits.

A conception of individual well-being which combines autonomy and value pluralism meets the liberal question of how a political pursuit of ideals of the good can be combined with an attitude of toleration and respect for individual freedom. Perfectionist liberalism has firm moral foundations. On the one hand, on this conception governments' function is to protect and promote, within the bounds of their competence, the well-being of people. On the other hand, we claimed that people prosper through a life of self-definition consisting of free choices among a plurality of incompatible but valuable activities, pursuits, and relationships, i.e. a plurality of valuable and incompatible styles and forms of life. This value pluralism, and not scepticism, or value neutrality, is the liberal bulwark against uniformity, against a society imposing through its government or otherwise a uniform vision of the ideal form of life on its population. Furthermore, given that the flourishing life is the self-created life, i.e. a life engaged in freely chosen valuable activities and pursuits, it is not a life which governments or anyone else can give to people, let alone impose on them. Autonomy speaks of an active life freely engaged in by the agent. It is incompatible with any vision of morality being thrust down people's throats.

Hence a government dedicated to pluralism and autonomy cannot make people good. To be autonomous, they have to choose their own lives for themselves. Governments, and other people generally, can help people flourish, but only by creating the conditions for autonomous life, primarily by guaranteeing that an adequate range of diverse and valuable options shall be available to all. Beyond that they must leave individuals free to make of their lives what they will.

The Importance of the Common Good

So far I have tried to draw a picture of perfectionist liberalism which bases the liberal respect for freedom on a political concern for the well-being of individuals. One of the virtues of this form of liberalism is that its doctrine of freedom is moored in a wider conception of the good person and the good society, rather than being cut off from them as is the case with liberal doctrines of moral neutrality and others. This is the clue to the way to rid liberalism of its association with self-centred individualism.

The clue is in the dependence of autonomy on the environment. The life of the autonomous person is distinctive not by what it is, but by how it came to be what it is. It is marked by the fact that it could have been otherwise and became what it is through the choices of that person. It is marked by the fact that the autonomous agent had many options which he rejected. To show that a person had an autonomous life, we have to look not only at him but also at his environment. One is autonomous only if one lives in an environment rich with possibilities. Concern with autonomy is concern with the environment.

The environment determines whether one has the conditions of autonomy, and it is the conditions of autonomy which are, up to a point, the charge of political institutions. Governments cannot make people have a flourishing autonomous life. That is up to each one to see to himself. But governments can help put people in conditions where they are able to have that kind of life by protecting and promoting the creation of the environment which makes such a life a possibility. Toleration as respect for individual freedom not only is consistent with, it in fact requires concern for and involvement with others.

It is important to see that this is not merely a moral requirement of concern for all. It is also, to a degree, a precondition of having the required environment oneself. The availability of options depends in part on private goods such as money. But options also depend on public goods, which are available to all and which serve all. Public goods lie at the foundations of most options. Options are to a considerable degree socially defined. A British coalminer is someone engaged in extracting coal. But he is also someone whose job involves certain patterns of relations with colleagues and bosses, certain patterns of work routines and leisure times, etc. And beyond all that he is someone whose fortunes are affected by the public images and myths of coalmining, the images of physical hard work, dirt and blackness, courage and danger, camaraderie, and a long tradition of loyalty and struggle, of belonging to the aristocracy of the working class, etc. Those for whom there is a real option of becoming a coalminer or of leaving the mines have a choice whose meaning is partly determined by a public culture which contributes to making mining what it is.

It is much the same not only for all occupations but also for all leisure activities, such as stamp-collecting, train-spotting, jazz music, and amateur photography, which are all recognized forms of social activity with their attendant rewards, traditions, and public images determining their social status and thus their meaning for individuals who may or may not choose to engage in them. The same is true of personal relations. Marriage, friendships, parenthood, and the others are all moulded and patterned by the common culture which determines to a very considerable degree the bounds of possible options available to individuals.[29]

The conditions of autonomy require an environment rich in possibilities. In that they require an appropriate public culture, for it is the public culture which to a considerable degree determines the nature and quality of the opportunities available in a society. But to the extent that the conditions of autonomy require a suitable public culture, they depend on the common good, that is, on a good which if available to one is available to all and whose benefits can be had by all without competition or conflict.

We should not, of course, underestimate the degree to which our society involves competition for resources. Nor should we underestimate the severity of the distributional problems which a morality of personal autonomy gives rise to, with its requirement that an adequate range of diverse and valuable options be within the reach of all. It is important, however, to see clearly the crucial role of a suitable common culture sustaining and defining the options available in a society. Recognition of the importance of such a common culture leads to the rejection of moral individualism. It also dispels any impression that an autonomy-based morality encourages self-centred and socially indifferent attitudes, or that it regards social relations as based on negotiated agreements.

An autonomy-sustaining common culture is a presupposition of the freedom of one and all. People concerned with their own autonomy must be concerned with the flourishing of the common culture. They must be concerned with the existence of one major condition for the autonomy of all.

Tolerating the Bad

A liberal democracy assigns its political institutions, in addition to the job of providing for basic needs when necessary, the tasks of marking sound boundaries within which individuals may act freely without the consent of all those who are affected by their actions, and of protecting and enhancing the common services and the common culture which will enable those

---

[29] In the dependence of valuable activities, relationships, and styles of life on the common culture lies what truth there is in the suggestion that morality depends on social practices. See above, p. 94.

individuals to pursue worthwhile options within the area in which they have the freedom to act.

The idea I am trying to convey is that people's preferences should be freely pursued only within certain bounds. They should be free to engage in valuable activities, pursuits, and relationships within the limits set by consideration for the interests of others. They should be free to do so because such activities, pursuits, and relationships contribute to their well-being. Thus, the function of government, besides the provision of a minimal protective net guaranteeing the satisfaction of basic needs, is to demarcate the boundaries of such freedom of action so as to enhance, inasmuch as is in its power, the quality of the options it makes available to people.

All this raises one major question. The picture this pluralistic and autonomy-based liberalism suggests is one in which the community and its institutions foster and encourage a wide range of diverse forms of life among which individuals are left freely to choose. But those are all good and valuable types of activity and forms of life. What of those which are immoral and ignoble? I do not mean merely those which are considered to be immoral or ignoble but which are in fact all right. People will be protected against the results of misjudgments by constitutional policies instilling caution and moderation. The question I am raising concerns the fate of those whose activities and preferences are really immoral or ignoble. Is it not the essence of liberalism that they too should be defended? The answer to this is a qualified yes. They should be defended to the extent that this is necessary for the protection of their autonomy.

The threat to their position arises out of the fact that autonomously choosing the immoral detracts from one's well-being. Given that governments' task is the promotion of well-being, and that they are required to protect and promote autonomy only to the extent that it contributes to people's well-being, it seems to follow that they need not respect people who pursue immoral or ignoble activities, and that such activities may be suppressed by governmental action. Where is liberal toleration now?

This argument is, however, fallacious and its intolerant conclusions exaggerated. It is true that the perfectionist liberal who encourages the community and its political institutions to foster pluralism and autonomy sees no value in the protection of immoral and demeaning options as such. The community and its institutions are fully justified in trying to discourage, as far as they can, the availability of such options. Both in fostering a common culture and in providing access to its opportunities, one should act with discrimination to encourage the good and the valuable and to discourage the worthless and the bad.

Discouragement should, however, be sensitive to the fact that the means must be appropriate to the ends, and that they must respect the basic principle that people should be allowed to pursue their well-being, i.e. that their autonomy be respected at all times. This principle requires discrimination in the means used by the authorities for discouraging victimless immoralities. Those means should not infringe people's autonomy, which is the foundation of their well-being. This means that governments should not use repressive measures, and in particular that they should neither criminalize nor employ coercion to discourage victimless immoralities. For such measures interfere with people's general standing as autonomous human beings. They do not merely make it more difficult for people to engage in a specific worthless activity. Criminalization and other repressive measures deny people, to a substantial degree, control over the course of their lives. By attaching the stigma of criminal conviction, by disrupting people's lives through the processes of trial and conviction, and often through imprisonment, they affect not merely the ability to engage in one particular activity but the general control one has over the course of one's life. Such an infringement of personal autonomy may be justified by the need to protect the autonomy of others. But when it is not justified by this need, when the matter concerns victimless offences, then respect for the autonomy of the individual dictates a policy of toleration which goes well beyond the recognition of the plurality of values and extends to tolerating victimless immoralities.

To conclude, the moral roots of our concern for individual freedom lie in an appreciation of the importance of personal autonomy to the prosperity of the individual. This leads both to an active encouragement of the freedom of people to guide their own lives by successive choices from an adequate range of valuable options and to a passive toleration of misguided choices, at least to the extent that, subject to the need to protect the interests of others, no measures will be adopted by the state which infringe the autonomy of individuals, however misguided their choices may be. For their autonomy is a condition of their prosperity in modern societies.[30]

Finally, because the value of political freedom lies in providing the conditions for personal autonomy and because personal autonomy can be realized only in a society which maintains an appropriate public culture, the freedom of one individual depends on the freedom of others. Of course, there are many conflicts of interests among individuals, and disputes as to whether the freedom of one should be purchased at a cost to others. But beyond this stands vindicated the traditional precept that no person can be free except in a society of free people. Concern for individual freedom leads directly to concern for the condition of society as a whole.

[30] My argument is confined to modern industrial societies. Moreover, as it stands, it does not apply to enclaves of traditional premodern communities within our societies.

6

National Self-Determination

In the controversy-ridden fields of international law and international relations, the widespread recognition of the existence of national rights to self-determination provides a welcome point of agreement. Needless to say, the core consensus is but the eye of a raging storm concerning the precise definition of the right, its content, its bearers, and the proper means for its implementation. This essay will not address such questions, though indirectly it may help with their investigation. Its concern is with the moral justification of the case for national self-determination. Its purpose is critical and evaluative; its subject lies within the morality of international relations rather than within international law and international relations proper.

It is assumed throughout that states and international law should recognize such a right only if there is a sound moral case for it. This does not mean that international law should mirror morality. Its concern is with setting standards that enjoy the sort of clarity required to make them the foundations of international relations between states, and fit for recognition and enforcement through international organs. These concerns give rise to special considerations that should be fully recognized in the subtle process of applying moral principles to the law. The derivation of legal principles from moral premises is never a matter of copying morality into law. Still, the justification of the law rests ultimately on moral considerations, and therefore those considerations should also help shape the contours of legal principles. That is why the conclusions of this essay bear on controversies concerning the proper way in which the law on this subject should develop, even though such issues are not here discussed directly.

Moral inquiry is sometimes understood in a utopian manner, i.e. as an inquiry into the principles that should prevail in an ideal world. It is doubtful whether this is a meaningful enterprise, but it is certainly not the one we are engaged in here. We assume that things are roughly as they are, especially that our world is a world of states and of a variety of ethnic, national, tribal, and other groups.[1] We do not question the justification for this state

First published in *The Journal of Philosophy*, 87/9 (Sept. 1990). I am grateful to Professor Avishai Margalit for generously agreeing to the inclusion of this essay. We are grateful to Lea Brilmayer, Moshe Halbertal, David Heyd, and the editors of the Journal for helpful comments on an earlier draft.

[1] This fact is doubly relevant. It is a natural fact about our world that it is a populated world with no unappropriated lands. It is a social and a moral fact that it is a world of nations, tribes, peoples, etc., i.e. that people's perception of themselves and of others and their judgments of the opportunities and the responsibilities of life are shaped, to an extent, by the existence of

of affairs. Rather, we ask whether, given that this is how things are and for as long as they remain the same, a moral case can be made in support of national self-determination.

I. ISOLATING THE ISSUE

The core content of the claim to be examined is that there is a right to determine whether a certain territory shall become, or remain, a separate state (and possibly also whether it should enjoy autonomy within a larger state). The idea of national self-determination or (as we shall refer to it in order to avoid confusion) the idea of self-government encompasses much more. The value of national self-government is the value of entrusting the general political power over a group and its members to the group. If self-government is valuable, then it is valuable that whatever is a proper matter for political decision should be subject to the political decision of the group in all matters concerning the group and its members. The idea of national self-government, in other words, speaks of groups determining the character of their social and economic environment, their fortunes, the course of their development, and the fortunes of their members by their own actions, i.e. by the action of those groups, inasmuch as these are matters which are properly within the realm of political action.[2] Given the current international state system, in which political power rests, in the main, with sovereign states,[3] the right to determine whether a territory should be an independent state is quite naturally regarded as the main instrument for realizing the ideal of self-determination. Consideration of this right usually dominates all discussions of national self-determination. To examine the justification of the right is the ultimate purpose of this essay. But we shall continuously draw attention to the fact that, as we shall try to show, the

such groups and their membership of them. It may be meaningful to claim that our views regarding national self-determination apply only to a populated world like ours. One may point to different principles that would prevail in a world with vast, unoccupied, fertile lands. Such speculation is utopian, but it may serve to highlight some of the reasons for the principles that apply in our condition. To speculate concerning a reality different from ours in its basic social and moral constitution is pointless in a deeper way. Such social facts are constitutive of morality. Their absence undercuts morality's very foundations. We could say that under such changed conditions people will have normative beliefs and will be guided by some values. But they are not ones for which we can claim any validity.

[2] This qualification is to take account of the fact that, according to doctrines of limited government, certain matters are outside the realm of politics, and no political action regarding them may be undertaken.

[3] Among the exceptions to this rule are the slowly growing importance of supranational, especially regional, associations, such as the European Union, the growth of a doctrine of sovereignty limited by respect for fundamental human rights, and the continuing (usually thinly veiled) claims of some states that they are not bound by the international law regarding the sovereignty of states.

right of self-determination so understood is not ultimate, but is grounded in the wider value of national self-government, which is itself to be only instrumentally justified.

The next section deals with the nature of the groups that might be the subject of such a right. Section III considers what value, if any, is served by the enjoyment of political independence by such groups. Section IV examines the case for conceding that there is a moral right to self-determination. This examination may lead to revising our understanding of the content of the right. It may reveal that moral considerations justify only a narrower right, or that the argument that justifies the right warrants giving it a wider scope. But the core as identified here will provide the working base from which to launch the inquiry.

Before we start, a few words about this way of identifying the problem may be in place. In two ways the chosen focus of our examination is narrower than many discussions of self-determination in international relations. First, we disregard the claims made, typically by third-world countries, in the name of self-determination, against the economic domination of multinational companies, the World Bank, or against powerful regional or world powers. The considerations canvassed here are relevant to such issues, but fall short of directly tackling them. To be complete, a discussion of a right must examine both its grounds and its consequences. This essay is concerned mostly with the grounds for the right of self-determination. It asks the question: Who has the right and under what conditions is it to be exercised? It does not go into the question of the consequences of the right beyond the assumption, already stated, that it is a right that a territory be a self-governing state. A good deal of the current turmoil in international law, and international relations, has to do with the exploration of that last notion. What is entailed by the fact that a state is a sovereign, self-governing, entity? The claims that economic domination violates the right to self-determination belong to that discussion. Our conclusions provide part of the grounds by which such claims are to be settled. But we do not propose to pursue this question here.

Second, claims of self-determination are invariably raised whenever one state invades and occupies another, or a territory belonging to another. Yet it is important to distinguish between the wrongness of military invasion or occupation, and the rights available against it, and the right (whatever it may turn out to be) to self-determination. In a word, the latter is a source of title, whereas the former is a possessory right based largely on public-order considerations. Any legal system, international law not excluded, recognizes certain ways as legitimate ways of solving disputes, and outlaws others. Subject to the exceptions of legitimate self-defence and self-help, the use of violence is forbidden. Violation of that prohibition gives rise to a right to have the status quo ante restored, before the deeper sources of the dispute between the parties are examined; that is, regardless of the soundness of one's title to a territory, one may not use force to occupy it. This is why the right to recover a territory lost by force is a possessory right. It does not depend on the ultimate soundness of one's title, and that is why it was said to be based on public-order considerations. A large part of its justification is in the need to establish that the proper means of dispute resolution should be the only ones resorted to.

Not surprisingly, invocation of this possessory right is, however, accompanied by a claim of good title (the merits of which are not immediately relevant). The underlying title is often the right to self-determination. Hence the temptation to confuse the two. But notice that, apart from the different justificatory foundations, the two are far from identical in consequence. They merely overlap. The claims of a people who have been for many years ruled by another cannot be based on the possessory right that applies only against a recent occupier. On the other hand, the occupation of portions of Antarctica, or of some uninhabited island, do violate the possessory right, but not the right of self-determination. The latter is that of the inhabitants, and does not apply when there are no inhabitants.[4]

II. GROUPS

Assuming that self-determination is enjoyed by groups, what groups qualify? Given that the right is normally attributed to peoples or nations, it is tempting to give that as the answer and concentrate on characterizing 'peoples' or 'nations'. The drawbacks of this approach are two: it assumes too much, and it poses problems that may not require a solution.

It is far from clear that peoples or nations, rather than tribes, ethnic groups, linguistic, religious, or geographical groups, are the relevant reference group. What is it that makes peoples particularly suited to self-determination? The right concerns determination whether a certain territory shall be self-governing or not. It appears to affect most directly the residents of a territory, and their neighbours. If anyone, then residents of geographical regions seem intuitively to be the proper bearers of the right. Saying this does not get us very far. It does not help in identifying the residents of which regions should qualify. To be sure, this is the crucial question. But even posing it in this way shows that the answer, 'the largest regions inhabited by one people or nation', is far from being the obvious answer.

We have some understanding of the benefits self-government might bring. We need to rely on this in looking for the characteristics that make groups

---

[4] The substantive right protected indirectly by the possessory right in cases of this kind is one of the other rights providing a title in a territory. The right to self-determination is only one of the possible sources of title.

suitable recipients of those benefits. We want, in other words, to identify groups by those characteristics which are relevant to the justification of the right. If it turns out that those do not apply to peoples or nations, we shall have shown that the right to self-determination is misconceived and, as recognized in international law, unjustified. Alternatively, the groups identified may encompass peoples (or some peoples) as well as other groups. This will provide a powerful case for redrawing the boundaries of the right. Either way, we shall be saved much argument concerning the characterization of nations which, interesting as it is in itself, is irrelevant to our purpose.

Having said that, it may be useful to take nations and peoples as the obvious candidates for the right. We need not worry about their defining characteristics. But we may gain insight by comparing them with groups, e.g. the fiction-reading public, or Tottenham Football Club supporters, which obviously do not enjoy such a right. Reflection on such examples suggests six characteristics that in combination are relevant to a case for self-determination.

1. The group has a common character and a common culture that encompass many, varied, and important aspects of life, a culture that defines or marks a variety of forms or styles of life, types of activity, occupation, pursuit, and relationship. With national groups we expect to find national cuisines, distinctive architectural styles, a common language, distinctive literary and artistic traditions, national music, customs, dress, ceremonies and holidays, etc. None of these is necessary. They are but typical examples of the features that characterize peoples and other groups that are serious candidates for the right to self-determination. They have pervasive cultures, and their identity is determined at least in part by their culture. They possess cultural traditions that penetrate beyond a single or a few areas of human life, and display themselves in a whole range of areas, including many which are of great importance for the well-being of individuals.

2. The correlative of the first feature is that people growing up among members of the group will acquire the group culture, will be marked by its character. Their tastes and their options will be affected by that culture to a significant degree. The types of career open to one, the leisure activities one has learned to appreciate and is therefore able to choose from, the customs and habits that define and colour relations with strangers and with friends, patterns of expectations and attitudes between spouses and among other members of the family, features of lifestyles with which one is capable of empathizing and for which one may therefore develop a taste—all these will be marked by the group culture.

They need not be indelibly marked. People may migrate to other environments, shed their previous culture, and acquire a new one. It is a painful and slow process, success in which is rarely complete. But it is possible, just as it is possible that socialization will fail and one will fail to be marked by the culture of one's environment, except negatively, to reject it. The point made is merely the modest one that, given the pervasive nature of the culture of the groups we are seeking to identify, their influence on individuals who grow up in their midst is profound and far-reaching. The point needs to be made in order to connect concern with the prosperity of the group with concern for the well-being of individuals. This tie between the individual and the collective is at the heart of the case for self-determination.

As one would expect, the tie does not necessarily extend to all members of the group, and failure of socialization is not the only reason. The group culture affects those who grow up among its members, be they members or not. But to say this is no more than to point to various anomalies and dilemmas that may arise. Most people live in groups of these kinds, so that those who belong to none are denied full access to the opportunities that are shaped in part by the group's culture. They are made to feel estranged, and their chances to have a rewarding life are seriously damaged. The same is true of people who grow up among members of a group so that they absorb its culture, but are then denied access to it because they are denied full membership of the group.

Nothing in the above presupposes that groups of the kind we are exploring are geographically concentrated, let along that their members are the only inhabitants of any region. Rather, by drawing on the transmission of the group culture through the socialization of the young, these comments emphasize the historical nature of the groups with which we are concerned. Given that they are identified by a common culture, at least in part, they also share a history, for it is through a shared history that cultures develop and are transmitted.

3. Membership in the group is, in part, a matter of mutual recognition. Typically, one belongs to such groups if, among other conditions, one is recognized by other members of the group as belonging to it. The other conditions (which may be the accident of birth or the sharing of the group culture, etc.) are normally the grounds cited as reasons for such recognition. But those who meet those other conditions and are yet rejected by the group are at best marginal or problematic members of it. The groups concerned are not formal, institutionalized groups, with formal procedures of admission. Membership in them is a matter of informal acknowledgment of belonging by others generally, and by other members specifically. The fiction-reading public fails our previous tests. It is not identified by its sharing a wide-ranging pervasive culture. It also fails the third test. To belong to the fiction-reading public all we have to do is to read fiction; it does not matter whether others recognize us as fiction-reading.[5]

---

[5] The fiction-reading public can take the character of a literary élite with mutual recognition as part of its identity. The importance of 'acceptability' in such groups has often been noted and analysed.

4. The third feature prepares the way for, and usually goes hand in hand with, the importance of membership for one's self-identification. Consider the fiction-reading public again. It is a historically significant group. Historians may study the evolution of the fiction-reading public, how it spread from women to men, from one class to others, from reading aloud in small groups to silent reading, from reliance on libraries to book buying, etc.; how it is regarded as important to one's qualification as a cultured person in one country, but not in another; how it furnishes a common topic of conversation in some classes but not in others; how belonging to the group is a mark of political awareness in some countries, while being a sign of escapist retreat from social concerns in another.

Such studies will show, however, that it is only in some societies that the existence of these features of the fiction-reading public is widely known. For the most part, one can belong to the group without being aware that one is a typical reader, that one's profile is that of most readers. Sometimes this is a result of a mistaken group image's being current in that society. Our concern is rather with those cases where the society lacks any very distinct image of that group. This indicates that, in such societies, membership of that group does not have a highly visible social profile. It is not one of the facts by which people pigeonhole each other. One need not be aware who, among people one knows, friends, acquaintances, shopkeepers one patronizes, one's doctor, etc., shares the habit. In such societies, membership of the fiction-reading public is not highly visible; it is not one of the things one will normally know about people one has contact with, one of the things that identify 'who they are'. But it happens in some countries that membership of the reading public becomes a highly visible mark of belonging to a social group, to the intelligentsia, etc. In such countries, talk of the recently published novel becomes a means of mutual recognition.

One of the most significant facts differentiating various football cultures is whether they are cultures of self-recognition: whether identification as a fan or supporter of this club or that is one of the features that are among the main markers of people in the society. The same is true of occupational groups. In some countries membership is highly visible, and is among the primary means of pigeonholing people, of establishing 'who they are'; in others it is not.

Our concern is with groups membership of which has a high social profile, that is, groups membership of which is one of the primary facts by which people are identified, and which form expectations as to what they are like, groups membership of which is one of the primary clues for people generally in interpreting the conduct of others. Since our perceptions of ourselves are in large measure determined by how we expect others to perceive us, it follows that membership of such groups is an important identifying feature for each about himself. These are groups members of which are aware of their membership and typically regard it as an important clue in understanding who they are, in interpreting their actions and reactions, in understanding their tastes and their manner.

5. Membership is a matter of belonging, not of achievement. One does not have to prove oneself, or to excel in anything, in order to belong and to be accepted as a full member. To the extent that membership normally involves recognition by others as a member, that recognition is not conditional on meeting qualifications that indicate any accomplishment. To be a good Irishman, it is true, is an achievement. But to be an Irishman is not. Qualification for membership is usually determined by non-voluntary criteria. One cannot choose to belong. One belongs because of who one is. One can come to belong to such groups, but only by changing, e.g. by adopting their culture, changing one's tastes and habits accordingly—a very slow process indeed. The fact that these are groups membership of which is a matter of belonging, and not of accomplishment, makes them suitable for their role as primary foci of identification. Identification is more secure, less liable to be threatened, if it does not depend on accomplishment. Although accomplishments play their role in people's sense of their own identity, it would seem that at the most fundamental level our sense of our own identity depends on criteria of belonging rather than on those of accomplishment. Secure identification at that level is particularly important to one's well-being.

6. The groups concerned are not small, face-to-face groups, members of which are generally known to all other members. They are anonymous groups, where mutual recognition is secured by the possession of general characteristics. The exclusion of small groups from consideration is not merely *ad hoc*. Small groups that are based on personal familiarity of all with all are markedly different in the character of their relationships and interactions from anonymous groups. For example, given the importance of mutual recognition to members of these groups, they tend to develop conventional means of identification, such as the use of symbolic objects, participation in group ceremonies, special group manners, or special vocabulary, which help quickly to identify who is 'one of us' and who is not.

The various features we listed do not entail each other but they tend to go together. It is not surprising that groups with pervasive cultures will be important in determining the main options and opportunities of their members, or that they will become focal points of identification, etc. The way things are in our world, just about everyone belongs to such a group, and not necessarily to one only. Membership is not exclusive, and many people belong to several groups that answer to our description. Some of them are rather like national groups, e.g. tribes or ethnic groups. Others are very different. Some religious groups meet our conditions, as do social classes and some racial groups. Not all religions or racial groups did develop rich and pervasive cultures. But some did, and those qualify.

III. THE VALUE OF SELF-GOVERNMENT

The Value of Encompassing Groups

The description of the relevant groups in the preceding section may well disappoint the reader. Some will be disappointed by the imprecise nature of the criteria provided. This would be unjustified. The criteria are not meant to provide operational legal definitions. As such, they clearly would not do. Their purpose is to pick on the features of groups which may explain the value of self-determination. As already mentioned, the key to the explanation is in the importance of these groups to the well-being of their members. This thought guided the selection of the features. They are meant to assist in identifying that link. It is not really surprising that they are all vague matters of degree, admitting of many variants and many nuances. One is tempted to say 'that's life'. It does not come in neatly parcelled parts. While striving to identify the features that matter, we have to recognize that they come in many shapes, in many shades, and in many degrees, rife with impurities in their mixing.

A more justified source of disappointment is the suspicion that we have cast the net too wide. Social classes clearly do not have a right to self-determination. If they meet the above conditions, then those conditions are at best incomplete. Here we can only crave the reader's patience. We tried to identify the features of groups which help explain the value of self-determination. These may apply not only beyond the sphere in which the right is commonly recognized. They may apply to groups that really should not possess it, for other reasons yet to be explored.

The defining properties of the groups we identified are of two kinds. On the one hand, they pick out groups with pervasive cultures; on the other, they focus on groups membership of which is important to one's self-identity. This combination makes such groups suitable candidates for self-rule. Let us call groups manifesting the six features *encompassing groups*. Individuals find in them a culture which shapes to a large degree their tastes and opportunities, and which provides an anchor for their self-identification and the safety of effortless, secure belonging.

Individual well-being depends on the successful pursuit of worthwhile goals and relationships. Goals and relationships are culturally determined. Being social animals means not merely that the means for the satisfaction of people's goals are more readily available within society. More crucially, it means that those goals themselves are (when one reaches beyond what is strictly necessary for biological survival) the creatures of society, the products of culture. Family relations, all other social relations between people, careers, leisure activities, the arts, sciences, and other obvious products of 'high culture' are the fruits of society. They all depend for their existence on the sharing of patterns of expectations, on traditions preserving implicit knowledge of how to do what, of tacit conventions regarding what is part of this or that enterprise and what is not, what is appropriate and what is not, what is valuable and what is not. Familiarity with a culture determines the boundaries of the imaginable. Sharing in a culture, being part of it, determines the limits of the feasible.

It may be no more than a brute fact that our world is organized in a large measure around groups with pervasive cultures. But it is a fact with far-reaching consequences. It means, in the first place, that membership of such groups is of great importance to individual well-being, for it greatly affects one's opportunities, one's ability to engage in the relationships and pursuits marked by the culture. Secondly, it means that the prosperity of the culture is important to the well-being of its members. If the culture is decaying, or if it is persecuted or discriminated against, the options and opportunities open to its members will shrink, become less attractive, and their pursuit less likely to be successful.

It may be no more than a brute fact that people's sense of their own identity is bound up with their sense of belonging to encompassing groups, and that their self-respect is affected by the esteem in which these groups are held. But these facts, too, have important consequences. They mean that individual dignity and self-respect require that the groups membership of which contributes to one's sense of identity be generally respected and not be made a subject of ridicule, hatred, discrimination, or persecution.

All this is mere common sense, and is meant to be hedged and qualified in the way our common understanding of these matters is. Of course, strangers can participate in activities marked by a culture. They are handicapped, but not always very seriously. Of course, there are other determinants of one's opportunities, and of one's sense of self-respect. Membership of an encompassing group is but one factor. Finally, one should mention that groups and their culture may be pernicious, based on exploitation of people, be they their members or not, or on the denigration and persecution of other groups. If so, then the case for their protection and flourishing is weakened, and may disappear altogether.

Having regard for this reservation, the case for holding the prosperity of encompassing groups as vital for the prosperity of their members is a powerful one. Group interests cannot be reduced to individual interests. It makes sense to talk of a group's prospering or declining, of actions and policies as serving the group's interest or of harming it, without having to cash this in terms of individual interests. The group may flourish if its culture prospers, but this need not mean that the lot of its members or of anyone else has improved. It is in the interest of the group to be held in high regard by others, but it does not follow that, if an American moon landing increases the world's admiration for the United States, Americans necessarily benefit from this. Group interests are conceptually connected to the interests of their members but such connections are nonreductive and generally indirect. For example, it is possible that what enhances the interest of the group provides opportunities for improvement for its members, or that it increases the chance that they will benefit.

This relative independence of group interest is compatible with the view that informs this essay: that the moral importance of the group's interest depends on its value to individuals. A large decline in the fortunes of the group may, for example, be of little consequence to its members. There is no a priori way of correlating group interest with that of its members or of other individuals. It depends on the circumstances of different groups at different times. One clear consequence of the fact that the moral significance of a group's interest is in its service to individuals is the fact that it will depend, in part, on the size of the group. The fortunes of a larger group may be material to the well-being of a larger number of people. Other things being equal, numbers matter.

The Instrumental Case

Does the interest of members in the prosperity of the group establish a right to self-determination? Certainly not, at least not yet, not without further argument. For one thing, we have yet to see any connection between the prosperity of encompassing groups and their political independence. The easiest connection to establish under certain conditions is an instrumental one. Sometimes the prosperity of the group and its self-respect are aided by, sometimes they may be impossible to secure without, the group's enjoying political sovereignty over its own affairs. Sovereignty enables the group to conduct its own affairs in a way conducive to its prosperity.[6] There is no need to elaborate the point. It depends on historical conditions. Hence the prominence of a history of persecution in most debates concerning self-determination. But a history of persecution is neither a necessary nor a sufficient condition for the instrumental case for self-government. It is not a necessary condition, because persecution is not the only reason why the groups may suffer without independence. Suffering can be the result of neglect or ignorance of or indifference to the prosperity of a minority group by the majority. Such attitudes may be so well entrenched that there is no realistic prospect of changing them.

Persecution is not a sufficient condition, for there may be other ways to fight and overcome persecution and because, whatever the advantages of independence, it may, in the circumstances, lead to economic decline, cultural

---

[6] This is not meant to suggest that there are not often drawbacks to self-rule. They will be considered below.

decay, or social disorder, which only make the members of a group worse off. Besides, as mentioned above, pernicious groups may not deserve protection, especially if it will help them to pursue repressive practices with impunity. Finally, there are the interests of non-members to be considered. In short, the instrumental argument (as well as others) for self-government is sensitive to counter-arguments pointing to its drawbacks, its cost in terms of human well-being, possible violations of human rights, etc.

We shall return to these issues below. First, let us consider the claim that the instrumental argument trivializes the case for self-government by overlooking its intrinsic value. Of the various arguments for the intrinsic value of self-government which have been and can be advanced, we examine one which seems the most promising.

An Argument for the Intrinsic Value of Self-Government

The argument is based on an extension of individual autonomy or of self-expression (if that is regarded as independently valuable). The argument unravels in stages: (1) People's membership of encompassing groups is an important aspect of their personality, and their well-being depends on giving it full expression. (2) Expression of membership essentially includes manifestation of membership in the open, public life of the community. (3) This requires expressing one's membership in political activities within the community. The political is an essential arena of community life, and consequently of individual well-being. (4) Therefore, self-government is inherently valuable; it is required to provide the group with a political dimension.

The first premiss is unexceptionable. So is the second, though an ambiguity might be detected in the way it is often understood. Two elements need separating. First, given the importance of membership to one's well-being, it is vital that the dignity of the group be preserved. This depends, in part, on public manifestations of respect for the group and its culture, and on the absence of ridicule of the group, etc., from the public life of the society of which one is a member. One should not have to identify with or feel loyalty to a group that denigrates an encompassing group to which one belongs. Indeed, one should not have to live in an environment in which such attitudes are part of the common culture. Second, an aspect of well-being is an ability to express publicly one's identification with the group and to participate openly in its public culture. An encompassing group is centred on mutual recognition and is inevitably a group with a public culture. One cannot enjoy the benefits of membership without participation in its public culture, without public participation in its culture.

Both elements are of great importance. Both indicate the vital role played by public manifestations of group culture and group membership among the conditions of individual well-being. To the extent that a person's well-being is bound up with his identity as a member of an encompassing group, it has an important public dimension. But that dimension is not necessarily political in the conventional, narrow sense of the term. Even where it is, its political expression does not require a political organization whose boundaries coincide with those of the group. One may be politically active in a multi-national, multicultural polity.

Here supporters of the argument for the intrinsic value of self-government may protest. The expression of membership in the political life of the community, they will say, involves more than its public expression. It involves the possibility of members of an encompassing group participating in the political life of their state, and fighting in the name of group interests in the political arena. Such actions, they will insist, may be not only instrumentally valuable to the group but intrinsically important to its politically active members. They are valuable avenues of self-fulfilment. These points, too, have to be readily admitted. There is no reason to think that everyone must take part in politics if his or her development is not to be stunted and personality or life is not to be deficient. In normal times, politics is but an option that people may choose to take or to leave alone. Although its availability is important, for its absence deprives people of valuable opportunities, its use is strictly optional. Even if it is possible to argue that one's personal well-being requires some involvement with larger groups, and the avoidance of exclusive preoccupation with one's own affairs and those of one's close relations or friends, that involvement can take non-political forms, such as activity in a social club or interest in the fortunes of the arts in one's region.

Politics is no more than an option, though this is true in normal times only. In times of political crises that have moral dimensions, it may well be the duty of everyone to stand up and be counted. In Weimar, Germans had a moral duty to become politically involved to oppose Nazism. There are many other situations where an apolitical attitude is not morally acceptable. But all of them are marked by moral crises. In the absence of crisis there is nothing wrong in being non-political.

Having said this, we must repeat that the option of politics must remain open, and with it the option of fighting politically for causes to do with the interests of one's encompassing groups. But there is nothing here to suggest that this should be done in a political framework exclusive to one's group or dominated by it. There is nothing wrong with multinational states, in which members of the different communities compete in the political arena for public resources for their communities. Admittedly, prejudice, national fanaticism, etc., sometimes make such peaceful and equitable sharing of the political arena impossible. They may lead to friction and persecution. This may constitute a good argument for the value of self-government, but it is an instrumental argument of the kind canvassed above. There is nothing in the need for a public or even a political expression of one's membership of an encompassing group which points to an intrinsic value of self-government.

The Subjective Element

In an indirect way, the attempt to argue for the intrinsic value of self-government does point to the danger of misinterpreting the instrumental approach to the question. First, the argument does not deny the intrinsic value of the existence of the political option as a venue for activity and self-expression to all (adult) members of society. We are not advocating a purely instrumentalist view of politics generally. The intrinsic value to individuals of the political option does not require expression in polities whose boundaries coincide with those of encompassing groups. That is the only point argued for above.

Second, the pragmatic, instrumentalist character of the approach advocated here should not be identified with an aggregating impersonal consequentialism. Some people tend to associate any instrumentalist approach with images of a bureaucracy trading off the interest of one person against that of another on the basis of some cost–benefit analysis designed to maximize overall satisfaction; a bureaucracy, moreover, in charge of determining for people what is really good for them, regardless of their own views of the matter. Nothing of the kind should be countenanced. Of course, conflicts among people's interests do arise, and call for rational resolution that is likely to involve sacrificing some interests of some people for the sake of others. Such conflicts, however, admit of a large degree of indeterminacy, and many alternative resolutions may be plausible or rational. In such contexts, talking of maximization, with its connotations of comparability of all options, is entirely out of place.

Furthermore, nothing in the instrumentalist and pragmatic nature of our approach should be allowed to disguise its sensitivity to subjective elements, its responsiveness to the perceptions and sensibilities of the people concerned. To a considerable extent, what matters is how well people feel in their environment: Do they feel at home in it or are they alienated from it? Do they feel respected or humiliated? This leads to a delicate balance between 'objective' factors and subjective perceptions. On the one hand, when prospects for the future are concerned, subjective perceptions of danger and likely persecution, etc., are not necessarily to be trusted. These are objective issues on which the opinion of independent spectators may be more reliable than that of those directly involved. On the other hand, the factual issue facing the independent spectators is how people will respond to their conditions, what will be their perceptions, their attitudes to their environment, to their neighbours, etc. Even a group that is not persecuted may suffer many of the ills of real persecution if it feels persecuted. That its perceptions are mistaken or exaggerated is important in pointing to the possibility of a different cure: removing the mistaken perception. But that is not always possible, and up to a point in matters of respect, identification, and dignity, subjective responses, justified or not, are the ultimate reality so far as the well-being of those who have them is concerned.

IV. A RIGHT TO SELF-DETERMINATION

It may seem that the case for self-government establishes a right to self-determination. That is, it establishes the reasons for the right sort of group, an encompassing group, to determine that a territory shall be self-governing. But things are not that simple. The case for self-government shows that sometimes, under certain conditions, it is best that the political unit be roughly an encompassing group. A group's right to self-determination is its right to determine that a territory be self-governing, regardless of whether the case for self-government, based on its benefits, is established or not. In other words, the right to self-determination answers the question 'who is to decide?', not 'what is the best decision?'. In exercising the right, the group should act responsibly in light of all the considerations we mentioned so far. It should, in particular, consider not only the interests of its members but those of others who may be affected by its decision. But if it has the right to decide, its decision is binding even if it is wrong, even if the case for self-government is not made.[7]

The problem in conceding the existence of such a right is, of course, not the possibility that a group that would best be self-governing does not wish to be so. Given the strong subjectivist element in the instrumentalist argument, such reluctance to assume independence would suggest that the case for its being self-governing is much weakened. The problem is that the case for self-government is hedged by considerations of the interest of people other than members of the groups, and by the other interests of members of the groups, i.e. other than their interests as members of the groups. These include their fundamental individual interests which should be respected, e.g. by a group whose culture oppresses women or racial minorities. These

---

[7] It should be made clear that these observations relate to the right to self-determination as it is commonly understood in the discourse of international relations and international morality. In principle, there could be a different right of self-determination, i.e. a right that, when the case for self-government is established, self-government should be granted, i.e. that all the international agents have a duty to take what action is necessary to grant self-government to the encompassing group regarding which the case for self-government has been established. That is, there could in principle have been a substantive right to have self-government when it is right that one should have it, rather than a 'who is to decide' right, that an encompassing group should be entitled to decide whether it should be self-governing. Below we touch briefly on the reasons that explain why the right of self-determination as we know it today is not of this kind.

considerations raise the question whether encompassing groups are the most suitable bodies to decide about the case for self-government. Can they be entrusted with the decision in a matter in which their group interests are in conflict with other interests of members of the group as well as with the interests of other people? At the very least this suggests that the right must be qualified and hedged to protect other interests.

More fundamental still is the question of how the right of self-determination fits within our general conception of democratic decision making. We are used to a two-level structure of argument concerning social issues such as just taxation or the provision of public education. First, we explore the principles that should govern the matter at issue. Second, we devise a form of democratic procedure for determining what shall be done. The first level answers the question 'what should be done?'. The second responds to the question 'who should decide?'.

On a simple majoritarian view, the issue of self-government seems to defy a democratic decision procedure. The question is 'what is the relevant democratic unit?' and that question cannot be democratically decided, at least not entirely so. In fact, of course, we are not simple majoritarians. We adopt a whole range of democratic procedures such as constitution-making privileged majorities, ordinary legislative processes, plebiscites, administrative processes, and decisions by special agencies under conditions of public accountability and indirect democratic control. We match various democratic processes with various social and political problems. This means that there is no universal democratic formula serving as the universal answer to 'who decides?' questions. Rather, we operate a mixed principled-democratic system in which principles, whose credentials do not derive entirely from their democratic backing, determine what form of a democratic procedure is suited for what problem. Within this mixed principled-democratic framework, the right to self-determination fits as just another qualified democratic process suited to its object.

What are the principles involved? It is tempting to see here a principle giving the part veto over the issue of membership in a larger whole. To form a new political unit, or to remain part of an existing one, all component parts should agree. To break up a political unit, or to foil the creation of a new one, all that is required is the will of the group that wants to secede or to stay out. This principle derives its appeal from its voluntaristic aura. It seems to regard the justification of all political units as based on consent. But this is an undesirable illusion. It is undesirable since, as was explained above regarding encompassing groups, the more important human groupings need to be based on shared history, and on criteria of non-voluntaristic (or at least not wholly contractarian) membership, to have the value that they have. The principle presents no more than an illusion of a contractarian principle, since it refers to groups, not to individuals. But the whole contractarian ethos derives its appeal from the claim that each individual's consent is a condition of the legitimacy of political units. Beyond all that, the principle simply begs the question that it is meant to answer, namely, what are the parts? Which groupings have the veto and which do not? Can the group of all the people whose surnames begin with a '*g*' and end with an '*e*' count for these purposes? Do they have the veto on membership in a larger political unit?

The right to self-determination derives from the value of membership in encompassing groups. It is a group right, deriving from the value of a collective good, and as such opposed in spirit to contractarian-individualistic[8] approaches to politics or to individual well-being. It rests on an appreciation of the great importance that membership in and identification with encompassing groups has in the life of individuals, and the importance of the prosperity and self-respect of such groups to the well-being of their members. That importance makes it reasonable to let the encompassing group that forms a substantial majority in a territory have the right to determine whether that territory shall form an independent state in order to protect the culture and self-respect of the group, provided that the new state is likely to respect the fundamental interests of its inhabitants, and provided that measures are adopted to prevent its creation from gravely damaging the just interests of other countries. This statement of the argument for the right requires elaboration.

1. The argument is an instrumental one. It says, essentially, that members of a group are best placed to judge whether their group's prosperity will be jeopardized if it does not enjoy political independence. It is in keeping with the view that, even though participation in politics may have intrinsic value to individuals, the shape and boundaries of political units are to be determined by their service to individual well-being, i.e. by their instrumental

---

[8] The reference is to moral individualism, or value individualism, not to methodological individualism. It is impossible here to deal with the matter adequately. Let us simply indicate our position briefly. There is no accepted characterization of the term. In *The Morality of Freedom*, 198, Raz identified moral individualism with the view that only individual goods, and no collective goods, have intrinsic values. According to individualism so understood, membership of encompassing groups, and the prosperity of such groups, cannot be of intrinsic value. But we believe that it is intrinsically valuable. Hence, on this definition our approach is not individualistic. In 'Three Grades of Social Involvement' (*Philosophy and Public Affairs*, 18 (1989), 133), George Sher characterizes moral individualism as the belief that moral justification proceeds through premises relating to individuals and their preferences. His characterization is too vague to be conclusively disputed (e.g. all holistic justifications will include premises relating to preferences as well as to everything else—does that make them individualistic?). But if Sher has in mind the standard type of (actual or hypothetical) contractarian justifications, then our approach is not individualistic. Because actual individual preferences heavily depend on social practices, there is no reason to give them justificatory primacy. The content of hypothetical preferences is either too indefinite to yield any results or is made definite by assuming a certain social context to give them meaning. Either way it cannot be endowed with justificatory primacy, though of course people's capacity to respond to various conditions, and to form various goals and attachments, is central to any moral justification.

value. In our world, encompassing groups that do not enjoy self-government are not infrequently persecuted, despised, or neglected. Given the
importance of their prosperity and self-respect to the well-being of their
members, it seems reasonable to entrust their members with the right to
determine whether the groups should be self-governing. They may sacrifice
their economic or other interests for the sake of group self-respect and
prosperity. But such a sacrifice is, given the circumstances of this world,
often not unreasonable.

One may ask why such matters should not be entrusted to international
adjudication by an international court, or some other international agency.
Instead of groups' having a right to self-determination which makes them
judges in their own cause, the case for a group's becoming self-governing
should be entrusted to the judgment of an impartial tribunal. This would
have been a far superior solution to the question 'who is to decide?'. Unfortunately, there simply does not exist any international machinery of enforcement that can be relied upon in preference to a right of self-determination
as the right of self-help, nor is there any prospect of one coming into
existence in the near future. In the present structure of international relations, the most promising arrangement is one that recognizes group rights
to self-determination and entrusts international bodies with the duty to help
bring about its realization, and to see to it that the limits and preconditions
of the right are observed (these are enumerated in the points 2–5 below).

2. The right belongs to the group. But how should it be exercised? Not
necessarily by a simple majority vote. Given the long-term and irreversible
nature of the decision (remember that, while independence is up to the
group, merger or union is not), the wish for a state must be shared by an
overwhelming majority, reflecting deep-seated beliefs and feelings of an
enduring nature, and not mere temporary popularity. The precise institutional requirements for the exercise of the right are issues that transcend the
topic of this essay. They are liable to vary with the circumstances of different
national and ethnic groups. Whatever they are, they should reflect the above
principle.

3. The right is over a territory. This simply reflects the territorial organization
of our political world. The requirement that the group be a substantial
majority of the territory stems from further considerations aimed at balancing the interest in self-government against the interests of nonmembers.
First, it is designed to ensure that granting self-government to a territory
does not generate a problem as great as it is meant to solve, by ensuring
that the independence will not generate a large-scale, new minority problem.
That risk cannot be altogether avoided. As was remarked before, numbers
count in the end.

A further factual assumption underlying this condition is that people are,
even today, most directly affected by the goings-on in their region. It is true

that one's economic conditions are affected by economic activities in far-away places. This, however, is more and more true of the international system generally. The ideal of economic autarchy died a natural death. (Correspondingly, the condition of economic viability which used to figure in theories of the states in international relations has little role in the modern world.) What can be secured and protected, and what vitally matters to the quality of life, is its texture as determined by the local culture and custom, the nature of the physical environment, etc. Hence the right is given only to a group that is the majority in a territory. The case for self-government applies to groups that are not in the majority anywhere, but they do not have the right to self-determination anywhere. Their members, like other people, may have a right to immigration on an individual basis to a territory of their choice. But their case is governed by general principles of freedom of movement and the sovereign rights of existing states. This means that their communal interests remain an important consideration to be borne in mind by the decision-makers, but they have no right: the decision is not up to them.

Do historical ties make a difference? Not to the right if voluntarily abandoned. Suppose that the group was unjustly removed from the country. In that case, the general principle of restitution applies, and the group has a right to self-determination and control over the territory it was expelled from, subject to the general principle of prescription. Prescription protects the interests of the current inhabitants. It is based on several deep-seated concerns. It is meant to prevent the revival of abandoned claims, and to protect those who are not personally to blame from having their life unsettled by claims of ancient wrongs, on the ground that their case now is as good as that of the wronged people or their descendants. Prescription, therefore, may lose the expelled group the right even though its members continue to suffer the effects of the past wrong. Their interest is a consideration to be borne in mind in decisions concerning immigration policies, and the like, but because of prescription they lost the right to self-determination. The outcome is not up to them to decide.

4. The right is conditional on its being exercised for the right reasons, i.e. to secure conditions necessary for the prosperity and self-respect of the group. This is a major protection against abuse. Katanga cannot claim a right to self-determination as a way of securing its exclusive control over uranium mines within its territory. This condition does not negate the nature of a right. The group is still entrusted with the right to decide, and its decision is binding even if wrong, even if the case for self-government does not obtain, provided the reasons that motivate the group's decision are of the right kind.

5. Finally, there are the two broad safeguards on which the exercise of the right is conditional. First, that the group is likely to respect the basic

rights of its inhabitants, so that its establishment will do good rather than add to the ills of this world. Secondly, since the establishment of the new state may fundamentally endanger the interests of inhabitants of other countries, its exercise is conditional on measures being taken to prevent or minimize the occurrence of substantial damage of this kind. Such measures, which will vary greatly from case to case, include free-trade agreements, port facilities, granting of air routes, and demilitarization of certain regions.

Two kinds of interest do not call for special protection. One is the interest of a people to regard themselves as part of a larger rather than a smaller grouping or country. The English may have an interest in being part of Great Britain, rather than mere Englanders. But that interest can be justly satisfied only with the willing co-operation of, for example, the Scots. If the other conditions for Scottish independence are met, this interest of the English should not stand in its way. Secondly, unjust economic gains, the product of colonial or other forms of exploitation of one group by another, may be denied to the exploiting group without hesitation or compensation (barring arrangements for a transitory period). But where secession and independence will gravely affect other and legitimate interests of other countries, such interests should be protected by creating free-trade zones, demilitarized areas, etc.

6. A right in one person is sufficient ground to hold some other person(s) to be under a duty.[9] What duties arise out of the right to self-determination? How is this matter to be settled? As the previous discussion makes clear, the right of self-determination is instrumentally justified, as the method of implementing the case for self-government, which itself is based on the fact that in many circumstances self-government is necessary for the prosperity and dignity of encompassing groups. Hence, in fixing the limits of the right, one has to bear in mind the existing system of international politics, and show that, given other elements in that system, certain duties can be derived from the right to self-determination, whereas others cannot. The first and most important duty arising out of the right is the duty not to impede the exercise of the right, i.e. not to impede groups in their attempts to decide whether appropriate territories should be independent, so long as they do so within the limits of the right. This duty affects in practice first and foremost the state that governs the territory concerned and its inhabitants.

There may be other duties following from the right of self-determination. In particular, there may be a duty on the state governing the territory to provide aid in exercising the right, and a duty on other states to aid the relevant group in realizing its right, and thus to oppose the state governing the territory if it impedes its implementation. But the extent of these duties

---

[9] See *The Morality of Freedom*, ch. 7, 'The Nature of Rights'. On the relations of moral and legal rights, see also ch. 11 below. Raz has applied this analysis to the case of constitutional rights in general in ch. 10 of *The Morality of Freedom*.

must be subject to the general principles of international morality, which indicate what methods may and may not be used in pursuit of worthwhile goals and in preventing the violation of rights. As indicated at the outset, the examination of the details of such implications of the right is beyond the scope of this essay.

This brings to an end our consideration of the outlines of the case for a right to self-determination and its limits. It is an argument that proceeds in several stages from fundamental moral concerns to the ways in which they can be best implemented, given the way our world is organized. The argument is meant to present the normal justification for the right. It does not claim that there could not be alternative justifications. But it does claim to be the central case, which alternatives presuppose or of which they are variations.[10]

Two conclusions emerge from this discussion. On the one hand, the right to self-determination is neither absolute nor unconditional. It affects important and diverse interests of many people, from those who will be citizens of the new state, if it comes into being, to others far away from it. Those who may benefit from self-government can not insist on it at all costs. Their interests have to be considered along with those of others. On the other hand, the interests of members of an encompassing group in the self-respect and prosperity of the group are among the most vital human interests. Given their importance, their satisfaction is justified even at a considerable cost to other interests. Furthermore, given the absence of effective enforcement machinery in the international arena, the interest in group prosperity justifies entrusting the decision concerning self-government to the hands of an encompassing group that constitutes the vast majority of the population in the relevant territory, provided other vital interests are protected.

---

[10] On the notion of a 'normal justification', and the reasons why it cannot be analysed as either a necessary or a sufficient condition, see ibid. ch. 3.

7

Free Expression and Personal Identification

I. THE PUZZLE

Freedom of expression is a liberal puzzle.[1] Liberals are all convinced of its vital importance, yet why it deserves this importance is a mystery. The source of the problem is simple. While a person's right to freedom of expression is given high priority, and is protected (or, in political morality, is held to deserve protection) to a far greater degree than a person's interest in having employment, or in not running a risk of an accident when driving along public roads, it is evident that most people value these interests, and many others which do not enjoy special legal protection, much more than they value their right to free expression. Worse still, there can be little doubt that most people are right not to value their right to free expression highly. With few exceptions, people's interest in their right to free expression is rather small.

The right of freedom of expression protects people's freedom to communicate in public. 'Communication' is to be understood broadly to include much more than the communication of propositional information. It includes any act of symbolic expression undertaken with the intention that it be understood to be such an act by the public or part of the public. Thus communication here covers not only all the forms of language-dependent communication but also pictorial and musical communication, and a whole range of symbolic acts such as picketing, displaying banners, wearing uniform. It does not cover acts of expression which are not convention-based symbolic expression, such as blushing, or expressing anger at one's competitor's success by setting fire to his shop.[2] Furthermore, to be protected communication has to be public, i.e. addressed to or made available to the public or any section of the public. It is essentially a right actively to participate in and contribute to the public culture.[3]

First published in the Oxford Journal of Legal Studies, 11/3 (1991). This essay benefited from comments on earlier drafts by John Finnis, John Gardner, Avishai Margalit, Sandra Marshall, Hans Oberdiek, Quentin Skinner, Andrew Williams, and participants in the political-thought seminar conducted by Professors Skinner and Dunn in the spring of 1990, and especially from the detailed comments of Ron Garet and Carl Wellman.

[1] In this essay 'Liberalism' refers to a political culture which dominates in some societies, or subcultures, and not to any particular philosophical doctrine.

[2] Many acts which carry a symbolic meaning also have some other standard consequences, e.g. pickets impede traffic. This may affect 'balancing tests' but does not exclude them from protection.

[3] Freedom of expression includes the passive freedom to listen and the corresponding negative freedoms, i.e. the freedom not to communicate and not to listen.

Given this understanding of the scope of the right the liberal puzzle is apparent. Rights protect interests and it is natural to expect the importance or stringency of the rights to reflect the importance to the right-holder of the interest that they protect.[4] But most people participate in public expression rarely if at all. For most of them, participation is confined to addressing local communities about local matters (for example, concern with the maintenance of street lights in one's neighbourhood expressed in a local paper or a local meeting). While that interest is important to a large number of people, it can be protected by a much weaker right than the one the liberal doctrine of free expression upholds. It is true that we have an interest in the freedom to engage in activities we are unlikely to engage in, but, other things being equal, that interest is proportionate to the likelihood, and for most people it is very small indeed.

I should be careful not to underestimate the interest people may have in the freedom to engage in public speech. It is not part of my case that most people have no interest in the freedom of public expression. All I am arguing is that many other interests most people have are much more valuable to them than their interest in this freedom. Yet it is the freedom to express oneself publicly, rather than the more valuable interests, which enjoys special protection.

The responses to the puzzle are numerous. Most of them fall into five categories. First is the contention that appearances are misleading and that people have a great interest in their own freedom of expression. It lies at the heart of their humanity, is a requirement of personhood or rationality, etc.

Second comes the contention that, while people's interest in their own freedom of expression may be small there is absolutely no reason, or only minuscule ones, for curtailing it. At least there can be no legitimate reason for curtailing it, since its possession and its exercise do no one any harm. Words do not kill. To the counter-argument that they do, the reply can be to redefine the right so that, where words infringe other people's interests (as in libel or invasion of privacy), there one's freedom does not stretch, or at least there it has to be balanced against other interests. A sophisticated version of this argument regards the right to free expression as a right against its curtailment for certain reasons, e.g. that what is expressed is false, or an abomination or repugnant. This allows one to restrict the freedom, provided this is done for other reasons.

Third comes the contention that, while people's interest may be small, the risk that curtailment will be unjustified is particularly great in this area. This could be because governments are worse judges of the justification of

---

[4] For a discussion of rights in general, see my *The Morality of Freedom*, ch. 5. Constitutional rights are discussed in ch. 8. The discussion in this essay relies on, and further develops, the framework discussed there.

public expression than they are of welfare and other matters, or because they have an institutional interest in restricting expression unjustifiably (it threatens their power), etc.

Fourth are the arguments which suggest that, while the likely harm to the right-holders in cases of curtailed freedom of public expression is not particularly great, the wrong done to them is great. The wrong done to them, according to this argument, is not to be measured in consequentialist terms. The very act of censorship insults the censored, denies their rationality, treats them as means rather than ends in themselves, etc.

Fifth come the arguments that a person's right to free expression is protected not in order to protect him, but in order to protect a public good, a benefit which respect for the right of free expression brings to all those who live in the society in which it is respected, even those who have no personal interest in their own freedom.

Of course these different avenues are not mutually exclusive, and quite a number of writers have buttressed their defence of the right to freedom of expression by combining arguments from different categories. In this article I will examine just one idea which leads to two arguments which belong respectively to the fifth and fourth types; both arguments regard free expression as a public good.

It is not my purpose to propose a comprehensive account of freedom of expression. The considerations I will put forward are insufficient in several respects to justify the right of free expression as it is practised in some Western democracies and advocated by some political theorists. One possible conclusion is that the liberal emphasis on free expression is overdone. Another is that there are other important considerations in support of the right which I will not consider. The second conclusion is certainly warranted, and possibly there is something in the first conclusion as well. All this will remain unexplored here.

Furthermore, I will not be concerned with questions of the outer boundaries of the right, not even inasmuch as these are affected by the considerations here examined. It seems to be a common philosophical mistake to think that the core justification of a right or any other normative institution is sufficient for fixing its boundaries. The boundaries of a right are greatly affected by existing local conventions and practices, and by institutional considerations. Rights are compatible with a variety of institutional arrangements. Contrary to some views, constitutional judicial review is but one possible institutional expression of the right of free expression. A strong common-law tradition is another, equally viable institutional framework for the right.[5] The traditions and prospects of different countries may well make

---

[5] I say that it is equally viable, meaning in principle. It is not my contention that the British courts do justice to freedom of expression.

one or another institutional framework the preferable one for that country at that time. But often there is no reason to prefer one institutional arrangement over another. This does not mean that different institutions will protect, should protect, or are capable of protecting the right within identical boundaries. It means that, so far as the core justification of the right goes, there is a flexible range of permissible or acceptable boundaries; the choice between them turns on their suitability for the institutional arrangements in the different societies.

II. FREEDOM OF EXPRESSION AS A PUBLIC GOOD

So much by way of general caution regarding the ambitions of my arguments and the hedges around them. As I said, they hold that, whatever else it may be, freedom of expression is a public good. Therefore the right to it is also a public good.[6] I believe that it is regarded as such in the common law, but would not argue for that conclusion.[7] Instead I will try to justify that view of freedom of expression first by removing a conceptual objection to the view that a fundamental civil and political individual right can be a justified as a public good, and second by pointing to one uncontroversial public good served by free expression.

The conceptual objection is encapsulated in the view which I have already expressed. The considerations which justify rights, I said, are that they protect an interest of the right-holder.[8] Furthermore, their importance depends entirely on the importance of the right-holder's interest which they protect.[9] Both propositions are true and wrong—wrong in excluding the relevance of other considerations. That the first proposition is true is hard to deny.[10] On the one hand stands the fact that rights are necessarily to what

---

[6] As will be emphasized below, it is important to distinguish between freedom of expression, as an actual social situation, and the right to it. The distinction does not avoid the present difficulty, for if freedom of expression is a public good so is the right to it if it does protect and promote it.

[7] As Mark Kelman remarked to me, the frequent invocation of the 'slippery slope' or the 'thin end of the wedge' argument in cases dealing with free expression itself lends some support to the view that the right is regarded as resting on the need to protect a public good rather than as a matter of protecting the right-holder from a violation of a very important interest of his in the case under consideration. This matter also has bearing on the availability of the right to corporations and other legal persons.

[8] A right protects an interest if and only if respecting it leads to the interest being better protected than it would be if the right did not exist. The argument for a right also shows that whatever disadvantages it brings to others are justified, given the interests it protects.

[9] More accurately, their importance is often thought to be a function of the net gain from respecting their existence, i.e. the benefit to the protected interest which such respect brings (compared with a situation in which the right does not exist) discounted by the loss to others, if any, resulting from restrictions it imposes on them.

[10] The so-called 'choice theory' of rights, most notably defended by H. L. A. Hart (see his *Essays on Bentham* (Oxford: Oxford Univ. Press, 1982)) does not deny it. One way of

is in the interests of the right-holders.[11] One cannot have a right to a dis-advantage, or to a penalty, etc. unless it is, at least in part, to one's advantage to have the disadvantage or the penalty. This cannot be just a coincidence. The natural explanation is that the reason for the right is (at least in part) that it serves the interest of the right-holder. Pointing to the interests of right-holders is the standard argument for rights. This would suggest that the importance of the right-holders' interest is a factor in assessing the importance of the right. But it does not establish it as the only factor.

There can be no denying that other people's interests are often served by behaviour which respects rights, and harmed by behaviour which violates them. Assault, or burglary, apart from harming the victims, also instils fear in others, with (sometimes) considerable consequences for their lives. Do the benefits of the right to people other than the right-holder count in assessing the importance of the right? I have argued elsewhere[12] that, when the benefits to others are the result of the benefit the right brings to the right-holder (rather than merely a coincidental independent effect), they do. Given that the right has these consequences, any consequentialist morality is committed to taking them into account. Indeed, any morality with a consequentialist component (i.e. one which allows that consequences matter even if they are not all that matters) is bound to take them into account. The most natural way to take them into account is to allow them to be reflected in our judgment of the importance of the right, respect for which secures these consequences.

Once we have gone that far, it is but one more step to suggest that the further benefits to third parties which respect for a right brings count, along-side the interest of the right-holder, towards establishing the claim that that person has a right. The problem is this. Rights exist only if the interest they protect is sufficient to hold another person to be under a duty to respect it. That is so only if the interests in question are greater than the disadvan-tages, if there are such, of being subject to the duty to respect them. Judgment of the existence of a right does, therefore, involve a comparison of interests protected and sacrificed. The question I gave an affirmative answer to is the question whether the interests of those who benefit from the fact that the

reinterpreting the choice theory, not one favoured by its supporters, is that it identifies the interest in choice as the only, or at any rate the primary, interest for the protection of which one may have a right. Nor does the view that rights are side-constraints (held, regarding some rights, by R. Nozick in *Anarchy, State and Utopia* (Oxford: Blackwell, 1978)) necessarily conflict with the first proposition. It is compatible with holding that only acts detrimental to the right-holders' interests can give rise to rights. The side-constraint view is, of course, incom-patible with the second proposition. It regards all rights as absolute, regardless of the importance of the right-holders' interest they protect. This understanding of rights, therefore, supports, but for other reasons, my rejection of the second proposition.

[11] Or, in the case of legal rights, only what the law considers to be in the interest of the right-holders can be so protected. See Ch. 11 below.

[12] *The Morality of Freedom*, ch. 10.

would-be right-holder's interest is respected count in the case for the exist-ence of a right. Again, the reason is that that seems to be the most natural response by every morality with a consequentialist component to the fact that respect for the interest of one person sometimes essentially serves the interests of others as well. To deny the relevance to the existence of a right of third-party interests which it so serves would be odd, since it amounts to asserting that considerations which affect the importance of a right are irrelevant to its existence.

Given that the interests of third parties count towards the justification of a right, we can begin to see how rights can be justified by their service to public goods. But the case for justifying rights by their service to public goods is not based merely on the abstract argument preceding. It relies in part on the fact that such justifications are deeply embedded in our prac-tices. After all, the argument we are engaged in at the moment, the argu-ment about the nature of rights, is an attempt to understand the basic structure of some of our practices. If it can be shown that those practices are not intelligible except on the assumption that rights are advocated and upheld by reference to their service to public goods, then that is strong evidence that such considerations are relevant.[13]

The paradigmatic public-good argument for freedom of expression is also the least problematic argument for the importance of the right. Freedom of expression is an integral part of a democratic regime, i.e. one based on some form of institutional arrangements designed to ensure significant responsiveness of government to the wishes of the governed. Whatever justification democratic government may have, and whatever form it may take, two implications are bound to emerge: (1) Governmental responsive-ness to the wishes of the governed is to be desired only if those wishes themselves are not entirely the product of manipulation by the government.[14] (2) Other things being equal, the better informed the governed are and the better able they are to evaluate the information at their disposal, the stronger the case for heeding their wishes.

These two considerations serve as a foundation for the democratic defence of freedom of expression. In contemporary multi-candidate electoral systems, these considerations lead to a right to the free dissemination of

---

[13] I have delineated the outline of such an argument in *The Morality of Freedom*, ch. 10. My argument is not 'intuitionist'. It is not based on accepting current moral views, and regarding their vindication as the aim of moral or political theory. I am merely saying that structural features of concepts should be recognized. It is the fact that what is, if a good at all, a public good counts towards the justification of rights that I am relying on, not the actual beliefs in the value of particular alleged public goods.

[14] It is perhaps arguable that there is nothing wrong in governments manipulating the interests of the people so that the perpetuation of those governments in power should be in the people's interests. My concern here is merely with manipulating information and the ability to judge it, and not with the manipulation of interests.

information and opinion which may affect judgment on matters of public policy, i.e. on issues which are, or may be, objects of a political decision. It has often been pointed out that democratic justification is insufficient to account for the full scope and importance of the constitutional protection of freedom of expression called for in liberal political theory. This is partly because that freedom extends to matters which are not subject to political decisions, nor likely to affect opinion on issues which are (such as publication of research on the burial customs of the ancient Egyptians), but also because the importance of the right in such theories does not reflect the importance of the information for political decisions (for example, the right is supposed to protect views about the authorship of the Gospels as much, if not more, than views about the causes of inflation, even though the latter are more relevant for political decisions). This is not a refutation of the democratic argument. There is no reason to think that just one consideration can provide a complete account of the right. My purpose in adverting to the democratic case for free expression is both to highlight this fact and to point out that it is a public-good justification.

From the point of view of the democratic argument, whatever value the right to free expression has for an individual right-holder derives from his interest in being able to participate in the democratic process. It is, however, notoriously difficult to show that people have a rational reason to cast a vote in any election with a sufficiently large electorate. Arguably, therefore, the value of the right to vote largely depends on the symbolic recognition of full membership in the community which it expresses, rather than arising out of the value of actually being able to vote. How does this reflect on the right of free speech? It carries, though to a lesser degree, the same symbolic value as the right to vote, i.e. its denial implies less than complete membership. Its actual exercise can be of greater value than the right to vote, since it may enable a person, like Springer, Murdoch, or a Kennedy, to affect the votes of many. But for most people the exercise of the right to free public political speech (by which I mean the right of free expression as justified by the democratic argument) has little value, and most people refrain from exercising the right in more than a minimal way.

This argument notwithstanding, the right is essential for the survival of democracy, and everyone has a great interest in the survival of democracy. The point is that this interest is not limited to those who have the vote or the right of free expression. Members of the public in general, be they infants or convicts without the vote, or without a right to free expression, have an interest in the prosperity of democracy, since we assume that democracy is a better form of government than its alternatives, and therefore more likely to ensure that people get what they deserve and are entitled to, and what would be good for them to have. This good, i.e. living in a democratic country, that most people have a personal interest in having is clearly a public good. Its existence is, in part, the existence of the right to free public political expression. Hence that right is a public good, a good not merely to its holders but to the public at large. Furthermore, it follows from the above that the right's service to this public good is a major reason for its importance, a reason of greater weight than the value of the right to each individual who has it.

III. THE CORE CASE: VALIDATING FORMS OF LIFE

With this clarification behind us, it is time to turn to the core case behind the two arguments to be presented here.[15] They are primarily arguments for freedom of expression, and only secondarily for a right to it, on the ground that that is a good way of protecting and promoting it.[16]

Much public expression, in books, newspapers, television, cinema, etc., portrays and expresses aspects of styles or forms of life. Views and opinions, activities, emotions, etc., expressed or portrayed, are an aspect of a wider net of opinions, sensibilities, habits of action or dressing, attitudes, etc., which, taken together, form a distinctive style or form of life.[17] An important case for the importance of freedom of expression[18] arises out of the fact that public portrayal and expression of forms of life validate the styles of life portrayed, and that censoring expression normally expresses authoritative condemnation not merely of the views or opinions censored but of the whole style of life of which they are a part.

The fact that much public expression expresses or portrays aspects of ways of life is often either overlooked or taken for granted as a trivial and irrelevant point. It is overlooked because often writers on freedom of expression focus attention on types of speech of which this is not true, or at least not true in any straightforward way. For example, claims about

---

[15] The view I wish to explore is closely related to the general position expressed by J. Nickel in 'Freedom of Expression in a Pluralistic Society', *Law and Philosophy*, 7 (1988/9), 281.

[16] I will talk both of rights and of duties as protecting interests. Duties protect interest inasmuch as their observance promotes the interests or their violation damages them. Rights protect interests inasmuch as they are the justifying reasons for duties which protect the interests.

[17] Though naturally any single act of expression can be an element of, or fit in with, various forms of life. The only point is that it does not fit with all. Note that nowhere do I define 'forms of life'. For the purpose of this argument the precise understanding of the term is immaterial. The only material points are that different aspects of activities, tastes, styles, and attitudes are seen to belong together, in the ordinary way in which we can distinguish the yuppy, or the middle class, or the 'Sloane Ranger', etc. Whatever other aspects of styles or forms of life are material to the argument will emerge as the argument of the essay develops.

[18] i.e. a situation in which freedom of expression occurs, not of a right to free expression.

the relative merit of high interest rates versus high taxation as a means of dampening consumer spending do not express any way of life. The same goes for publication of an academic article about the origin of galaxies, etc. Discussion of such cases normally focuses on the importance of the information conveyed and of being free to convey it. But these cases have an additional aspect. Engaging in such speech is part of the normal activities of economists, politicians, journalists, or scientists. Prohibiting or censoring such speech distorts and impedes these activities, and if such measures are they render those activities impossible and can constitute their public condemnation. This is true of interference with much free expression. It points to the fact that public expression is itself an element of several styles of life.

Of course, this fact in itself is no argument for the *special* protection of free expression. Many non-speech activities are integral to many different styles of life. One should be aware of this factor whenever the state criminalizes or otherwise impedes various activities. It would be wrong, however, to dismiss this consideration just on the ground that it is not unique to acts of expression. Even though it applies to other cases too, it may justify greater protection of free expression than of freedom to engage in other activities, if only for the reason that the justification of each freedom involves comparing good and ill, merits and demerits; and the demerits, the disadvantages of engaging in various activities, are not the same. Prayer may be part of a religion which involves ritual bodily mutilation of young children. Respect for this religious style of life may weigh equally in favour of tolerating both prayer and mutilation. But the arguments against tolerating the two practices are far from equal, and the result need not be the same.

The argument that I wish to explore covers cases in which the very act of expression is an element of a way of life as a special case. It covers also speech by people who do not share the style of life about aspects of which they express themselves. That is why I refer to portrayals or descriptions of ways of life as the paradigmatic, though not the only, case to which my argument applies. These include cases in which the concern is not with the interest of the speaker and the way his speech is an aspect of his life, but the way it reflects, expresses, or describes the life of others.

A typical example of this is a portrayal of a family in a television sitcom. Let us say, a husband and wife have two children, an adolescent girl, romantic and full of dreams about poetry, her boyfriend, her studies, her tennis, and a younger boy, continuously quarrelling with the neighbours' children, making his first steps as a computer hack, teasing his older sister to tears. While such portrayals are typical of the kind of expression I am concerned with, they are not the only ones. The argument extends to discussion and comments on activities, beliefs, attitudes, and of responses to them. It also, and most importantly, extends to pornography, to prayer-books, and to much else which, while only sometimes portraying ways of life, are always meant to be used as part of certain ways of life.

The reason to focus on acts of expression of this type is that they fulfil important functions in contemporary societies.[19] Three are of prime concern to my argument:

1. They serve to familiarize the public at large with ways of life common in certain segments of the public.
2. They serve to reassure those whose ways of life are being portrayed that they are not alone, that their problems are common problems, their experiences known to others.
3. Finally, they serve as validation of the relevant ways of life. They give them the stamp of public acceptability.

I shall talk of portrayal in the public media as validating the experience or way of life portrayed or expressed, as a shorthand to refer to all three functions of such expression. The use of the term 'validation' suggests the direction of the argument.

That public portrayal has an important validating function is a contingent fact of human nature. But, although contingent, it is deeply rooted and of great importance to the preservation of any culture. Even traditional homo-geneous societies, in which individuals find themselves enmeshed in close-knit social networks, depend for the legitimation of their culture and its transmission and renewal on its expression and portrayal in the public arena. The difference is that contemporary pluralistic societies place a high value on recognizing the existence of a plurality of valuable ways of life, and of the possibility of change and the generation of novel, valuable forms of life. Furthermore, we depend more than ever before on a culture which saturates us with images and messages through the public media, which have acquired a great power both to encourage and to stifle and marginalize activities, attitudes, and the like.

To a large extent the validating functions of public expression acquire their contemporary importance from two much-discussed aspects of con-temporary societies, their urban anonymity, and their cultural and ethical pluralism. These mean that people depend more than ever on public com-munication to establish a common understanding of the ways of life, range of experiences, attitudes, and thinking which are common and acceptable in their society. They also depend on finding themselves reflected in the public media for a sense of their own legitimacy, for a feeling that their problems and experiences are not freak deviations.[20]

---

[19] By 'contemporary societies' I mean societies like ours. Many past societies shared these features, and some contemporary ones lack them. But it seems to me important to start from the here and now, and not from an abstract enumeration of relevant features.

[20] For the existence of the problem consider the proliferation of support groups for people who are drug-abusers, smokers, teenage mothers, fat, thin, etc.

IV. THE FIRST ARGUMENT: TOLERATING AND ENCOURAGING VALIDATION

Freedom of expression touches on the validation of ways of life in two ways, yielding two distinct arguments for it. First, while it exists and inasmuch as it is exercised, ways of life which are portrayed and expressed are validated through their portrayal and expression. People get the reassurance that others know of their problems, experiences, attitudes, etc., and that they are acceptable in the society. Second, because of this significance of expression, censorship and criminalization acquire a wider negative significance. They express not merely disapproval of the particular act of expression which is censored. They express disapproval of the whole way of life (of all the ways of life) of which it is a part. In contemporary societies, public portrayal validates ways of life, whereas censorship is authoritative public condemnation of the way of life. The first argument for freedom of expression arising out of these considerations asserts that freedom of expression renders a great service to people's well-being. This service takes three forms.

First, validation of a way of life through its public expression is of crucial importance for the well-being of individuals whose way of life it is. It helps their identification with their way of life, their sense of its worth, and their sense that their way of life facilitates rather than hinders their integration into their society.

Second, such validation is important for making ways of life a real option for people. Absence of validation makes them suspect, and unattractive, and jeopardizes the chances that people will choose them.

Third, public validation is an essential element in the process of cultural transmission, preservation, and renewal. It is one of the central arenas for the assertion of traditions, and for challenging traditions and experimenting with new forms of relationships, attitudes, and styles of life.

This argument shows freedom of expression to be a public good, a constitutive element of a public culture. It points to a strong, positive case for free expression. It points to the importance not only of the absence of censorship but of providing access to the means of public expression to those who portray various ways of life, and express different points of view.[21] At the same time the argument supports only a weak, overridable right. Like all public-good arguments, it is weak on setting boundaries. No major difficulty arises if one allows, say private television stations to deny access to certain views, so long as those views can find other avenues of

---

[21] At its most abstract level, the argument does not distinguish between privately owned and publicly owned means of expression (such as land, newspapers, public halls, or television stations). It establishes a reason for all those who control means of public expression to allow access to them. But in establishing the ways such abstract reasons are to receive institutional support and become enforceable by law, it may be reasonable to distinguish between privately owned and publicly owned means of expression and to impose lesser duties on the former. Such matters cannot be determined in the abstract.

expression. No major problem arises from restricting the areas in towns in which demonstrations can be held, so long as the areas available provide for a reasonably effective way of expressing views and displaying the intensity with which they are felt.

V. THE SECOND ARGUMENT: CENSORSHIP AS INSULT

To a certain extent the issue of boundaries is helped by a second argument. It derives from the evil of censorship and criminalization, which extends a good deal beyond denying people the benefits of a culture in which expression is free. Because of the validating function of public expression, pure content-based censorship[22] has acquired a symbolic meaning. It expresses official, authoritative disapproval and condemnation of the style of life of which the censored communication is a part.[23]

People's relations with the society in which they live is a major component in their personal well-being. It is normally vital for personal prosperity that one should be able to identify with one's society, should not be alienated from it, should feel a full member of it. The importance of this factor derives from two concerns. First, a significant part of the activities and pursuits through which people prosper (or fail to prosper) involves engagement with larger groups (their workplace or trade association, their city, sports or other leisure association, a variety of civic activities, in support of the homeless, single mothers, war veterans, etc.). Full membership in the society is essential for free participation in the activities of such groups (except in those which are dedicated to achieving full membership for certain subgroups—membership of such subgroups sometimes presupposes absence of full membership in one's country's society). Second, the very ability to identify with one's society is an independent background good, and feeling alienated from it is a significant handicap. They have a considerable, often imperceptible impact on people's ability to engage in activities involving relations with other people, or contributions to their well-being or to the common good. Official denunciation or condemnation of one's way of life

---

[22] 'Pure' content-based censorship is marked by the reasons for the censorship. Censorship is pure content-based if the reason for it is the disapproval of the content of the act of expression, rather than merely an attempt to avoid undesirable consequences of its publication. Prohibition of the publication of military secrets is content-based but not 'purely' content-based. 'Content' is meant to include style: expressing a view by the use of violent language or gesture has, for the purposes of this discussion, a different content from its expression in polite academic language. This follows from the fact that attitudes, emotions, etc., and not merely a cognitive content, are covered by 'expression'. Pure content-based censorship can take the form of prior restraint, criminalization, or regulation. But the last is characteristically based on desire to minimize the consequences of the act of expression, and is only very rarely purely content-based. Criminalization and prior restraint can be either purely content-based or based on a perceived reason to avoid or mitigate the consequences of the speech.

[23] I use this expression to indicate both acts of expression which are themselves a part of a form of life and those which portray, describe, discuss, etc., aspects of forms of life. Both are covered by the arguments advanced here.

is a major obstacle to identification with one's society, and this is a powerful argument against it.

Just like the first argument, the second rests on a public-good case for free expression. The evil to be avoided is not a specific harm to the interests of the right-holder caused by denying him free expression. It is a harm to the common interest of all, and especially of those whose interests are served by the condemned way of life and its prosperity. Because this is the meaning of *every* act of content-based censorship, and of *every* content-based criminalization of acts of symbolic public expression, the second argument solves many of the boundary problems which the first argument generates.

In some ways this second argument is the more powerful of the two. Content-based censorship and criminalization are a public and authoritative condemnation. Their repudiation of ways of life which they reject is insulting and hurtful, and their negative meaning is a stronger reason against censorship and criminalization than the reason for free expression deriving from the value of the validation of styles of life through their public portrayal. In a culture in which expression is free, validation is provided by people exercising their freedom. They provide validation and not the state, not society using its authoritative voice. Society's official attitude welcomes and facilitates such validation, but it is given only where members of that society wish to give it through their exercise of freedom of expression. Content-based censorship and criminalization not only deny individuals the opportunity to provide validation but constitute official condemnation of the way of life aspects of which are censored or criminalized.

The symbolic meaning of content-based censorship and criminalization gives the second argument considerable weight where it applies. But its range is limited compared with the first argument. The symbolic meaning of condemnation of the style of life to which the expression belongs is a feature of pure content-based prohibitions. It is not typical of other restrictions on free expression, such as banning demonstrations from the vicinity of churches during the high holidays, out of respect for the feelings of worshippers, or banning them on certain highways during the rush hour, in order to facilitate commuters' journeys home. Similarly, the interest of would-be speakers in having access to the public has to be reconciled with the interest of the public not to be made a captive audience, a reconciliation which requires many pragmatic compromises between speakers who wish to address people where they are likely to be and members of the public who wish to be able to use public arenas without being subjected to acts of expression which they regard as odious.[24] The second argument does not

---

[24] Of course, members of the public also have an interest in easy access to information which they wish to receive. The conflict I am alluding to is not between speakers and the public. It is between speakers and the sections of the public who wish to have easy access to them and other sections of the public who wish to be free of their intrusion.

extend to such cases, and while the first argument does it establishes only a weak right, which is subject to compromises when it clashes with such legitimate concerns.

The weight and scope differences between the two arguments should not be exaggerated. Limited acts of prior restraint by a minor official, even though content-based, do not carry the message of official condemnation to the same degree as major legislation extensively criminalizing the portrayal of a group's way of life. Even pure content-based censorship is a matter of degree, though this is normally relevant to the degree of wrongness of the act rather than to its justification. Justification is, however, at stake in mixed cases. Often criminalization or prior restraint[25] is based both on pure content-based reasons and on a perceived reason to avoid the consequences of acts of expression. Furthermore, given that the underlying reasons for such criminalization and prior restraint are so commonly mixed, almost every content-based criminalization or prior restraint is perceived as expressing in part official condemnation of the content of expression.[26] Since the evil is in the public perception, almost every content-based criminalization and prior restraint is subject to the considerations of my second argument.

These observations presuppose that the public meanings of permitting and prohibiting are not contraries. Whereas prohibition (i.e. censorship and criminalization) condemns the prohibited conduct, permission does not endorse what is permitted, it merely tolerates it. How should facilitating actions be judged? How should one judge state subsidies to science? Does their denial to astrology amount to its condemnation? How should access to the media be judged? Does the provision of television time to Muslims and its non-provision to Buddhists constitute condemnation of the latter and endorsement of the former? The main point to bear in mind is that the issue is factual, not logical. It is not to be resolved by arguing, say, that subsidies are a positive interference, like censorship, and not merely a non-interference, like permissions, and that therefore they are an endorsement, whereas a refusal to facilitate is no condemnation. Nor would it do to argue that, since no effective access is likely to be possible to some ideas or ways of life (since they have no rich supporters), it follows that refusal to facilitate is condemnation. The only issue is what is the public meaning of certain acts, and the same act can have different meanings in different societies.[27] The meaning may depend on considerations of the kind mentioned, and on

---

[25] I have in mind all content-based criminalization and prior restraint, pure or impure, i.e. excluding only those which are designed merely to enforce regulatory measures rather than to stop all expression of a certain content.

[26] The exceptions are instances where the importance of the non-content-based reasons is clear, as with vital military secrets.

[27] More awkwardly for setting the boundaries of the right, it may have different meanings to different groups in the same society.

many others (the reasons for lack of facilitation being obvious ones,[28] as are the normal expectations in that society). I am assuming that, generally, providing access to the public media in our society does not speak of approval but of toleration. And that its denial does not amount to condemnation by the society. Therefore, the second argument does not support a positive right of access to the means of public expression. The state's failure to give philosophers an assured access to the means of expression does not amount to an authoritative condemnation of philosophy by the state, whereas censorship and criminalization of philosophical publications are such a condemnation.

Broadly speaking, the position is this. Regulatory restrictions are subject to the first argument only. In general, content-based criminalization and prior restraint are subject to the second argument, for in most cases they express condemnation of the way of life portrayed or expressed. Where the restriction is pure content-based, the argument is normally decisive. Where the restriction is based also on good reasons to avoid certain consequences of the act of expression, the need for such restriction has to be assessed against the reasons against it adumbrated above.

Finally, neither of the two arguments protects most acts of expression about particular individuals. Similarly, the democratic argument for free expression does not concern, with some obvious exceptions, speech regarding identifiable ordinary persons. Naturally, it does protect many comments regarding individuals who are holders of or candidates for public office, or who are otherwise involved in politics. Similarly, the arguments I am considering here do protect speech about individuals who become symbols of certain cultures, or ideologies, or who have acquired a status of paradigmatic representatives of styles of life, cultures, etc. But, with these exceptions, the right to freedom of expression does not conflict with the law of libel and right of privacy.

VI. PROTECTING BAD SPEECH

Any doctrine of freedom of expression must face the question: why should society respect people's freedom to express false, worthless, degrading, depraved, etc., views and opinions? It is an essential aspect of any doctrine of free expression that it purports to justify the freedom to what we can generically call bad speech (by which I do not mean that it must justify the freedom to express anything, however bad). Does my argument do that? Does it not depend on the value of the protected speech? This objection misunderstands the nature of my argument. It does indeed depend on the

---

[28] Compare denying subsidies to Buddhists on the ground that there are none in the country with their denial on the ground that Buddhism is repugnant, or morally corrupting.

value to be found in the ways of life of which protected speech is a part. But bad speech is often a part[29] of a good way of life, or at any rate one which should not be condemned by society through its official organs. This point is important not only for the justification of freedom of expression but for any doctrine of toleration.

Take two examples. First, an atheist may say that, since there is no God, it is permissible to censor public expression avowing belief in the existence of God, or propagating arguments purporting to prove His existence since they only spread error. Second, a person of cultivated taste may say that the high volume of rock music detracts from its value, and the law may, perhaps even should, restrict the volume at which it is played, for to do so can only improve people's taste and the quality of their lives. Let us assume that we agree with the atheist about the non-existence of God, and with the finely cultivated person about the worthlessness of loud music. Does it follow that censorship is justified?

Of course not. There are many other questions which have to be faced. Is such speech protected by other principled arguments for free speech? Can we trust the legislature with the power to take such decisions? Even if right in these cases, is it not likely that wrong conclusions may be reached more often than not? Would the consequences of restriction of speech have the desired results? Or will it lead to enhancing the appeal of the forbidden speech by lending it the aura of anti-establishment heroism? Will restrictions have undesired side-effects (undermining confidence in the government, providing the police with excessive powers which invite abuse, etc.)? There is always also the consideration, which elsewhere[30] I made much of, that any prohibition of victimless crimes brings with it punishments which infringe people's life, and deny their autonomy in ways which exceed the authority of the state, since they cannot be justified on the ground that they are necessary to protect the autonomy of others. For the purpose of the present argument I want, however, to leave all these considerations on one side and concentrate on a question of first principle. Do the considerations I canvassed above establish any reason of principle against the state curtailing free expression in the two examples we are discussing?

They do, for by curtailing these acts of bad speech the state condemns, and impedes the existence of, good ways of life of which the acts of bad speech are parts. I am assuming here that we will all agree that the religious life, and the life of rock fans, are valuable despite the presence in them of these objectionable features.[31] The real question is one of separability. Can

---

[29] Either in being strictly speaking a part of, or in portraying something which is part of, a bad style of life.

[30] In *The Morality of Freedom*.

[31] Two caveats: first, I am not assuming that all religions embody valuable ways of life, only that at least one does. The same goes for the life of the rock fans. Second, while the notion

it not be said that in condemning these aspects of these ways of life one does not condemn the whole way of life? It is to be welcomed, and even encouraged, but it should be purged of its objectionable features.

It cannot be said that it is impossible for people to go to church, perform church music, continue with the complex social, charitable, and educational activities of their churches, but abandon their belief in the existence of God. There is good reason to think that this is indeed the way that quite a few people conduct themselves. Similarly, it cannot be said that rock music is not improved if played at lower volumes. Yet such claims are beside the point. For the believer, belief in God is an essential part of the religious life. For the rock fan, volume is essential to his favourite music and to its significance for his life. We can say to them that there is an alternative way of life which is better, but we cannot deny them sovereignty over defining what their way of life is, and what is integral to it. This question is answerable entirely from the point of view of those whose way of life it is. *Their* way of life is the activities, practices, and attitudes which are meaningful and rewarding in their life.[32]

The censoring government can say that it does not intend to condemn the style of life as a whole, that it rejects only the censored aspect of it. But such response, even when truthful, is inadequate. What is condemned is an objective matter, which does not altogether depend on the government's intentions. The perceived significance of the act is more sweeping. For reasons which are not hard to seek, it is reasonably seen as a condemnation of that way of life as it is. Given that that is the social significance of such acts of censorship, that they are perceived as condemning the way of life as a whole, such censorship constitutes condemnation. The defence 'we did not intend to condemn' is of no avail. What counts is what the government did, not what it intended to do.

These observations relate to the second of my two arguments. Similar considerations apply to the first argument. In denying public expression to aspects of a way of life, the government restricts and impedes the ability of that way of life as a whole, and not just the offending aspect, to gain public recognition and acceptability.

---

of a religious life is familiar, there is no equivalent term to describe the disjunctive set of features which make one or the other styles of life in which rock music features importantly. But the absence of a handy phrase does not mean that rock music is not an important part of the lifestyles of many people.

[32] And it is not determinable in the abstract. It depends on the actual practices of real people. This is consistent with allowing that individuals may make mistakes about what is meaningful in their lives. They do not enjoy an epistemically privileged position. But I mean styles of life to be understood flexibly, to include more or fewer aspects of a person's life. All that matters for this argument to apply to any act of expression is that it reflects or portrays an aspect which is either pervasive in itself or is an integral element in a pervasive aspect of that person's life.

Does all this matter? It is conceded that the ways of life my argument intends to protect are deficient, and that they can be improved by changing them in appropriate ways, or by substituting alternative way of life which preserve much of the good but avoid the shortcomings of the ones portrayed in the offending speech. Does not that provide sufficient grounds for restricting free expression? Assuming that the bad speech expresses or portrays elements of a valuable way of life, does not the fact that there are better alternative ways of life justify restrictions of free expression if they are likely to encourage a change to the better alternatives? There is nothing wrong in principle in governments trying to promote valuable ways of life, and to improve them. But here the proposed measures to that end include impeding or denying public recognition to a good (though imperfect) way of life, or its public, authoritative condemnation. Such measures cannot be justified. They are wrong in themselves.[33]

So the arguments I am advancing provide reasons to protect much bad speech. But they do not protect all bad speech. To be protected by these arguments, it has to be an expression or portrayal of something which is a part of a valuable way of life. Some ways of life are without redeeming features. Some of their aspects have no place in any worthwhile way of life, and their expression or portrayal is not protected by the arguments advanced here.

This is not the place to discuss in detail what makes a way of life totally unacceptable. This is one of the central questions of ethics. But it is worth noting that the task is not straightforward. Moral philosophy tends to concentrate on single items: which acts are wrong or right, which character traits are admirable and which are not. The character of a way of life depends on evaluating a much broader canvas, of practices, character traits, attitudes, beliefs, and so on. It raises questions rarely discussed by theorists. Some tests seek perfection, and would disallow any but forms of life without any blemish. They are based on a misunderstanding of the task. It is not to imagine perfect or saintly lives, but good and worthwhile ones. Other tests, while sensible in their motivation, may be deemed too lenient. For example, it may be suggested that any form of life which may enhance the quality of life of a person, while not involving him in any major sin, is acceptable. By this test, which is admittedly too vague to be accepted without much further development, even Nazism is acceptable. Many youngsters were rescued from a life of drifting and petty criminality, were transported into organized, spirited activities in Nazi youth clubs, enjoyed camaraderie and a sense of proud membership in their nation, partaking of its culture and traditions, as well as a sense of purpose in their life, while being lucky enough never to

---

[33] Remember that the first of my two arguments is subject to adjudication between conflicting goods. The second argument is different, and it seems that only extraordinary circumstances will justify overriding it.

have become involved in Nazi crimes. Such cases raise difficult issues which I will leave on one side.[34] One sufficient condition for the unacceptability of a style of life is that the activities essential and distinctive to its pursuit are rightly forbidden by law. But this test is incomplete, and in any case merely defers the question. For it all depends on what is rightly forbidden by law.

VII. ATTACKING SPEECH

For more than two years now, Britain's liberal conscience has been shaken by the Rushdie case. The thought that a novelist may find himself pursued by murder gangs, that he should go into hiding, lose contact with people and places, that his creative life no less than his personal life will be for ever indelibly marked by a campaign of mass hysteria and hatred, shocked and horrified the public. Personally I was touched by another aspect of the affair. I suddenly found myself living among neighbours some of whom believe that they have a duty to kill Rushdie if the opportunity comes their way. Liberal-minded people everywhere found themselves torn between their belief in free expression and their abhorrence of racism and acceptance of pluralism. How were they to react to the claims of many Muslims that Rushdie, under the protection of an alien and hostile culture, had blasphemed, and had also grossly defamed their religion?

The Muslim response to Rushdie, where even moderates called for the banning of the book, on the one hand, and the campaigns by gays and lesbians for gay culture to find expression in the public arena, were the main triggers for the thoughts I have been outlining in this essay. Both highlight the considerations on which I based my arguments, i.e. the validation of ways of life through their public expression. The Muslim campaign to suppress speech which attacks and vilifies their religion raised the question of the limits of the protection. Do not the very considerations I pointed to suggest that, while positive portrayal of ways of life, or aspects of them, should be tolerated, a critical or hostile discussion or portrayal of them is to be banned?

There are two tempting mistakes in understanding these arguments. One is to invoke a presumption of freedom. After all, we are told, no one is compelled to read novels, or newspaper articles, or to watch films or television. I remarked at the outset that acts of expression have consequences, even as acts of expression, for the life of others. One important interest which all people share is an interest in the character of their environment,

---

[34] One response, suggested to me by Anthony Duff, is to distinguish between morally mistaken and morally evil beliefs. The latter can perhaps be said to diminish the quality of one's life, as well as one's character, even if one does not act wrongly as a result of such beliefs.

cultural and social as well as natural and physical. It is short-sighted to condemn the reaction of the Muslim community to a culture which is critical of their religion as meddling in things which are of no concern to them, since they can avoid reading the offensive literature. It is a legitimate concern of gays that our culture is swamped with displays of heterosexual relations, whereas homoerotic ones are *de facto* denied public expression. These facts do undermine the public acceptability of gay relations, or of Muslim culture.

But it is wrong to react by embracing the other mistake, and censor critical or hostile portrayals of Muslims or gays. Two considerations establish the need to tolerate hostile speech. First, while content-based censorship or criminalization is an expression of authoritative condemnation of the views censored and the way of life they are a part of, criticism, hostility, or neglect on the part of individuals or sections of the public express only their hostility or condemnation. They do not carry the authoritative voice of society. This again is a matter of fact, a matter of the social significance of our acts of toleration in the public culture of free societies. It is otherwise in illiberal societies. Since in them only those who express approved views are allowed to express them, the fact that an opinion is tolerated shows that it has authoritative endorsement. By their very nature this is not true of free societies.[35] Hence the second argument for protecting free expression does not tend to censorship of private hostility and condemnation. Second, criticism of rival ways of life is a part of any way of life, in the sense that it is implied by it, and is felt by its adherents. Hence the arguments I advanced for protecting free expression also protect expressions of critical and hostile views and attitudes.[36]

One needs to distinguish here between incompatible and rival ways of life. Two ways of life are incompatible if they cannot both be adopted by the same person.[37] Many incompatible styles of life are displayed in any society. For example, the way of life of town-dwellers is incompatible with the way of life of the inhabitants of the prairies or of remote mountains. There is no inconsistency in approving of different ways of life just because they are incompatible. Rival ways of life are ones which it is inconsistent to approve of without reservation. Islam and Christianity offer rival ways of life. A Christian can approve of the way of life of the Muslim, and vice versa, in that they can and should find each other's way of life valuable and worthwhile. But not without reservations. There are aspects of the other's practices, attitudes, and beliefs that each of them must take exception to,

[35] Though it is worth remembering that freedom is a matter of degree, and so is the social significance of toleration.

[36] As mentioned in the section above, there is always a need for a compromise between the interest in addressing the public and the interest of individuals in not being rendered a captive audience. This applies to offensive and hostile speech as well. The rules which apply to, say, books will therefore differ from those which apply to television in a country where there are only a few television stations and thus less choice for members of the public.

[37] Throughout a whole lifetime. Within limits, people can change from one to another.

must disagree with. Disagreement, condemnation, and even hostility to certain aspects of rival ways of life is an essential element of each way of life. That is why the argument of this essay protects its expression.

The argument for a right of free expression I am defending is 'perfectionist' in the sense that it is based on the need to fashion legal institutions to promote people's ability and prospects of having worthwhile, good lives. But it is not perfectionist in the more ordinary sense of the term. It recognizes that imperfect ways of life may be valuable. Moreover, imperfect ways of life may be the best which is possible for people, given the society to which they belong and the course of their life to date. This view is strongly pluralistic. It recognizes the value of many incompatible ways of life, but also the value of many rival ways of life. Strong pluralism of this kind finds itself, as the Rushdie case illustrates, approving as valuable, though imperfect, ways of life which themselves deny the truth of pluralism. Of course the anti-pluralistic views which underlie such ways of life are regarded as wrong, and the ways of life that they inform are correspondingly imperfect. They are rival ways of life, but none the less recognized as valuable, i.e. as enabling those who follow them to have good and rewarding lives, and as being for some people, due to their circumstances, the best kind of life possible.

Where a dominant pluralistic outlook leads to the recognition of the value of rival ways of life, conflict is inevitable. The pluralist, while finding value in the ways of life informed by some wrong beliefs, must inevitably differ from the people who have those wrong beliefs about what precisely is valuable in their lives and why. The Christian will regard his life as good because he is following the word of God. The atheist will approve of that person's life because it is informed by respect for human beings, or because it values religious art and therefore manifests aesthetic sensibility.

The respect that the pluralist shows for the anti-pluralist may disguise the difference of values, even from the eyes of the pluralist. The seeming harmony is fractured when cases such as Rushdie's make it plain. At such moments the anti-pluralists challenge the sincerity of the pluralists. You never really respected us, they say. You only approved of us when it suited your outlook. But you never respected our views out of respect for them, for the truth they express. All along you were merely enforcing your views on us, allowing us to go our own way only when it suited you. Your claim of pluralism is therefore a sham. You enforce your toleration of Rushdie on us in an intolerant spirit (since you do not tolerate our rejection of him), and at the same time you object to us, the anti-pluralists, enforcing our beliefs in the name of a toleration of other people's views.[38] Pluralists often feel

---

[38] There are, of course, other claims made in this context. One of them, that if one is to tolerate other cultures then one should censor attacks on them, has been dealt with above.

uncomfortable when faced with such accusations. They feel that their pluralism is indeed inadequate, for they do not allow (when they have the
political power to decide such matters) the anti-pluralist cultures, which
they claim to respect, to have their way of life (including its anti-pluralist
aspects) fully enacted. They pick and choose what to allow and what to
disallow.

But the accusation is groundless. The accusers seize on aspects of the
pluralist position while misunderstanding their significance. Pluralists have
the virtue of recognizing the value of rival ways of life. But such recognition
does not stem from abandonment of judgment, or from general scepticism.
Such positions are incoherent.[39] Consistent pluralists have their own firm
views about the qualities which make for a good life. They are distinctive
in recognizing the plurality of incompatible and even rival but none the less
valuable ways of life. Pluralism is misunderstood when it is assumed that
it is committed to approval and support of every aspect of ways of life it
recognizes as valuable, or that it is committed to taking these ways of life
at their own estimation. Because it recognizes the value of ways of life
which it (partly) disagrees with, pluralism is committed to a society in which
conflicting ideologies and beliefs are accepted, and tolerated. But it is an
illusion to think that accepting conflict is a way of avoiding conflict. This is
the substance of the accusation of hypocrisy against the plurality, that in the
end he has his own position which he is willing to back against those he
'pretended' to tolerate. So he does; so does anyone who has a coherent
position. Pluralist toleration is real enough, but it is no recipe for the avoidance of social conflict. Conflict is avoided not by pluralist toleration but by
repressive perfectionist uniformity.

There is, of course, the question of how conflict should be conducted.
Should the supporters of rival views be allowed to use the law to promote
their views? This question finds its answer in each of the rival views out of
its own internal logic. The attempt by some thinkers[40] to find an extra or
meta-position from which to reconcile the conflicting views does not seem
to hold much promise. The views explored here are the implications of a
pluralist position for the question of using the law to suppress free expression. It shows that freedom of expression can be supported as part of a
pluralist argument for using the law to promote pluralism in the society.

VIII. THE CASE FOR SPECIAL PROTECTION

So far this essay has advanced a case for respecting freedom of expression.
I have said nothing about the justification of a right to freedom of expression,

---

[39] See Chs. 3 and 4 above.   [40] Most notably Rawls.

let alone of a constitutional right. This concluding section will briefly address this last issue. The point I wish to highlight is that the stringency and the constitutional standing of the right need not be justified by showing that freedom of expression is more important than relative economic prosperity, or full employment. The right can be justified on the ground that the institutional arrangements best suited for the protection of freedom of expression are best operated through the institution of a constitutional right.

As indicated at the outset, the institutional arrangements proper for the protection of freedom of expression depend to a considerable extent on the tradition and practices of different countries. But some general observations about contemporary societies can be made. First let it be noted what the argument of this essay does *not* establish. It does not establish that freedom of expression should never be compromised. As noted above, the second of the two arguments I presented comes close to doing so, but it applies only to pure content-based censorship and criminalization, which is but a small part of the protected acts of expression. Second, the arguments do not even establish that free expression should be protected as a matter of individual right of the speaker. The arguments are public-good arguments. The case for a right is institutional. Vesting speakers with a right to free expression is an efficient way of protecting freedom of expression in the community, for it enables people whose freedom to express themselves is restricted to invoke the law, rather than relying exclusively on governmental institutions whose motivation to protect freedom of expression is often suspect. Furthermore, giving individuals a legal right to free expression is one way of making the courts guardians of this freedom, and as we shall see there are institutional reasons for doing so. With all that, it still seems to me that the protection of freedom of expression should not in most states rest entirely on the individual right to free expression. It requires additional recognition in public culture and legal institutions.

Needless to say, my arguments do not establish a universal moral right to freedom of expression. Nor do they establish that the value of freedom of expression is universal to all human societies. The core considerations on which the arguments rest apply to most familiar societies. But even they are not universal, and certainly the ramifications of the arguments depend on cultural features which vary from country to country. Finally, while the arguments of this essay do not cover all aspects of the conventional liberal doctrine of free expression, their implications are not confined to freedom of expression. They may have special force in cases of expression, but they can be applied to condemn some forms of moral paternalism, such as forcing people to refrain from sexual activities which are, let us assume, immoral.

All that being said, the arguments do point to the great importance of free expression. They turn on the fundamental need for public validation of one's way of life, and on the need for public recognition as a way of transmitting, preserving, and developing ways of life. In the circumstances of contemporary life these considerations touch the very foundations of pluralistic societies. In this respect, the argument I have adumbrated joins three other arguments to form the foundation of a liberal doctrine of free expression. The other three are: (1) freedom of expression as a prerequisite of a democratic government; (2) freedom of expression as vital for the prosperity of a pluralistic culture; (3) freedom of expression as a crucial element in controlling possible abuses and corruption of power. All four arguments point to the need to make freedom of expression a foundational part of the political and civic culture of pluralistic democracies.

There is reason to favour legal arrangements which provide institutional recognition for the distinction between everyday, short-term politics and those aspects of our political life which protect the basic features of our culture. Freedom of expression belongs to the latter, and should receive the kind of institutional protection given to the fundamentals of our culture. One way of doing so, suited for countries with a strong tradition of the rule of law, and a politically sophisticated and enlightened judiciary, is by assigning primary responsibility for the protection of this freedom to the courts. This is the main justification for its inclusion in entrenched bills of rights. The significance of such entrenchment is that it removes the matter from the short-term pressures of ordinary political decision-making. It places decisions in the hands of courts which enjoy, under the doctrine of the rule of law, independence from everyday political pressures. This does not mean that decisions about freedom of expression are apolitical or undemocratic. They are political through and through, both in their implications and in the reason underlying them, which all too often have to do with striking compromises between conflicting interests. They are also democratic, in that the courts are properly responsive to public opinion. But they are responsive to public opinion, not as expressed in public opinion polls but as expressed in the public culture of their country. That culture may have implications which do not curry favour with the public, implications which remain unpopular for a long time. In respecting those implications the courts avoid degeneration of the public culture, which does, by definition, enjoy public support.

The entrenchment and special protection of legal rights, we thus learn, can be a reflection of the institutionalized arrangements for settling disputes concerning them, and not only a reflection of the importance of their subject-matter.

8

Multiculturalism: A Liberal Perspective

I was grateful for being invited to participate in this conference, and frightened by my acceptance of the invitation. Grateful for the honour—and for the opportunity to explore further the implications of the liberal political theory I have faith in for the way contemporary democracies should treat multiculturalism. Frightened at my own presumption in addressing my thoughts to the condition of a country of whose problems I know little, and to the situation under Dutch law of which I know nothing. I was emboldened by my hosts, who reassured me that by the time my turn comes the conference will be suffused with expert knowledge of Dutch law and the most comprehensive understanding of the social condition of the Netherlands. My job is that of the generalist who can talk about everything without knowing anything. For he is a philosopher dealing with immortal ideas.

I should perhaps explain that I do not really believe that political philosophy provides us with eternally valid theories for the government of all human societies. To my mind political philosophy is time-bound. It is valid—if it is valid at all—for the conditions prevailing here and now. Its conclusions apply also to similar situations. But we cannot set the precise boundaries for their application. There are two principled reasons for this limitation.

First, it is in principle impossible to articulate comprehensively all the relevant moral considerations which we are aware of, and impossible to state in general how much they weigh against each other in situations of conflict. Saying this is to emphasize that moral knowledge is practical in a special sense, i.e. that it is embodied in our practices, and acquired by habituation. We often know what to do when faced with the situation in which action is called for when we could not have known what to do ahead of time. My point is not that there is ineffable moral knowledge. Everything we know can be articulated, can be expressed in words. But it cannot be exhaustively expressed in general abstract formulae. The situation is analogous with that of a person who embarks on a journey to a distant destination.

This essay is an extended version of the talk I gave at the conference on Multiculturalism and the Law, organized by Professor Max Brod in Leiden in Oct. 1992. It retains the conversational style of the original talk. Given the aim to survey a wide range of the problems multiculturalism raises for contemporary liberalism, I indulged in expressing views only sketchily supported by arguments. Some of the missing arguments can be found in *The Morality of Freedom*, and in chs. 5 and 6 above. I am grateful to Dr P. A. Bulloch for trenchant and helpful objections to an earlier version.

Ask him ahead of time to describe the route and he will be unable to do so. Yet as he progresses along the road he recalls at every stage how to proceed at that point. Not everything we know can be exhaustively stated in the abstract. Moral knowledge escapes such formulation, and that means that moral theories are to be taken as mere approximations. Those who apply them inflexibly are fanatics heading for disaster.

The second reason for the fact that political morality is bound to the here and now and lacks universal validity is that there are principled limitations to our ability to conceive how society will develop. The problem is not merely due to the complexity of the social conditions which may prevail in the future, a complexity which defeats our ability to apply our principles to those conditions. The problem extends further. Social situations can change in such a way that the very concepts we employ to understand and analyse them become inapplicable, thus making the principles both of (so-called descriptive) social science and of (so-called) evaluative political morality inapplicable.

I start my reflections with these remarks on the contextuality of political theory for two reasons. First, my reasons for belief in contextuality presuppose value pluralism, which lies at the heart of the problem of multiculturalism. Second, contextuality highlights the complicated relations of contemporary liberalism to its classical ancestry. That relationship is not that of identity. Seventeenth- and eighteenth-century liberalism was, by and large, right for its time and place. Those of us who adhere today to liberal political theories should do so not by adhering to the theories of Locke or Kant but by embracing contemporary theories, valid for our conditions, which descend in spirit from those of their classical forefathers. This is important for a reflection on the importance of community for individual well-being.

The migration of labour familiar since the rise of capitalism, and accelerated to undreamt-of proportions by the combined effect of contemporary mass media and means of communications and of easy transportation, has led to unprecedented levels of communal disintegration and individual alienation. The nineteenth-century bourgeoisie reacted to the migrations from the country to the cities by developing a rich urban culture, a culture of anonymity and bureaucratic impartiality. This is the culture we are all children of, a culture in which people resent charity and insist on entitlements to social services and social benefits financed by strangers whom they never meet, and administered by faceless, rule-applying officials. Ours is a culture in which we feel more comfortable on a beach, in a park, a restaurant, or a concert-hall bustling with strangers, observing them as they observe us. We are more likely to feel uncomfortable and restless on a lonely beach, or in an empty restaurant. We feel at ease in an apartment block served by lifts which keep its residents unseen by each other, and we feel stifled and oppressed in a closely knit local community where everyone knows us, and our history, and where every deviation from our daily routine is noted behind neighbouring curtains and every one of our visitors is closely observed by our neighbours. This way we can choose our friends, and do not have to befriend people just because they are neighbours, nor be subject to their approval and disapproval of our actions and friends.

The advantages of the culture of urban anonymity are many. But it is inadequate to cope with the multiculturalism which started emerging in many countries as a by-product of the decolonization movement, and is gathering pace all the time. The culture of urban anonymity could absorb individual migrants, escaping oppressive or disintegrating societies, and wishing to find their home in a new society. It is tempting to exaggerate and say that it was made for such people, be they internal or external migrants. But this culture cannot adequately cope with the conditions of today. The threatening results of this failure are the development of a subculture of anomie, of accelerating alienation from society and its institutions, and the emergence of a growing underclass.

Hence the development of a third liberal response to multiculturalism. I call it a third approach for two others can be seen as part supplements, part rivals to it.

First was the attitude and policy which I will dub 'toleration'.[1] It consists in letting minorities conduct themselves as they wish without being criminalized, so long as they do not interfere with the culture of the majority, and with the ability of members of the majority to enjoy the life-styles of their culture. To a considerable degree this limitation meant restriction of the use of public spaces and public media by the minority. It also usually means that all activities of a minority are to be financed out of the resources of that community, in addition to its contribution through taxation to the maintenance of the general culture.

Two types of argument are commonly advanced to support toleration. First, principled reasons for restricting the use of coercion. The Harm Principle, for example, prescribes that no one may be coerced except in order to restrain him from causing harm to others or to punish him for causing harm to others. By this principle, conduct of members of minority cultural groups which does not harm others may not be criminalized. Arguments of the second type, commonly relied upon to justify toleration, appeal to considerations of public peace, social harmony, and the legitimation of the system of government, all of which may be jeopardized by the resentment and hostility of minorities which are not allowed to continue with their religious and cultural activities and practices.

---

[1] do not mean to suggest that the concept of toleration cannot be applied to other policies. I have offered a more comprehensive analysis of toleration in *The Morality of Freedom*. Here I am using the term to capture the spirit of one fairly familiar attitude to minorities.

Toleration was eventually supplemented, perhaps even supplanted,[2] by a second liberal policy towards minorities, one based on the assertion of an individual right against discrimination on national, racial, ethnic, or religious grounds, or on grounds of gender or sexual preference. Non-discrimination rights are a natural extension of the classical liberal conception of constitutional civil and political rights. They also fit that strand of liberalism made popular by the writings of Rawls, according to which the principles on which the constitution is based and which are used to justify political action should make no reference to any specific conception of the good life.

Non-discrimination rights go well beyond toleration. They have far-reaching consequences which intrude on and affect the way the majority community leads its own life. Most obviously, it is no longer free to exclude members of the minority from its schools, places of employment, residential neighbourhoods, etc. Usually non-discrimination rights are interpreted to allow each community control over certain exclusive institutions. They also normally tolerate a measure of discrimination in one's private dealings. But under a regime of scrupulous non-discrimination a country's public services, its education, and its economic and political arenas are no longer the preserve of the majority, but common to all its members as individuals.

The third liberal approach to the problem of minorities is the affirmation of multiculturalism. It is advanced as suitable in those societies in which there are several stable cultural communities both wishing and able to perpetuate themselves. It does not apply, for example, to a country which receives many immigrants from diverse cultures, but where those from each culture are few in number or, even if numerous, do not wish to keep their separate identity. Perhaps even their very migration to the host country is an expression of their rejection of the culture or group from which they emigrated. Finally, multiculturalism should not be pursued regarding cultural groups which have lost their ability to perpetuate themselves. This could happen, for instance, where the ossification of their culture and the allure of the surrounding cultures means that the vast majority of their young people wish to assimilate in the majority culture and rebel against their parents' culture.

In what follows I will continue to use 'multiculturalism' ambiguously. On the one hand it is a predicate which indicates a society in which the conditions set out in the previous paragraph obtain. On the other hand it is a policy of saying yes to this situation. For the discussion that follows it is important to distinguish two types of multicultural society. In one the different communities live in the main in separate geographical regions (e.g. the Inuits in Canada and the Scots in Britain). The other type obtains where, even though the communities may be disproportionately concentrated in

---

[2] Arguably, all that toleration guarantees is also protected by non-discrimination rights.

different residential neighbourhoods, there is in the main no geographical separateness. In that case, for the most part the different communities share the same public places and common services, and they mix in workplaces and in leisure facilities. It is this second condition which characterizes societies whose multiculturalism is of relatively recent vintage, resulting from the ever-growing migrations of the modern era. The discussion of this essay should be understood to be focused on the second type, that of multiculturalism without territorial separation.

The policy of multiculturalism differs from that which relies exclusively on non-discrimination rights in rejecting the individualistic bias of the latter. While endorsing non-discrimination rights, multiculturalism emphasizes the importance to political action of two evaluative judgments. First, the belief that individual freedom and prosperity depend on full and unimpeded membership in a respected and flourishing cultural group. Multiculturalism as an evaluative approach is anchored in a belief in the interdependence of individual well-being and the prosperity of the cultural group to which those individuals belong. Second, multiculturalism arises out of a belief in value pluralism, and in particular in the validity of the diverse values embodied in the practices which constitute the diverse and in many ways incompatible values of different societies.

Given those beliefs, multiculturalism requires a political society to recognize the equal standing of all the stable and viable cultural communities existing in that society. This includes the need for multicultural political societies to reconceive themselves. There is no room for talk of a minority problem or of a majority tolerating the minorities. A political society, a state, consists—if it is multicultural—of diverse communities and belongs to none of them. While the relative size of the different communities affects the solutions to conflicts over resources and public spaces among them, none of them should be allowed to see the state as its own, or to think that the others enjoy their standing on sufferance.

The purpose of my remaining discussion is to elaborate and defend this brief description of multiculturalism. I will do so from a liberal perspective. Not everyone in the liberal camp—if I may call it that—will agree to these views. Liberal doubts about multiculturalism stem from three main sources. First, there is the view of liberalism as the bastion of individual freedom, and correspondingly a fear that multiculturalism supports the power of communities to hold on to reluctant members against their will. Second, there is the view of the superiority of the secular, democratic, European culture, and a reluctance to admit equal rights to inferior, oppressive, religious cultures, or ones whose cultural values tend to be limited and less developed. These perceptions feed the fear that flirting with multiculturalism leads liberals to contradict their own fundamental values. Why should liberals give succour to cultures based on the repudiation of liberal values?

Finally, there is the fear that a common culture is the cement of society. Without it society will fall apart. Living in one political society entails a willingness to suffer for the sake of other members of society. The resentment of West Germans, let alone other Europeans, at the prospect of having to make sacrifices to solve the social and economic problems of the eastern part of Germany illustrates that the willingness to make sacrifices is an attitude of mind which is hard to gain. I will first state briefly the liberal case for multiculturalism, and then deal with the three objections.

The brief argument is that denial of multiculturalism in today's Western societies, far from keeping liberal ideals pure, leads to their degeneration into supermarket liberalism. Before I venture a brief explanation, I would like to clarify the spirit permeating my observations. It is not one of utopian hope. It is not one of a vision of the great future to which liberalism holds the key, a future in which the noblest human hopes will come to fruition. It is the spirit of pessimism nourished by perception of conflict as inevitable, and its resolution as less than ideal, regardless of who wins.

II. THE CASE FOR MULTICULTURALISM

When I was invited to the conference my first thought was admiration for the organizers, who are already thinking of the problems of a post-Maastricht Europe. That will, of course, be a multicultural Europe in which the Netherlands will be one minority community striving to protect its standing.

I soon realized that I mistook the problem they had in mind. But it occurred to me that, when one thinks in the Netherlands or in Britain of the right way to deal with cultural groups within our countries, one should always imagine what one would want to happen had the question affected not the Turks, let us say in the Netherlands, or the Bangladeshis in Britain, but the Dutch or the British in Europe. If we always start by applying this procedure and transferring the answer to the case of cultural communities within our countries, subject to the modifications which are really required by the differing circumstances, then we will not go far wrong.

This is in brief my view about multiculturalism. I doubt that what follows improves it. But at least it makes it more explicit. So let me carry on.

Liberalism is more than just a political morality. It is a political morality which arises out of a view of the good of people, a view which emphasizes the value of freedom to individual well-being. Liberalism upholds the value for people of being in charge of their life, charting its course by their own successive choices. Much Liberal thought has been dedicated to exploring the ways in which restrictions on individual choices, be they legal or social, can be removed, and obstacles to choice—due to poverty, lack of education, or other limitations on access to goods—overcome. An aspect of freedom which has fallen into disrepute in some circles used to be known as the difference between freedom and licence. Freedom, said Spinoza, Kant, and others, is conduct in accord with rational laws. Licence is arbitrary choice, in disregard of reason. There is no denying that the slogan that freedom is not licence was often abused, and abused to impose unreasonable restrictions on freedom. I believe, however, that, when correctly understood, this view is right. Moreover, once it is reinstated and its implications are understood, the justification of multiculturalism becomes obvious.

To a considerable degree the claim that freedom is action in accordance with reason is no more than a consequence of the fact that freedom presupposes the availability of options to choose from, and that options—all except the very elementary ones—have an internal structure, an inner logic, and we can exercise our freedom by choosing them only if we comply with their inner reason. A simple illustration will make the point. One cannot play chess by doing what one wants, say, by moving the rook diagonally. One can only play chess by following the rules of chess. Having to do so may look like a limitation of his freedom to a child. But that is the tempting illusion of licence. In fact, complying with the rules of chess and of other options is a precondition of freedom, an inescapable part of its realization.

Of course, games are unlike the practice of medicine or law, the profession of teaching, or the role of parents, spouses, friends, etc. Relative to the options which make up the core of our lives they are simple, relatively one-dimensional, and tend to be governed by relatively explicit rules. The options which make the core of our lives are complex and multidimensional, rely on complex unstated conventions, and allow extensive room for variation and improvisation. One doctor's bedside manner is not like another's. But there are things which every doctor should do, one way or another, and others no doctor may do. And so on.

Freedom depends on options which depend on rules which constitute those options. The next stage in the argument shows that options presuppose a culture. They presuppose shared meanings and common practices. Why so? the child may ask; why must I play chess as it is known to our culture, rather than invent my own game? Indeed, the wise parent will answer, there is nothing to stop you from inventing your own game. But— the philosophically bemused parent will add—this is possible because inventing one's own games is an activity recognized by our culture with its own form and meaning. What you cannot do is invent everything in your life. Why not? the child will persist, as children do. The answer is essentially that we cannot be children all the time. It is impossible to conduct one's life on the basis of explicit and articulated rules to govern all aspects of one's conduct. The density of our activities, their multiplicity of dimensions and aspects make it impossible to consider and decide deliberately on all of them. A lot has to be done, so to speak, automatically. But to fit into a pattern that automatic aspect of behaviour has to be guided, to be directed and channelled into a coherent meaningful whole. Here then is the argument.

The core options which give meaning to our lives—the different occupations we can pursue, the friendships and relationships we can have, the loyalties and commitments which we attract and develop, the cultural, sporting, or other interests we develop—are all dense webs of complex actions and interactions. They are open only to those who master them, but their complexity and the density of their details defy explicit learning or comprehensive articulation. They are available only to those who have or can acquire practical knowledge of them, that is, knowledge embodied in social practices and transmitted by habituation.

So far I have been talking of social practices which constitute options as if they come one by one. The reality is, and practically speaking has to be, different. Social practices are interlaced with each other. Those constituting language are also elements of all others; the practices of parenting and other social relationships intersect. Not only do many people naturally move from one role to another, but even where such transitions are not expected, the different family roles are at least in part defined by analogy and contrast to each other. Similarly with occupations. Our common ways of distinguishing groups of them, such as the professions, clerical jobs, those belonging to trade and commerce, or the caring professions, are each marked by common and overlapping practices. Such conglomerations of interlocking practices which constitute the range of life options open to one who is socialized in them is what cultures are. Small wonder, therefore, that membership in cultural groups is of vital importance to individuals.

Only through being socialized in a culture can one tap the options which give life a meaning. By and large one's cultural membership determines the horizon of one's opportunities, of what one may become, or (if one is older) what one might have been. Little surprise that it is in the interest of every person to be fully integrated in a cultural group. Equally plain is the importance to its members of the prosperity, cultural and material, of their cultural group. Its prosperity contributes to the richness and variety of the opportunities the culture provides access to. This is the first of three ways in which full membership in a cultural group and its prosperity affect one's own prospects in life.

The second is the fact that sameness of culture facilitates social relations, and is a condition of rich and comprehensive personal relationships.[3] One particular relationship is especially sensitive to this point. Erotic attraction, economic or certain raw emotional needs can often help overcome even the greatest cultural gaps. But in one's relations with one's children and with one's parents, a common culture is an essential condition for the tight

---

[3] Please do not understand this point as suggesting that people belonging to two nations, or two social classes, say a Frenchman and a Dutch person, cannot be friends. What I am suggesting is that there is a considerable common cultural background to people from diverse but culturally neighbouring groups.

bonding we expect and desire. A policy which forcibly detaches children from the culture of their parents not only undermines the stability of society by undermining people's ability to sustain long-term intimate relations, it also threatens one of the deepest desires of most parents, the desire to understand their children, share their world, and remain close to them.

The third way in which being a member of a prosperous cultural community affects individual well-being takes us to a further dimension not yet considered. For most people, membership in their cultural group is a major determinant of their sense of who they are; it provides a strong focus of identification; it contributes to what we have come to call their sense of their own identity. This is not really surprising: given that one's culture sets the horizon of one's opportunities, it is natural to think of it as constituting one's identity. I am what I am, but equally I am what I can become or could have been. To understand a person we need to know not just what he is but how he came to be what he is, i.e. to understand what he might have been and why he is some of those things and not others. In this way one's culture constitutes (contributes to) one's identity. Therefore slighting one's culture, persecuting it, holding it up for ridicule, slighting its value, etc., affect members of that group. Such conducts hurts them and offends their dignity. This is particularly offensive if it has the imprimatur of one's state or of the majority of official culture of one's country.

So this is the case for multiculturalism. It is a case which recognizes that cultural groups are not susceptible to reductive analysis in terms of individual actions or states of mind. Cultural, and other, groups have a life of their own. But their moral claim to respect and to prosperity rests entirely on their vital importance to the prosperity of individual human beings. This case is a liberal case, for it emphasizes the role of cultures as a precondition for, and a factor which gives shape and content to, individual freedom. Given that dependence of individual freedom and well-being on unimpeded membership in a respected and prosperous cultural group, there is little wonder that multiculturalism emerges as a central element in any decent liberal political programme for societies inhabited by a number of viable cultural groups.[4]

III. THE DIALECTICS OF PLURALISM

The Unstable Tensions of Competitive Pluralism

One of the difficulties in making multiculturalism politically acceptable stems from the enmity between members of different cultural groups, especially

---

[4] The preceding argument summarizes and highlights some aspects of the argument of *The Morality of Freedom*, and of ch. 6 above.

when they inhabit one and the same country. Such enmity is quite universal. When relations between two communities are at their most amicable they are accompanied by disapproval of the other culture, be it for its decadence, its vulgarity, lack of sense of humour, its treatment of women, or something else. It would be comforting to think that such enmity is sometimes justified, and that in the other cases it is due to ignorance and bigotry which can be eradicated. I believe, however, that this optimism is unwarranted, and that conflict is endemic to multiculturalism.

It is, in fact, endemic to value pluralism in all its forms. Belief in value pluralism is the view that many different activities and forms of life which are incompatible are valuable. Two values are incompatible if they cannot be realized or pursued to the fullest degree in a single life. In this sense value pluralism is a familiar mundane phenomenon. One cannot be both a sprinter and a long-distance runner, both valuable activities, for they require the development of different physical abilities, and also tend to suit different psychological types. Philosophers do not make good generals and generals do not make good philosophers. One cannot pursue both the contemplative and the active life, and so on and so forth.

The plurality and mutual exclusivity of valuable activities and forms or styles of life is a commonplace. It becomes philosophically significant the moment one rejects a still pervasive belief in the reducibility of all values to one value which serves as a common denominator to the multiplicity of valuable ways of life. In our day and age, with its sometimes creeping, sometimes explicit, subjectivism, the reduction is most commonly to the value of feeling happy, or having one's desires satisfied. Value pluralism is the doctrine which denies that such a reduction is possible. It takes the plurality of valuable activities and ways of life to be ultimate and ineliminable. This radically changes our understanding of pluralism. On a reductive-monistic view, when one trades the pleasures (and anxieties) of a family life for a career as a sailor one is getting, or hoping to get, the same thing one is giving up, be it happiness, pleasure, desire-satisfaction, or something else. So long as one plans correctly and succeeds in carrying out one's plans there is no loss of any kind. One gives up the lesser pleasure one would derive from family life for the greater pleasure of life at sea. If value pluralism is correct, this view is totally wrong. What one loses is of a different kind from what one gains. Even in success there is a loss, and quite commonly there is no meaning to the judgment that one gains more than one loses. When one was faced with valuable options and successfully chose one of them, then one simply chose one way of life rather than another, both being good and not susceptible to comparison of degree.

Theoretically the plurality of valuable ways of life asserted by pluralism need not manifest itself in the same society. We may value the different cultures of Classical Greece without its opportunities and ways of life being options for us. But typically in our day and age pluralism exists within every society, indeed within every culture. That generates conflict between competing and incompatible activities and ways of life. When valuable alternatives we do not pursue are remote and unavailable, they do not threaten our commitment to and confidence in the values manifested in our own life. But when they are available to us and pursued by others in our vicinity they tend to be felt as a threat. I chose A over B, but was I right? Skills and character traits cherished by my way of life are a handicap for those pursuing one or another of its alternatives. I value long contemplation and patient examination; these are the qualities I require to succeed in my chosen course. Their life requires impetuosity, swift responses, and decisive action. People whose life requires these excellences despise the slow contemplative types as indecisive. They almost have to. To succeed in their chosen way they have to be committed to it, and to believe that the virtues it requires should be cultivated at the expense of those which are incompatible with them. They therefore cannot regard those others as virtues for them. By the same token, it is only natural that they will value in others what they choose to emulate themselves. Hence a variety of dismissive attitudes to the virtues of the competing ways of life. People who chose my way of life are in a similar position, only with contrary commitments.

Conflict is endemic. Of course, pluralists can step back from their personal commitments and appreciate in the abstract the value of other ways of life and their attendant virtues. But this acknowledgement coexists with, and cannot replace, the feelings of rejection and dismissiveness towards what one knows is in itself valuable. Tension is an inevitable concomitant of accepting the truth of value pluralism. And it is a tension without stability, without a definite resting-point of reconciliation of the two perspectives, the one recognizing the validity of competing values and the one hostile to them. There is no point of equilibrium, no single balance which is correct and could prevail to bring the two perspectives together. One is forever moving from one to the other from time to time.

The Transforming Effect of Multiculturalism

The inescapable tension between acceptance and rivalry between competing valuable ways of life, which forever threatens to destabilize, is common to all forms of value pluralism, where plural incompatible options coexist in the same society. It exists in homogeneous as well as in multicultural societies. Admittedly, the latter tend to generate a heightened awareness of the tension because they polarize it along cultural–ethnic divides. But it is equally acute in societies with strong class divisions, for example. The next form of dialectics of pluralism I want to focus on is special to multiculturalism.

Multiculturalism is often a result of a transition from life in a relatively homogeneous society to life in a multicultural one. It is a result of conquest of a territory and subjugating its indigenous population, or of large-scale migrations such as the migration of East African Indians to Britain, or Turks to the Netherlands. Sometimes it arises as a consequence of political union of people from neighbouring, but culturally distinct, countries, as in the case of Czechoslovakia, or Great Britain. In all these cases the constituent cultures face great pressures to change in their new multicultural societies as a result of their interaction with the other groups in the society. Naturally they wish to resist the pressure for change. The desire to resist change is particularly felt by small communities when the change is perceived to be the impact of coexistence with much larger groups whose cultures dominate the atmosphere in the public arena.

The view that I advocate may be expected to be sympathetic to such conservationist trends. After all, the whole idea of multiculturalism is to encourage communities to sustain their own diverse cultures. But while this is so, and while it is of the essence of multiculturalism that different communities should enjoy their fair share of opportunities and resources to maintain their cultures and develop them in their own way, multiculturalism as I see it is not inherently opposed to change, not even to change which is induced by coexistence with other cultural groups. On the contrary, as we will see in what follows, multiculturalism insists that members of the different groups in a society should be aware of the different cultures in their society, and learn to appreciate their strengths and respect them. This in itself leads to inevitable developments in the constituent cultures, especially those which have developed in relative isolation and ignorance of other cultures.

Furthermore, multiculturalism calls on all the constituent communities in a society to tolerate each other. Some of these communities have a culture which is itself intolerant, or whose toleration of others is inadequate. Such cultures will face a great pressure for change in a multicultural society.

Finally, as we will see, multiculturalism insists on a right of exit, that is, the right of each individual to abandon his cultural group. Many cultures do all they can to stop their members from drifting away, or leaving their communities. On this front again they will find themselves under pressure to change in a liberal multicultural society.[5]

This tension in multiculturalism, between a policy of protecting a plurality of cultures and recognizing and sometimes encouraging change in them, may surprise some. But it should not. Liberal multiculturalism does not arise out of conservative nostalgia for some pure exotic cultures. It is not a policy of conserving, fossilizing some cultures in their pristine state. Nor is it a

---

[5] At this point it is particularly important to recall that this discussion is confined to multicultural societies where the different communities are not geographically segregated.

policy fostering variety for its own sake. It recognizes that change is inevitable in today's world. It recognizes that fossilized cultures cannot serve their members well in contemporary societies, with their generally fast rate of social and economic change. Liberal multiculturalism stems from a concern for the well-being of the members of society. That well-being presupposes, as we saw, respect for one's cultural group and its prosperity. But none of this is opposed to change.

Change is resisted most when it is seen as a result of hostility of the majority, or of the dominant culture, to minority cultures. It is also resisted when it arouses fear that one's culture will disappear altogether by being diluted and then assimilated by others. It is to be hoped that, in a country where multiculturalism is practised by the government and accepted by the population, the first fear will be generally felt to be unfounded. The second is less easily laid to rest. Furthermore, it has to be admitted that liberal multiculturalism is not opposed in principle to the assimilation of one cultural group by others. In some countries some of the constituent cultures may lose their vitality and be gradually absorbed by others. So long as the process is not coerced, does not arise out of lack of respect for people and their communities, and is gradual, there is nothing wrong in it. The dying of cultures is as much part of normal life as the birth of new ones. But the process is much slower and rarer than those who trumpet their fears of the death of their cultures proclaim. What they most commonly have in mind is resistance to change, masquerading, innocently or otherwise, as a fight for survival.

In these remarks I display again the non-utopian character of the liberal multiculturalism which I advocate. It is non-utopian in rejecting any ideal which wishes to arrest the course of time, the pressures for change, some moment of perfection. Indeed, it refuses to have any truck with notions of perfection. Furthermore, it is non-utopian in seeing as endemic the continuation of conflict, between cultures and, within every one of them, between those favouring change and those resisting it.

Do Not Take Cultures at Their Own Estimation

Finally, the earlier discussion has already brought into the open the most fundamental dialectical element in liberal multiculturalism. While it respects a variety of cultures, it refuses to take them at their own estimation. It has its own reasons for respecting cultures, reasons like those expressed in the first part of this essay. These are likely to vary from the reasons provided in most cultures for their value. For example, religious cultures will justify themselves in theological terms. The justification of those very same cultures in the eyes of liberal multiculturalism is humanistic, not theological. In particular multiculturalism urges respect for cultures which are not themselves liberal cultures—very few are. As we shall see, it does so while imposing liberal protection of individual freedom on those cultures. This in itself brings it into conflict with the cultures it urges governments to respect. The conflict is inevitable because liberal multiculturalism recognizes and respects those cultures because and to the extent that they serve true values. Since its respect of cultures is conditional and granted from a point of view outside many of them, there is little surprise that it finds itself in uneasy alliance with supporters of those cultures, sometimes joining them in a common front while at others turning against them to impose ideals of toleration and mutual respect, or to protect the members of those very cultures against oppression by their own group.[6]

IV. OBJECTIONS TO MULTICULTURALISM

Protecting Inferior Cultures?

It is time to return to the objections to multiculturalism mentioned at the outset. The one I can do least justice to is that which says: 'Some cultures are inferior to others. By encouraging their prosperity one is acting against the interests of their members. To serve their interests best one should discourage those cultures and encourage rapid assimilation of their members in our superior culture.' I believe that very often judgments about the inferiority of other cultures are based on bigotry and ignorance, and that in truth many cultures simply cannot be compared in those terms. Each of them is valuable. Each of them can be improved in a way consistent with its own spirit and out of its own resources. But none of them can be judged superior to the others. But these views can only be justified by plunging into a discussion of the foundations of ethics, which we are mercifully absolved from on this occasion. Instead I will address three subsidiary points.

First, some people fear, consciously or unconsciously, that if our culture is not superior to others we are not entitled to love it as much as we do. If it is not the best, they feel, then it is irrational to be so dedicated to its preservation and cultivation. Moreover, if it is not the best then our ignorance of other cultures is inexcusable. We should, if they are all good and none is superior, be equally knowledgeable and interested in all of them.

It is not my wish to discourage people from taking an interest in other cultures, and, as will be discussed below, one should be acquainted with the cultures which inhabit one's country—and this is so whether or not they are the equal of one's own. That requirement is a result of the duties of citizenship, and has nothing to do with the merits of any culture. Putting

---

[6] The Rushdie affair in Britain exemplified the dialectics of liberal toleration in its most acute form. See on this issue ch. 6 above.

these considerations on one side for the moment, let it be said that one's devotion to and love of one's culture in no way depends on believing it to be better than others. It is rational and valid whether or not it is better than others, so long as one loves one's own culture for what is truly good in it.

Compare one's attitude to one's culture with one's love of one's children. We rightly ridicule parents who feel that their devotion to their children requires holding them to be little geniuses, much better than other children. One loves one's children because they are one's children.[7] The same is true with all personal attachments. The people one loves need not be, nor need they be thought to be, better than others to make one's love rational. So long as one loves them for the right reasons, and admires in them their virtues rather than their vices, one's love and friendship are sound.

Nor need one feel obliged to learn and become acquainted with all valuable cultures. To do so is the desire of some people and it is a worthy desire. But it is not one which all people must share. There is no reason to know of or share in everything that is valuable. This too is an aspect of value pluralism. According to it there is plenty valuable in the world and we have no reason to pursue, nor any real possibility of pursuing, all of it.

Second, I would not wish to deny that some cultures, or aspects of some cultures, are unacceptable, and should not benefit from the positive attitude to a plurality of cultures which multiculturalism stands for. There are various dimensions by which cultures or aspects of them can be compared and judged. I will mention only one whose importance is obvious. Some cultures repress groups of either their own members or of outsiders. Slave cultures, racially discriminatory cultures, and homophobic cultures are obvious examples. Such cultures may be supported only to the degree that it is possible to neutralize their oppressive aspects, or compensate for them (for example, by providing convenient exit from the oppressive community to members of the discriminated-against group).

The test of oppression should be carefully considered. One needs to distinguish between it and occasional failure of socialization leaving an individual member of a cultural group alienated from his culture, and unable to find fulfilment within it. Occasional failures of socialization are endemic to all cultures. Oppression differs from them in being a result of a structural feature of that culture which systematically frustrates the ability of people, or groups of people, to fulfill or give expression to an important aspect of their nature within that society. Not all people will be affected by oppressive aspects of society. Many will not belong to the oppressed group, where the oppression is based on racial, religious, or some such grounds. Others will not have such great need to express the repressed aspect of

---

[7] And I do not mean genetically one's own. I mean that they are children one has brought up and is attached to.

their personality, or they will find ways of making do with substitutes or alternatives. In all sexually oppressive societies, such as homophobic ones, many people learn to do without much sex. In societies which repress the spirit of free inquiry or of imaginative creativity, many find that their need to engage in them is limited and can be suppressed without too much difficulty. Adjustability is never complete, and repression invariably leads to much suffering. But even those who adjust suffer. Their lives and person-alities become stunted, and do not reach full expression. When this is a result of a systematic feature of their culture, the fault is with the culture. In serious cases it may justify suppressing the oppressive cultures. In others it will call for reform, and for mitigating actions in the multicultural society of which they are a part.

Third, and finally, even when cultures are at fault, and certainly when they are inferior without being oppressive, we have reason for supportive toleration. People bred and socialized within such cultures often knew no better, and had no choice. Moreover, by the time they are grown up their ability to transplant themselves and become a part of another culture is limited. The limits differ from case to case and are a matter of degree. It is easier to acquire a home in a new cultural community when it does not differ too much from one's original cultural group, and when one has self-generated motives to do so. It is more difficult when the distance between the cultures is great and when the reason for the transition is externally imposed. Given that even oppressive cultures can give people quite a lot, it follows that one should be particularly wary of organized campaigns of assimilation and discrimination against inferior and even oppressive cul-tures. For many of their members they provide them with all that they can have, as it may be too late for them to make a transition.

In saying this I am not going back on my earlier view that oppression should not be tolerated. I am merely urging restraint and consideration in thinking of the means by which it is to be countered.

More on Oppressive and Intolerant Cultures

Oppression of members of the cultural group was the second objection introduced at the outset. We have already considered it, and conceded its force, because repression and repressive oppression are among the criteria affecting the relative merits of various cultures. It is worth adding here that existence in a multicultural society often makes cultural groups more repres-sive than they would be were they to exist in relative isolation. The insecurity of existence in multicultural societies, especially where there is real or per-ceived discrimination against the group, tends to encourage conservative elements in cultural groups, resisting all change in their culture which is equated with its dilution to the point of extinction. They also tend to increase pressure on members of the group to turn inward and reduce their contact with the external world, as an inward outlook is perceived as the only guarantee against defection from the group. Such conservative and repressive pressures can lead to bitter intergenerational conflicts.

Furthermore, the significance of various social practices may change by being brought into the new context of a multicultural society. The status of women is a case in point. Set aside the various cultures which repressed women. Probably all cultures known to us, even those which did not repress women, distinguished between men and women in that a large array of social relationships, occupations, leisure activities, educational and cultural opportunities, and the like were gender-specific. Provided such separation does not carry with it the implication of an inferior status, and provided the opportunities available to either men or women are adequate for their full development and self-expression, there is nothing wrong with such gender-sensitive cultures so long as they succeed in socializing the young to a willing acceptance of their ways. But once such a cultural group is transplanted to a different environment in which the dominant cultures accept gender determination of opportunities only in exceptional cases, the transplanted group is transformed into an oppressive one. In the new environment it is bound to fail in socializing all its young to accept its ways and reject the ideas prevalent in the general culture. In contemporary broadly liberal societies, the prevailing notions of gender non-discrimination and the debate about feminism is bound to filter across the cultural barriers. It will affect the self-understanding of the young, and not only the young. It will inform their perceptions of their own native cultural practices. When this happens, the meaning of the gender-based practices of the culture changes. It is understood by many of its own members as consigning women to an inferior status. The protestations that that is a perversion of the meaning of those practices are to no avail. The true meaning of social practices is their social meaning. Thus existence of a cultural group in a new multicultural environment can lead to a change in the meaning of some of its practices and make them oppressive.

A positive attitude to multiculturalism can be thought to be committed to lending support to the conservative strands in various communities, at least when they become the dominant voice of the community. But to my mind this is a mistake. As was remarked above, cultures are bound to undergo changes as a result of existing within a multicultural society. The fact that members of cultural groups intermix to a considerable degree[8] is bound to have its impact on the different groups in the society. The preservation of their culture is justified only in terms of its contribution to the well-being

---

[8] Remember again that societies in which cultural groups enjoy considerable geographical and economic separation have been excluded from consideration here.

of people. This requires an adjustment of each of the cultural groups to the conditions of a relatively harmonious coexistence within one political society.

As will be emphasized below, peaceful coexistence and participation in one political society require becoming acquainted with the customs of all the people and ethnic groups in one's country. This creates opportunities, sometimes it creates the temptation, to drift out of one's native cultural group and into another. Attempts to prevent people from having these opportunities undermine the possibility of mutual peaceful existence.

Moreover, the opportunity to exit from a group is a vital protection for those members of it who are repressed by its culture. Given that most cultures known to us are repressive to a lesser or greater degree, the opportunity of exit is of vital importance as a counter to the worry that multiculturalism encourages repressive cultures to perpetuate their ways. I have already indicated that political societies are entitled, indeed required, to discourage repressive practices in their constituent cultural groups. The groups should be encouraged to change their repressive practices. But this is a very slow process. Opportunities of exit should be encouraged as a safeguard, however imperfect, for members who cannot develop and find adequate avenues for self-expression within their native culture.

Solidarity

The final objection to multiculturalism was that it undermines social solidarity, which is invariably built on the possession of a common culture. Without a deep feeling of solidarity, a political society will disintegrate into quarrelling factions. Solidarity is required for people to feel concerned about each other's fortunes, and to be willing to make sacrifices for other people. Without such willingness the possibility of a peaceful political society disappears. There is a lot of truth in the argument. Civic solidarity is essential to the existence of a well-ordered political society. Where the argument is too quick is in asserting that a common culture is essential to solidarity, and that multiculturalism is inconsistent with the existence of a common culture.

Let me take the last point. The truth is that multiculturalism, while endorsing the perpetuation of several cultural groups in a single political society, also requires the existence of a common culture in which the different coexisting cultures are embedded. This is a direct result of the fact that it speaks for a society in which different cultural groups coexist in relative harmony, sharing in the same political regime. First, coexistence calls for the cultivation of mutual toleration and respect. This affects in a major way first and foremost the education of the young in all the constituent groups in the society. All of them will enjoy education in the cultural traditions of their communities. But all of them will also be educated to understand

and respect the traditions of the other groups in the society. This will also apply to the majority group, where such a group exists. Its young will learn the traditions of minority groups in the society. Cultivation of mutual respect and toleration, of knowledge of the history and traditions of one's country with all its communities, will provide one element of a common culture.

A second element will result from the fact that members of all communities will interact in the same economic environment. They will tap the same job market, the same market for services and for goods. Some communities may be over-represented in some sectors of the market, as either consumers of goods and services or their producers and providers. But by and large they will inhabit the same economy. This means that they will have to possess the same mathematical, literary, and other skills required for effective participation in the economy.

Finally, members of all cultural groups will belong to the same political society. They will all be educated and placed to enjoy roughly equal access to the sources of political power and to decision-making positions. They will have to acquire a common political language, and common conventions of conduct, to be able to compete effectively for resources and to be able to protect their group as well as individual interests in a shared political arena. A common political culture will be the third major component of a common culture that will be generated in liberal multicultural societies.

The emergence of such a common culture is still to an extent an aspiration, for while elements of it are already evident in some multicultural societies, none has reached the level of development of a common culture that is evident in some culturally homogeneous societies. Whether the sort of common culture I have outlined is sufficient to form a basis for the social solidarity required to secure the cohesion and stability of modern political societies remains, therefore, a moot point. But I think that it may serve this purpose successfully, and should be given a chance to do so.

It remains the case that, while the liberal common culture of pluralistic societies remains to be developed, a swift social change towards multiculturalism may well severely test the existing bonds of solidarity in a society, and threaten disintegration or a backlash of rabid nationalism. This, while it does not pose an objection of principle to liberal multiculturalism, requires great caution in the method and speed with which multicultural policies are implemented.

V. FINAL WORDS

Multiculturalism, in the sense of the existence within the same political society of a number of sizeable cultural groups wishing and in principle able to maintain their distinct identity, is with us to stay. In so far as one can discern the trend of historical events, it is likely to grow in size and importance. Liberal multiculturalism, as I called it, as a normative principle affirms that, in the circumstances of contemporary industrialist or post-industrialist societies, a political attitude of fostering and encouraging the prosperity, cultural and material, of cultural groups within a society, and respecting their identity, is justified by considerations of freedom and human dignity. These considerations call on governments to take action which goes beyond that required by policies of toleration and non-discrimination. While incorporating policies of non-discrimination, liberal multiculturalism transcends the individualistic approach which they tend to incorporate, and recognizes the importance of unimpeded membership in a respected an flourishing cultural group for individual well-being.

This doctrine has far-reaching ramifications. It calls on us to reconceive society, changing its self-image. We should learn to think of our societies as consisting not of a majority and minorities, but of a plurality of cultural groups. Naturally such developments take a long period to come to fruition, and they cannot be secured through government action alone, as they require a widespread change in attitude. The current attitude of the population at large, and the speed with which it accepts the precepts of multiculturalism, set limits on the practicability and good sense of proceeding with various concrete policies to advance and implement liberal multiculturalism. But we must think long-term to set short-term policies within a sensible context. The size of cultural groups and their viability is another variable affecting the way various concrete measures should be pursued. Where publicly funded pro-grammes are called for, relative size is inevitably a consideration. So is viabil-ity. There is no point in trying to prop up by public action cultures which have lost their vitality, which have become moribund and whose communities—usually their young members—drift away from them. Of course multicultural-ism changes the prospects of survival for cultures it supports. That is its aim. But it recognizes that deliberate public policies can serve a useful purpose only if they find response in the population they are meant to serve. They can serve to facilitate developments desired by the population, but not to force cultural activities down the throats of an indifferent population.

The more concrete policies, which become appropriate gradually, as developments justify, include measures like the following.

1. The young of all cultural groups should be educated, if their parents so desire, in the culture of their groups. But all of them should also be educated to be familiar with the history and traditions of all the cultures in the country, and an attitude of respect for them should be cultivated.

2. The different customs and practices of the different groups should, within the limits of toleration we have explored earlier, be recognized in law and by all public bodies in society, as well as by private companies and

organizations which serve the public, be it as large employers, providers of services, or otherwise. At the moment petty intolerance is rife in many countries. In Britain people still have to fight to be allowed to wear traditional dress to school or to work, to give one example.

3. It is crucial to break the link between poverty, undereducation, and ethnicity. So long as certain ethnic groups are so overwhelmingly over-represented among the poor, ill-educated, unskilled, and semi-skilled workers, the possibilities of cultivating respect for their cultural identity, even the possibility of members of the group being able to have self-respect and to feel pride in their cultures, are greatly undermined.

4. There should be a generous policy of public support for autonomous cultural institutions, such as communal charities, voluntary organizations, libraries, museums, theatre, dance, musical or other artistic groups. Here (as in education) the policy calls for allocation of public resources. In the competition for them the size of the groups concerned is an important factor. It works in two ways. By and large it favours the larger groups with a more committed membership. But it also calls for disproportionate support for small groups which are strong enough to pass the viability test. Given that the overheads are significant, the per capita cost of support for small viable cultural groups is greater than for large ones.

5. Public space, streets, squares, parks, shopping arcades, etc. (as well as air space on television) should accommodate all the cultural groups. Where they differ in their aesthetic sense, in their preferences for colours, patterns, smells, music, noise, and speed, the solution may involve dividing some public spaces between them, as often happens without direction in ethnic neighbourhoods, while preserving others as common to all.

Of course, all such measures are designed to lead to relatively harmonious coexistence of non-oppressive and tolerant communities. They therefore have their limits. But it is important not to use false standards as tests of the limits of toleration. The fact that the Turkish government does not tolerate certain practices of the Kurds, let us say, in Turkey, is no reason why the Kurds from Turkey should not be allowed to continue with the practice when they settle in Europe. Similarly, the fact that tolerating certain practices of immigrant communities will lead to a change in the character of some neighbourhoods or public spaces in one's country is no reason for suppressing them. The limits of toleration are in denying communities the right to repress their own members, in discouraging intolerant attitudes to outsiders, in insisting on making exit from the community a viable option for its members. Beyond that, liberal multiculturalism will also require all groups to allow their members access to adequate opportunities for self-expression and participation in the economic life of the country, and the cultivation of the attitudes and skills required for effective participation in the political culture of the community.

The combined effect of such policies is that liberal multiculturalism leads not to the abandonment of a common culture, but to the emergence of a common culture which is respectful towards all the groups of the country, and hospitable to their prosperity.

PART II
BETWEEN LAW AND MORALITY

9

The Problem about the Nature of Law

It is characteristic of philosophical disciplines that among their major concerns is the clarification and delimitation of their own subject matter. The theory of knowledge attempts to clarify the nature of knowledge, the philosophy of logic examines the definition of logic, moral philosophy reflects on the nature and boundaries of morality, and so on. Since the identity of such disciplines depends on the identity of their subject matter, preoccupation with their own self-identity is typical of many philosophical inquiries. Philosophy of law is no exception. It too is partly engaged in an investigation of the nature of law and of the boundary of the legal, and thus it is perennially reflecting upon its own nature.[1]

The persistence of such self-reflexive questioning is testimony to the importance of formulating precise questions and of choosing one's starting-point. The inability of philosophers to agree on a common answer is partly due to differences in their perception of the nature of the problems involved in the question. Such differences reflect themselves in differing unstated assumptions and unconscious starting-points chosen in answering the philosophical questions concerned. Here I shall describe and comment upon three current approaches to the question of the nature of law. To explain them and justify my comments I shall have to venture some remarks towards a theory concerning the nature of law, but these will be, in the present context, both incomplete and incidental to the main task of clarifying the problem about the nature of law.

I. THE LINGUISTIC APPROACH

Both among the classical exponents of legal philosophy[2] and among its modern practitioners[3] one finds philosophers who took the inquiry

First published in *Contemporary Philosophy: A New Survey*, 3 (1983) and in the *University of Western Ontario Law Review*, 21 (1983).

[1] H. L. A. Hart has repeatedly commented on this feature of legal philosophy. See *Definition and Theory in Jurisprudence* (Oxford: Oxford Univ. Press, 1953) and *The Concept of Law* (Oxford: Oxford Univ. Press, 1961), ch. 1.

[2] See e.g. John Austin's treatment of the question in *The Province of Jurisprudence Determined* (1832).

[3] For reasonably sophisticated discussions of the linguistic approach see G. Williams, 'The Controversy Concerning the Word "Law" ', in P. Laslett (ed.), *Philosophy, Politics and Society*, 1st ser. (Oxford: Blackwell, 1967), and R. Wolheim, 'The Nature of Law', *Political Studies* (1954), 128.

concerning the nature of law to be an attempt to define the meaning of the word 'law'. The linguistic approach was boosted by the anti-essentialist spirit of much of modern analytical philosophy, and in particular by its tendency in its early years to regard all philosophical questions as linguistic questions.

Recently philosophers have grown dissatisfied with the linguistic approach, and I introduce it first only to dismiss it by surveying some of the flaws and defects associated with it. The first and most common response to the linguistic approach is that philosophers are not lexicographers. This, though true, is obviously incomplete. What then are philosophers of law after? The answer will be found in our examination of the other two approaches to be discussed below. Yet even while allowing that the final verdict on the linguistic approach must await the emergence of a viable alternative, we can examine the internal weakness of the linguistic approach itself.

Traditionally, those who adopted the linguistic approach concentrated on the word 'law'. They encountered the overwhelming problem that that word is used in a multiplicity of non-legal contexts. We have laws of nature and scientific laws, laws of God and of thought, of logic and of language, etc. Clearly the explanation of 'law' has to account for its use in all these contexts, and equally clearly any explanation which is so wide and general can be of very little use to legal philosophers.

Only on one assumption can the explanation of 'law' hope to provide the answer to the legal philosopher's inquiry into the nature of law. That assumption is that the use of 'law' in all contexts but one is analogical or metaphorical or in some other way parasitical on its core meaning as displayed in its use in one type of context, and that that core meaning is the one the legal philosopher has at the centre of his inquiry. Unfortunately, the assumption is mistaken. Its implausibility is best seen by examining the most thorough and systematic attempt to provide an analysis of 'law' based on this assumption, that proposed by John Austin in *The Province of Jurisprudence Determined*. For the failure of Austin's analysis does not depend on his espousal of a general command model of law. Quite independently of the shortcomings of the command theory, Austin was doubly wrong. First, there is no reason to regard discourse about purely theoretical laws, like laws of nature, as parasitical extensions of discourse about purely practical laws, such as legal rules. Second, when considering purely practical laws there seems no reason to give legal rules and their special features preferred status compared with that of, say, moral laws.

The fate of the linguistic approach is not yet sealed. The explanation of the meaning of the word 'law' has little to do with legal philosophy,[4] but

---

[4] Lon Fuller (see esp. *The Morality of Law* (New Haven, Conn.: Yale Univ. Press, 1964; rev. edn. 1969) represents an interesting line. He is totally uninterested in the special features of legal systems. His theory is best seen as an inquiry into some putative features of practical laws

it is possible that the meaning of some other terms is closely associated with the concerns of legal philosophers. The most promising candidates are 'legal' and 'legally'. They are not used in theoretical contexts, and in practical contexts seem to be excluded from moral and all other usages apart from those which directly concern legal philosophy.

'Legally' is, *inter alia*, a sentence-forming operator on sentences. The claim that its semantics explains the nature of law amounts to saying that 'legally *p*' is the general form of all legal statements. To examine the claim one should consider the five types of sentence standardly used to make legal statements.

First, some other legal operators such as 'It is the law that . . .' and 'According to law . . .' are roughly synonomous with 'Legally . . .'.[5] The main other legal operator, 'There is a law that . . .' though not synonomous with 'legally . . .', can be explained by its use. 'There is a law that *p*' is logically equivalent to 'Legally, there is a rule that *p*'.

Second, 'legal' can be defined in terms of 'legally'. '*x* has a legal duty' (or 'a legal right' or 'legal authority', etc.) is logically equivalent to 'Legally, *x* has a duty' (or 'a right' or 'authority', etc.). Similarly 'This is a legal transaction' is logically equivalent to 'Legally this is a transaction', and so on.

Third, purely legal predicates are predicates such as 'a mortgage', 'a share', 'a copyright', 'fee simple' which, we intuitively judge, are used only to make legal statements. Any sentence containing a purely legal predicate should, therefore, count as a legal sentence even though it does not display the form 'Legally *p*'. However, any sentence '*p*' containing a purely legal predicate is logically equivalent to 'legally *p*'. For example, 'He has the copyright' is logically equivalent to 'legally he has the copyright'.

Fourth, semi-legal predicates are predicates which are normally used to make legal statements but which can also be used in other contexts. 'Ownership', 'marriage', 'contract' are semi-legal. 'They make a contract', 'They are married', 'He owns the house', 'The house is his' are normally used to make what we intuitively judge to be legal statements. But my son is right in saying that his books are his, even if in law they are mine, and Marian Evans could quite sensibly regard herself as G. H. Lewes's wife, not merely consider that she deserves to be. In contrast, if it is not the case that

---

generally, whether legal or not. In following this line he may have been influenced, consciously or unconsciously, by the linguistic approach focusing on 'law'. If the philosophy of law is the study of 'law', then why bother with any finer demarcations? It should instead study all kinds of practical law.

[5] Note that 'The rule is legally valid' is logically equivalent to 'Legally, the rule is valid', In equating 'legally . . .', 'According to law . . .' and 'It is the law that . . .' I do not mean to deny that there are stylistic and conversational differences between them which make one or the other of them more appropriate than the others in different contexts. Being here concerned merely with their semantic properties, I shall disregard such differences, and use 'legally' even in contexts where one of the others will be conversationally more apposite.

according to law one has the copyright then it is not true that one has the copyright, however much one deserves to have it. Given these facts about semi-legal predicates, it is clear that the condition specified above respecting legal predicates does not apply to them. Sentences containing semi-legal predicates are *not* logically equivalent to the sentences resulting from them by prefixing 'legally' to them.

At the same time it is true that any legal statement made by the use of a sentence '*p*' containing a semi-legal predicate is logically equivalent to the statement standardly made by the use of 'Legally *p*'.

Fifth, legal statements are often made by the use of ordinary deontic sentences where the content of the sentence and the context of its utterance indicate that it is used to make a legal statement (e.g. 'It is prohibited to park here'). Here again, all one can say is that, when such a deontic sentence '*p*' is used to make a legal statement, the statement thus made is logically equivalent to the one standardly made by 'Legally *p*'.

Consideration of the first three points may suggest that all sentences standardly used to make legal statements are, or are logically equivalent to, sentences of the form 'Legally *p*'. The fourth and fifth points, however, disprove any such suggestion. It is true that all the foregoing observations strongly suggest that all legal statements can be expressed by sentences having the form 'legally *p*', yet this judgment is based on an intuitive notion of 'legal statement' which is not itself explained by reference to 'legally'. One may therefore conclude that any theory of the nature of law must observe the Linguistic Condition:

LC   All legal statements are statable by the use of sentences of the form 'Legally *p*'.

But one must at the same time reject the claim that the theory of the nature of law is simply an investigation of the meaning of 'legally'.

This claim is also defeated by an independent argument. The argument above shows that not all the sentences frequently used to make what we intuitively judge to be legal statements can be analysed in terms of 'legally'. It can also be shown that not all the statements standardly made by the use of sentences of the form 'Legally *p*' are intuively judged to be legal statements in the sense relevant to legal philosophy. 'Legally *p*'-sentences can be used to make statements of religious law or of international law or, indeed, of the law of some other kinds of powerful social association, but the credentials of such statements as legal statements in the relevant sense (whatever that may be) is not a question which philosophers will allow to be settled by the appropriateness of the use of 'legally' in such cases. To say this is essentially no more than to reassert that philosophy is not lexicography.

II. THE LAWYER'S PERSPECTIVE

The upshot of the discussion so far is that linguistic considerations impose a constraint on the acceptability of legal theories but that the inquiry into the nature of law is not a study of the meaning of any term or family of terms. What, then, is the object of such an inquiry? Many legal philosophers start from an unstated basic intuition:

BI   The law has to do with those considerations which it is appropriate for courts to rely upon in justifying their decisions.

I have left the formulation vague because it is meant to capture a common basic intuition. Many legal philosophers accepting the basic intuition as an unconscious starting-point regard their task as refining it to yield a philosophical theory of the nature of law which is in fact an elaboration of the basic intuition.

It may be thought, and the thought may have influenced various philosophers, that the basic intuition is justified by the linguistic approach (or perhaps even by LC). It may be thought, in other words, that 'legal rules' and 'legal facts' mean the same as 'the considerations that it is appropriate for courts to rely upon'. But this cannot be accepted on the strength of linguistic usage. The case of constitutional conventions in English law provides a good counterexample.[6] In England constitutional conventions constitute a major part of the English constitution, regulating as they do the relations between the organs of government. An example is the convention that the monarch is not entitled to refuse royal assent to a bill properly passed by Parliament. According to most standard theories of English constitutional law, one defining feature of conventions is that they are not considerations on which courts can base decisions. If this is so, then according to the basic intuition they are not legal rules. This indeed was Dicey's view, and it is shared by many other legal theorists. But this conclusion cannot be supported by linguistic usage, since many native English speakers would not hesitate to dub various conventions 'legal rules'. Having rejected the linguistic approach above, it will be clear that I am not presenting the case of constitutional convention as a refutation of the basic intuition, but merely as a refutation of the suggestion that it is necessitated by the linguistic approach. In fact it is at odds with facts about linguistic usage, and although it is compatible with LC it is by no means justified or required by it.

---

[6]   The classical discussion of constitutional conventions is in A. V. Dicey, *Introduction to the Study of the Law of the Constitution* (London: Macmillan, 1885). For an interesting recent discussion see G. Marshall and G. C. Moodie, *Some Problems of the Constitution*, 4th edn. (London: Hutchinson, 1967), esp. ch. 2.

I shall assume, and will say a little below to justify the assumption, that BI is true. This still leaves unexplained the question why it should have been taken by so many as an unexamined assumption which serves, mostly unconsciously, to define their own subject and thus gives shape to their theories. If I am right in suggesting that many tended to regard BI as justified by linguistic usage, this provides a partial explanation for the willingness to adopt BI without further questioning. But since this belief is so evidently ill-founded there must be additional reasons, if only to explain why legal philosophers were so myopic in their perception of linguistic usage. The explanation is simple. Most theorists tend to be by education and profession lawyers, and their audience often consists primarily of law students. Quite naturally and imperceptibly they adopted the lawyer's perspective on the law. Lawyers' activities are dominated by litigation in court, actual or potential. They not only conduct litigation in the courts. They draft documents, conclude legal transactions, advise clients, etc., always with an eye to the likely outcome of possible litigation in which the validity of the document or transaction or the legality of the client's action may be called into question. From the lawyer's point of view, the law does indeed consist of nothing but considerations appropriate for courts to rely upon.[7]

The lawyer's perspective consists of the unquestioning acceptance of BI as the starting-point for legal philosophy and as determining its subject-matter. But perhaps BI need not be accepted unquestioningly. Perhaps it can be justified by more fundamental assumptions. Therefore, accepting BI does not commit one to accepting the lawyer's perspective.

Kelsen can be taken as an instructive example of a philosopher who adopts the lawyer's perspective without being aware of this. That if he did so he was unaware of this would probably be generally conceded. Indeed, most of Kelsen's interpreters either did not notice or underplayed the point. This is quite natural. Kelsen himself says he is following a combination of the linguistic approach and the institutional approach:

Any attempt to define a concept must take for its starting-point the common usage of the word denoting the concept in question. In defining the concept of law we must begin by examining the following questions: Do the social phenomena generally called law present a common characteristic distinguishing them from other social phenomena of a similar kind? And is this characteristic of such importance . . . that it may be made the basis of a concept serviceable for the cognition of social life?[8]

---

[7] My 'sociological' generalizations should be regarded as crude approximations to the truth; e.g. there are specialist constitutional lawyers who advise on the application of constitutional conventions. But such exceptions to the general rule do not affect the thrust of the argument.

[8] H. Kelsen, *General Theory of Law and State* (New York: Russell and Russell, 1945), 4, and see further 5, 14 f.

But in fact Kelsen is merely paying lip-service to what he regards as a proper methodological procedure. He never seriously examined any linguistic evidence and he assumed dogmatically, and in the face of all the glaring evidence to the contrary, that law is the only social institution using sanctions (other than divine sanctions).[9]

The clue to the methodological approach he was in fact pursuing is in his insistence that legel theory must be a pure theory. He regarded it as doubly pure. It is pure of all moral argument and it is pure of all sociological facts. We shall return to the purity from morality below. For the time being let us concentrate on purity from social facts. By this Kelsen indicates his belief that the analysis of legal concepts and the determination of the content of any legal system depends in no way at all on the effects the law has on the society or the economy, nor does it involve examination of people's motivation in obeying the law or in breaking it. The picture of law dictated by the methodology of the Pure Theory is of law in the books, of an analysis of law using as the raw material only law reports and statute-books. Now the only possible justification for legal studies to ignore the social realities behind the law is a conception of law and legal studies which concentrates on the lawyer's perspective.

On the assumption that Kelsen embraces the lawyer's perspective, it is easier to understand why Kelsen was tempted by two of his best-known doctrines. If the law consists of considerations appropriate for courts to rely upon, it is tempting to regard all laws as addressed to courts. Furthermore, if one thinks of every law as determining the result of a (class of) potential disputes, it is tempting to regard every law as stipulating a remedy (Kelsen says that every law stipulates a sanction, but his notion of a sanction is wide enough to cover all remedies excepting declaratory judgments). After all, every litigation is about the applicability or non-applicability of certain remedies. I am not suggesting that these doctrines are plausible nor that they are necessitated by the lawyer's perspective, merely that they are made comprehensible on the assumption that Kelsen endorsed this perspective.

The basic intuition says that law has to do with reasons for courts' decisions. It does not say that *all* the considerations that courts may rely upon are legal considerations. Nor does it reject such a view. Kelsen himself, however, rejected it. He regarded law as consisting of enacted law, case law, and customary law, and he acknowledged that there are other considerations on which courts may rely. These are extralegal considerations. So far as the law is concerned, the courts are left with discretion when the

---

[9] It is not my claim that law does not resort to sanctions, merely that sanctions play a major role in informal social norms and in non-legal organizations as well. See further my *Practical Reason and Norms*. 154–62; H. Oberdiek, 'The Role of Sanctions and Coercion in Understanding Law and Legal Systems', *American Journal of Jurisprudence* (1977).

law runs out and other considerations come into play. Kelsen's reasons for such a position have nothing to do with BI. They derive from the other aspect of the purity of legal theory: its purity from moral considerations.

For Kelsen it is self-evident that legal theory is free of all moral considerations. Given his essentially emotivist theory of ethics, this is a prerequisite for legal theory to be 'scientific'. But this argument, quite apart from its dependence on a particular view of the nature of morality, is clearly misconceived. The task of legal theory is clearly to study law. If law is such that it cannot be studied scientifically, surely the conclusion must be that legal theory is not 'a science'. One can even accept the conclusion that, if the law does involve moral considerations and therefore cannot be studied scientifically, then legal theory will study only those aspects of the law which can be studied scientifically. What one cannot conclude is that, since only morally neutral considerations can be studied scientifically, therefore the law is such that its study does not involve moral considerations.

Since Kelsen has no good reason to insist that legal theory should be free from moral considerations, he has no good reason to delimit the law in the way he does. He is aware that courts do rely on moral considerations. He regards enacted law, case law, and customary law as exhausting the content of the law, even though he is aware that courts quite appropriately rely on moral considerations not incorporated in legislation, custom, or precedent. I remarked above that BI does not require that such considerations be taken as law. But since BI postulates that at least some of the considerations appropriate for courts are legal, it imposes a burden on anyone who claims that some such considerations are not legal to explain what difference between them and legal considerations makes them non-legal and why. Kelsen has no such explanation. The logic of his own doctrines can be used against him: if enacted and case law can be represented as instructions for courts to apply sanctions in certain circumstances, so can those moral considerations which it is appropriate for courts to rely upon. If all the considerations which guide courts in applying sanctions are legal considerations, why are not moral considerations which do so part of the law, even if they are not incorporated in legislation, precedent, or custom?

Legal theory in America has always been dominated by the thought that law is just what the courts do. American theorists not only embraced the lawyer's perspective but jumped to the conclusion that all the considerations which courts may use are legal. The most sophisticated and accomplished representative of this tradition is R. M. Dworkin who, in a series of articles during the last fifteen years, developed a theory of law out of a theory of adjudication.[10] In fact he developed a theory of adjudication and

---

[10] Most of Dworkin's articles are collected in his *Taking Rights Seriously* (London: Duckworth, 1977). See also his 'No Right Answer' in P. M. S. Hacker and J. Raz (eds.), *Law, Morality, and Society* (Oxford: Oxford Univ. Press, 1977).

regards it willy-nilly and without further argument as a theory of law. Dworkin points out that judges must use moral considerations in addition to enacted and case law. He argues that the moral considerations which they should use are those which belong to a moral theory justifying the enacted and case law binding on them, i.e., that moral theory which constitutes the ideology of the law.[11] One may agree or disagree with this theory of adjudication. Either way one has to ask a separate question: which of all these considerations constitute the law? Dworkin, however, does not pause to ask this question. He unquestioningly assumes, without ever stating the assumption or providing any reason for it, that all the considerations which courts legitimately use are legal considerations.

Dworkin's identification of a theory of adjudication with a theory of law looks, however, very natural from the lawyer's perspective. Lawyers' activities, as we saw, revolve, directly or indirectly, round litigation in the courts. From the lawyer's perspective all the considerations pertaining to judicial reasoning are equally relevant. A lawyer has to concern himself not only with legislation and precedent but also with other considerations relevant to judicial reasoning. A lawyer, therefore, fortified in virtue of BI with the knowledge that the law has to do with judicial reasoning, finds no reason from the perspective of his own professional preoccupations to stop short of identifying the theory of law with a theory of adjudication.

III THE INSTITUTIONAL APPROACH

I have suggested that from the lawyer's perspective in the disagreement between Kelsen and Dworkin the latter must be declared winner. But we have also seen that neither the basic intuition BI nor the linguistic constraint LC contributes to this verdict. They are compatible with both Kelsen's and Dworkin's theories of law.[12] It is the lawyer's perspective which delivers the verdict. Yet there is something inherently implausible in adopting the lawyer's perspective as one's fundamental methodological stance. There is no doubting the importance of the legal profession and of the judicial system in society. It is entirely appropriate to make them the object of a separate study and to regard legal theory as that study. It is, however, unreasonable to study such institutions exclusively from the lawyer's

---

[11] Cf. 'Hard Cases' in *Taking Rights Seriously*. See also my explanation and criticism in 'Prof. Dworkin's Theory of Rights', *Political Studies* (1978).

[12] It is arguable that further linguistic evidence may provide support for one or the other theory. I believe, however, that the linguistic evidence in itself, without the backing of theoretical considerations, is likely to remain indecisive. See my *The Authority of Law* (Oxford: Oxford Univ. Press, 1979), ch. 3.

perspective. Their importance in society results from their interaction with other social institutions and their centrality in the wider context of society. The law is of interest to students of society generally, and legal philosophy, especially when it inquires into the nature of law, must stand back from the lawyer's perspective, not in order to disregard it, but in order to examine lawyers and courts in their location in the wider perspective of social organization and political institutions generally.

The institutional approach has had many representatives in the history of legal philosophy. Its influence on English legal philosophy is due principally to the influence of John Austin (who combined it with the linguistic approach). He, following Bentham, first explains the nature of the political system and then proceeds to explain the nature of law by placing it within the political system. H. L. A. Hart is a prominent practitioner of this approach today.[13] In his discussion of the emergence of secondary rules and of the minimum content of natural law, as well as in his discussion of the separateness of states, he examines the law as involving the emergence of new kinds of political institution, both legislative and judicial, against the context of social and political needs.[14]

The institutional approach, subjected to the restriction of LC, seems much superior to its two rivals. The linguistic approach, though useful as imposing restrictions and suggesting insights, is bound to yield inconclusive results. The lawyer's perspective, though based on a sound intuition, is arbitrary as an ultimate starting-point.

The institutional approach strives to present an analysis of a central political institution which, since its analysis conforms to LC, should be accepted as the analysis of law. From its point of view BI is a justifiable consequence, and the disagreement indicated above between Kelsen and Dworkin is resolved in favour of Kelsen. In order to illustrate this last point, I shall deviate from the purely methodological reflections of these pages to indicate in broad outline some of the features of a theory based on the institutional approach, features relevant to the issue between Kelsen and Dworkin.[15]

From the institutional point of view the basic intuition is the starting-point for further critical reflection. It is entirely plausible to regard the notion of

---

[13] See his *The Concept of Law*; and 'Kelsen's Doctrine of the Unity of Law' in Howard E. Kiefer and Milton K. Munitz (eds.), *Ethics and Social Justice* (New York State Univ. NY Press 1970).

[14] See generally on Hart's theory of law P. M. S. Hacker, 'Hart's Philosophy of Law' in Hacker and Raz (eds.), *Law, Morality, and Society*. For critical discussion of relevant aspects of Hart's theory see J. M. Finnis, 'Revolution and Continuity of Law' in A. W. B. Simpson (ed.) *Oxford Essays in Jurisprudence* (Oxford: Oxford Univ. Press, 1973); Dworkin, *Taking Rights Seriously*, ch. 2; Raz, *The Authority of Law*, chs. 5, 9.

[15] I have further discussed these ideas in *Practical Reason and Norms*, ch. 4, and in *The Authority of Law*, ch. 3.

law as bound up with that of a judicial system, but what are the essential characteristics of a court and why are they important to the political organization of society? Three features characterize courts of law:

1. They deal with disputes with the aim of resolving them.
2. They issue authoritative rulings which decide these disputes.
3. In their activities they are bound to be guided, at least partly, by positivist authoritative considerations.

The first point does not imply that courts of law do not engage in other activities than settling disputes. They often administer estates and bankruptcies, conduct the affairs of certain categories of people, etc. The first point simply asserts that, however many other activities lawcourts engage in, they are courts because, among other things, they strive to settle disputes. This point, when juxtaposed with BI, can be read as saying that it is as courts, i.e. as settling disputes, that they are crucial to our understanding of law. But I am not at all confident that this is so. It seems more plausible that what is crucial for the existence of law are the other two features of lawcourts (features which can be and in many legal systems are shared by other, though perhaps less important, institutions). However, I shall not argue this point here.

The second limb of the above definition of a court of law, i.e. that it issues authoritative rulings, may seem self-evident. A few words of explanation concerning the sense of 'authoritative' rulings may nevertheless be called for. First, let me make clear that both here and below I am using 'authoritative' as short for 'claimed to be authoritative', i.e. by the court or person concerned or the organization to which they belong or which they represent. There is no suggestion that the claim is morally warranted. A court's opinion on the merits of a dispute is authoritative and binding in a way in which my opinion is not, not because I have no opinion on such disputes (which I sometimes have), not because my opinion is not an expert's opinion (which it may be), nor again because courts never err (they sometimes do). The reason is that the court's very utterance of its opinion is claimed by it to be a reason for following it, whereas my utterance of my opinion is not claimed to be a reason for following it. At best it amounts to informing the persons concerned of the existence of reasons which are themselves quite independent of my utterance.

The need for the third limb of the definition, that courts of law be, at least partly, guided by authoritative positivist considerations, is clearly seen by contemplating its negation. There are forms of arbitration in which the arbitrator is instructed merely to judge the merits of the case and to issue a just judgment, without being bound to follow any authoritative positivist standard. We can imagine a purely moral adjudication taking the same form. Positivist considerations are those the existence and content of which

can be ascertained without resort to moral argument.[16] Statutes and precedents are positivist considerations whereas the moral principles of justice
are not. A moral adjudicator will rely in his deliberation on the existence of
positivistic standards, but he is not bound to regard them as authoritative.
But one does not have a court of law unless it is bound to take as authoritative some positivist standards such as custom, legislation, or precedent.

So much we can learn from our intuitive understanding of the nature of
courts of law as a political institution. How can we use this understanding
as a base on which to anchor a complete doctrine on the nature of law? The
clue is in the emergence of authoritative positivist considerations as crucial
to our conception of courts of law which, in accordance with BI, provide
the institutional key to the nature of law. We can formulate an additional
constraint on an adequate doctrine of the nature of law.

AP   Law consists only of authoritative positivist considerations.

An analogy with personal action will help to explain the point. It is possible
to distinguish between a deliberative and an executive stage in a person's
attitude to the prospect of a certain action. The deliberative stage, in which
the person considers the merits of alternative courses of action, terminates
when he reaches a conclusion as to what he should do. It is followed by
an executive stage if and when he forms an intention to perform a certain
act. In the executive stage he is set to act if and when the occasion arrives.
When an intention is formed deliberation will terminate, though it may
be restarted and the intention suspended or even revoked. Sometimes
the intention will harden into a decision, indicating reluctance to reopen
deliberation. In any case, the existence of an intention indicates that the
question what to do has been settled and that the person is ready to act.

Not every action is preceded by both stages or by one of them. Sometimes one just acts without prior deliberation or intention. Sometimes one
or the other stage exists without the other, and very often when both exist
the boundaries between them are extremely fuzzy. Yet the general distinction is of great importance: just as the deliberative stage is necessary for
people to be able to form considered views on the merits of alternative
courses of action, so the executive stage is necessary to enable people to
plan ahead, to determine themselves to act in advance of the occasion for
the action. For large organizations a distinction between deliberative and
executive stages is essential to secure planned and efficient institutional
action. In institutions such division often includes a division of responsibility between different persons. Some will be responsible for deliberating and deciding, others for executing those decisions. In general, social

---

[16] Note that it is not required that the standard will be capable of being applied without
recourse to moral argument. A statute instructing the courts to act as if they are moral legislators is a positivistic standard.

co-operation, either negative (people refraining from hurting each other) or positive, can be viewed as a form of social action decided upon by some social institutions and carried out by individuals. Some societies allow individuals a share in deciding on their schemes of co-operative action and other plans. But even they have to distinguish between the deliberative stage, where individuals contribute to the decision-making process, and the executive stage, where perhaps those very same individuals are bound to observe those decisions.

In the deliberative stage the question what is to be done is open to argument based on all sorts of considerations. Reasons of a moral character will often dominate. Once the matter has been decided to the satisfaction of the social institution involved, its appropriate organ will formulate 'the social intention', i.e. it issues an authoritative instruction. Since this instruction represents the conclusion of the deliberative stage and belongs itself to the executive stage, it will be identifiable without resort to further moral argument. Those belong by definition to the deliberative stage. Only positivist considerations can belong to the executive stage. Furthermore, executive considerations are authoritatively binding. Those subject to them are not normally allowed, by the social institution concerned, to challenge or query their validity or conclusiveness. To do so is to reopen the deliberative process, and unless there are limitations on the freedom with which this can be done the considerations cannot be regarded as executive. So long as argument is free the executive stage has not been reached.

Executive considerations are, therefore, authoritative positivist considerations. This brings us back to the definition of courts of law. It included the fact that they are guided in part by authoritative positivist considerations, and that they issue authoritative rulings (which, being issued by the action of members of the court, are themselves authoritative positivist rulings). This suggests that the law consists of the authoritative positivist considerations binding on the courts and belongs essentially to the executive stage of the political institution (the state, the church, etc.) of which it is a part. The resulting picture has the courts applying both legal (i.e. authoritative positivist) and non-legal considerations. They rely both on executive and deliberative reasons, yet the law belongs to the first kind only.

The two-stage picture presented above may make one surprised with a doctrine by which the courts are guided by considerations belonging to both stages. But the surprise is due merely to the oversimplification in the representation of the two stages above. Consider again the case of the individual. A person may stagger the process of decision-making, moving towards the 'pure' executive stage in several separate steps. First, for example, he decides to act on the balance of economic considerations and to discount considerations of prestige. Then he decides that one of the half-dozen alternatives open to him is to be rejected, since at least one of the others is better supported by economic considerations, etc. The law often proceeds in a similar way. On many issues statutes represent but the first step towards a 'pure' executive stage. They may have to be supplemented by delegated legislation and perhaps even by further administrative action. Sometimes litigation reaches the courts in matters which have not reached a 'pure' executive stage in the matter at issue and the courts have to resort to non-legal, i.e. non-executive, considerations to resolve the dispute. Even this picture is oversimplified. It suggests, for example, that the survival of a deliberative stage down to the adjudicative level is always to be regretted. This is far from the truth. It is often advantageous for a person while form-ing a general intention in advance (I'll stay the night in Nottingham) to leave the precise details to the last moment (I'll choose a hotel when there). The same kind of reason suggests that often, especially when dealing with very broad categories, it is better not to fix too inflexibly the precise details in advance. It is better to settle for executive reasons, i.e. laws, which fix the framework only and leave the courts room to apply deliberative reasons within that framework.

Be that as it may, our concern here is not to comment on various law-making policies but on the nature of law. Our analysis has yielded only one element: the law consists of authoritative positivist considerations enforce-able by courts. Clearly, not all the considerations which meet this condition are part of the law. Other conditions have to be added. However, the fact that law consists of considerations enforceable by courts (as required by BI) which are authoritative and positivist is suggested by the definition of a legal court, and is supported by the common distinction between the two functions of the courts as law-makers and law-appliers which roughly coincides with the distinction between cases where the law is unsettled and those where it is not. It is further supported by the fact that any analysis of law based in part on this feature focuses on a distinction of paramount importance to social organization: the distinction between the deliberative and the executive stages.

IV. IS LEGAL PHILOSOPHY VALUE-FREE?

The analysis outlined above is intended to show how, at the level of highest philosophical abstraction, the doctrine of the nature of law can and should be concerned with explaining law within the wider context of social and political institutions. It shows how the lawyers' perspective is an arbitrary starting-point for legal philosophy, disregarding the wider political context in which the law is moored. It also shows how, from this point of view, the inclination to identify the theory of law with a theory of adjudication and legal considerations with all the considerations appropriate for courts is based on a short-sighted doctrine overlooking the connection of law with the distinction between executive and deliberative considerations.

It may be thought that the arguments of the last section support legal positivism against natural law. But this is not so. It is true that positivists do generally regard legal considerations as authoritative and positivist.[17] But they are not the only ones. The theories of several prominent natural lawyers conform with all the features contributing to a doctrine of the nature of law mentioned above.[18] There still remains the general question about the moral character of the doctrine of the nature of law. Is it a moral doctrine based on moral considerations or not?

Clearly, a theory of adjudication is a moral theory. It concerns all the considerations affecting reasoning in the courts, both legal and non-legal. In pronouncing which extralegal considerations have force and how much weight is due to them, it is engaged in moral argument. When the doctrine of the nature of law is identified with a theory of adjudication, it becomes itself a moral theory. The question what is the law of England is identified with the question which considerations should courts rely upon. This is clearly a question of political morality, at least inasmuch as it concerns the content of one or the other of the extralegal considerations. For example, the question whether an English court today is entitled to declare a ministerial regulation null and void on the ground that it violates human rights is clearly a moral and political question. It is a question one may expect an answer to from a complete theory of adjudication which specifies all the considerations judges should use and their force. If a theory of adjudication is a theory of law, if all the considerations to be used by courts are legal considerations, the theory of the nature of law is a moral theory.

A different conclusion emerges if one follows the arguments presented above based on the institutional approach. Since law belongs to the executive stage, it can be identified without resort to moral arguments, which belong by definition to the deliberative stage. The doctrine of the nature of law yields a test for identifying law the use of which requires no resort to moral or any other evaluative argument. But it does not follow that one can defend the doctrine of the nature of law itself without using evaluative (though not necessarily moral) arguments. Its justification is tied to an evaluative judgment about the relative importance of various features of social organizations, and these reflect our moral and intellectual interests and concerns.

---

[17] Though see for doubts as to whether Hart conforms with this condition: P. Soper, 'Legal Theory and the Obligation of a Judge: The Hart–Dworkin Dispute', *Michigan Law Review,* 75 (1977), 473, and D. Lyons 'Principles, Positivism and Legal Theory: Dworkin, *Taking Rights Seriously*', *Yale Law Journal* (1977), 415.

[18] See e.g. Fuller, *The Morality of Law,* and J. M. Finnis, *Natural Law and Natural Rights* (Oxford: Oxford Univ. Press, 1980).

10

Authority, Law, and Morality

H. L. A. Hart is heir and torch-bearer of a great tradition in the philosophy of law which is realist and unromantic in outlook. It regards the existence and content of the law as a matter of social fact whose connection with moral or any other values is contingent and precarious. His analysis of the concept of law is part of the enterprise of demythologizing the law, of instilling rational critical attitudes to it. Right from his inaugural lecture in Oxford[1] he was anxious to dispel the philosophical mist which he found in both legal culture and legal theory. In recent years he has shown time and again how much the rejection of the moralizing myths which accumulated around the law is central to his whole outlook. His essays on 'Bentham and the Demystification of the Law' and on 'The Nightmare and the Noble Dream'[2] showed him to be consciously sharing the Benthamite sense of the excessive veneration in which the law is held in common-law countries, and its deleterious moral consequences. His fear that in recent years legal theory has lurched back in that direction, and his view that a major part of its role is to lay the conceptual foundation for a cool and potentially critical assessment of the law are evident.

This attitude strikes at the age-old question of the relation between morality and law. In particular it concerns the question whether it is ever the case that a rule is a rule of law because it is morally binding, and whether a rule can ever fail to be legally binding on the ground that it is morally unacceptable. As so often in philosophy, a large part of the answer to this question consists in rejecting it as simplistic and misleading, and substituting more complex questions concerning the relation between moral worth and legal validity. Let us, however, keep the simplistic question in mind; it helps to launch us on our inquiry.

Three theses with clear implications concerning the relation between law and morality have been defended in recent years. They can be briefly, if somewhat roughly, stated as follows:

The sources thesis: All law is source-based.

The incorporation thesis: All law is either source-based or entailed by source-based law.

First published in *The Monist*, 68/3 (1985).

[1] *Definition and Theory in Jurisprudence* (Oxford: Oxford Univ. Press, 1953).

[2] See his *Essays on Bentham* (Oxford: Oxford Univ. Press, 1982) ch. 1; *Essays in Jurisprudence and Philosophy* (Oxford: Oxford Univ. Press, 1983).

The coherence thesis: The law consists of source-based law together with the morally soundest justification of source-based law.[3]

A law is source-based if its existence and content can be identified by reference to social facts alone, without resort to any evaluative argument. All three theses give source-based law a special role in the identification of law. But whereas the parsimonious sources thesis holds that there is nothing more to law than source-based law, the other two allow that the law can be enriched by non-source-based laws in different ways. Indeed, the coherence thesis insists that every legal system necessarily includes such laws.

The main purpose of this essay is to defend the sources thesis against some common misunderstandings[4] and to provide one reason for preferring it to the other two. The argument turns on the nature of authority, which is the subject of the first section. In the second section some of the implications of this analysis are shown to be relevant to our understanding of the law. Their relation with the three theses is then examined. The connection between law and authority is used to criticize Dworkin's support of the coherence thesis, as well as the incorporation thesis advocated by Hart and others. The rejection of these views leads to the endorsement of the sources thesis. The essay concludes with some observations concerning the relations between legal theory, law, and morality. Throughout, the argument is exploratory rather than conclusive.

I. AUTHORITY AND JUSTIFICATION

Authority in general can be divided into legitimate and *de facto* authority. The latter either claims to be legitimate or is believed to be so, and is effective in imposing its will on many over whom it claims authority, perhaps because its claim to legitimacy is recognized by many of its subjects. But it does not necessarily possess legitimacy. Legitimate authority is either practical or theoretical (or both). The directives of a person or institution with practical authority are reasons for action for their subjects, whereas the advice of a theoretical authority is a reason for belief for those regarding whom that person or institution has authority. Though the views here expressed apply to theoretical authorities as well, unless otherwise indicated

---

[3] These formulations of the theses aim to preserve simplicity and comparability, and pay the price of crudeness. The coherence thesis is distorted most. Its advocates may insist that only a holistically conceived soundest theory enables us to interpret accurately many, perhaps even all, of the sources of law and to identify which law is based on them. This point will be taken up below.

[4] I have defended the thesis before. See *The Authority of Law*, ch. 3, *The Concept of a Legal System*, 2nd edn. Ch. 8 above.

I shall use 'authority' to refer to legitimate practical authority. Since our interest is in the law we will be primarily concerned with political authorities. But I shall make no attempt to characterize the special features of those, as opposed to practical authorities in general or legal features of those, as opposed to practical authorities in general or legal authorities in particular.

The distinction between reasons for action and reasons for belief may be sufficient to distinguish between practical and theoretical authorities, but it is inadequate to distinguish between authorities and other people. Anyone's sincere assertion can be a reason for belief, and anyone's request can be a reason for action. What distinguishes authoritative directives is their special peremptory status. One is tempted to say that they are marked by their authoritativeness. This peremptory character has other led people to say that in accepting the authority of another one is surrendering one's judgment to him, that the acceptance of authority is the denial of one's moral automony, and so on. Some have seen in these alleged features of authority a good deal of what often justifies submitting to authority. Many more derived from such reflections prove that acceptance of authority is wrong, or even inconsistent with one's status as a moral agent. Elsewhere[5] I have developed a conception of authority which accounts for its peremptory force while explaining the conditions under which it may be right to accept authority. Let me briefly repeat the main tenets of this conception of authority. Its details and the arguments in its support cannot be explored here.

Consider the case of two people who refer a dispute to an arbitrator. He has authority to settle the dispute, for they agreed to abide by his decision. Two features stand out. First, the arbitrator's decision is for the disputants a reason for action. They ought to do as he says because he says so. But this reason is related to the other reasons which apply to the case. It is not just another reason to be added to the others, a reason to stand alongside the others when one reckons which way is better supported by reason. The arbitrator's decision is meant to be based on the other reasons, to sum them up and to reflect their outcome. He has reason to act so that his decision will reflect the reasons which apply to the litigants. I shall call reasons of the kind which apply to the arbitrator dependent reasons. I shall also refer to his decision as a dependent reason for the litigants. Notice that in this second sense a dependent reason is not one which does in fact reflect the balance of reasons on which it is based. It is one which is meant to, i.e. which should, do so.

This leads directly to the second distinguishing feature of the example. The arbitrator's decision is also meant to replace the reasons on which it depends. In agreeing to obey his decision, the disputants agreed to follow his judgment of the balance of reasons rather than their own. Henceforth

---

[5] 'Authority and Justification', *Philosophy and Public Affairs*, 14 (1985), 3.

his decision will settle for them what to do. Lawyers say that the original reasons merge into the decision of the arbitrator or the judgment of a court, which, if binding, becomes *res judicata*. This means that the original cause of action can no longer be relied upon for any purpose. I shall call a reason which displaces others a pre-emptive reason.

It is not that the arbitrator's word is an absolute reason which has to be obeyed come what may. It can be challenged and justifiably disobeyed in certain circumstances. If, for example, the arbitrator was bribed, was drunk while considering the case, or if new evidence of great importance unexpectedly turns up, each party may ignore the decision. The point is that reasons that could have been relied upon to justify action before his decision cannot be relied upon once the decision is given. Note that there is no reason for anyone to restrain their thoughts or their reflections on the reasons which apply to the case, nor are they necessarily debarred from criticizing the arbitrator for having ignored certain reasons or for having been mistaken about their significance. It is merely action for some of these reasons which is excluded.

The two features, dependence and pre-emptiveness, are intimately connected. Because the arbitrator is meant to decide on the basis of certain reasons, the disputants are excluded from later relying on them. They handed over to him the task of evaluating those reasons. If they do not then reject those reasons as possible bases for their own action, they defeat the very point and purpose of the arbitration. The only proper way to acknowledge the arbitrator's authority is to take it to be a reason for action which replaces the reasons on the basis of which he was meant to decide.

The crucial question is whether the arbitrator's is a typical authority, or whether the two features picked out above are peculiar to it, and perhaps a few others, but are not characteristic of authorities in general. It might be thought, for example, that the arbitrator is typical of adjudicative authorities, and that what might be called legislative authorities differ from them in precisely these respects. Adjudicative authorities, one might say, are precisely those in which the role of the authority is to judge what are the reasons which apply to its subjects and decide accordingly, i.e. their decisions are merely meant to declare what ought to be done in any case. A legislative authority, on the other hand, is one whose job is to create new reasons for its subjects, i.e. reasons which are new not merely in the sense of replacing other reasons on which they depend but in not purporting to replace any reasons at all. If we understand 'legislative' and 'adjudicative' broadly, so the objection continues, all practical authorities belong to at least one of these kinds. It will be conceded, of course, that legislative authorities act for reasons. But theirs are reasons which apply to them and which do not depend on, i.e. are not meant to reflect, reasons which apply to their subjects.

The apparent attractiveness of the above distinction is, however, mis-guided. Consider an Act of Parliament imposing on parents a duty to maintain their young children. Parents have such a duty independently of this Act, and only because they have it is the Act justified. Further argument is required to show that the same features are present in all practical authorities. Instead, let me summarize my conception of authority in three theses:

> The dependence thesis: All authoritative directives should be based, among other factors, on reasons which apply to the subjects of those directives and which bear on the circumstances covered by the direc-tives. Such reasons I shall call dependent reasons.[6]

> The normal justification thesis: The normal and primary way to establish that a person should be acknowledged to have authority over another person involves showing that the alleged subject is likely better to com-ply with reasons which apply to him (other than the alleged authoritative directives) if he accepts the directives of the alleged authority as author-itatively binding, and tries to follow them, than if he tries to follow the reasons which apply to him directly.[7]

> The pre-emption thesis: The fact that an authority requires performance of an action is a reason for its performance which is not to be added to all other relevant reasons when assessing what to do, but should replace some of them.

The first and the last theses generalize the features we noted in the arbitra-tion example. The normal justification thesis replaces the agreement be-tween the litigants which was the basis of the arbitrator's authority. Agreement or consent to accept authority is binding, for the most part, only if condi-tions rather like those of the normal justification thesis obtain.

The first two theses articulate what I shall call the service conception of authority. They regard authorities as *mediating* between people and the right reasons which apply to them, so that the authority judges and pronounces what they ought to do according to right reason. The people on their part take their cue from the authority whose pronouncements replace for them the force of the dependent reasons. This last implication of the service conception is made explicit in the pre-emption thesis. The mediating role

---

[6] The non-dependent reasons authorities may act for are those which make them better able to satisfy the normal justification thesis, i.e. reasons which make their directives reflect more closely the dependent reasons. Because of the circumstances of their action, a direct attempt to pursue all the dependent reasons and no other is likely to backfire. All bureaucracies have to adopt rules which deviate from the underlying reasons in detail in order better to conform with them overall.

[7] The normal justification thesis specifies only the reasons for recognizing an authority. It says nothing on the reasons against doing so. These exist to various degrees depending on the nature of the case. They determine how strong the case for recognizing the authority has to be. It must be sufficient to overcome the reasons to the contrary.

of authority cannot be carried out if its subjects do not guide their actions by its instructions instead of by the reasons on which they are supposed to depend. No blind obedience to authority is here implied. Acceptance of authority has to be justified, and this normally means meeting the conditions set in the justification thesis. This brings into play the dependent reasons, for only if the authority's compliance with them is likely to be better than that of its subjects is its claim to legitimacy justified. At the level of general justification the pre-empted reasons have an important role to play. But once that level has been passed and we are concerned with particular action, dependent reasons are replaced by authoritative directives. To count both as independent reasons is to be guilty of double counting.

This is the insight which the surrender of judgment metaphor seeks to capture. It does not express the immense power of authorities. Rather it reflects their limited role. They are not there to introduce new and independent considerations (though when they make a mistake and issue the wrong decrees they do precisely that). They are meant to reflect dependent reasons in situations where they are better placed to do so. They mediate between ultimate reasons and the people to whom they apply.

II. AUTHORITY AND THE LAW

I will assume that necessarily law, every legal system which is in force anywhere, has *de facto* authority. That entails that the law either claims that it possesses legitimate authority or is held to possess it, or both. I shall argue that, though a legal system may not have legitimate authority, or though its legitimate authority may not be as extensive as it claims, every legal system claims that it possesses legitimate authority. If the claim to authority is part of the nature of law, then whatever else the law is it must be capable of possessing authority. A legal system may lack legitimate authority. If it lacks the moral attributes required to endow it with legitimate authority then it has none. But it must possess all the other features of authority, or else it would be odd to say that it claims authority. To claim authority it must be capable of having it, it must be a system of a kind which is capable in principle of possessing the requisite moral properties of authority. These considerations, I shall argue, create a weighty argument in favour of the sources thesis. Let us review them step by step.

The claims the law makes for itself are evident from the language it adopts and from the opinions expressed by its spokesmen, i.e. by the institutions of the law. The law's claim to authority is manifested by the fact that legal institutions are officially designated as 'authorities', by the fact that they regard themselves as having the right to impose obligations on their subjects, by their claims that their subjects owe them allegiance, and that their subjects ought to obey the law as it requires to be obeyed (i.e. in all cases except those in which some legal doctrine justifies breach of duty). Even a bad law, is the inevitable official doctrine, should be obeyed for as long as it is in force, while lawful action is taken to try and bring about its amendment or repeal. One caveat needs be entered here. In various legal systems certain modes of conduct are technically unlawful without being so in substance. It is left to the prosecutorial authorities to refrain from prosecuting for such conduct, or to the courts to give absolute discharge. Where legally recognized policies direct such authorities to avoid prosecution or conviction, the conduct should not be regarded as unlawful except in a technical sense, which is immaterial to our considerations.

Does the fact that the law claims authority help us understand its nature in any way, beyond the sheer fact that the law makes this claim? If of necessity all legal systems have legitimate authority, then we can conclude that they have the features which constitute the service conception of authority. But it is all too plain that in many cases the law's claim to legitimate authority cannot be supported. There are legal systems whose authority cannot be justified by the normal justification thesis or in any other way. Can it not be argued that, since the law may lack authority, a conception of authority cannot contribute to our understanding of what it is, except by showing what it claims to be? This conclusion is at the very least premature. It could be that, in order to be able to claim authority, the law must at the very least come close to the target, i.e. that it must have some of the characteristics of authority. It can fail to have authority. But it can fail in certain ways only. If this is so, there are features of authority that it must have. If so, we can learn from the doctrine of authority something about the nature of law.

Note that nothing in this suggestion assumes that all the necessary features of the law are necessary features of every practical authority. The law may well have others. Indeed, I am already assuming that the law does have others, since it is not necessary that every person who has legitimate authority claims to have it, as the law necessarily does. All that we are trying to establish is whether some necessary characteristics of law are necessary characteristics of authority, which the law must have if it is to be capable of claiming authority.

I suggested above that only those who can have authority can sincerely claim to have it, and that therefore the law must be capable of having authority. This claim is so vague that, even if correct, it cannot be more than a gesture towards an argument. What might that be? Consider the fact that the law is a normative system. If it were not, it would be incapable of having practical authority. If the law were a set of propositions about the behaviour of volcanoes, for example, then it would not only lack authority over action, it would be incapable of having such authority. The statement that a normative system is authoritatively binding on us may be false, but at least it makes sense, whereas the claim that a set of propositions about volcanoes authoritatively determines what we ought to do does not even make sense.

But cannot one claim that a person X has authority which it would make no sense to attribute to X? The claim makes sense because we understand what is claimed, even while we know that it is not merely false but is necessarily, or conceptually, false. For example, what cannot communicate with people cannot have authority over them. Trees cannot have authority over people. But someone whose awareness of what trees are is incomplete, a young child, for example, can claim that they do have authority. He is simply wrong. Similarly, even if he is aware of the nature of trees, he may make an insincere claim to that effect. Perhaps he is trying to deceive a newly arrived Martian sociologist. Notice, however, that one cannot sincerely claim that someone who is conceptually incapable of having authority has authority if one understands the nature of one's claim and of the person of whom it is made. If I say that trees have authority over people, you will know that either my grasp of the concepts of authority or of trees is deficient or that I am trying to deceive (or, of course, that I am not really stating that trees have authority but merely pretending to do so, or that I am play-acting, etc.).

That is enough to show that since the law claims to have authority it is capable of having it. Since the claim is made by legal officials wherever a legal system is in force, the possibility that it is normally insincere or based on a conceptual mistake is ruled out. It may, of course, be sometimes insincere or based on conceptual mistakes. But at the very least in the normal case the fact that the law claims authority for itself shows that it is capable of having authority.

Why cannot legal officials and institutions be conceptually confused? One answer is that while they can be occasionally they cannot be systematically confused. For given the centrality of legal institutions in our structures of authority, their claims and conceptions are formed by and contribute to our concept of authority. It is what it is in part as a result of the claims and conceptions of legal institutions. This answer applies where the legal institutions themselves employ the concept of authority. But there may be law in societies which do not have our concept of authority. We say of their legal institutions that they claim authority because they claim to impose duties, confer rights, etc. Not having the concept they cannot be confused about it, though we can be confused in attributing the claim of authority to them.

The argument of the last four paragraphs has established, first, that one can fail to have authority because one is incapable of possessing authority (though even those capable of having authority may fail to have it), second, that since the law claims authority it is capable of having authority. There are two kinds of reason for not having authority. One is that the moral or normative conditions for one's directives being authoritative are absent. Typically, this will be either because the normal justification, explained above, is unavailable or because, though available, it is insufficient to outweigh the conflicting reasons which obtain in this particular case. The second kind of reason for not having authority is that one lacks some of the other, non-moral or non-normative, prerequisites of authority, for example, that one cannot communicate with others.

It is natural to hold that the non-moral, non-normative conditions for having authority are also the conditions of the ability to have authority. A person's authority may be denied on the ground that he is morally incompetent or wicked. But such facts do not show that he is incapable of having authority in the way that trees are incapable of having authority. Nazi rules may not be authoritatively binding, but they are the sort of thing that can be authoritatively binding, whereas statements about volcanoes cannot. Most arguments about the authority of governments and other institutions revolve around their moral claim to the obedience of their subjects. The existence of the non-moral qualifications is taken for granted. The argument does not start except regarding persons and institutions who meet those other conditions. That is why they are thought of as the conditions which establish capacity to possess authority.

If this view is correct then, since the law necessarily claims authority, and therefore typically has the capacity to be authoritative, it follows that it typically has all the non-moral, or non-normative, attributes of authority. The remainder of my argument, however, does not depend on this strong conclusion. We will concentrate on two features which must be possessed by anything capable of being authoritatively binding. These two features will then be used to support the sources thesis.

It is convenient to concentrate attention on instructions or directives. The terms are used in a wide sense which can cover propositions, norms, rules, standards, principles, doctrines, and the like. In that sense the law is a system of directives, and it is authoritative if and only if its directives are authoritatively binding. Likewise, whoever issues the directives has authority if and only if his directives are authoritatively binding because he makes them, that is (1) they are authoritative, and (2) part of the reason is that he made them.

The two features are as follows. First, a directive can be authoritatively binding only if it is, or is at least presented as, someone's view of how its subjects ought to behave. Second, it must be possible to identify the directive as being issued by the alleged authority without relying on reasons or considerations on which directive purports to adjudicate.

The first feature reflects the mediating role of authority. It is there to act

on reasons which apply to us anyway, because we will more closely conform to those reasons if we do our best to follow the directives of the
authority than if we try to act on those reasons directly. Hence, though the
alleged authoritative instruction may be wrongly conceived and misguided,
it must represent the judgment of the alleged authority on the reasons
which apply to its subjects, or at least it must be presented as the authority's
judgment. Otherwise it cannot be an authoritative instruction. If fails not
because it is a bad instruction, but because it is not an instruction of the
right kind. It may be an instruction given for some other occasion, or in jest,
or an order or threat of a gangster who cares for and considers only his own
good. Strictly speaking, to be capable of being authoritative a directive or
a rule has actually to express its author's view on what its subjects should
do. But given that this element is one where pretence and deceit are so
easy, there is little surprise that appearances are all one can go by here, and
the concept of *de facto* authority, as well as all others which presuppose
capacity to have authority, are based on them. If the rule is presented as
expressing a judgment on what its subjects should do, it is capable of being
authoritative.

The second feature too is closely tied to the mediating role of authority.
Suppose that an arbitrator, asked to decide what is fair in a situation, has
given a correct decision. That is, suppose there is only one fair outcome,
and it was picked out by the arbitrator. Suppose that the parties to the
dispute are told only that about his decision, i.e. that he gave the only
correct decision. They will feel that they know little more of what the
decision is than they did before. They were given a uniquely identifying
description of the decision and yet it is an entirely unhelpful description.[8]
If they could agree on what was fair they would not have needed the
arbitrator in the first place. A decision is serviceable only if it can be identified by means other than the considerations the weight and outcome of
which it was meant to settle.

This applies to all decisions, as much to those that a person takes for
himself as to those taken for him by others. If I decide what would be the
best life insurance to buy, it is no good trying to remind me of my decision
by saying that I decided to buy the policy which it is best to buy. It means
that I have to decide again in order to know what I decided before, so the
earlier decision might just as well never have happened. The same applies
to the subjects of any authority. They can benefit by its decisions only if
they can establish their existence and content in ways which do not depend
on raising the very same issues which the authority is there to settle.

Can it not be objected that my argument presupposes that people know

---

[8] I am disregarding possible complications—e.g. if the parties believed that theirs is an
honest disagreement about what is fair in the case, the information they were given leaves
them where they were. If they knew that one of them is trying to take advantage of the other,
the answer they were given may be more meaningful to them.

the normal justification thesis, and the others which go with it? To be sure such an assumption would not be justified. Nor is it made. All I am assuming is that the service conception of authority is sound, i.e. that it correctly represents our concept of authority. It is not assumed that people believe that it does.

It is worth noting that a set of conditions rather like the pair I have argued for can be derived from a much weaker assumption than that of the service conception of authority explained above. I will call this the alternative argument. Its premiss is nothing more than the claim that it is part of our notion of legitimate authority that authorities should act for reasons, and that their legitimacy depends on a degree of success in doing so. Even those who reject the service conception of authority will accept conditions similar to the two I have argued for if they accept that legitimacy depends on (a degree of) success in acting for reasons. It is obvious that this weak assumption is enough to hold that only what is presented as someone's view can be an authoritative directive.

Instead of the second condition, that directives be capable of independent identification (i.e. independent of the reasons they should be based upon), two weaker conditions can be established. I will assume that authorities make a difference, i.e. the fact that an authority issued a directive changes the subjects' reasons. It follows that the existence of reasons for an authority to issue a directive does not by itself, without the directive having actually been issued, lead to this change in the reasons which face the subjects. Therefore, the existence of reasons which establish that a certain directive, if issued, would be the right one to have issued cannot show that such a directive exists and is binding. Its existence and content, in other words, cannot depend exclusively on the reasons for it. The existence and content of every directive depend on the existence of some condition which is itself independent of the reasons for that directive. Moreover, that further condition cannot simply be that that or some other authority issued another directive. Often the existence of one law is a reason for passing another. But we have just established that the existence of a law cannot depend simply on the existence of reasons for it, on reasons showing that it would be good if people behaved in the way it prescribes, or that it would be good if the law required them to do so. Therefore, the existence of one directive, though it may show that another is desirable or right, cannot by itself establish its existence.

III. THE COHERENCE THESIS

The previous section argued that, even though the law may lack legitimate authority, one can learn quite a lot about it from the fact that it claims legitimate authority. It must be capable of being authoritative. In particular it must be, or be presented as, someone's view on what the subjects ought to do, and it must be identifiable by means which are independent of the considerations the authority should decide upon.

It is interesting to note that legal sources meet both conditions. To anticipate and simplify, the three common sources of law, legislation, judicial decisions, and custom, are capable of being sources of authoritative directives. They meet the non-moral conditions implied in the service conception of authority. Legislation can be arbitrary, and it can fail to comply with the dependence thesis in many ways. But it expresses, or is at least presented as expressing, the legislator's judgment of what the subjects are to do in the situations to which the legislation applies. Therefore, it can be the product of the legislator's judgment on the reasons which apply to his subjects. The same is true of judicial decisions. Judges may be bribed. They may act arbitrarily. But a judicial decision expresses a judgment on the legal consequences of the behaviour of the litigants. It is presented as a judgment on the way the parties, and others in the same circumstances, ought to behave. Similarly with custom. It is not normally generated by people intending to make law. But it can hardly avoid reflecting the judgment of the bulk of the population on how people in the relevant circumstances should act. Source-based law can conform to the dependence thesis. It therefore conforms to the first of our conditions which are entailed by the fact that the law claims authority.

Legal sources also conform with the second of our two conditions, since they are capable of being identified in ways which do not rely on the considerations they are meant to decide upon. An income-tax statute is meant to decide what is the fair contribution of public funds to be borne out of income. To establish the content of the statute, all one need do is to establish that the enactment took place, and what it says. To do this one needs little more than knowledge of English (including technical legal English), and of the events which took place in Parliament on a few occasions. One need not come to any view on the fair contribution to public funds.

As was noted above, all three rivals, the coherence, the incorporation, and the sources theses, are united in attributing a special significance to source-based law. The preceding simplified account illustrates the way central features of the law can mesh in with and acquire a special significance from the service conception of authority and the two necessary features of law which it entails. It does not follow that these are the reasons normally given for the centrality of source-based law. The coherence thesis represents an account which is at the very least indifferent to the considerations outlined above. I have identified it as the view that the law consists of source-based law together with the morally best justification of the source-based law. This may look an unholy mixture of disparate elements. But it need not be. In the hands of its best advocate, R. M. Dworkin, it embodies a powerful and intriguing conception of the law.

Dworkin's conception of the law, expressed in various articles over many years, is not easy to ascertain. Some points of detail which are nevertheless essential to its interpretation remain elusive. Many readers of his celebrated 'Hard Cases' (1975) took it to express a view of law which can be summarized in the following way:

> To establish the content of the law of a certain country one first finds out what are the legal sources valid in that country and then one considers one master question: Assuming that all the laws ever made by these sources which are still in force, were made by one person, on one occasion, in conformity with a complete and consistent political morality (i.e. that part of a moral theory which deals with the actions of political institutions), what is that morality?

The answer to the master question and all that it entails, in combination with other true premises is, according to this reading of Dworkin, the law. The master question may fail to produce an answer for two opposite reasons, and Dworkin complicates his account to deal with both. First, there may be conflicts within a legal system which stop it from conforming with any consistent political morality. To meet this point Dworkin allows the answer to be a political morality with which all but a small number of conflicting laws conform. Second, there may be more than one political morality meeting the condition of the master question (especially once the allowance made by the first complication is taken into account). In that case Dworkin instructs that the law is that political morality which is, morally, the better theory. That is, the one which approximates more closely to ideal, correct or true morality.

In his 'Reply to Seven Critics' (1977) Dworkin returns to the question of the nature of law. He gives what he calls too crude an answer, which can be encapsulated in a different master question:

> To establish the content of the law of a certain country one first finds out what are the legal sources valid in that country and then one considers one master question: What is the least change one has to allow in the correct, sound political morality in order to generate a possibly less than perfect moral theory which explains much of the legal history of that country on the assumption that it is the product of one political morality?

That (possibly less than perfect) political morality is the law. Both master questions depend on an interaction of two dimensions. One is conformity with ideal morality, the other ability to explain the legal history of the country. The new master question differs from its predecessor in two important respects. First, its fit condition concerns all the legal history of the country. Acts of Parliament enacted in the thirteenth century and repealed fifty years later are also in the picture. They also count when measuring the degree to which a political morality fits the facts. The earlier test refered only to law still in force. Only fitting in with them counted. Second, the new master question gives less weight to the condition of fit. It is no longer the case that the law consists of the political morality which fits the facts best, with ideal morality coming in just as a tie-breaker. Fit (a certain unspecified level of it) now provides only a sort of flexible threshold test. Among the (presumably numerous) political moralities which pass it, the one which is closest to correct morality is the law.

I hesitate to attribute either view to Dworkin. The articles are not clear enough on some of the pertinent points, and his thought may have developed in a somewhat new direction since these articles were written. Luckily, the precise formulation of the master question does not matter to our purpose. Enough of Dworkin's thought is clear to show that its moving ideas are two. First, that judges' decisions, all their decisions, are based on considerations of political morality. This is readily admitted regarding cases in which source-based laws are indeterminate or where they conflict. Dworkin insists that the same is true of ordinary cases involving, say, simple statutory interpretation or indeed the decision to apply statute at all. This does not mean that every time judges apply statutes they consider and re-endorse their faith in representative democracy, or in some other doctrine of political morality from which it follows that they ought to apply these statutes. It merely means that they present themselves as believing that there is such a doctrine. Their decisions are moral decisions in expressing a moral position. A conscientious judge actually believes in the existence of a valid doctrine, a political morality, which supports his action.

If I interpret Dworkin's first leading idea correctly and it is as stated above, then I fully share it. I am not so confident about his second leading idea. It is that judges owe a duty, which he sometimes calls a duty of professional responsibility, which requires them to respect and extend the political morality of their country. Roughly speaking, Dworkin thinks that morality (i.e. correct or ideal morality) requires judges to apply the source-based legal rules of their country, and, where these conflict or are indeterminate, to decide cases by those standards of political morality which inform the source-based law, those which make sense if it is an expression of a coherent moral outlook.

Notice how far-reaching this second idea is. Many believe that the law of their country, though not perfect, ought to be respected. It provides reasonable constitutional means for its own development. Where reform is called for, it should be accomplished by legal means. While the law is in force it should be respected. For most, this belief depends to a large degree on the content of the law. They will deny that the laws of Nazi Germany deserved to be respected. Dworkin's obligation of professional responsibility is different. It applies to every legal system simply because it is a legal system, regardless of its content. Furthermore, it is an obligation to obey not merely the letter of the law but its spirit as well. Judges are called upon to decide cases where source-based law is indeterminate, or includes un- resolved conflicts, in accordance with the prevailing spirit behind the bulk of the law. That would require a South African judge to use his power to extend apartheid.

Problems such as these led to the weakening of the element of fit in the second formulation of the master question. But then they also weaken the duty of professional responsibility. There is an attractive simplicity in hold- ing that morality requires any person who joins an institution to respect both its letter and its spirit. If this simple doctrine does not apply to judges in this form, if their respect for their institution, the law, is weakened from its pure form in the first master question to that of the second, then one loses the theoretical motivation for such a duty, at least if it means more than saying that one ought to respect the legal institutions of a particular country because their structure and actions merit such respect, or to the extent that they do.

These are some of the doubts that Dworkin's second leading idea raises. My formulations of the two leading ideas (and of the doubts concerning the second) are mere sketches. They are meant to outline an approach to law which gives source-based law a special role in the account of law on grounds other than those explained in the previous section. It is easy to see that Dworkin's conception of law contradicts the two necessary features of law argued for above. First, according to him there can be laws which do not express anyone's judgment on what their subjects ought to do, nor are they presented as expressing such a judgment. The law includes the best justi- fication of source-based law, to use again the brief description given in the coherence thesis of which Dworkin's master questions are different inter- pretations. The best justification, or some aspects of it, may never have been thought of, let alone endorsed by anyone. Dworkin draws our atten- tion to this fact by saying that it requires a Hercules to work out what the law is. Nor does Dworkin's best justification of the law consist of the implied consequences of the political morality which actually motivated the activities of legal institutions. He is aware of the fact that many different and incompatible moral conceptions influenced different governments and their officials over the centuries. His best justification may well be one which was never endorsed, not even in its fundamental precepts, by anyone in govern- ment. Much of the law of any country may, according to Dworkin, be unknown. Yet it is already legally binding, waiting there to be discovered. Hence it neither is nor is presented as being anyone's judgment on what the law's subjects ought to do.

Second, the identification of much of the law depends, according to

Dworkin's analysis, on considerations which are the very same considerations which the law is there to settle. This aspect of his theory is enhanced by his second master question, but it makes a modest appearance in the first as well. Establishing what the law is involves judgment on what it ought to be. Imagine a tax problem on which source-based law is indeterminate. Some people say that in such a case there is no law on the issue. The court ought to ask what the law ought to be and to decide accordingly. If it is a higher court whose decision is a binding precedent, it will have thereby made a new law. Dworkin, on the other hand, says that there is already law on the matter. It consists in the best justification of the source-based law. So in order to decide what the tax liability is in law, the court has to go into the issue of what a fair tax law would be and what is the least change in it which will make source-based law conform to it. This violates the second feature of the law argued for above.

It is important to realize that the disagreement I am pursuing is not about how judges should decide cases. In commenting on Dworkin's second leading idea I expressed doubts regarding his view on that. But they are entirely irrelevant here. So let me assume that Dworkin's duty of professional responsibility is valid and his advice to judges on how to decide cases is sound. We still have a disagreement regarding what judges do when they follow his advice. We assume that they follow right morality, but do they also follow the law or do they make law? My disagreement with Dworkin here is that, in saying that they follow pre-existing law, he makes the identification of a tax law, for example, depend on settling what a morally just tax law would be, i.e. on the very considerations which a tax law is supposed to have authoritatively settled.

For similar reasons Dworkin's theory violates the conditions of the alternative argument, the argument based on nothing more than the very weak assumption that authorities ought to act for reasons and that the validity of authoritative directives depends on some degree of success in doing so. This assumption leads to the same first condition, i.e. that the law must be presented as the law-maker's view on right reasons. As we have just seen, Dworkin's argument violates this condition. He also violates the other condition established by the alternative argument, that the validity of a law cannot derive entirely from its desirability in light of the existence of other laws. Dworkin's theory claims that at least some of the rules which are desirable or right in view of the existence of source-based law are already legally binding.

Dworkin's theory, one must conclude, is inconsistent with the authoritative nature of law. That is, it does not allow for the fact that the law necessarily claims authority and that it therefore must be capable of possessing legitimate authority. To do so it must occupy, as all authority does, a mediating role between the precepts of morality and their application by people in their behaviour. It is this mediating role of authority which is denied to the law by Dworkin's conception of it.

IV. THE INCORPORATION THESIS

The problem we detected with the coherence thesis was that, though it assigns source-based law a special role in its account of law, it fails to see the special connection between source-based law and the law's claim to authority, and is ultimately inconsistent with the latter. It severs the essential link between law and the views on right action presented to their subjects by those who claim the right to rule them. In these respects, the incorporation thesis seems to have the advantage. It regards as law source-based law and those standards recognized as binding by source-based law. The approval of those who claim a right to rule is a prerequisite for a rule being a rule of law. Thus the law's claim to authority appears to be consistent with the incorporation thesis.[9]

I should hasten to add that many of the supporters of the incorporation thesis do not resort to the above argument in its defence. Nor do they interpret the centrality of source-based law to their conception of law in that way. They regard it as supported by and necessary for some version of a thesis about the separability of law and morals. Jules Coleman, for example, is anxious to deny that there is 'a necessary connection between law and morality'.[10] He mistakenly identifies this thesis with another: 'The separability thesis is the claim that there exists at least one conceivable rule of recognition and therefore one possible legal system that does not specify truth as a moral principle as a truth condition for any proposition of law.'[11] If this were a correct rendering of the separability thesis stated by Coleman in the first quotation above, the incorporation thesis entails separability. But Coleman's rendering of his own separability thesis is mistaken. A necessary connection between law and morality does not require that truth as a moral principle be a condition of legal validity. All it requires is that the social features which identify something as a legal system entail that it possess moral value. For example, assume that the maintenance of orderly social relations is itself morally valuable. Assume further that a legal system can be the law in force in a society only if it succeeds in maintaining orderly social relations. A necessary connection between law and morality

---

[9] Works recommending the incorporation thesis include Philip Soper, 'Legal Theory and the Obligation of a Judge: The Hart–Dworkin Dispute', *Law Review*, 75 (1977), 511–12; Jules L. Coleman, 'Negative and Positive Positivism', *Journal of Legal Studies*, 11 (1982), 139, 160, 162; D. Lyons, 'Moral Aspects of Legal Theory', in P. A French *et at.* (eds.), *Midwest Studies in Philosophy*, 7 (Minneapolis: Univ. of Minnesota Press, 1982), 237.

[10] Coleman, 'Negative and Positive', 140.   [11] Ibid. 141.

would then have been established, without the legal validity of any rule being made, by the rule of recognition, to depend on the truth of any moral proposition.

Supporters of the incorporation thesis may admit that, while it is not sufficient to establish the separability thesis, at least it is necessary for it, and is therefore supported by it. The separability thesis is, however, implausible. Of course the remarks about orderly social relations do not disprove it. They are much too vague and woolly to do that. But it is very likely that there is some necessary connection between law and morality, that every legal system in force has some moral merit or does some moral good even if it is also the cause of a great deal of moral evil. It is relevant to remember that all major traditions in Western political thought, including both the Aristotelian and the Hobbesian traditions, believed in such a connection.[12] If the incorporation thesis seems much more secure than the separability thesis, it is because if seems to be required by the fact that all law comes under the guise of authority, together with the considerations on the nature of authority advanced in the previous sections. The law is the product of human activity because if it were not it could not be an outcome of a judgment based on dependent reasons, that is, it could not provide reasons set by authority.

There may, of course, be other cogent reasons for favouring the incorporation thesis. They will not be explored here. Instead I will argue that the thesis ought to be rejected, and that the support it seems to derive from the argument about the nature of authority is illusory. In fact the incorporation thesis is incompatible with the authoritative nature of law. To explain the point let us turn for a moment to look at theoretical authority.

Suppose that a brilliant mathematician, Andrew, proves that the Goldbach hypothesis, that every integer greater than two is the sum of two prime numbers, is true if and only if the solution to a certain equation is positive. Neither he nor anyone else knows the solution of the equation. Fifty years later that equation is solved by another mathematician and the truth of the

---

[12] The following are some of the authors who advocated versions of the necessary connection thesis which are all compatible with the incorporation thesis: H. L. A. Hart, *The Concept of Law* (Oxford: Oxford Univ. Press, 1961), ch. 9 (on the minimum content of natural law); L. Fuller, *The Morality of Law* (New Haven, Conn.: Yale Univ. Press, Mass.: 1964), and 'Forms and Limits of Adjudication', *Harvard Law Review*, 92 (1978); J. M. Finnis, *Natural Law and Natural Rights* (Oxford: Oxford Univ. Press, 1980). I have discussed this approach in *Practical Reason and Norms*, 162–70. It has been considered by P. Soper in 'Legal Theory and the Obligation of a Judge: The Hart–Dworkin Dispute', *Michigan Law Review*, 75 (1977), and by D. Lyons in 'Moral Aspects of Legal Theory', 223, 226—though surprisingly he advances, albeit tentatively, the view that the facts which determine the existence and content of law do not guarantee it any moral value (p. 251). This, as I said, seems implausible. What does appear true is that the necessary connection between law and morality which is likely to be established by arguments of the kind canvassed by the above-mentioned authors is a weak one. It is insufficient e.g. to establish a prima-facie obligation to obey the law.

Goldbach hypothesis is established. Clearly we would not say that Andrew proved the hypothesis, even though he made the first major breakthrough and even though the truth of the hypothesis is a logical consequence of his discovery. Or suppose that Betty is an astrophysicist who demonstrates that the big bang theory of the origin of the universe is true if and only if certain equations have a certain resolution. Again, their resolution is not known at the time, and is discovered only later. It seems as clear of Betty as it was of Andrew that she cannot be credited with proving (or disproving) the big bang theory even though the truth (or falsity) of the theory is entailed by her discovery. Now imagine that Alice tells you of Andrew's discovery, or that Bernard tells you of Betty's. Alice and Bernard are experts in their respective fields. They give you authoritative advice. But Alice does not advise you to accept the Goldbach hypothesis. She merely advises belief in it if the relevant equation has a positive solution. The fact that the truth of the hypothesis is entailed by her advice is neither here nor there. The same applies to Bernard's advice based on Betty's work.

All this is commonplace. Nor is it difficult to understand why one cannot be said to have advised acceptance of a particular proposition simply on the ground that it is entailed by another proposition acceptance of which one did advise. People do not believe in all that is entailed by their beliefs. Beliefs play a certain role in our lives in supporting other beliefs, in providing premises for our practical deliberations. They colour our emotional and imaginative life. More generally, they are fixed points determining our sense of orientation in the world. Many of the propositions entailed by our beliefs do not play this role in our lives. Therefore they do not count amongst our beliefs. One mark of this is the fact that had people been aware of some of the consequences of their beliefs, rather than embrace them they might have preferred to abandon the beliefs which entail them (or even provisionally to stick by them and refuse their consequences, i.e. embrace inconsistencies until they found a satisfactory way out). This consideration explains why we cannot attribute to people belief in all the logical consequences of their beliefs. It also explains why a person cannot be said to have advised belief in a proposition he does not himself believe in. (Though it is possible to advise others to take the risk and act as if certain propositions are true even if one does not believe in them and equally possible to advise believing in a proposition if it is true.)

Advice shares the mediating role of authoritative directives. It too is an expression of a judgment on the reasons which apply to the addressee of the advice. Because the advice has this mediating role it can include only matters on which the adviser has a view, or presents himself as having one (to cover cases of insincere advice). Since a person does not believe in all the consequences of his beliefs he does not, barring special circumstances, advise others to believe in them either.

The analogy with authority is clear and hardly needs further elaboration. The mediating role of authority implies that the content of an authoritative directive is confined to what the authority which lends the directive its binding force can be said to have held or to have presented itself as holding. It does not extend to what it would have directed, given a chance to do so, nor to all that is entailed by what it has directed. It will by now be clear why the incorporation thesis must be rejected if the law does necessarily claim authority. The main thrust of the incorporation thesis is that all that is derivable from the law (with the help of other true premisses) is law. It makes the law include standards which are inconsistent with its mediating role, for they were never endorsed by the law-making institutions on whose authority they are supposed to rest. The mistake of the incorporation thesis is to identify being entailed by the source-based law with being endorsed by the sources of law.

Law is a complex social institution, and some of its complexities help mask the incorporation thesis's mistake. When thinking of a piece of advice or of an authoritative directive we tend to think of them as having one author. In the law, as in other hierarchical institutions, matters are complicated in two respects. First, authoritative directives are typically issued by institutions following an elaborate process of drafting and evaluation. Second, they are often amended, modified, and their content amplified and changed by a succession of subsequent legislative, administrative, and judicial actions. A convention of reference sometimes exists which allows one to refer to a statute, or to the original judicial decision, when citing a legal rule, even though they are no more than the starting-point in the development of the rule, which is in a very real sense the product of the activities of several bodies over a period of time.

These complications mean, of course, that the rule as it is now may include aspects which cannot be attributed to its original creator. They are part of the rule because they are attributable to the author of a later intervention. For example, typically successive judicial interpretations change or add to the meaning of statutes. Likewise, though we attribute beliefs and intentions to institutions and corporations on the basis of the beliefs and intentions of their officials, the attributing functions may sometimes sanction holding a corporate body to have had a belief or an intention which none of its officials had. This is not the place to inquire into the rules of attributions invoked when we talk of the intentions or beliefs of states, governments, corporations, trade unions, universities, etc. All that is required for our present purposes is that attribution is made in a restrictive way which does not allow one to attribute to such a body all the logical consequences of its beliefs and intentions. Restrictions to all the foreseen or foreseeable consequences are the ones most common in the law. This is enough to show that the incorporation thesis receives no sustenance from the institutional complexities of the law, since it insists that the law includes all the logical consequences of source-based law.

In disputing the incorporation thesis I am not denying two other points which are asserted by D. Lyons in the most thoroughgoing defence of this position. First, I agree with him that judges who work out what is required by, for example, the due process provision of the American constitution are engaged in interpreting the constitution. Lyons is mistaken, however, in thinking that it follows from that that they are merely applying the law as it is (at least if they succeed in discovering the right answer). Judicial interpretation can be as creative as a Glen Gould interpretation of a Beethoven piano sonata. It is a mistake to confuse interpretation with paraphrase or with any other mere rendering of what the interpreted object is in any case. Second, Lyons is quite right to think that there is more to the law than is explicitly stated in the authoritative texts. Authorities can and do direct and guide by implication. It does not follow, however, that they imply all that is entailed by what they say, let alone all that is entailed by it with the addition of true premises. The limits of the justifiable imputation of directives are no wider, I have argued above, than the limits of the imputation of belief.

V. THE SOURCES THESIS

The last section established that not all the moral consequences of a legal rule are part of the law.[13] But it leaves open the possibility that some are: that some moral consequences of a legal rule can be attributed to the author of that legal rule as representing its intention or meaning and thus being part of the law. I will not present a refutation of this possibility. The purpose of the present section is more modest. It argues that the authoritative nature of law gives a reason to prefer the sources thesis. It leaves open the possibility that additional considerations lead to a complex view of the law lying between the incorporation and the sources theses.

Let us distinguish between what source-based law states explicitly and what it establishes by implication. If a statute in country A says that income earned abroad by a citizen of A is liable to income tax in A, then it only implicitly establishes that I am liable to such tax. For my liability is not stated by the statute but is inferred from it (and some other premises). Similarly, if earnings abroad are taxed at a different rate from earnings at home, the fact that the proceeds of export sales are subject to the home rate is implied rather than stated. It is inferred from this statute and other legal rules on the location of various transactions.

---

[13] By the same reasoning it also established that not all the factual consequences of a rule of law are part of the law.

The two examples differ in that the statement that I am liable to tax at a certain rate is an applied legal statement depending for its truth on both law and fact. The statement that export earnings are taxed at a certain rate is a pure legal statement, depending for its truth on law only (i.e. on acts of legislation and other law-making facts). The sources thesis as stated at the beginning of this chapter can bear a narrow or a wide interpretation. The narrow thesis concerns the truth conditions of pure legal statements only. Pure legal statements are those which state the content of the law, i.e. of legal rules, principles, doctrines, etc. The wide thesis concerns the truth conditions of all legal statements, including applied ones. It claims that the truth or falsity of legal statements depends on social facts which can be established without resort to moral argument.

The fact that the law claims authority supports the narrow sources thesis because it leads to a conception of law as playing a mediating role between ultimate reasons and people's decisions and actions. To play this role the law must be, or at least be presented as being, an expression of the judgment of some people or of some institutions on the merits of the actions it requires. Hence, the identification of a rule as a rule of law consists in attributing it to the relevant person or institution as representing their decisions and expressing their judgments. Such attribution need not be on the ground that this is what the person or institution explicitly said. It may be based on an implication. But the attribution must establish that the view expressed in the alleged statement is the view of the relevant legal institution. Such attributions can only be based on factual considerations. Moral argument can establish what legal institutions should have said or should have held but not what they did say or hold.

We have already traced one source of resistance to this conclusion to the assumption that if attribution is on factual rather than moral grounds then it must be a non-controversial, easily established matter which requires at most the application of a procedure of reasoning having the character of an algorithm to some non-controversial simple facts. The assumption that only moral questions can resist easy agreement or solution by algorithmic procedures has nothing to recommend it, and I in no way share it. The case for saying that attribution of belief and intention to their author is based on factual criteria only does not rest on the false claim that such attributions are straightforward and non-controversial. A second source of resistance, also noted above, derives from overlooking the greater complexity involved in attributing views or intentions to complex institutions whose activities spread over long stretches of time, and the tendency to think that nothing more is involved in these cases than is involved in attributing beliefs or intentions to individuals.

But there is a third difficulty with the view I am advocating which must be addressed now. One may ask: if an authority explicitly prohibited e.g.

unfair discrimination, is not the fact that certain cases display unfair discrimination evidence enough for attributing their prohibition to the authority? Two considerations are usually brought to support the view that these
reasons are sufficient to determine the content of the law on such matters.
I shall try to rebut this view by showing that these supporting considerations are mistaken. First is the claim that the only alternative view holds that
the law is determined only regarding cases which the law-maker actually
contemplated and had in mind when making the law. This, let it be conceded right away, is not merely false but very likely an incoherent view.
Second (and it does not matter that this point may be incompatible with the
first), it is sometimes said that the only alternative view assumes that the
law-makers intend their particular view of what is unfair discrimination to
become law even if they are wrong.

Suppose that the fathers of the constitution outlawed cruel punishment.
Suppose further that it is beyond doubt that they thought that flogging is
not cruel, and finally, that in fact (or in morals) it is cruel. Are we to assume
that the law-makers' intention was to exclude flogging from the scope of
the constitutional prohibition of cruel punishments? Would not the correct
view be that in making cruelty a bench-mark of legality the law-makers
intended their own judgment to be subject to that criterion, so that, though
believing flogging not to be cruel, they expressed the view that if it is cruel
it is unlawful?

Both points have a *déjà vu* aspect. They depend on the unimaginative
assumption that either the law is determined by the thoughts actually entertained by the law-maker when making the law or it must include all the
implications of those thoughts. Since it must be granted, and I do grant, that
it is not the first, the second is supposed to be the case. This was the
structure of Lyons's argument regarding the explicit content thesis. As he
saw it, either the law is confined to its explicit content or it contains all its
implications. Since Hart rejects the second alternative he was saddled by
Lyons with the first. Since Lyons sees, as everyone must, that the first is
wrong, he embraces the second. The two considerations explained above
are the psychological variants of Lyons's linguistic dichotomy. They contrast
not actual language with its implications but actual thoughts with their
implications.

The answer to both arguments is the same: the dichotomy is a false one.
There are other possibilities. Sometimes we know of a person that, for
example, if only he realized that certain forms of psychological abuse are
cruel, would not be so indifferent to them. At others we know that if he
were convinced that they are cruel he would find some other way to justify
them. He would come to believe that cruelty is sometimes justifiable. In
attributing such views to people, one does not endorse either of the two
unacceptable views mentioned above. Naturally it is often impossible to

impute any such view to a person. The question whether he would have maintained his intention to prohibit cruel punishment had he known that capital punishment is cruel (assuming for a moment that it is) may admit of no answer.

Furthermore, and this is often overlooked, the sources thesis by itself does not dictate any one rule of interpretation. It is compatible with several. It is compatible, for example, with saying that, if it is known that the law-makers prohibited cruel punishment only because they regarded flogging as not cruel, then that law does not prohibit flogging. It is also compatible with the rule that the law is confined in such cases to the intention expressed by the law-maker. This is to prohibit cruel punishment. Since, by this rule of interpretation, no more specific intention is attributable to the law-maker, the law gives discretion to the courts to forbid punishments they consider cruel (this reflects the lack of specificity in the law) and instructs them to forbid those which are cruel.[14] Which of these, or of a number of alternative interpretations, is the right one varies from one legal system to another. It is a matter of their own rules of interpretation. One possibility is that they have none on this issue, that the question is unsettled in some legal systems. The only point which is essential to the sources thesis is that the character of the rules of interpretation prevailing in any legal system, i.e. the character of the rules for imputing intentions and directives to the legal authorities, is a matter of fact and not a moral issue. It is a matter of fact because it has to sustain conclusions of the kind: 'That is in fact the view held by these institutions on the moral issues in question.'

Two further points have to be made to avoid misunderstanding. First, none of the above bears on what judges should do, how they should decide cases. The issue addressed is that of the nature and limits of law. If the argument here advanced is sound, it follows that the function of courts to apply and enforce the law coexists with others. One is authoritatively to settle disputes, whether or not their solution is determined by law. Another additional function the courts have is to supervise the working of the law and revise it interstitially when the need arises. In some legal systems they are assigned additional roles which may be of great importance. For example, the courts may be made custodians of freedom of expression, a supervisory body in charge both of laying down standards for the protection of free expression and adjudicating in disputes arising out of their application.

Second, it may be objected that relying on the mediating role of authority becomes an empty phrase when it comes to legal rules which have evolved through the activities of many hands over a long time. The fact that we implicitly or explicitly endorse rules of attribution which sanction talk of the intention of the law where that intention was never had by any one

---

[14] See for a detailed explanation Ch. 10 below.

person does not support the argument from the mediating role of the law. It merely shows it to be a formalistic, hollow shell. This objection, like some of the earlier ones, seems to betray impatience with the complexities, and shortcomings, of the world. Every attribution of an intention to the law is based on an attribution of a real intention to a real person in authority or exerting influence over authority. That intention may well relate to a small aspect or modification of the rule. If the intention of the law regarding the rule as a whole differs from that of any single individual, this is because it is a function of the intentions of many. Sometimes, but by no means always, this leads to reprehensible results. Be that as it may, the view propounded here will in such circumstances highlight the indirect and complex way in which the law has played its mediating role.

All the arguments so far concern the narrow sources thesis only. Nothing was said about its application to applied legal statements. I tend to feel that it applies to them as well, since they are legal statements whose truth value depends on contingent facts as well as on law. If one assumes that contingent facts cannot be moral facts, then the sources thesis applies here as well. That is, what is required is the assumption that what makes it contingently true that a person acted fairly on a particular occasion is not the standard of fairness, which is not contingent, but the 'brute fact' that he performed a certain action describable in value-neutral ways. If such an assumption is sustainable in all cases, then the sources thesis holds regarding applied legal statements as well.

The considerations adumbrated above dispel some of the misunderstandings which surround the sources thesis. First, it does not commit one to the view that all law is explicit law.[15] Much that is not explicitly stated in legal sources is nevertheless legally binding. Second, the sources thesis does not rest on an assumption that law cannot be controversial. Nor does it entail that conclusion. Its claim that the existence and content of the law is a matter of social fact which can be established without resort to moral argument does not presuppose nor does it entail the false proposition that all factual matters are non-controversial, nor the equally false view that all moral propositions are controversial. The sources thesis is based on the mediating role of the law. It is true that the law fails in that role if it is not, in general, easier to establish and less controversial than the underlying considerations it reflects. But this generalization is exaggerated and distorted when it turns into the universal, conceptual dogmas of the explicit content or the non-controversiality theses.

The sources thesis leads to the conclusion that courts often exercise discretion and participate in the law-making process. They do so when their decisions are binding on future courts (even where the decisions can be

---

[15] See the discussion of this distinction in Lyons, 'Moral Aspect's of Legal Theory', 238 ff. Lyons mistakenly attributes to Hart and to me commitment to what he calls the explicit content thesis. See my discussion in the works mentioned in n. 4 above.

modified or reversed under restrictive conditions) and where their decisions do not merely reflect previous authoritative rulings. Saying this does not mean, however, that courts in exercising their discretion either do or should act on the basis of their personal views on how the world should be ideally run. That would be sheer folly. Naturally judges act on their personal views, otherwise they would be insincere. (Though the fact that these are their views is not their reason for relying on them. Their reasons are that those propositions are true or sound, for whatever reason they find them to be so.) But judges are not allowed to forget that they are not dictators who can fashion the world to their own blueprint of the ideal society. They must bear in mind that their decisions will take effect in society as it is, and the moral and economic reasons they resort to should establish which is the best or the just decision given things as they are rather than as they would be in an ideal world.

Finally, the sources thesis does not presuppose a non-naturalist ethical position. Even if a certain social fact entails certain moral consequences it can still be a source of law. It is a source of law as the social fact it is, and not as a source of moral rights and obligations. It is a source of law under its naturalistic rather than under its moral decription.[16]

VI. THE ROLE OF VALUES IN LEGAL THEORY

According to R. M. Dworkin, legal positivists endorse the model of rules because of a political theory about the function of law which they think is to 'provide a settled public and dependable set of standards for private and official conduct, standards whose force cannot be called into question by some individual official's conception of policy or morality'.[17] The argument of this article shows that something like Dworkin's description applies to my argument. But notice that Dworkin's remark suggests that legal positivists endorse the non-controversiality and the explicit contents theses, which I do not share. Besides, it is misleading to regard the thesis and argument explained here as moral ones. The argument is indeed evaluative, but in the sense that any good theory of society is based on evaluative considerations in that its success is in highlighting important social structures and processes, and every judgment of importance is evaluative.[18]

---

[16] That is why the sources thesis refers to social facts which can be described without resort to moral argument, and not to 'a social fact which does not entail any moral consequences'. This point is misunderstood by Lyons, 'Moral Aspects of Legal Theory'.

[17] *Taking Rights Seriously* (Cambridge, Mass.: Harvard Univ. Press, 1977), 347.

[18] 'Moral Aspects of Legal Theory', 245, without page references to my work to support this interpretation of it, attributes to me the following argument: 'The social order is liable to break down if substantive moral arguments used in adjudication are counted as helping to interpret the law because that would encourage members of the society to break the law in hope of avoiding the legal consequences by challenging the justification of the standard.' I am happy to say that nothing remotely like this ever crossed my mind or my pen.

Let me exemplify the difference between my conception of the role of evaluation in explaining the nature of law and that of Dworkin by considering one central objection to the sources thesis. Some people object, not to the attribution of intention to legislators or interpreters of the law in itself, but to the presupposition of the sources thesis that whenever one is faced with valid legislation one can also find an intention behind it. Is it always the case? Do we not know that sometimes Members of Parliament vote knowing nothing and intending only to get home as early as possible? An adequate answer to this and related questions has to await a comprehensive treatment of interpretation and the role of intention within its context. A brief indication of the direction in which an answer is to be sought will have to do.

Let us start by considering the view which denies the importance of the law-makers' intention to our understanding of the law. To the question: 'why should one assign any importance to a particular text as legally binding?' that view will reply: 'because is was endorsed by the proper constitutional procedure.' To the question 'how should the text be interpreted other than by reference to the intentions of its author or of those whose action maintains its force as law?' the answer would refer to existing conventions of interpretation which need not refer to anyone's intention. There is nothing wrong with these replies. They merely raise further questions. Why does the endorsement of a certain text in accord with those procedures endow it with a special status? Is it some form of magic or fetishism?

That procedure is a way of endowing a text with legal force because it is a procedure designed to allow those in authority to express a view on how people should behave, in a way which will make it binding. That it is such a procedure, and not just any arbitrarily chosen ritual, is part of what makes it into a legal procedure. The law-making procedure includes conventions of interpretation. A change in the conventions of interpretation of a legal system changes its law. Consider the simple example of a change from an understanding of 'person' to include only people to a reading of it which covers foetuses as well. Law-makers need not intend anything other than that the bill should become law with the meaning given it by the conventions of interpretation of their country. To deny them that intention is to deny that they know what they are doing when they make law.

How is this sketchy reply to the objection to be defended? It turns on evaluative conceptions about what is significant and important about central social institutions, i.e. legal institutions. But in claiming that these features are important one is not commending them as good. Their importance can be agreed upon by anarchists who reject any possibility of legitimacy for such institutions. All that is claimed is the centrality to our social experience of institutions which express what they claim to be the collective and binding judgment of their society as to how people should behave.

Given the centrality of that feature, it is justified to interpret the action of law-makers who are in a hurry to get back home, who vote without paying attention to what they are voting for, in the way described. Two features stand out. First, while this is an evaluative judgment, it is not a judgment of the moral merit of anything. Second, its application depends on the fact that the perception of importance of the feature focused upon is shared in our society, that it is shared, among others, by the law-makers themselves.

The concept of law is part of our culture and of our cultural traditions. It plays a role in the way in which ordinary people as well as the legal profession understand their own and other people's actions. It is part of the way they 'conceptualize' social reality. But the culture and tradition of which the concept is a part provide it with neither sharply defined contours nor a clearly identifiable focus. Various, sometimes conflicting, ideas are displayed in them. It falls to legal theory to pick on those which are central and significant to the way the concept plays its role in people's understanding of society, to elaborate and explain them.

Legal theory contributes in this respect to an improved understanding of society. But it would be wrong to conclude, as D. Lyons has done,[19] that one judges the success of an analysis of the concept of law by its theoretical sociological fruitfulness. To do so is to miss the point that, unlike concepts like 'mass' or 'electron', 'the law' is a concept used by people to understand themselves. We are not free to pick on any fruitful concepts. It is a major task of legal theory to advance our understanding of society by helping us understand how people understand themselves.

To do so it does engage in evaluative judgment, for such judgment is inescapable in trying to sort out what is central and significant in the common understanding of the concept of law. It was my claim in this chapter that one such feature is the law's claim to authority and the mediating role it carries with it. The significance of this feature is both in its distinctive character as a method of social organization and in its distinctive moral aspect, which brings special considerations to bear on the determination of a correct moral attitude to authoritative institutions. This is a point missed both by those who regard the law as a gunman situation writ large and by those who, in pointing to the close connection between law and morality, assume a linkage inconsistent with it.

---

[19] *Ethics and The Rule of Law* (Cambridge: Cambridge Univ. Press, 1983), 57–9.

11

The Inner Logic of the Law

Lawyers, both academic and practising, are fond of talking of the life of the law, its spirit, or its inner logic. In part these expressions refer to the unwritten conventions of the legal profession. These extend beyond habits and manners, and affect the presentation of argument. They include conventions of interpretation and a sense of propriety in the conduct of cases which may be decisive in determining their outcome. There is no doubt that, because of the importance of the legal profession and its conventions in contemporary legal systems, any study of the law which disregards them is liable to produce a distorted picture. Often, however, references to the logic of the law have a different and a more ambitious purpose. It is sometimes claimed that legal thought or legal reasoning are subject to a special legal logic. This is sometimes taken to mean that legal reasoning is not subject to logical laws. But more often it indicates a belief that there are additional rules of logic which apply to legal reasoning only.

Although I will assume that both these claims about legal logic are false, I will consider neither of them here. My purpose is to examine another view often expressed by talk of the inner logic of the law, a belief in the inner dynamism of the law, its internal momentum for development. My purpose is to clarify and explain this belief, inasmuch as there is truth in it.

I. CLARIFICATIONS

The conventional picture is reasonably clear. Legal positivism is held to present a static view of the law. Legal positivists, such as Kelsen and Hart, regard the law as a system of rules, or norms. The rules may be changed from time to time. But they are changed by external political intervention 'from outside' the law. So far as one is concerned with legal reasoning as such, its point and purpose can only be the interpretation of existing law. Any change or development in the law requires an extralegal injection. It requires input from outside the legal system.

This, it is claimed, is a one-sided picture. It is true that legislation is typically an effecting of a change in the law which, though authorized by

First published in *Materiali per una storia della cultura giuridica*, 14/2 (1984); first published in English in Torstein Eckhoff, Lawrence M. Friedman, and Jyrki Uusitalo (eds.), *Vernunft und Erfahrung im Rechtsdenken der Gegenwart* (Reason and Experience in Contemporary Legal Thought), *Rechtstheorie* supplementary vol. x (Berlin: Duncker and Humblot, 1986).

law, is motivated by extralegal considerations. Legislation typically reflects political concerns, be they social, economic, technological, or bureaucratic. But, the claim goes, the same is not true of the so-called judge-made law. The courts do indeed develop the law, but they do so not as political agents but by working out the implications of internal legal considerations. Courts in developing the law do not give expression to their personal views, nor do they reflect external social or political forces. Rather, they unravel the spirit of the law, unfold its hidden force and reveal its meaning.

Though the conventional picture is clear, its meaning and validity are not. How can the law provide the impetus for its own development? If the law itself points to a certain rule as the right legal rule, is not that rule a legal rule now? If it is, then recognizing it and acting on it is merely acting on existing law. It is not a case of developing and changing the law. But, on the other hand, if acting on, recognizing, or enforcing the rule does change the law, if the rule is not yet a legal rule but will be made legal by its recognition, then how can it be that existing law points to it as the correct legal rule to adopt? Must all law be explicitly enacted? Surely one can enact by referring to certain rules and dictating that they should be deemed valid law. What is the difference between enactment by reference, which makes the referred-to binding, and a pointing to a rule as the right one without making it thereby into a binding law? Unless supporters of the view of the inner dynamics of the law can resolve this puzzle, their thesis cannot even be held to be false. It is merely incoherent.

The puzzle may be thought easy to solve, but some solutions are too easy. The law is, for example, an inspirational source for its own development. Ideas embodied in the law may suggest solutions to new social or legal problems. Knowledge of how certain legal institutions, or legal solutions, have fared in practice may suggest ways of improving them. These facts are not in contention. We all know that reflection on the law and its practical impact has been a major source of proposals and ideas for reform and improvement. In a sense, this is a way in which the law provides an impetus for its own development, but this is not a sense relevant to the argument between legal positivists and their opponents. Clearly, neither side has any difficulty in accounting for these facts, for this sense of the dynamism of the law.

As a source of ideas for its own development the law suggests what reasons for action (i.e. for reforming action) there are. It does not itself constitute a reason for its own development. But the very existence of the law, or of certain parts of it, is a reason for introducing certain changes in the law. The existence of for example a local property tax and of a national income tax is a reason for not introducing a separate system of local income tax. To do so would duplicate existing bureaucracies, and would lead to inefficiencies and to a great increase in complaints from the public.

Similarly, the existence of a duty to pay income tax is a reason for instituting a duty to report one's income to the authorities. Failing to do so will lead to large-scale tax evasion, which is harmful to the exchequer, unjust towards honest tax-payers, and which undermines respect for the law and for the government.

These are examples of one legal rule or institution providing a reason for instituting or for maintaining another legal rule or institution. This way of pointing to possible or desirable changes in the law is of major importance for the understanding of legal history generally and of the development of judge-made law in particular. Elsewhere I have argued that considerations of this kind explain one of the most important differences between the role of the courts and the role of Parliament in their activities as law-makers. (That is, it is sufficient to explain why they behave differently when they have power to change the law. It does not explain the differences between the occasions on which they have power to change it.) Because of the importance of the point to our present purpose, let me briefly summarize that argument.

Suppose that rules C and D are currently the law. The court believes that replacing them with rules A and B respectively will be a great improvement. It is sitting in a case which involves C but not D. Let us further assume that the court has power to replace rule C with rule A (suppose e.g. that both C and D are common-law rules, and that the court involved is the House of Lords). The court believes that rule A is far better than C and yet it may rightly conclude that it should not change it. The reason may be that, though A is better than C, A and D are worse than C and D. It is true that in such a situation there is likely to be another rule, e.g. B, such that A and B are better than C and D. But since a court can only change rules the application of which is possible in the case before it, our court cannot replace D with B. Not knowing when an opportunity to do so will arise, it may well judge, and judge correctly, that it should not replace C with the better rule A. Sometimes in such circumstances the court may find another rule, A' which, though inferior to A, is such that it with D is an improvement over C and D. If so, the court will choose to replace C with A'. To do so is in a sense to settle for a second best. But it may be the best course of action open to the court in the circumstances.

It would be wrong to suggest that considerations of this character never apply to legislation by Parliament. But since the courts have little control over the cases coming before them, and since therefore they cannot control the opportunities available to them for changing the law, their reasoning is often dominated by considerations of this kind, i.e. by what I have called the dilemma of partial reform. I have claimed that the dilemma of partial reform explains why the development of the law in the hands of the judges tends to be gradual and organic. For radical reform in a short period of time one has to look to Parliament.

The dilemma of partial reform, despite its fundamental impact on the law, is simple in structure. Because the courts lack control over their opportunities for changing the law, the existence of the rest of the law, which is currently beyond their reach, is a major constraint on their reforming activities. The existence of the law is a reason for or against the acceptability of certain possible reforms.

Elsewhere I have distinguished between two kinds of reason, operative and auxiliary. Put loosely, operative reasons are those which, if accepted, provide the motivating force. They point to the need for action in pursuit of a certain goal. Auxiliary reasons connect a certain course of action to that goal by showing it to be a route to its achievement. That getting wet and cold is bad for one is an operative reason. That by leaving the house one will get cold and wet because there is a storm outside is an auxiliary reason, which in combination with the operative reason just mentioned points to staying at home as the thing to do. Similarly, a promise to convey certain information to a friend is an operative reason. The fact that he is now at home and reachable by phone is an auxiliary reason. Both together point to telephoning the friend as the thing to do.

These explanations beg many questions and require much refinement. But they will do for our purpose. It seems clear that the existence of legal rules and institutions is, as explained above, an auxiliary reason for certain legal reforms and against others. Given certain operative reasons which set certain goals of social justice or welfare to be achieved, the existence of certain legal rules or institutions points to the conclusion that certain legal changes would or would not be desirable. Can the existence of legal rules and institutions ever constitute an operative reason for the development of law? Even though it is true that legal theorists have often been guilty of neglecting the many important ways in which the law serves as an auxiliary reason for its own development, it has to be admitted that the main theoretical problem is whether it can form an operative reason for its own development.

II. DIRECTED POWERS

Consideration of ordinary legislative powers suggests a sense in which the law can provide reasons for its own development. Legislative powers are granted by laws which may confer limited or unlimited legislative powers, that is, they may make any rule made by the designated authority valid, or they may make only rules which meet certain conditions valid. One special kind of condition may be that the rule was made in order to promote certain designated objectives, or that it does in fact promote certain designated objectives. But the possession of legislative powers, be they limited or not, is no reason for using them. If I possess a certain power then I can use it (at least on certain occasions). This raises the question whether I should do so and how, a question which would have been out of place had I lacked the power. Possessing the power cannot in itself provide an answer to this question. Even if I have the power only if I use it for a certain purpose (as when a knight in shining armour can defeat his enemy only if he fights to defend the honour of his lady), it is no reason to use it for that purpose. The law can, however, combine the grant of a power to legislate with the imposition of a duty to use it in a certain way.

Most commonly we are free to use legal powers as we please. Indeed, often it is the purpose of the grant of a legal power that its holder shall use it as he wishes. The power to make contracts is an obvious example of such a power. Yet legal powers can be coupled with duties concerning their exercise. In some countries (e.g. Australia) the power to vote in elections is coupled with a duty to do so. This duty does not dictate how one should use one's vote. But duties concerned with the exercise of other legal powers do precisely that. Agents ought to use their power to represent their principals in accord with their instructions, company directors are duty-bound to use their powers in the interests of the shareholders, and there are detailed rules specifying some of the particular duties this involves, etc.

Subordinate legislators are often subjected to legal duties as to how they should exercise their legislative powers. Just as the conditions limiting legal powers can be of many shapes or forms, so the duties regulating their use can vary greatly in content. I am concerned with one kind of duty. It is a duty to legislate, and to legislate rules which promote or protect certain ends and none other. We have already seen that there could be a limitation on a legislative (or any other) power which has an analogous form. The legislation may be valid only if it does, or if it is undertaken in order to, promote some specified aims. Very often both the limitation of a legislative power and the duty concerning its use are imposed by one and the same enactment. Often the same words used in a statute are interpreted to have the dual meaning and effect of limiting the legislator's power and of directing him to use it to achieve a certain purpose. All this is common enough, but it should not obscure the distinction between a limitation on a power and a duty concerning its exercise.

For our present purpose we want to concentrate on a law-making power coupled with a duty to use it, and to use it to achieve certain objectives and only them, regardless of whether or not this power is limited in the corresponding way. I shall call such a power and the duties attached to it a *directed power.*

Directed powers are the paradigmatic case of the law providing for its own development. Here we find the law providing reasons for the introduction of new legal rules, yet those are not part of the law until enacted by the empowered authority. It is important to understand the reason why in such cases the rules the authority is directed to make are not legally binding, are not law, until enacted by it. The reason is not that the direction as to which rules to enact is imprecise and therefore cannot be said to identify a specific rule as the one to be enacted. The directions can but need not be imprecise. They can be as precise as, for example, a law that 'the Secretary of State for Social Welfare shall, by regulation, increase old age pensions and unemployment benefits annually by the rate of inflation during the preceding year'. Even in such a case, the new rate of the specified benefits does not come into force until the Secretary of State approves the required regulation.

The general function of directed powers is to introduce and maintain a certain division of power and of labour between various authorities. In my example, Parliament could have enacted for automatic augmentation of old-age pensions and unemployment benefits according to its chosen formula. It chose to make such increases dependent on ministerial regulation, thus sharing some of its legislative power with the Secretary of State. The law of the E.C. provides an interesting illustration of this point. Many provisions in the Treaty of Rome which were drafted and ratified with the intention that they shall constitute directed powers requiring action by the member states were, especially since the second decade of the existence of the Community, interpreted by the European Court of Justice as directly applicable, that is, as complete rules already in force, rather than as directives to the member states to introduce new rules. The purpose and effect of this development in the jurisprudence of the Court was to diminish the power of the governments of the member states, in order to reduce their ability to frustrate the goals of the Community as set out in the Treaty of Rome.

The general function of laws creating directed powers is to effect a certain division of power and of labour. The reasons why such a division is thought desirable are many and varied, and need not detain us here. It is important, however, to distinguish between two kinds of directed power. The one kind includes all those cases where the directions for the use of the legislative power may require the exercise of some moral judgment on the part of the authority. The second kind includes all the other cases, i.e. those where the legal directions as to how the legislative power is to be exercised can always be followed without the empowered authority resorting to any moral propositions or arguments. A case where power is given to make rules for the protection of public safety and the freedom of the individual belongs to the first kind. In making such rules the legislator may have to settle conflicts between public safety and individual liberty, and this cannot be done other than by the exercise of moral judgment. Furthermore, even the question of what actions affect individual liberty is a moral question. The definition of one's concept of individual liberty is in itself a moral issue.

It may be thought that my earlier example of increasing social benefits in line with inflation is a case of the second kind. The duty imposed on the legislator is to enact a rule the content of which can be calculated without resort to any moral reasoning. But this is a mistake. Though in this case there is less room for the legislator to exercise moral judgment, he may yet have to do so. The question of what is the best measure of inflation is more than a purely factual question. It may well involve moral judgment. (In Britain after the 1979 election the government introduced a new index which reflected the change in the combined level of prices plus taxes as a truer measure of inflation than the ordinary cost-of-living index.) Even questions of how much evidence is required to establish a point of fact may well be a moral question, a point familiar to anyone who reflects on the difference in the level of proof required by law in criminal and civil cases.

Though directed powers of the second kind can exist, it is perhaps not surprising that they are rather rare. Administrative powers whose use is subject to duties which do not require the exercise of moral judgment are much more common. An example of such a power is that of certain officials to issue licences for holding TV receivers. Those officials are under a duty to issue the licence upon payment of a fixed fee and then only. All they have to do to follow their instructions is to collect the fee. They are not called upon to exercise any moral judgment. Indeed, it is precisely the exclusion of any moral judgment which marks these powers as a special class, known as mandatory powers, which is contrasted with discretionary administrative powers. The latter are not to be confused with absolute powers. Their use is subject to legal duties (the minimal duty imposed on all administrative discretionary powers in English law is that they be exercised in good faith). But these are duties whose discharge requires moral judgment.

III. THE DIRECTED POWERS OF COURTS

Directed powers of both kinds mentioned above are the model for the law's ability to provide for its own development. It is by an analogy with legislative directed powers that one can understand the often-discussed inner logic of the law, i.e. the ability of the courts to change the law by following guidelines set by the law itself. This analogy also solves the puzzle mentioned at the outset: how can the law provide for a new rule without that rule being already part of the law in virtue of the fact that it is legally provided for?

Let us use as examples two legal doctrines. First, a contract that tends to corruption in public life is illegal. Second, a person owes a duty of care to another 'where the circumstances of the time, place and person would create in the mind of a reasonable man in those circumstances such a probability of harm resulting to other persons as to require him to take care to avert that probable result' (*Nova Mink Ltd.* v. *Trans Canada Airlines* [1951] 2 DLR 241 at 254). Consider the following two hypothetical decisions which (purport to) apply these doctrines:

1. A contract wherein a property developer agrees to contribute to the election campaign funds of a candidate in a local election in return for a commitment that, if elected, the candidate will propose the construction of a road connecting two housing estates is held to be illegal.
2. It is held that surveyors owe a duty of care to anyone who commissions a survey and to anyone whom they authorize to use it, but to no one else.

Two points I will take for granted. First, that the decision in the first case, though couched in specific language referring to a particular case, is based on a general proposition which applies to a class of cases. This much is entailed by the universal requirement that judicial decisions be reasoned. (This requirement should not be confused with the duty to give reasons. Juries are not required to give reasons but they are required to reach reasoned decisions.) Second, that in all legal systems judicial decisions are a source of law, i.e. that the legal propositions in the two examples will become part of the law of the land if a judicial custom to follow them is established. In some countries, such as England, there is a formal doctrine of precedent which allows for a short cut: judicial decisions can establish binding rules of law even before they crystallize in a judicial custom. Doctrines of precedent often enable a single decision of a superior court to establish a new rule of law. But in all legal systems, even those which do not have a doctrine of precedent, judicial custom is a source of law.

Many theorists, myself included, have argued that the law is an institutionalized normative system administered by judicial institutions, and have explained why this entails that courts have law-making powers, even where none is expressly granted. Let me just note that this does not deny that courts can make mistakes in law. It is well known that customs can emerge by action which itself offends against the previously existing customs. To revert to our EC. example: the European Court of Justice may well have been acting against the law when it declared Article 119 of the Treaty of Rome to be directly applicable. But since its decision has now hardened into a customary rule of the Court, and of the national courts when applying Community law, it has become a rule of the Community.

Let us return to my two examples of the illegality of some contracts fettering administrative discretion and the duty of care of surveyors. Do the decisions described in them change the law? The two points I am taking for granted establish only that the decisions can change the law, not that they do so. They can change the law because, being reasoned, they are based on a general rule or principle, and because it is necessarily the case that judicial decisions, at least once they harden into a judicial custom, are a source of law. But these points do not establish that the decisions, even if they crystallize a judicial custom, do in fact change the law. It could be that they merely reflect the way the law has been all along. Remember that the same is true of parliamentary legislation. It is a source of law, but not every Act of Parliament changes the law. Some Acts are consolidation Acts, merely re-enacting in one statute provisions previously found in several. To establish that the decisions in our examples change the law, we have to establish not just that they are sources of law but also that they do more than simply repeat existing law.

In arguing that these decisions do change the law I am assuming that they either set a binding precedent or crystallize a judicial custom. I am also assuming that, apart from the general doctrines set out above, which they (purport to) apply, there are not other legal rules directly determining the outcome of the issues decided in these cases. Given these assumptions, any argument to the effect that the instanced decisions do not change the law will have to claim that they merely reiterate what is implicit in the two general doctrines set out above. It is, of course, possible that the two decisions misapply the doctrines which they purport to apply. They may have reached conclusions which are at odds with these doctrines. In that case, given that they are sources of law, it has to be admitted that they change the law. They do so by mistake, but nevertheless they do so. The interesting case, however, is the one in which the courts do not fail to apply the doctrines correctly.

This case opens up two possibilities. The decisions of the court may have been the ones required by the general doctrines or the doctrines may have been indeterminate on the issue in question. For the sake of argument let us assume that the first doctrine, that contracts which tend to corruption in public life are illegal, dictates the result in the first case, i.e. that a contract exchanging contributions to an election campaign for a commitment how to behave when elected is illegal. And let us assume that the second doctrine, that one's duty of care is determined by what a reasonable man would have judged right in the circumstances, is indeterminate on the question of whether a surveyor owes a duty of care to people whose reliance on the survey was not authorized by him.

In making these assumptions we are not assuming that the first doctrine is not indeterminate in any way. All that is assumed is that it gives a definite answer to the case in our first example. The second doctrine, it is assumed, fails to give an answer to the second case. This does not mean that it is indeterminate on all cases. By dictating that the duty of care follows the judgment of the reasonable man, it determines the fate of many cases in which there are sound arguments to establish what the view of a reasonable man would have been. It is merely assumed that it is indeterminate on the case in the second example, i.e. there is no sound argument as to what the reasonable man would think in *that* case.

If the doctrine in the second case is indeterminate on the issue of the case, then it neither entails the rule decided upon in it nor entails its negation. Since the rule is established in the case and since it was not established law before it, the second case does, given our assumptions, develop the law. It is true that one is intuitively more hesitant to say that the law was changed in the case. This is because 'a change' is often used to convey a change of direction, or an alteration to the existing situation which is significant enough to make the changed object substantially or significantly different from before. In this sense no change occurred. The law was modified in a matter of detail which merely develops it in the same direction and in the same spirit it had before. This is shown also by the fact that we are willing to refer to the court in this case as applying the doctrine even though it does not dictate the result of the case. We do so because the decision is not only consistent with the doctrine but was designed to be so, and because either no rival doctrine has been avowed by the court as guiding it in reaching its decision or, if one was avowed, it was taken to be lexically subordinate. Yet the decision changes the law if this means just that, as a result of the decision, the law on one particular point is not exactly as it was before. Where it was indeterminate it is now determined.

The more difficult case is the first one. A correct application of the doctrine that contracts that tend to corrupt public life are invalid does yield the rule that a contract securing a contribution to an election fund in return for a promise how one would use one's powers if elected is illegal. It yields these rules through a chain of reasoning concerning the likely effects of recognizing the validity to such contracts and of their moral desirability. I shall assume that in that chain of reasoning two considerations are prominent. First, that it is undesirable that office-holders will assume their powers while under legal obligations which stop them from changing their views on issues of public concern once they assume office. Second, that ideally one's wealth should not determine one's political influence.

My argument is that in such a case the new decision does change and develop the law. The rule it establishes is a new rule and there was no law to that effect before. In saying that I mean to say nothing more than what is the common view of the legal profession: I am merely repeating generally acknowledged facts. (The reasons why the views of the legal profession should be taken as determining such legal facts cannot be explored here.) This is clear both when we survey a course of such decisions and when we anticipate them. When we survey the development of the American Supreme Court decisions on, say, freedom of expression, and even when we confine our atention to those which correctly apply the First Amendment of the American Constitution, we are aware that the general view is that those decisions have greatly developed the legal protection of freedom of expression in the USA and that many of the doctrines which govern freedom of expression have become part of the law in recent times. They correctly apply the First Amendment. But they were not legally binding until enshrined in the jurisprudence of the court.

Similarly, when we anticipate such a decision in a case of first impression we are aware that we anticipate a new development in the law. An attorney advising a client as to the legality of the contract in our example before the case comes to litigation for the first time will tell him of the general doctrine, and will advise him that this means that the court ought to declare that such contracts are illegal. But he would also warn his client that this is a case of first impression, that there is no legal authority on the issue, and that given that the law is as yet unsettled much depends on the political and moral convictions of the judges. The case, he may say, will set an important new precedent, and may help develop a dormant legal doctrine in new directions.

I have dwelt on these familiar reactions, for they are the foundation of the assertion that decisions like the one in our example change the law. But these common perceptions, though very persuasive, are less than decisive in themselves. They may be susceptible to different interpretations, and in any case we may refuse to follow them if we believe that they do not reflect any distinction of importance or that they are confused or incoherent. But the described reactions reflect a distinction which is both cogent and important.

Clearly, many general legal statements are true even though they do not repeat verbatim the contents of statutes or precedents. They are true because they are entailed by other legal statements which do directly describe the contents of enactments or of precedents, perhaps together with some further true factual premises. A statement that contracts such as the one in our example are illegal was not true until the decision to that effect was given. It is not entailed by an existing legal doctrine with the addition of further true *factual* premises. Its justification calls for and relies upon moral reasoning, especially on the propositions concerning the undesirability of allowing one's wealth to affect one's political power and of having public officials assume office shackled with prior legal undertakings as to the way they will exercise this power. In other words, the reactions we have described reflect a belief in what I have elsewhere dubbed the Sources Thesis, i.e. the view that the law is capable of being identified by social facts without resorting to moral argument. Prior to the decision establishing the illegality of such contracts, there was no way of arguing that there was a legal rule rendering the contracts illegal except by relying on moral argument. Therefore there was no such law.

Does the sources thesis capture an important fact about the law? The general importance of the divide between moral and non-moral discourse (and its importance does not presuppose that the distinction is sharp or that the categories are entirely exclusive) suggests that a distinction based on it is likely to be viable and important. But its importance is often misinterpreted by its own supporters. They often see it as based on certainty, and regard moral arguments as inherently uncertain. This, I think, is a mistake. At best there is here a complex difference of degree. Many moral propositions are more certain and less controversial than many factual ones (that murdering a healthy and innocent person is wrong is much more certain and uncontroversial than any economic theory). The insight embodied in the sources thesis is the importance of the distinction between those (valid or invalid) moral considerations which have received authoritative public endorsement and those which have not. But as I and others have discussed this point before, let us leave it here and return to our main problem.

I have spent a long time arguing that the decision in my example changes and develops the law because once this point is established the similarity between the courts' legal situation in such cases and that of a subordinate legislator subject to a directed power is evident and striking. We have already mentioned that both have power to make law. In the situations illustrated by the example the courts' powers are directed, i.e. they are subject to duties prescribing the ends which alone must be served by the exercise of the powers and enjoining the courts to use their powers to those ends. The ends are embodied in the general doctrines, e.g. declaring the illegality of all contracts tending to corruption in public life. In dealing with cases falling under this doctrine the courts may develop the law, but only in order to achieve the end set by the doctrine. We expect the courts to be guided by the general doctrines applicable when developing the law to meet the circumstances of different cases. We judge their efforts by their success in doing so. And we regard them as having failed in their duties if their decisions fail to serve the governing doctrines.

It has been suggested by R. M. Dworkin, and accepted by many who disagree with his views on almost all other points, that courts can change the law only where the pre-existing law fails to indicate one solution as the uniquely correct solution to the legal question in litigation. Elsewhere I have shown that this is a misconception which overlooks the fact that the courts may have power not only to fill in gaps in the law but also to reserve a valid legal rule and replace it with another. The prevalence of directed legislative powers points to another misconception in Dworkin's suggestion. A subordinate legislator subject to a directed power often has a legal duty to enact one particular rule. If he fails to do so or if he enacts a different rule, he is guilty of breach of duty. Most commonly there are no legal remedies against such breach of duty. But occasionally legal remedies are available, and they may include an order of mandamus or a positive injunction demanding that the legislator shall enact the rule he has a duty to enact. What is not in doubt is that, despite the fact that in a sense this is a situation in which the law points to one uniquely correct rule, that rule is not law until enacted.

That much is uncontroversial. What is overlooked is the fact that the same is often true of the courts when they are subject to a directed power. There is then a uniquely correct solution to the case, but it is not law until given legally binding force by the court. Until then it may be the case that the law imposes a duty on the court to establish a new legal rule, but that rule is no more legally valid prior to the courts' decision than is a piece of subordinate legislation, which an official has a legal duty to enact, legally valid before its enactment.

IV. DIRECTED POWERS AND DEFEASIBLE RULES

Our task is largely complete. We have in the notion of a directed power the key to the way in which the law provides (operative) reasons for its own development. Directed legislative powers are confined to subordinate legislation, and their existence normally depends on specific statutory provisions which expressly or implicitly direct the exercise of the legislative power. Directed judicial law-making powers are much more pervasive. They exist in all cases in which judicial decisions are a source of law (either as precedent or as judicial custom) and in which the courts are legally required to apply certain moral considerations to the determination of the case. They then have a power to make law, and a duty to do so in accord with those moral considerations. Indeterminacy may result in the law failing to single out any specific rule as the one the courts ought to establish. But many cases are not affected by indeterminacy, and there the courts' duty uniquely points to one specific rule as the one they ought to establish. But it is not law until established as such by the courts. And thus it is that we have here a legal reason for changing the law.

To leave the subject at this point, however, would suggest that doctrines such as 'Contracts tending to corruption of public life are invalid' are instructions to the courts and nothing more. This is a mistake. It is true that a statutory provision establishing a directed legislative power is addressed to the relevant legislator and to him alone. But general legal doctrines which call for the exercise of moral judgment in their application, while they do confer directed powers on the courts, do also address themselves to the public. They also confer rights, duties, powers, status, etc., or deny them to members of the public.

The doctrine of the illegality of certain contracts which we have been examining determines, even before any decision applying it, that people do not have the legal power to make contracts tending to corruption in public life. The first Amendment to the American Constitution that 'Congress shall make no law . . . abridging the freedom of speech' establishes everyone's right to free expression. In this respect these judicial directed powers differ from legislative powers. If Article 119 of the EEC. Treaty were not directly applicable, it would have established a directed legislative power. This would have meant that women workers in the Community would have had a right that their government enact laws guaranteeing them equal pay. But they would not have had a right to equal pay until such laws were enacted. The ECJ decision in *Defrenne* v. *Sabena* 43/75 (1976) that the Article is in part directly applicable has two direct results. First, women workers have a right to equal pay even prior to specific state legislation. Second, the courts (as well as the states' legislatures) have a directed power to make rules implementing the doctrine.

The legal significance of holding women workers to have a legal right to equal pay is self-evident. It means, first, that they enjoy those particular rights which can be derived from the general right without relying on moral argument. Thus a woman has a right not to receive half the pay enjoyed by a man employed under the same conditions to do the same job. Second, it means that they can approach the courts and demand that they use their directed powers to make rules for the implementation of the right to equal pay which will be applied in their case. They cannot do so if Article 119 is not directly applicable. That is the reason for holding that, if the Article is not directly applicable and merely grants directed legislative powers, then it only grants women a right against the state to adopt equal pay legislation. Since, however, it is directly applicable, it not only establishes directed powers in the courts but also, and for the reason stated, grants women a right to equal pay against their employers and a duty on the latter to respect it.

In common-law jurisdictions, and perhaps in all precedent-recognizing legal systems, legal doctrines governing the use of the directed powers of the courts are defeasible to a particularly high degree. All legal rules are defeasible in at least three ways. First, they may be overridden by other conflicting legal rules. Second, they are overridden by the specific decrees rendered in final judicial judgments purporting to apply them to the parties before the court, which in fact misapply them through a judicial mistake. Third, they are overridden, in circumstances similar to those of the second case, by general rules adopted by the courts which have the force of precedent (or which have hardened into a judicial custom). Common-law systems restrict defeasibility of the third kind. The fact that a judicial decision misinterpreted or misapplied a statute, or even a common-law doctrine, may deny it its binding force, or at any rate weaken it (in a case in which the judicial mistake may not have been decisive in determining the rule adopted in the case. Cf. *Conway* v. *Rimmer* [1968] AC 910 on the misunderstanding of Scottish law in *Duncan* v. *Cammell, Laird & Co. Ltd.* [1942] AC 624). No such restrictions on the force of a decision as a binding precedent apply when its misapplication of the existing law consists in faulty moral reasoning, or in accepting the wrong moral premisses. This is the clear implication of e.g. *Miliangos* v. *George Frank (Textiles)* [1975] 3 All ER 801. Therefore, legal doctrines directing the law-making powers of the courts are particularly defeasible.

The structure which emerges is therefore this. The law provides for its own development by granting directed powers. The typical case is of directed judicial law-making powers governed by a general doctrine, which applies to ordinary law-subjects as well, and therefore provides them with access to the courts.

V. THE SYSTEMATIC NATURE OF LAW

What is it that makes a legal system into a system rather than a haphazard collection of legal rules? To this ancient question there are two kinds of answer. The first refers to the criteria of membership in the system which determine what belongs to it and what does not. These criteria determine the formal unity of the system. They are presupposed by any discussion of what may be called material unity. But they do not themselves account for it. They cannot explain the way in which one legal system has a certain character which marks it off from other legal systems.

One should not be carried away by talk of the spirit or character of a particular legal system. Many modern legal systems are far from being all of a piece. They reflect different and often conflicting attitudes to human life and to social co-operation as well as to the legal methods of handling them. Furthermore, to a large extent talk of the distinctive character of one legal system is but a flowery reference to the fact that its arrangements and institutions are different from those found in other legal systems. But there is more to it than that. Talk of the nature of the common-law legal systems as against those based on the Roman-law tradition, of their different character and different approach to legal problems, means more than the obvious fact that they differ in their legal institutions. It also refers to their tendency to develop along different routes, their tendency to provide different solutions to similar problems.

In this chapter I have touched on the three main factors which account for these facts. First, there are the traditions, conventions, and practices of the legal profession. These do extend to style of argument and the kinds of argument allowed in court. They thus have a very significant impact on the role of the court in developing the law. An example of such a factor is the willingness of American courts to admit arguments based on social research and to take note of social statistics. Such arguments are not allowed in English courts. Therefore decisions such as *Brown* v. *Bd. of Education* 347, VS 483 (1954) or many apportionment cases could not have been reached, at least not on the same grounds, in England.

The second factor is the impact of the existence of certain legal institutions and arrangements on the desirability of introducing certain reforms, and of avoiding others. This factor, i.e. the law as an auxiliary reason for its own development, explains, I have claimed, the importance of the widespread use of analogy in judicial reasoning. It thereby explains why the courts are essentially a conservative force, conserving existing institutions by gradually modifying their details to conform to the perceived social and economic conditions.

Lastly, the law provides operative reasons for its own development. It does so primarily by conferring directed judicial powers which are reasons for the courts to develop the law in certain ways and not in others.

All three factors help to explain the feeling that different legal systems have a different character by explaining how they tend to perpetuate their own institutions and legal traditions. The importance of such factors is great, but it is exaggerated by those who regard it as sufficient by itself to explain the development of judge-made law.

I started the article by referring to a view common in certain quarters that, while legislated developments in the law reflect political, social, and economic forces, developments in judge-made law are not to be explained by reference to such forces but by the inner logic of the law. I have done my best to explain this view (by reference to the three above-mentioned factors) and to defend it inasmuch as it is defensible. For at the end of the day it has to be rejected as a distorting exaggeration.

This is particularly clear in so far as the impact of directed powers on the development of the law is concerned. Those, as I have argued above, require the courts to use extralegal considerations in developing the law. They refer them to moral considerations and thus open them to the influence of social and political considerations. The degree to which this is so depends on the extent to which the courts have power to develop the law at all, and the degree of discretion they are given and the kind of direction in its use they are provided with. These are empirical matters which vary between different legal systems. But as it is a necessary fact that courts have law-making powers, it is also a universal fact that in exercising them they base their actions on moral and political tendencies, and that they are directed by law to do so.

12

Legal Rights

What are legal rights? How do they relate to moral rights? It is common for philosophers to turn to the law for a model for their analysis of rights in general. Several leading legal philosophers, such as W. N. Hohfeld and H. L. A. Hart,[1] have proposed explanations of legal rights without establishing whether they apply to non-legal rights as well. They have thus assumed that the nature of legal rights can be established independently, that the success of an account of legal rights does not depend on its applicability (possibly somewhat modified) to other rights. Other philosophers like L. Becker, C. Welman, and R. Flatham,[2] make some account of legal rights, usually Hohfeld's, the starting-point for their explanation of rights in general.

This mode of approach is not, and has never been, universal. J. Feinberg and R. M. Dworkin are but two prominent contemporary writers who base their analysis of legal rights on an explanation of rights in general.[3] Elsewhere I have proposed a general account of rights.[4] Its gist is that to say of an individual or a group that he or it has a right is to say that an aspect of their well-being is a ground for holding another to be under a duty. My purpose here is to show that this account applies to legal rights and to defend my approach, which regards moral, rather than legal, rights as the model for a general explanation of the concept. The essay does not attempt a classification of legal rights. Nor does it offer an analysis of special kinds of rights. Its sole concern is the general idea of a legal right.

First published in the *Oxford Journal of Legal Studies*, 4/1 (1984). I am grateful to P. A. Bulloch and to the Editor for helpful comments on the draft of this essay and to Wayne Sumner for a very useful discussion of a much earlier draft.

[1] See Hohfeld, *Fundamental Legal Conceptions* (New Haven, Conn.: Yale Univ. Press, 1919); Hart, *Definition and Theory in Jurisprudence* (Oxford: Oxford Univ. Press, 1953); 'Bentham on Legal Rights' in A. W. B. Simpson (ed.), *Oxford Essays in Jurisprudence*, 2nd ser. (Oxford: Oxford Univ. Press, 1973).

[2] See L. Becker, *Property Rights* (London: Routledge and Kegan Paul, 1977); C. Wellman, 'A New Conception of Human Rights' in E. Kamenka and A. E. S. Tay (eds.), *Human Rights* (London: Arnold, 1979); R. Flatham, *The Practice of Rights* (Cambridge: Cambridge Univ. Press, 1976). Cf. also T. D. Perry, 'A Paradigm of Philosophy: Hohfeld on Legal Rights', *American Philosophical Quarterly*, 14 (1977). Those deontic logicians who consider rights at all tend to base their work on Hohfeld's.

[3] See J. Feinberg's *Rights, Justice and the Bounds of Liberty* (Princeton, NJ: Princeton Univ. Press, 1980), essays 6–8. Dworkin, *Taking Rights Seriously* (London: Duckworth, 1977).

[4] 'The Nature of Rights', *Mind* (1984).

I. AGAINST THE INSTITUTIONAL MODEL

Not all writers who have been inspired by a legally based account of rights, like that of Hohfeld, have chosen to base on it their explanations of rights in general by reason of its foundation in the law. Many of them simply saw it as a promising starting-point. Since any complete theory of rights has to apply both to legal and to non-legal rights, it may be thought unimportant whether a writer's source of inspiration is reflection on the law or not. The issue does, however, suggest a few points which deserve attention.

Some non-legal rights resemble legal rights more than others. Closest to them are institutional rights. These are rights conferred by the rules of associations such as political parties, trade unions, educational institutions, and sports associations. They share with the law several of its defining characteristics. They are normative systems regulated by adjudicative institutions and by rules of recognition determining membership of the system.[5] Just as the law is a particular type of institutional normative system, so legal rights are a particular type of institutional rights.

Some other rights are custom-based. They derive from rules, customs, and conventions observed in a certain community. Institutional rights are custom-based. But not all custom-based rights are institutional. Many social rules and conventions do not belong to systems of rules identified by rules of recognition and enforceable in courts or tribunals.[6]

It is at least arguable that many rights are not custom-based. People who believe in fundamental human rights usually believe that these rights do not derive from social practices which recognize and implement them even where such practices exist. They further believe that people have such rights even in societies in which the rights are neither recognized nor respected.

It is plausible to regard the law as the model for the analysis of institutional systems generally. The reason is not its greater importance but its greater self-conscious articulateness. Modern law is not just an institutional normative system, it is also a bureaucratic system. Its institutions are manned, for the most part, by professionals. Its proper functioning depends on full-time judges, barristers, solicitors, and other legal officials, their professional associations, law schools, and the like. Though legal systems have preceded their bureaucratization, contemporary law relies heavily on bureaucratic processes, many of which are designed, at least in part, to give conscious, explicit, and complete articulation to the law. This makes it a particularly clear instance of an institutional normative system.

---

[5] See on institutional systems generally and on the law as a special kind of such systems, my *The Authority of Law*, essay 6.

[6] This way of distinguishing customary from other rights is crude and unsatisfactory, but will do for present purposes.

This high degree of self-conscious articulation may also incline one to regard legal rules and institutions as a paradigmatic example of all rules and normative arrangements. And, therefore, to view legal rights as a basis for the analysis of all rights. This tendency is, however, not without risks. The danger is that it will lead to an account based on the specific institutional features of legal rights and will distort our conception of rights in general.

One family of explanations which suffer from this pitfall is that comprising accounts basing rights on normative powers to enforce duties or to apply sanctions for disregarding them. Because the law is an institutional system, it is concerned primarily with those rights and duties which it is willing to enforce or following the violation of which it is willing to provide remedies or sanctions. Let us examine the reasoning leading to this conclusion. Being an institutional normative system means being a system consisting of source-based rules which certain adjudicative bodies are bound by their rules of recognition to recognize and apply. That is, institutional systems consist of rules which are subject to adjudication before official bodies. Such adjudication is normally undertaken to obtain remedies or secure sanctions for violation of rights or for breach of duties, or to prevent such behaviour. The only important exception in modern legal systems is litigation to obtain a declaratory judgment. But even that is usually undertaken to facilitate or make unnecessary action for enforcement, remedies, or sanctions, or in circumstances where by convention it is respected as if it were an ordinary enforcement or remedial action.[7]

Since litigation is almost invariably either for the enforcement of rights or duties or for remedies or sanctions for disregarding them, it is tempting to think that only rights and duties which can be litigated with a view to such results can be legal rights and duties. This is a mistake. There are legal rights and duties which cannot be enforced and violation of which does not give rise to action for penalties or remedies. The most important class of such exceptional legal rights and duties is certain rights and duties of or against officials. Rights and duties of officials and rights against them regulate the activities of courts and other legal officials, and are therefore subject to adjudication. That is why they can meet the conditions for being legal rights and duties. But they are not always themselves protected by action in the courts. The law determines what appeals the highest Court of Appeal has a right to hear, but if it decides to hear an appeal that it has no right to hear then no one can take legal action to stop it. I do not claim that the law must contain unprotected rights and duties, merely that all legal systems in fact contain them. They are, however, clearly exceptional and in a sense parasitical on rights and duties which are enforceable or which do give rise, when disregarded, to actions for remedies or for sanctions. Therefore, their

---

[7] As is the case in action against the Crown in Britain.

existence does not disprove the statement that the law is primarily concerned with rights and duties which it is willing to enforce, or for the violation of which it is willing to provide remedies or sanctions.

Moreover, the law typically, though not invariably, endows right-holders with power to take legal action to enforce their rights or obtain redress for their violations. This is normally a very sound policy. There are strong reasons for limiting access to court. If anyone could go to court to complain of the violation of any right regardless of whose right it was, the result would be that individuals would often face action alleging that they had transgressed someone's rights when the action was frivolous or malicious or based on no evidence. Right-holders are those most directly affected. They have in most cases the motivation to protect their rights and good access to available evidence. It is far better to give them access to the court and deny it to all others. We all know the flaws in any argument that the initiative for all legal actions to protect rights should rest exclusively with the right-holder. Our present interest is not, however, with these considerations of legal policy, but with their unfortunate impact on certain theories of rights.

Some writers on legal rights, seeing that most legal rights are protected by remedies, sanctions, and enforcement measures and that right-holders normally have legal power to invoke such protective measures, have concluded that to have a legal right (or at least to have one kind of legal right) is to have control over its corresponding duty, i.e. to have legal powers to take protective legal action. Other writers, who found their accounts of rights generally on some such explanation of (one kind of) legal rights, have concluded that all (or one kind of) rights are no more than the possession of a normative power to control duties corresponding to the right. They have, therefore, looked for non-legal analogues of legal remedies and sanctions and of legal rules of *locus standi*.

The results were only too often a distorted view of morality. In the search for analogues of legal sanctions and remedies, expressions of views about the rightness or wrongness of actions were often interpreted as sanctions. People's judgments that they had behaved badly were often regarded as internal sanctions. Pangs of conscience were compared with jail sentences.[8] Of course, people sometimes punish themselves or each other for wrong-doing. Of course, we all recognize obligations to compensate the victims of our wrongdoings. But punishment and demands for compensation are based on and justified by judgments about wrongdoings. Neither the formation of such judgments nor their natural expression (be it through their open avowal, through feelings of shame or rage or whichever emotion is appropriate to one's belief, or through the natural expression of such feelings in word or

[8] See on these points P. M. S. Hacker's important article 'Sanction Theories of Duty' in A. W. B. Simpson (ed.), *Oxford Essays in Jurisprudence* (Oxford: Oxford Univ. Press, 1973).

action) should be confused with punishment. Punishment is a deliberate act intended to hurt because of a (believed) wrongdoing by the punished (or, in the case of collective punishment, by one of the punished). It is distinct both from the belief on which it is based and from its natural expression in words or deeds.[9]

Such distortions cannot be dismissed as aberrations which do not undermine credence in an account of (all or some kinds of) rights as the possession of a power to control a duty. Without these aberrations this account loses its appeal. Any sound morality recognizes rights whose purpose is not to protect economic interests, rights whose violation does not cause harm nor gives rise to a right to punish or to obtain compensation. Many people believe in a right not to be deceived by members of one's family, a right not to be insulted or treated with contempt by anyone, and many other rights which derive from recognition of a person's dignity rather than a need to spare his feelings or his pocket. But their belief is not merely false but incoherent if rights consist in controlling another's duty by being able to punish its violation or demand compensation.

Some philosophers draw an analogy between legal *locus standi* rules and moral rules concerning the appropriateness of complaints about wrongdoings. While some similarity exists, it cannot be used to provide an account of rights as power to control duties without leading to exaggeration and distortion. Many conventions about the propriety of poking one's nose in other people's affairs are mere matters of etiquette or of good manners, and cannot affect underlying moral rights. Some moralities, while recognizing rights, impose no moral restrictions on the right to punish their violation or to demand that compensation be given to the victims. Everyone is morally entitled, or even required, to do so, if his action is likely to be helpful. Where moral restrictions on the right to complain exist, they often fail to point to the right-holder. According to certain moral theories children are not allowed to complain of violations of (some of) their rights. Furthermore, such restrictions may exist even where no right is violated. For example, breach of certain religious duties or of duties to the public at large is often not viewed as a violation of any right, and yet only the head of the family or the priest may be allowed to punish or demand compensatory action.

II. LEGAL JUSTIFICATIONS

I have dwelt on the shortcomings of one family of explanations of rights to illustrate the dangers in taking legal rights as the model for an explanation

---

[9] Though, of course, people can, and occasionally do, punish each other by expressing views in order to hurt, on the ground that the wrongdoer deserves such treatment.

of rights in general, the danger of basing one's account on the institutional features of the law which are absent in non-institutional rights. My proposed account of rights generally as grounds for holding others to be subject to duties is certainly free of this danger. It identifies rights by their role in practical reasoning. They indicate intermediate conclusions between statements of the right-holder's interests and another's duty. To say that a person has a right is to say that an interest of his is sufficient ground for holding another to be subject to a duty, i.e. a duty to take some action which will serve that interest, or a duty the very existence of which serves such interest. One justifies a statement that a person has a right by pointing to an interest of his and to reasons why it is to be taken seriously.[10] One uses the statement that a right exists to derive (often with the aid of other premises) conclusions about the duties of other people towards the right-holder.[11]

Such an account of rights certainly does not rely on any institutional features of law. When coming to use it to explain legal rights, one encounters the opposite problem. The law, one may say, like other institutional systems, is primarily concerned with aspects of individual behaviour which can be adjudicated in courts and tribunals. It is, consequently, a system of rules for the guidance of behaviour. It is not a system of practical reasoning, but of operative, action-guiding rules. An explanation of rights in terms of their role in practical reasoning is, therefore, incapable of explaining legal rights.

To prepare the ground for applying my general account of rights to legal rights it is, therefore, important to consider briefly the extent to which the law, as well as other institutional normative systems, are systems of practical reasoning. To regard them as such is compatible with thinking of them as normative systems, i.e. as systems of rules. All that is involved is the view that legal rules are sometimes hierarchically nested in justificatory structures. That the law is a system of practical reasoning means no more than that it follows from this fact that belief in the normative force of some of the legal rules commits one to belief in the normative force of some of the others.

To say of the law that it is a system of practical reasoning is, then, to claim that it consists of rules some of which justify some of the others. It is a statement of the logical properties of the law. It is not a psychological or sociological statement about people's beliefs about the law or their attitude to it. Nor is it a moral or other value judgment about the value or merit of the law.

Lawyers commonly conceive of the law as made of sets of nested rules

[10] One cannot specify in the abstract what importance those reasons must assign to the interest except circularly, by saying 'sufficient to justify the conclusion that that person has a right'. One can and should, of course, develop a theory of which interests are protected by rights and when.

[11] A duty is towards a certain person if and only if it is derived from his right.

linked by justificatory chains. One rule in a set justifies one or more of the others which in turn justify a few of the rest, and so on. A rule enacted by a Minister of the Crown derives its legal force from an Act of Parliament. Anyone who believes that the Act of Parliament is normatively binding[12] is committed to believe that so is the ministerial rule, since that conclusion is entailed by his premiss (together with certain true factual premisses). This illustrates the fact that the law is a structure of authority. The authority of some of its rules is vindicated by the fact that they were created in modes authorized by other of its rules.

There is no reason to think that each legal system is a pyramid of authority leading to one apex, to one supreme legal rule which authorizes all the others. I am merely pointing to the familiar fact that some rules of law authorize the creation of some others. Many legal rules can be grouped by their common origin. In Britain statutory law, for example, derives its authority from the authority of Parliament to make law, whereas case law derives its authority from the power of the higher courts to do the same. Borrowing Hart's terminology,[13] we can call the type of justificatory nexus we have considered so far 'content-independent justification'. In our example it was assumed that the ministerial regulation is normatively binding regardless of its content, because it was issued by a person who had authority to do so.[14] But some legal rules provide content-dependent justification for some others.

Consider the relation between the following three (hypothetical) legal rules:

1. Every person has a right to freedom of expression.
2. No person shall be subject to a duty restraining the publication of a sincerely held opinion or of true information without his consent, unless such restriction is necessary for reasons of security of state or of the maintenance of essential public services.
3. Publication of details of the working of an essential public service such as the water supply cannot be prohibited by law, even if possession of such information can assist anyone who may wish to disrupt such service, unless there is a clear and immediate danger that it may be used for such a purpose.

I should emphasize that it is not my claim that these rules either are or should be law. They are merely useful since they resemble several actual

---

[12] I use the expression 'normatively binding' where others may have used 'morally binding'. Though on occasion I will refer to moral force or to moral justifications, 'moral' is often used in a narrower sense in which 'moral' considerations are only one kind of normative consideration.

[13] H. L. A. Hart, 'Moral and Legal Obligations', in A. I. Melden (ed.), *Essays in Moral Philosophy* (Seattle: University of Washington Press 1958), and *Essays on Bentham* (Oxford: Oxford Univ. Press, 1982), 254.

[14] Though his authority may be, and usually is, limited to rules which meet certain conditions.

rules and they illustrate typical justificatory relations between rules. Each of these rules justifies the ones that follow it. They therefore form a justificatory hierarchy. The first rule is the most general. It justifies not only the other two but many more. For example, it justifies the rules:

4. There is no legal duty protecting the reputation of the dead.
5. Journalists have a right not to disclose the sources of their information except when this is necessary to secure prosecution and conviction for an offence for which the maximum penalty is five years or more.

Rule 2 justifies 3 but not 4 or 5. It is, therefore, lower in the justificatory hierarchy than I but higher than 3. The justificatory structures these rules exemplify are content-dependent. In this they differ from structures of authority which are content-independent justificatory structures. But otherwise they greatly resemble them. Both determine partial ordering among certain legal rules and yet neither is a connected relation.

They can be said to divide the law into (possibly overlapping) groups of rules in each of which one (or several in combination) provide a justification for the rest. When the justification is content-independent the groups are identified by their common, direct or indirect, source. When the justification is content-dependent the groups it creates are based on doctrinal unity. They are all articulations and implementations of one or more core doctrines.

Let me try and explain the justificatory relation I have been referring to more precisely. All legal statements can be expressed by 'It is the law that P' sentences where 'P' is replaced by a (non-legal) sentence. Let us define a relation of legal justification as follows. The statement 'It is the law that P' legally justifies the statement 'It is the law that R' just in case 'It is the law that P' is true and there is a set of true statements (legal or non-legal) <Q>, such that <Q> and it is the law that P state a complete reason to believe that R (and <Q> by itself does not state such a reason).

I shall refer to the embedded statement P of a legal statement 'It is the law that P' as its content. The content of a legal statement may be true even if the legal statement itself is false and vice versa. It is true that one ought to keep one's promises but false that it is the law that one ought to do so. It is (in many legal systems) true that it is the law that one may kill one's pets at will but it is false that one may do so. The sentence-forming expression 'it is the law that . . .' is not a truth functional operator. To establish the truth of a legal statement one has to establish not that its content is true but that it has legal status, that it has the force of law. Justifying a legal statement is not to be confused with proving or establishing its truth. It concerns the truth of its content. Since in normal discourse part of a reason, i.e. an incomplete reason, is a reason, a legal statement justifies another legal statement if it states a reason to believe in the truth of its content. But while the justifying statement provides a reason for believing in the truth of the content of the justified one, it falls short of proving its truth. The reason it provides need not be a conclusive reason. It may rely on inductive or on practical (deontic) inferences both of which are defeasible.

We can define a conclusive justification as follows. One legal statement, it is the law that P, conclusively justifies a second legal statement, it is the law that R, if there is a set of true premises <Q> which does not entail R but such that <Q> and 'it is the law that P' entails 'R'. Finally a justification should be distinguished from a complete justification. A complete justification of a legal statement is the set of all the non-redundant premises which constitute a complete reason to believe in the content of the justified statement.

As our examples illustrate, the justificatiory relation between legal rules[15] is not that of a complete justification. The doctrine of free speech stated in rule 1 is not a complete reason for believing in the content of rule 2, nor is 2 itself a complete reason for believing in the content of 3. The route from 1 to 2 goes through additional premises. Some elaborate and explain 1, its scope and its point. They may be premises which explain what is an act of expression and what counts as a restriction on its freedom. They also include explanations of why it matters. They will lead to the conclusion (which 1 by itself does not yield) that suppression of sincerely held opinion is worse than the suppression of the publication of opinions not held by the speaker, or that 1 protects only unconsented-to restrictions on publication (or at least that consent to a restriction on publication makes it less objectionable). Beside these premises, rules such as 2 and 3 reflect the force of other doctrines which conflict with 1, doctrines such as:

6. The public interest in the maintenance of essential services warrants measures necessary to guarantee their continued operation.

Rules 2 and 3 reflect the legal resolution of conflicting legal doctrines. They do not just apply their general justifying doctrines such as 1. They also indicate their limits and allow for certain exceptions to them.

When we refer to one rule as justifying another, we rarely have a complete justification in mind. Nor do we always assume the justification to be successful. I can reject the suggestion that 1 justifies 2 if I believe that the additional premises which are required to entail the contents of 2 are false. I may then say that it is a mistake, albeit a common one, to think that 1 justifies 2. Here 'justifies' means successfully justifies. But in another key I can say that the rule that the suitability of a person to have custody of his child depends entirely on the interest of the child is the justification of the legal practice of denying custody to homosexuals, without regarding the

---

[15] One legal rule justifies another in case the statement of the one justifies the statement of the other.

justification as successful. Here 'justification' means what is taken by the courts, or the law, or by people generally, to justify. In what follows this will be the sense in which 'justifies' will normally be used.

III. LEGAL JUSTIFICATION AND VALIDITY

A legal system can be regarded as a system of practical reasoning, for many of its rules are nested in justificatory structures. Rules are so nested if, of any two of them, one legally justifies the other. The relation of legal justification between legal rules is just an instance of a wider relation of legal justification between legal statements. It holds between 'it is the law that P' and 'it is the law that q' if and only if 'it is the law that p' is true and there is a set of true statements <Q> such that <Q> and 'it is the law that p' are a complete reason to believe that q. In other words, one legal statement justifies a second legal statement just in case it is a reason to believe in the content embedded in the second.

It should be obvious why the justificatory relation is said to exist between legal statements if the justifying legal statement is a reason for accepting *the content* of the justified one. A rule should have the force of law only if its content is successfully justified—whether by another legal rule (i.e. by a legal justification) or not is immaterial. This necessary condition can be strengthened into a sufficient condition as follows: if p is justified and if the matter it deals with should be regulated by law, then it should be the case that it is the law that p.[16] The general justificatory relation helps in the evaluation of the merit of the law. Our specific interest here is in legal justification only, i.e. those justifications based on legal premises. We are concerned only with the way one legal rule justifies another.

Where the justification starts from non-legal premises, it is clear that it cannot establish the truth of a legal statement or the validity of a legal rule. At best, it is part of an argument for its desirability. But where a successful legal justification is concerned, does it not establish the validity of a legal rule by showing that its content is entailed by another legal rule and other true premises? Is not this precisely the way that the validity of delegated legislation is established? Consider 7 and 7*a*:

7. Everyone has a legal right to his good name (i.e. it is the law that everyone has a right to his good name).

7*a*. Jimmy has a legal right to his good name.

Is not the fact that 7*a* is legally justified by 7 the only way in which its truth can be established?

---

[16] This of course does not entail that it is now best to change the law to that effect. Though it is best that p has the force of law, it may be wrong to enact it because of the consequences of the very act of introducing the change.

This crucial and difficult problem has not received as much explicit attention as it deserves. I do not know of anyone who denies that a successful legal justification does, under certain conditions, establish the truth of the justified legal statements. Kelsen came close to doing this. He denied that content-dependent justification can ever establish the truth of the justified legal statement.[17] He would have denied that the truth of 7a can be learnt from that of 7. His reasons for this view, if consistently pursued, would, however, lead to the conclusion that content-independent justifications also fail to establish the truth of the justified statement. That means that the validity of delegated legislation cannot be established by reference to the authorizing statutes but depends on judicial declarations of their validity. But this undermines the very emphasis on the structure of authority which is the backbone of Kelsen's theory of law. It also raises questions about the authority of the courts to make decisions validating delegated legislation. That authority itself rarely rests on the historically-first constitution. It depends on the very chain of reasoning that Kelsen is committed to reject.

I am not sure whether anyone has advocated the opposite view: that all successful legal justifications establish the truth of the justified statement. It is possible that this is R. M. Dworkin's view. My own view is determined by the Sources Thesis. It says that the existence and contents of the law can be determined without resorting to any moral argument. In its widest and strongest interpretation, the thesis applies not merely to the existence and content of all legal rules but, more generally, to the truth and content of all legal statements. It follows that a successful legal justification can establish the truth of the justified legal statement only if it does not resort to moral arguments (i.e. if no moral premises are among the additional premises <Q> which form part of the complete justification concerned).[18] Subject to that condition, it is true that a successful legal justification establishes the truth of the justified statement.

Therefore, content-independent justification which does not involve moral premises does indeed establish the validity of the delegated legal rules. Similarly, the truth of 7a can be established by reference to 7. On the other hand, while 1 justifies 2 it cannot establish its legal validity. If 2 is valid law, it is so in virtue of courts' decisions which have adopted it and which have the force of precedent, or in virtue of being incorporated into a statute. It cannot be regarded as valid law just on account of being successfully justified by 1.

A successful justificatory relation between one legal statement and another is of great legal significance even when it does not by itself establish

---

[17] See H. Kelsen, 'Law and Logic', in *Essays in Legal and Moral Philosophy* (Dordrecht: Reidel, 1973).

[18] See *The Authority of Law*, ch. 3; *The Concept of a Legal System*, 2nd edn., 210–16.

the truth of the justified statement.[19] If the justified statement is not a true statement of law, the justification provides a reason for changing the law so as to make the justified statement true. As has already been noted, it is not necessarily a conclusive reason. Though the change is shown by the justification to be desirable, its introduction may have undesirable aspects or consequences which outweigh the reason for it. If, on the other hand, the justified legal statement is already the law, then the justification shows that it is a morally valid law. A morally valid law may not be a good law if its validity derives from an authority-based, content-independent justification. The moral validity of a rule means that it has the moral force that it purports to have. If a rule imposing a certain duty on its subjects is morally valid, then its subjects have the duty it imposes on them. It does not follow that it is best that they should have it. They may have it because of the authority of the person who made the rule, but he may have made a mistake in making the rule, which should be rectified by changing it.

A content-dependent successful legal justification of an existing legal rule does establish not merely that it is morally valid but also that it is good that it exists. It is therefore a reason against changing it, but once more this is not necessarily a conclusive reason. The very introduction of a change, even one substituting a less satisfactory rule for the existing one, may have aspects and consequences which make it desirable and which may outweigh the reasons against it.

We now have a reasonably complete picture of the sense in which law is a system of practical reasoning. First, some legal rules justify some others. In this they illuminate their point and purpose. The former are invaluable guides to the interpretation of the latter, and they help decide what weight to give the latter when these conflict with others. Secondly, legal rules constitute legal reasons for developing the law in certain ways. The importance of the fact that they are *legal* reasons for developing the law is that they are reasons on which courts are required to act, given the appropriate opportunity. Elsewhere I have likened them to directed administrative powers.[20] Consider a case in which an administrative authority is given the power to grant certain privileges and rights (say, grant planning permission) and directed to do so if certain conditions are met (e.g. the development proposed preserves the character of the neighbourhood, meets the required safety standards, and will not significantly increase the traffic in the area). The authority is required by law to use its powers as directed. The fact

---

[19] The following remarks assume that the justification proceeds from a morally justified legal rule. (That is, they represent the perspective of a person who is willing to make the justifying legal statement in a committed way. I am using the distinction between committed and detached legal statements explained in *The Authority of Law*, essay 8.) This is normally the point of view of the courts; hence its importance to legal analysis.

[20] See Ch. 10 above.

that one legal statement successfully justifies another which does not yet have the force of law is a reason for courts, which have the power to do so, to give it legal effect. It makes their power to change and develop the law into a directed power.

IV. LEGAL RIGHTS AND LEGAL JUSTIFICATIONS

If rights are protected interests, in that a person has a right if and only if an interest of his is a sufficient ground for holding another to be subject to a duty, then legal rights are legally protected interests. Such an account gives 'rights' the same sense in legal as in non-legal contexts. It presupposes that the law is (at least in part) a system of practical reasoning. The previous two sections explained the sense in which this is so. How do their conclusions help to clarify the nature of legal rights?

An explanation of legal rights has to include two parts. It has to explain how it is possible to come to have legal rights and it has to explain what can be the legal consequences of having a right. People can come to have legal rights in the same ways in which they can come to have duties, powers, liabilities, or any other legal condition. Legal right-statements are either pure or applied. A legal right-statement is pure if its truth can be established by reference to the existence of certain laws alone. Other legal right-statements are applied statements. Their truth can only be established by facts which include facts other than the existence of law. It should be remembered that both kinds of legal right-statement are subject to the condition imposed by the Sources Thesis, namely that their truth can be established without using moral argument.

Consider the following examples:

8.   Everyone has a right to damages against anyone who defames him without lawful excuse.
8a. Jim has a right to damages against anyone who defames him without lawful excuse.
9.   Jim has a right to £1,500 defamation damages against Smith.
9a. Smith has a duty to pay Jim £1,500.
10.   Children have a right to maintenance against their parents.
10a. Jill has a right to maintenance against her mother.
11.   Jill has a right that her mother pay for her piano lessons.
11a. Jill's mother has a duty to pay for her piano lessons.

Of these, 8 and 10 are pure legal right-statements. So is 7. 7 justifies 8. It is wrong, however, to think that 8 is applied. Its legal force is due to the legal sources, precedents, and statutes which establish it in law. Its justification by 7 presupposes moral arguments and is therefore incapable of establishing its legal force. Common lawyers are more likely to say that 7 is inferred from 8. The common law is preoccupied with providing remedial rights. But the reasoning used by the courts shows clearly that they regard the remedies as justified by a right to reputation. The choice of remedies and their adequacy is assessed (in part) by their adequacy in protecting that right. Given the discussion of the previous section, there is no surprise in one rule which creates a right justifying another such rule, which derives its legal force not from that justification but from independent legal sources. Nor is there any surprise that 7*a*, 8*a*, and 10*a*, which are justified respectively by the rules 7, 8, and 10 without recourse to any moral argument, derive their very legal force from that justification, and are applied legal statements.

The crucial question is how one can tell that an enactment or a precedent establishes a right. We normally think that the question arises only if the language adopted in legislation or in a judicial decision is obscure or ambiguous. Otherwise it all depends on the language of the enacted rule. But though, where the language is plain, the question may be easy to answer, it still requires an answer. Why do we say that the rule made is the one expressed by the language of the enactment understood in its ordinary meaning, or in the meaning its language has, according to legal rules and conventions? The reason lies, crudely speaking, in the fact that where a law is laid down by authority its meaning is dictated by the intentions of that authority. If it were not so, then there would have been little reason to ascribe law-making power to that authority.[21] This lesson is particularly important when the issue is, not what precisely is the duty or the right that the law creates, but does the rule in question impose a duty or does it merely set a condition for one's ability to achieve certain consequences? Does it grant a power or a right? And suchlike doubts about the very type of legal condition the law creates.

Hart has shown that one cannot tell the difference between a duty breach of which incurs, say, a fine, and an activity one is free to undertake but has to pay a tax if one does, except by reference to the intentions of the law, i.e. of the legal institutions which have created and which enforce the rule.[22] In a similar vein I have argued that one cannot identify a legal power with the ability to perform an act which has legal consequences. This would yield the paradoxical consequence that people have legal power to break the law. (Do we need legal powers for *that*?) A legal power can only be identified by the reasons which led the law (i.e. the institutions which make and sustain it) to attach those legal consequences to the act. The act is an exercise of a legal power only if the reason for attributing to it the legal

---

[21] Needless to say, this brief answer is a rough one. Among many complications let me mention that this answer cannot be the whole story regarding old laws. But the details of a doctrine of interpretation need not concern us here.

[22] H. L. A. Hart, 'Kelsen Visited', *UCLA Law Review*, 10 (1963).

consequences it has is that it is held desirable to enable people to perform that act as a means to achieve those consequences, if they so wish.[23]

Similarly, a law creates a right if it is based on and expresses the view that someone has an interest which is sufficient ground for holding another to be subject to a duty. One way of creating a right is therefore by the use of the term 'right'. (For example: 'An employer shall have the right to. . .'.) This is an obvious way for the law to confer rights, for given that 'a right' means that an interest is sufficient for holding another to be subject to a duty, its use is a natural way to express that thought. But, as Bentham pointed out long ago, this is neither the only nor the most common way in which the law creates rights. It may do so by the use of specific technical terms such as 'a holding' or 'a share'. Or it may do so by imposing duties with the intention to protect someone's interest, thus endowing him with a legal right.

An individual has a right, if an interest of his is sufficient, to hold another to be subject to a duty. His right is a legal right if it is recognized by law, that is, if the law holds his interest to be sufficient ground to hold another to be subject to a duty. This is the core of the account here proposed. It explains why I said above that a rule is identified as a right-conferring one by the reasons for its adoption. To be a rule conferring a right it has to be motivated by a belief in the fact that someone's (the right-holder's) interest should be protected by the imposition of duties on others.

The other aspect of the explanation of legal rights follows naturally from the core idea. If a legal rule creates a legal right, its consequences are that others have duties to protect an interest of the right holder. Such duties are the consequences of a right in the sense that it legally justifies those duties. This legal justification can have either of the two results we distinguished in the previous section. If the justification does not involve any resort to moral argument, the justification establishes the justified duty as a legal duty. In this way, if A has a right to £5 against B, then B has a duty to give £5 to A. But very commonly the right can justify the duty only in conjunction with other moral premises. In this case the legal right is insufficient to endow the duty with legal force. But the legal right is a reason for giving that duty legal force, for making it into a legal duty.

Consider statements 9, 9a, 11, and 11a above. 9a is justified by 9 and 11a is justified by 11 without resort to moral argument. But while both 9 and 9a are justified by 8, and 11 and 11a are justified by 10, these justifications do involve moral judgments about the adequacy of certain payments. Therefore the rights and duties specified in 9, 9a, 11, and 11a are not legally binding until there is a decision in the court, or an agreement between the parties to that effect. But 8 and 10 provide powerful reasons for reaching such agreements and for rendering these judicial decisions.

---

[23] Cf. *Practical Reason and Norms*, s. 8, and *The Authority of Law*, 17–18.

An important part of our understanding of legal rights consists in grasping their logical consequences. These are, as we have just seen, that they legally justify other rights and duties. Some of these derive legal force from this justification. Others will be legal rights and duties established by independent legal sources. Others still are not yet legally binding. These last consequences of legal rights deserve special attention, since they show legal rights to constitute legal reasons for giving the justified rights and duties legal force. They establish the dynamic aspect of rights. Legal rights can be legal reasons for legal change. They are grounds for developing the law in certain directions. Because of their dynamic aspect legal rights cannot be reduced, as has often been suggested, to the legal duties which they justify. To do so is to overlook their role as reasons for changing and developing the law.[24]

V. LEGAL RIGHTS AND MORAL PRINCIPLES

The core account of legal rights presented above requires further explanation and refinement. These can best be supplied by examining a few of the objections which are liable to be raised to it. This section explores two groups of objections concerned with the relations between law and morality.

Legal Rights Need Not Be Recognized Moral Rights

The Objection. According to the account proposed above, every legal right is a legally recognized pre-existing moral right. This assumes a stronger connection between law and morality than in fact exists. It also misconstrues the nature of this connection. There are two reasons why a legal right may not be the giving of legal force to a pre-existing moral right. First, the law may quite deliberately create a right where none existed. There was no right to initiate the liquidation of a company or to obtain planning permission prior to their creation by law. Secondly, while intending to recognize a pre-existing right the law may fail to do so. It may detect an interest which deserves protection where none exists. Alternatively, the interest may exist but may be insufficient to be the ground of a duty on another. Where a legal right does not recognize a pre-existing moral right, it may yet create a moral right based not on the interest of the right-holder but on the reasons we have or may have to obey that law. On the other hand, where such reasons are absent or insufficient no moral right is created by the law, but it does create a legal right, one with no moral force.

The Reply. To begin to respond to this complex objection it is useful to

---

[24] I have discussed this point in *The Concept of a Legal System*, 225–7.

remind ourselves of the different kinds of legal discourse. There is the sociological description of social institutions and of people's attitudes and beliefs which H. L. A. Hart called discourse from the external point of view. In this way we talk of the beliefs and actions of courts and legislators. Occasionally sentences such as 'x has a right to y' are used in such discourse to state that legal institutions hold x to have a right to y.

Much more common is the use of such right-sentences to make statements which Hart described as internal, or statements made from the internal point of view, and which I called committed statements.[25] Committed right-statements state that the right-holders do have those rights, that they are, if you like, moral rights or rights that morality recognizes as valid. (One should remember that in this essay 'morality' is used very widely to include binding normative considerations of any kind.) The important point is that a committed statement that someone has a legal right simply means that that person has a right which is recognized in law, i.e. by the legal institutions.

The elucidation offered above explained 'legal rights' as used in committed statements, for they are the central type of legal discourse. First, not only is it the type of discourse most commonly employed in discourse concerning the law in countries in which the population is not estranged from the government, but it is also the normal mode of discourse in the sense that the law claims normative force and validity to itself. It is treated as it requires to be treated only by people who recognize its normative force and are therefore normally talking of it in committed discourse. Second, in every legal system, the officials manning its legal institutions have the internal point of view and are normally using committed statements to describe the law.

Finally, the non-committed modes of discourse are parasitical on the committed discourse. This is evident in the case of external statements. It is also true of the third common type of legal discourse, which I call 'detached discourse'. A statement is a detached normative statement if it describes a normative situation as seen from a committed point of view without being committed to it. A person who asserts the existence of legal rights in a detached way is not committed to the moral or normative validity of those rights. His statement is true if it would have been true had the law moral or normative force. Saying that there can be legal rights which have no moral force, or even such that are immoral, is saying that one can make true detached statements about legal rights while morally condemning them and being right to do so.

There is another point raised by the objection which is still to be met. While some legal rights are legally recognized moral rights (for example,

[25] See H. L. A. Hart, *The Concept of Law* (Oxford: Oxford Univ. Press, 1961), 55–6, 86–8; J. Raz, *The Authority of Law*, 140–3, 153–7.

one's right to a good name) other legal rights are legally created moral rights. They are moral rights one has because the law has granted them. The account of legal rights which I have offered fails to explain these cases.

There are three types of case where a legal right can be thought of as a legally created moral right. My explanation of legal rights adequately accounts for two of them. It requires a certain natural extension to apply to the third.

First is the case where the law changes a person's interests. Thereby it changes his moral rights, which it then proceeds to recognize. Strictly speaking, this is not a case where the law creates the moral right; it merely creates the interest which is the foundation of the right. Consider the following example. Until planning restrictions were introduced, everyone was free to build on his land as he liked. Then the law prohibited building without planning permission, and appointed planning authorities with powers to grant such permission. This created for some people an interest they did not have before, i.e. to obtain planning permission. Given general moral principles and the circumstances of those people, it is probable that some of them had a (moral) right to be given planning permission. In some countries the law recognizes those rights by giving a legal right to planning permission when certain conditions obtain, and where these conditions are those which morally entitle the applicants to the permission. It may look as if the law creates a moral right to planning permissions, for the whole of planning law is the law's creation. But upon inspection we can see that the law creates an interest which is the basis of a moral right which is in turn recognized by the law. This combination is in fact very common in technical legal areas such as company law or licensing law.

Second, the possession of some rights depends on the consent or authority of others. I have a right to be on your premises if you consent to my being there. In such cases the right is there to protect some interest of the right-holder. But that interest is sufficient to justify holding another subject to a duty only if the condition is met. My interest in being on your premises if I wish is insufficient by itself to establish a duty on you to let me do so unless you consent to my being there. Your consent removes certain objections to holding you bound to respect my interest, and it thus enables the interest to found a right.

Similarly, there are many cases where a moral right exists only if it is recognized by authoritative legal institutions. Sometimes they even have a duty to give their recognition to the right in order to bring it into existence (both as a moral and as a legal right), just as sometimes you ought to consent to my being on your premises, even though I do not have a right to be there unless you consent. In all cases where the consent of a legal authority is a moral condition for the existence of a moral right, a legal right *is* a legally recognized moral right. The legal recognition is self-referential:

it recognizes that once it (i.e. the legal recognition) is given, a moral right comes into force.

The third type of case involves an extension of the core account. It concerns legal rights which, though they purport to be recognized rights, fail to be so, and yet they create a morally recognized legal right. Suppose that in a certain country Parliament enacts a legal right to use contraceptives. Some people believe that there is no moral right to use contraceptives, not even a moral right conditional on legal recognition. They recognize, of course, that Parliament in granting this legal right assumes otherwise. But they do not agree. Yet they think that Parliament's authority carries such moral force as to entail that once the legal right is granted people are morally bound to respect it and not to stop others from using contraceptives. On my account, strictly speaking this is not a case of a moral right. One's moral duty not to prevent the use of contraceptives which is the consequence of the law is not based on the interest of the right-holder, but on respect for the authority of Parliament. But since this is respect for Parliament's mistake about moral rights, and since its moral consequences are to give individuals all they would have had, had they a right to contraceptives, it is a natural extension of the concept to regard such legislation as conferring a (legal) right. (Though of course it is, in the eyes of the anti-contraceptionists, a right to do wrong, and therefore one which should not be exercised.)[26]

If Rights are Subject to the Sources Thesis, Then in Many Areas There Are No Legally Justified Rights

The Objection. Legal rights have two kinds of legal implication. They justify other existing legal rights and duties, and they are legal reasons for developing the law by creating further rights and duties where doing so is desirable in order to protect the interests on which the justifying rights are based. The second objection concerns the first implication—the role of legal rights in providing legal justification for other existing legal rights and duties. The objection arises out of the claim that, in accordance with the Sources Thesis, all rights and duties can be identified without resort to any moral argument.

Legally justified legal rights are legally valid either because they are successfully legally justified without recourse to moral argument or because they have been directly enacted or acquired the force of precedent. Let us take the first case first. Can a right ever derive legal validity from the fact that it is successfully justified by another legal right? The objection is that this cannot happen in a way consistent with the Sources Thesis for the

---

[26] These objections are suggestive rather than conclusive. For an excellent detailed discussion of the issue see J. Waldron, 'A Right to Do Wrong', *Ethics*, 92 (1981) 21.

justification of any right requires moral argument. Consider the right of a child to be maintained by his parents. To conclude that in virtue of it he has any more specific right (to three meals a day, to proper clothing, etc.), one has to engage in moral argument on the purpose of the right and its place among other moral concerns: is it a right to minimal or to optimal support, is the level of support required relative to the parents' ability to pay, or to their life-style (they may be rich people who lead very simple lives), is it relative to the parents' moral beliefs (so that they may deny him certain experiences or opportunities because they object to them)? Does it include moral as well as material support? The right to maintenance against one's parents has no specific implications which do not involve answering these or some similar questions. These questions cannot be answered without using moral argument. Therefore, no legal right has concrete legal implications if the Sources Thesis is to be believed.

Turning to the other class of legally justified legal rights, those which derive their legal force from statute or precedent, even they cannot be explained in conformity with the Sources Thesis. At least, such explanation is impossible in those areas of the law where rights are liable to be over-ridden by moral considerations. This is true, it could be claimed, of all equitable remedies and equity-based rights. It is also true wherever considerations of public policy or public morality entitle the courts to override otherwise established rights. It is arguable that the courts have an inherent jurisdiction to this effect in all cases brought before them. Wherever they have this discretion, no concrete rights or duties can be attributed to the legislated right which is thus deprived of content. Its content can be restored only if we allow that the content of the law and of legal rights is determined by moral considerations.

The Reply. Both parts of the objections are based on simple mistakes. The fact that a given right can be overridden by moral considerations, just like the fact that it can be overridden by another legal right, shows nothing except that it is not an absolute right which defeats all contrary considerations. But legal rules rarely, if ever, have absolute force. In general they are liable to be overridden by contrary legal considerations where such exist, and where the law gives them greater force. Often, it is true, they are liable to be overridden by certain moral considerations as well, for often the law provides for this. But the account offered in the previous section is an account of defeasible rights. It does not presuppose that they have absolute force.

As to the objection concerning legal rights which derive their legal force from being justified by other legal rights, it is simply incorrect that all such justifications depend on moral assumptions. Suppose that it is morally right that parents can do with their children whatever they think is in the children's best interest (including killing them). If so, it is false that children have a right to maintenance against their parents. One cannot argue that this is what that right means. One cannot argue that a child's right to maintenance is respected by a parent who starves him because he, the parent, sincerely but falsely believes that this is in the best interests of the child. 'A right to maintenance' has as part of its meaning a descriptive content which can be established without use of moral argument. It establishes the legal force of those rights and duties which can be justified in virtue of its core descriptive content without invoking other moral principles.

VI. FURTHER OBJECTIONS

In order further to explain and defend my account of legal rights I will briefly consider three other possible objections to it which, unlike the objections considered above, do not turn on the relation between legal and moral rights.

Legal Rights as Reasons for Legal Change

The Objection. Much play was made in Section IV of the fact that legal rights not only justify other existing legal rights and duties but also direct the courts to develop the law in certain ways. They are legal reasons for creating new laws, new rights, and duties. They are therefore not reducible to a compendium statement of existing duties. One may object to this and claim that a statement that someone has a right to something is logically equivalent to a statement of existing duties. The dynamic aspect of rights, the fact that they are reasons for new duties, simply means that there is an existing duty on the courts to impose certain new duties on other people in certain circumstances. A's right to x is a reason for the court to allow him to x, to stop others from hindering him, etc.

The Reply. The courts may have reasons to do all that they are required to do in order to protect a right, but these reasons are based on different grounds. They may be based on considerations of general welfare or of public safety, or public order, etc. Sometimes their duty is grounded on A's rights. The nature of the grounds for the courts' duties is clarified by a right statement, but lost by the reduction. Stating the legally recognized ground of the court's reason for certain actions is no mere rhetoric. It may, for example, be crucial for determining the weight the court is allowed to attribute to this reason when it conflicts with others.

Rights of Officials and Corporations

It could be objected that even if my account explains individual rights it cannot explain official rights, nor those of corporations. Their rights are not meant to protect their interests, but the interests of others who are not the right-holders. This objection is based on a misunderstanding. Rights protect the interests of the right-holders. But these interests need not be intrinsically valuable. The reason for protecting them may be that by doing so one does protect the interests of others. Officials have interests. They are determined by their powers and duties, for their interest is to be able to use their powers and to discharge their duties. Corporations also have interests determined similarly by their purposes, powers, and duties. It is true that protecting these interests is not intrinsically valuable. Nevertheless, corporations and officials have rights in the same sense as other individuals. They have rights if and only if their interests are sufficient to justify holding others to be subject to duties.

Liberty Rights

Some may object that at best I have explained one sense of 'rights', that in which they correspond to duties. But there is a second quite separate sense of rights, i.e. the absence of duty. One has a right to x if it is neither wrong for one to x nor is it wrong if one does not.

The issue of the so-called liberty rights is a complex one. Here I will confine myself to a few brief and rather dogmatic observations. The absence of duty does not amount to a right. A person who says to another 'I have a right to do it' is not saying that he has no duty not to or that it is not wrong to do it. He is claiming that the other has a duty not to interfere. It is not necessarily a duty not to interfere in any way whatsoever. It is, however, a claim that there are some ways of interference which would be wrong because they are against an interest of the right-holder. 'I have a right to do it and you have a right to stop me if you can' is paradoxical only if it means 'if you can with no holds barred'.

The difficulty is that, though a statement of a right to do something is not a statement that it is right to do so, it is sometimes impossible to decide whether the speaker claims one or the other. The difficulty is all the greater because people rarely say, 'I am acting wrongly but I have a right to do what I am doing'. Nevertheless, they can say this. There is no contradiction in this statement. It is paradoxical, for if I know that I am acting wrongly why don't I stop? Consider, however, the past tense of the same sentence: I acted wrongly but I had a right to do what I did. This is not only in perfect logical order, it lacks the air of paradox. In fact it is quite a common thing to say. It is used when one concedes that one should not have done what one did and yet claims that none the less the other had no right to interfere. Such statements exemplify the fact that to have a right to x is not the same as to have no duty to x or not to x.

Though the objection is based on a mistake, it points to an important distinction which is yet to be introduced. We need to distinguish between legal rights and what I shall call 'legally respected rights'. It is arguable that the right to privacy is respected by English law. This means that there are no legal duties compliance with which violates the right to privacy. If this is so, then the right to privacy fares better than the right to establish a family because in England immigration officials have a duty to prevent entry into the country of husbands and fiancés of some women who have a right of permanent residence in England. This duty violates the right to establish a family. Though the right to privacy is respected (in the technical sense I have given this expression) in English law, it is not a legal right in England. The courts refuse to use it as a ground for imposing duties on officials or on other citizens to stop them from invading privacy.[27] Nor is it used by the courts to justify already existing rights.

Failure to distinguish between a legal right and a legally respected right may lead to the view that mere absence of a duty is a right. But if so, then privacy is a legal right in English law, and everyone agrees that this is not so.

[27] See *Re X (a minor)* [1975] 1 All ER 703 (CA) and *Malone* v. *Comnr of Police of the Metropolis (No. 2)* [1979] 2 All ER 620. One important aspect of the right to privacy is at least partially recognized as a legal right in English law: the right to confidentiality.

13

The Relevance of Coherence

Coherence is in vogue. Coherence accounts of truth and of knowledge have been in contention for many years. Coherence explanations of morality and of law are a newer breed. I suspect that, like so much else in practical philosophy[1] today, they owe much of their popularity to John Rawls. His writings on reflective equilibrium,[2] while designed as part of a philosophical strategy which suspends inquiry into the fundamental questions of moral philosophy, had the opposite effect. They inspired much constructive reflection about these questions, largely veering toward coherence as the right interpretation both of reflective equilibrium and of moral philosophy. In legal philosophy, Ronald Dworkin's work contributed to an interest in coherence accounts of law and of judicial reasoning.[3]

There were, however, other important influences on the growing popularity of coherence accounts in law and morality. They came from the application of a Davidsonian approach to ethics by Wiggins and McDowell.[4]

First published in the *Boston University Law Review*, 72/2 (Mar. 1992). This essay is an expanded version of a lecture given in the Boston University School of Law Distinguished Lecturer Series in Oct. 1991. I am grateful to Brian Bix, Penelope Bulloch, Michael Harper, Robert Bone, Avishai Margalit, Sidney Morgenbesser, and Kenneth Simons for comments on earlier drafts.

[1] Practical philosophy includes moral, legal, social, and political philosophy, especially when they are conceived of as so many aspects of the general problem of rationality in action, emotion, attitudes, etc.

[2] See John Rawls, *A Theory of Justice* (Cambridge, Mass.: Harvard Univ. Press, 1971); 'The Independence of Moral Theory', *American Philosophical Association Proceedings*, 48 (1974–5). For a sympathetic discussion of Rawls, see Norman Daniels, 'Wide Reflective Equilibrium and Theory Acceptance in Ethics', *Journal of Philosophy*, 76 (1979). An incisive critique of Rawls's doctrine can be found in James Griffin, *The Project of Ethics* (Oxford: Oxford Univ. Press, forthcoming), ch. 1. I attempted some critical reflections in 'The Claims of Reflective Equilibrium', *Inquiry*, 25 (1982).

[3] Interestingly, neither Rawls nor Ronald Dworkin (in his earlier writings) presents or discusses his work as coherence-based. For writers explaining Dworkin's as a coherence-based account, see Kenneth J. Kress, 'Legal Reasoning and Coherence Theories: Dworkin's Rights Thesis, Retroactivity, and the Linear Order of Decision', *California Law Review*, 72 (1984), 398–402; S. L. Hurley, *Natural Realism* (Oxford: Oxford Univ. Press, 1989), 262; 'Coherence, Hypothetical Cases, and Precedent', *Oxford Journal of Legal Studies*, 10 (1990). The degree to which Dworkin's theory relies on considerations of coherence is examined in the Appendix to this chapter.

[4] See e.g. David Wiggins, *Needs, Values, Truth*, rev. edn. (Oxford: Blackwell, 1991); John McDowell, 'Are Moral Requirements Hypothetical Imperatives?', *The Aristotelian Society*, 52 (suppl. 1978); 'Virtue and Reason', *The Monist*, 62 (1979); 'Aesthetic Value, Objectivity and the Fabric of the World', in Eva Schaper (ed.), *Pleasure Preference and Value*, i (Cambridge: Cambridge Univ. Press, 1983); 'Values and Secondary Qualities', in Ted Honderich (ed.), *Morality and Objectivity: A Tribute to J. L. Mackie* (London: Routledge, 1985). The influence of Wiggins

Their work points to the way coherence accounts chime in a vaguer, more pervasive way with the current philosophical climate. Coherence accounts fit well with the rejection of the Cartesian approach to philosophy. For one thing they seem a natural conclusion of the rejection of foundationalism, with its commitment to the view that all justified beliefs are justified by their relations to some incorrigible beliefs. Even those who accept that some beliefs are incorrigible would reject that. Moreover, under the impact of Quine's dual rejection of empiricism (with its belief in incorrigible foundations for all justified beliefs) and the analytic/synthetic distinction, many philosophers embraced holism, that is, the view that everything depends on everything. Coherence accounts, while not logically entailed by holism, seem to go well with it. If everything depends on everything, how is one to distinguish between truths and falsehoods if not by a test of coherence?

All this leads naturally to a frame of mind which, once one gets used to it, turns out to be oddly reassuring. We are all in mid-ocean on Neurath's ship.[5] We cannot disembark and make a fresh start with a sound vessel, accepting only safe beliefs. We must use what we have, repairing our ship from within, jettisoning that which, in the light of our current beliefs, corrigible and possibly mistaken as each one of them may be, seems mistaken. 'What is reassuring here?' you may ask. Is that not a recipe for scepticism? Not if one is convinced by Wittgenstein, or alternatively by the very different and incompatible argument of Davidson, that such scepticism is incoherent. Davidson's, rather than Wittgenstein's, arguments show the way toward coherence. Davidson concludes that it is incoherent to suppose that all or most of one's beliefs are false. Instead, he argues that to understand people presupposes accepting their beliefs as largely true. This confidence in the essential soundness of Neurath's ship seems to point to coherence as the inescapable solution to our puzzles.

I am not trying to describe a specific thesis here. My aim is to indicate some of the leading elements in the philosophical climate of opinion which make it congenial to coherence-based accounts—which make the air buzz with coherence. I will consider the merit and relevance of coherence in explaining the nature of law and of adjudication. In doing so, I will mention

and McDowell is evident in Mark Platts, *Ways of Meaning* (London: Routledge, 1979), and S. Hurley, *Natural Realism*. The merging of more traditional epistemic considerations with Rawlsian influences is seen in David Brink, *Moral Realism and the Foundations of Ethics* (Cambridge: Cambridge Univ. Press 1989), ch. 5. A hankering after coherence in morality, differently understood, and deriving from independent sources, is also manifested in Germain Grisez *et al.*, 'Practical Principles, Moral Truth, and Ultimate Ends', *American Journal of Jurisprudence*, 32 (1987).

[5] 'No tabula rasa exists. We are like sailors who must rebuild their ship on the open sea, never able to dismantle in dry-dock and to reconstruct it there out of the best materials.' Otto Neurath, 'Protocol Sentences' (trans. George Schick), in Alfred J. Ayer (ed.), *Logical Positivism* (Glencoe, Ill.: Free Press, 1959), 199, 201.

points derived from the writings of theorists who favour coherence. These borrowings notwithstanding, this is not an essay about the work of any particular theorist. It is an exploration of the role and value of an idea, and of some of the different forms that it can take.

Herein lies a difficulty. How can one make sure that the main, the most promising and interesting uses of coherence have been examined? That is the claim I make for my discussion, but I know of no way to prove it. It is possible that there are other more interesting and promising uses of coherence in explanations of law and adjudication than those here considered. With that caveat let us begin.[6]

I. AGAINST EPISTEMIC COHERENCE THEORY

Coherence explanations can feature in theories of knowledge. As such, they hold coherence to be the condition of justified belief. But coherence explanations are also advanced as explanations of what makes a judicial decision correct or what makes a legal proposition true. Because a justified belief can be false, epistemic, and constitutive (as I shall call coherence accounts of what makes propositions true or decisions correct), coherence-based explanations do not coincide. Rather, they respond to different concerns. Because one can be justified in holding a belief or taking an action which is, in fact (though unknown to one), wrong or mistaken, epistemic theses appear more moderate than constitutive ones, and therefore perhaps more appealing. But it would be wrong to think of them as being on a scale of moderation. Appearances to the contrary notwithstanding, the epistemic theses are more straightforwardly flawed than their constitutive counterparts. For most of this essay I will be concerned with constitutive coherence theories of law and adjudication, which claim that coherence makes legal propositions true or judicial decisions right. But to show constitutive coherence-based explanations to best advantage, and to clarify their difference from epistemic employment of coherence, I will begin with a consideration of the latter.

The first thing to note is that epistemic coherence-based explanations are not specifically legal. They claim that one's belief is justified (or that one's decision is justified) if it coheres better than any alternative with one's other beliefs generally, legal and non-legal alike. The reason is simple. A decision which coheres best with all legal propositions one believes may cohere less well than some alternative with all of one's believed propositions.[7] Of course, it is possible to argue either (1) that general coherence accounts

---

[6] I have put forward some considerations relevant to this issue before. See 'The Rule of Law and Its Virtue', in *The Authority of Law*, and Ch. 11 above.

[7] Or, for that matter, it may cohere less well than some alternative with all known propositions.

entail specifically legal coherence accounts of justified legal beliefs or legal decisions because they regard local coherence (i.e. coherence among one's beliefs about the law and adjudication) as in itself a strong constituent component of general coherence, strong enough to make the divergence impossible or at least very unlikely, or (2) that justification lies in coherence between beliefs of a certain class only, that is, that only beliefs about the law matter for the justification of legal decisions or of beliefs about the law. But those who uphold the epistemic force of coherence must have a reason for the exclusion of other beliefs, or for making coherence in a certain area the test for overall coherence. That reason will inevitably show that considerations other than coherence matter to justification, for only such considerations can lead to a deviation from a uniform account of coherence. Such explanations are only partially based on coherence. There is nothing objectionable in this, but as I am not aware of any reason favouring such a limited view of epistemic coherence, I will abandon that possibility and consider only general coherence-based epistemic explanations.

Their appeal derives not simply from the positive connotation of 'coherence'. Coherence conveys a specific good, the value of which is undeniable. What is incoherent is unintelligible, because it is self-contradictory, fragmented, disjointed. What is coherent is intelligible, makes sense, is well-expressed, with all its bits hanging together. Let us leave on one side the question of the relative importance of coherence. (Does it make sense to say: 'I prefer him not to be so coherent, for only then does he succeed in expressing his free spirit which is his best aspect'?) Can anyone doubt the value of coherence itself?

One can if one is a philosopher. I do not mean that philosophers can be expected to say any silly thing. I mean that philosophers, some philosophers, have taken 'coherent' to mean not just 'intelligible', but something (some things) quite different. Nobody would think that a text ought to be believed just because it is intelligible. But some philosophers think that it ought to be believed just because it is coherent. So let us leave on one side the undoubted value of coherence as intelligibility. We are after the philosophical notion of coherence. Realizing this is the first step in breaking the enchantment with coherence theories. In denying them, one is not denying the undoubted, familiar value of coherence (= intelligibility). The argument is about a technical notion of coherence and its systematic use in some philosophical theories.

I should not exaggerate the point. The philosophical notion, while deviating from the ordinary significance of 'coherence', is continuous with it. This is readily seen when we consider coherence-based epistemic theories of justified belief.[8] To say that a belief is justified is to say that it is epistemically

---

[8] Among the most instructive discussions of coherence theories of epistemic justification are: Keith Lehrer, *Theory of Knowledge* (London: Routledge, 1990), chs. 5–7; Gilbert Harman, *Change in View* (Cambridge Mass.: MIT Press, 1986); John L. Pollock, *Contemporary Theories of*

permissible to hold it, that there is no epistemic defect in holding it. The notion is vague, perhaps even obscure. But we need do no more than use it intuitively to see the appeal of coherence theories of belief justification.

How so? Because in epistemic theories philosophers use 'coherent' to mean something like 'mutually supporting'. Two beliefs coherent if each makes belief in the other more reasonable than its rejection. Opinions vary as to what relations must exist among beliefs in order for them to be mutually supporting. Let us say that if beliefs fit together they are mutually reinforcing, using 'fit together' in place of whatever relation(s) between propositions makes them cohere, i.e. makes them mutually reinforcing.[9] I will return to this problem later on. At the moment all we need to do is to acknowledge the force of this idea. It recognizes a relation of justification which is not linear and asymmetrical, but is circular and symmetrical. This may appear puzzling. If A justifies B, surely A cannot be justified by B. Justification must be asymmetrical, must it not? But, in fact, the thought that justification is circular and symmetrical is deeply rooted in our ordinary understanding of justification.

Suppose I believe (1) that John was seen going into Emily's house. Suppose further that I believe (2) that John has long wanted to visit Emily. My belief about John's desire to visit Emily tends to reinforce my belief that the reported sighting of John is correct. At the same time, if someone questions John's desire to visit Emily, I am likely to rely on the reported sighting as confirmation. The two beliefs 'fit together'—in this case because (2) explains (1), but we need not worry about what makes various beliefs 'fit together' at the moment—and they are therefore mutually supporting or reinforcing. All this is common sense. But in this example 'fitting together' is not an isolated and independent factor sufficient in itself to justify believing either proposition. I was told, by Jill, who is known to me to be trustworthy, that John was seen going into Emily's house, and I have reasons for holding that he has long since wanted to visit her. It is, one is inclined to say, only because of these further factors that I am justified in regarding the two beliefs as mutually reinforcing.

This seems sensible, but, as the advocate of the coherence theory of

---

Knowledge (London: Hutchinson Educ., 1986). For an attempt to justify epistemic coherence with special reference to moral beliefs, see Brink, *Moral Realism and the Foundations of Ethics*. Not all these authors have the same aim. Some are interested in the notion of justified belief for its own sake. Others are concerned primarily with an explanation of knowledge in which 'justified' belief features. Harman advances an account of rational belief change. The discussion is aimed at the employment of coherence in accounts of justified belief only, and does not affect Harman's explanations in *Change in View*.

[9] Should one not say that philosophers use 'coherent' as meaning 'fitting together', claiming what is coherent (= fits together) is mutually reinforcing as their substantive conclusion? I do not think so. The procedure seems to be the reverse. One starts by regarding coherence as a justificatory relation (i.e. as meaning mutually reinforcing) and proceeds to find what substantive relations make propositions or beliefs coherent in that sense. The main conclusion which defines the coherence theorist is that there is nothing to justification other than coherence.

knowledge will point out, it does not show that there is anything more to justification than coherence. This point establishes only that coherence requires a larger circle to carry much weight. To justify my belief that it was John who was seen going into Emily's house, my belief about John's desire to visit her has itself to fit other of my beliefs (e.g. about his general conduct toward Emily and his feelings about her). In order for my belief that John was seen going into her house to justify my view about his desire to visit Emily, it also must fit other of my beliefs (e.g. that the person who claims to have seen him knows him). It is all a matter of coherence, except that coherence works in larger, rather than smaller circles.

At this point things become problematic. Do we add nothing but further beliefs and further 'fitting' relations to the two beliefs from which we started? Surely it matters that the reliable Jill told me that someone, call him Jim, saw John go into Emily's house. In other words, the fact that some beliefs were reliably acquired—that they are not tainted by superstition, prejudice, rashness, jumping to conclusions, or other epistemic defects in the way they were reached or in the way that they are held, as well as their 'fitting together'—matters to the justification of holding them.

At this juncture the advocate of epistemic coherence theories may try his master argument. He may dismiss the objection on the ground that there is no escape from relying on the way one's beliefs relate to each other, for beliefs are all we have. What can one rely on in justifying one's beliefs other than further beliefs one has? Of course, he will concede that some of my beliefs may have been reliably reached, while others may not. But these facts cannot help me to justify my beliefs. In trying to justify my beliefs, all I have to go on are my own beliefs about the ways I arrived at them and their reliability. In asking when is a belief justified, we are asking when is it justified for a person to hold it.

How is one to judge between the coherence theorist and his opponent? At first blush it would appear that we are offered here two rival and coherent (= intelligible) ways of understanding 'justified belief'. The coherence theorist holds a belief to be justified if and only if something within the resources of the person who holds that belief provides better support for it than for other competing beliefs. The coherence theorist further holds that the resources of people which are relevant to the justification of their beliefs consist entirely of their other beliefs, including their beliefs about the ways they formed, the ways they hold their beliefs.

Against the coherence theorist is the view that there are epistemic defects in the ways beliefs are formed or held: for example, that they were formed through prejudice or superstition, or by people who are not competent to judge the matters concerned, which render beliefs affected by them unjustified, even when the person whose beliefs they are has no inkling that his beliefs are so affected. A belief is justified if the person who has it is not epistemically at fault, if he has done what can be expected of him, or something to that effect.[10]

Both accounts of justified belief allow that justified beliefs can be false. I think that both regard justification as person-relative, i.e. dependent on the state of the believer. They differ, however, on the basic features of justification of beliefs. They each have ramified implications and presuppositions, examination of which helps settle the dispute. They feed into one's account of reasoning and deliberation, they affect one's view of the nature of knowledge, and they reflect familiar differences of opinion concerning the presuppositions of responsibility. It is on the last aspect of the problem that I will comment.

I proceed on the assumption that we are interested in explicating the notion of justified belief which is part of our common epistemic vocabulary. The first step in the clarification is to identify justified belief with belief that one is not epistemically at fault in holding, belief that one may properly hold. The coherence theorist proceeds from here to claim that if one's other beliefs support the belief in question better than any of its alternatives, the condition of epistemic blamelessness is satisfied. What else can one expect of a person?[11] His opponent replies that we also can expect that a person should not be rash, or gullible, or prejudiced, or superstitious. That is, he upholds (in addition to coherence) objective conditions of epistemic blamelessness. People are to blame—epistemically speaking—when they fail to

---

[10] Notice that for a belief to be justified it is not necessary that the believer has a justification for it. It is merely necessary that the believer is justified in holding it. I am wary of attributing such considerations to any particular theorist. Many treatises in epistemology are inexplicit about the way they understand the nature of their endeavours.

[11] Two comments on the wider aspect of the problem will help clarify the comments that follow. First, we need to distinguish between holistic views of epistemic justification and coherence accounts of justified belief. Holistic views of justification hold that any belief may (depending on what else one justifiably believes) bear on the justification of holding any other belief. Holism implies (1) that there are no incorrigible beliefs and (2) that beliefs cannot be compartmentalized (by subject-matter or otherwise) into mutually invulnerable sets of beliefs. Holism is logically independent of coherence accounts, i.e. it neither implies them nor is it implied by them. Coherence accounts of justified belief imply that if a belief-set can be made more coherent by replacing one of its members by another which is inconsistent with it, this should be done. Holism does not sustain this conclusion. My discussion here is aimed against coherence accounts, and has no bearing one way or another on holism. One may say, following Pollock, that its real target is the doxastic assumption, i.e. the view that justification of a person's beliefs depends exclusively on that person's other beliefs. See Pollock, *Contemporary Theories of Knowledge*. In other words, the discussion is aimed as much against foundationalism as against coherence accounts. I avoid referring to foundationalism as a possible alternative to coherentism. I find, however, most discussions of the subject confused. Some versions of foundationalism are not committed to the doxastic assumption (here belong those who believe that perception is a source of knowledge, whereas hallucination, let us say, is not). Other accounts of foundationalism are firmly committed to the doxastic assumption. They understand the foundations to be beliefs identifiable by their form or content, rather than by their sources. While I hold no brief for either variant of foundationalism, the arguments advanced in the main text apply against the last variant only.

meet these standards. In these cases their epistemic functioning is at fault. The coherence theorist will acknowledge that when we do not function epistemically well we are more likely to fall into error. But when we have no inkling that we suffer from such failings we are not, according to him, to blame, and when our beliefs are blameless they are justified even when they happen to be false.

When we think of justified beliefs in this light, that is, as turning on whether the believer is at fault, whether he is responsible for holding a false belief, several observations become evident. First, it is simply false that we hold as justified beliefs conceived in prejudice and superstition, or entertained because of gullibility, obstinacy, or similar cognitive defects of the believer. The racist's belief in the untrustworthiness of members of a certain race, bred of prejudice, is not justified even if it coheres best with all the racist's other (mostly racist) beliefs. Coherence theory may seem plausible when attention is focused on the believer alone. But it is seen to be plainly false to our entrenched understanding of justified belief when we consider our judgment on the beliefs of others. We agree that people's beliefs are justified even when false, when they hold them in a reasonable way, on adequate evidence, and so on, but we regard them as unjustified when their cognitive processes or capacities are at fault, when they should have known better.

Second, the prejudiced, gullible, obstinate, etc., can avoid their mistake. They can acknowledge that they are prejudiced, gullible, obstinate, etc.—many people are aware of possessing such faults—and can counteract the effects by double-checking their evidence, consulting others, refusing to come to any conclusions, etc. One suspects that coherence theories appeal in part because there seems no alternative. If a belief coheres best with one's other beliefs, there is nothing to alert one to its defects. This is true so far as it goes. But it does not follow that one could not have known, or could not have suspected that it is not safe. It is a *non sequitur* to conclude that because one did not question a belief, one could not have, or that one could not have known what one's other beliefs did not provide (sufficient) reason to suspect. Justification and absence of blame may follow from an impossibility of knowing that one's belief is suspect. They do not follow where there was an epistemic fault which could have been avoided.[12]

Third, it seems likely, though no firm conclusion can be reached without examining closely what the 'fitting' relation consists of, that coherence is not only insufficient for justification but not necessary either. For example, you see your friend, John, out of your window. You believe, therefore, that he is in town. This contradicts your other belief that he is on holiday in Spain,

---

[12] Notice that not all flaws in the way a belief is acquired or held render it unjustified. Sometimes, for example, the believer cannot avoid falling prey to a trick or being taken in by unusual circumstances.

and various other beliefs which you have about his actions and plans. As it happens, you momentarily forgot about his holiday and all the rest, and are not in the least surprised to see him out of your window. There is no doubt in my mind that your belief that John is in town today is justified. At least on superficial examination, however, that belief does not fit as well with your other beliefs as the belief that you are mistaken in thinking that you saw John in the street.[13] If so, then coherence theory leads to the erroneous conclusion that your belief that John is in town is unjustified. It seems to me, though I am not confident about this, that there is no way of explaining what counts as 'fitting together' which will avoid the conclusion that the belief that he was in town did not fit best with one's other beliefs, though one will have to construct careful counterexamples to various possible articulations of that relation.

Fourth, another reason for rejecting coherence as necessary for justified belief becomes evident when we consider cases when one is justified in accepting or holding inconsistent beliefs. It is true that all true propositions are necessarily consistent. But it is false that any coherent set of propositions is closer to the truth than any incoherent set. It is not even the case that every consistent set of propositions is closer to the truth than any inconsistent one. This is so even when we confine ourselves to two sets which largely overlap in content, except that one is consistent and the other is inconsistent.[14] Even under these circumstances we have no reason to believe that the consistent set is necessarily closer to the truth. (Inconsistent though the Fregean articulation of the foundations of arithmetic was, it was closer to the truth than many of its consistent rivals.) Bear in mind here that, because we are concerned with believed propositions and because people do not believe all that is entailed by their beliefs, I am referring to sets of propositions which are not closed under entailment, i.e. which do not include all that they entail.

Given the possibility that a contradictory set is closer to the truth than a consistent alternative, the move to consistency can be a move in the wrong direction: the consistent set of beliefs replacing the inconsistent one may be both false and further away from the truth than the inconsistent one. Given that one knows that, it would hardly seem epistemically justified to move from the inconsistent to the consistent beliefs—at least not without further information, i.e. information which goes beyond indications of consistency to identify either which set is more likely to be true or which of the propositions

[13] I believe that Burns wrote the *Waverley* novels. But last week, when asked who their author was I could not remember. It does not follow that at that time I had lost my incorrect belief. My failure was of recall, of the ability to tap my memory, to activate it when the need arose.

[14] I am assuming that we can establish the overlap in content even though the set is inconsistent.

yielding the contradiction is in fact false. Again, it is possible, but seems to me unlikely, that an articulation of a relationship of 'fitting together' can be found to avert this possibility.

Finally, the last two points depend on the following proposition: while coherence theory, to make sense at all, must relate to the totality of one's beliefs, and not merely to what one is thinking of at the time, many of one's beliefs are not accessible to one at will. Much of what we believe we do not remember and cannot recall at will. Furthermore, many of the implications of our remembered beliefs elude us. This brings out the inherent incoherence of coherence theories. Their appeal depends on rejecting, as irrelevant to the justification of belief, everything other than a person's beliefs, on the ground that those other factors are not available to him. But by the same reasoning most of his beliefs are to be discounted as well. On the other hand, as we saw, sometimes what is not available could have been available. In many cases one could have come to recognize the existence of various epistemic defects, such as biases, prejudices, or incompetence to judge the matter at hand, much more easily than one could have come to remember certain of the things one knows which bear on the matter, or to work out their implications. Indeed, a defect one may be able to realize one suffers from is precisely this difficulty in remembering information of a certain type, or in realizing its consequences when one is under stress, and so on. Hence, sometimes one can know that one cannot remember correctly more easily than one can remember. But this shows that coherence theories are guilty of greatly exaggerating one's voluntary control over one's beliefs, as well as of espousing excessively voluntaristic notions of responsibility and justification. It is this excessive voluntarism which renders coherence theories ultimately incoherent.

II. FROM EPISTEMIC TO CONSTITUTIVE COHERENCE: REDEFINING COHERENCE

So far I have been concerned to refute the view that coherence provides the key to the justification of belief. You may, of course, say that all this is irrelevant because my topic is coherence and the law. Writers who have advanced coherence theories of law and justification did not offer them as epistemic accounts but as explanations of the nature of law and of correct adjudication. So why deviate from the view that coherence provides the key to the objective constitution of the law, to the view that it is the key to the justification of belief? There are three reasons for the detour. The first is rhetorical. Coherence enjoys such a good name that we should be on our guard: coherence may be the key to the solution of some problems, but it is not the solution to all the problems it is invoked to solve. This touches on the second reason for the detour. It is not always clearly understood that the jurisprudential theories of coherence are not epistemic, but constitutive. It is important to make clear that coherence is invoked in several distinct contexts, and that its success in some of them may well be logically independent of its success in others.

This brings us to the last reason for the detour. It may be thought (though I do not know of anyone actually making this claim) that the success of the coherence account of the law follows directly from the coherence theory of justification of belief. Roughly speaking, the claim would be that if justified beliefs form a coherent whole then so does the reality they represent. The subjective and the objective, the beliefs and the reality they are about must, when the beliefs are true, mirror each other. Whatever the independent problems with this argument, it can be put aside given the rejection of theories of epistemic coherence.[15]

I stated at the outset that constitutive coherence theories of law and adjudication are more plausible than coherence theories of justified belief. While by now my reasons for finding epistemic views suspect are clear, it may still be puzzling how constitutive theories can be taken seriously. Coherence may be a desirable feature of an intellectual system, the objector may say. We may prefer theories which display more coherence to those which display less. But this is all either a matter of intellectual satisfaction in one mode of presenting results rather than others, or a value judgment of some sort. Such judgments and preferences, the objector will continue, are irrelevant to an inquiry into the nature of law.[16] When we ask about the nature of law we aim to discover how things are independently of us. I do not mean that the law is as it is independently of human beings and their activities, only that what it is is independent of my, or anyone else's, inquiry into its nature. Therefore, our preferences or value judgments are immaterial. Our account of the law should be faithful to the nature of legal phenomena. And while it is possible that some legal systems display considerable coherence, there surely cannot be a general reason to suppose that they all do. There is no reason to suppose that the law lives up to our preferences or values.

In the end, this objection may very well prove decisive. Butt things are not that simple. To begin with, we need to recharacterize the way coherence is understood when it is advanced as a constitutive thesis about the nature of law, or as a thesis about correct adjudication. The epistemic

---

[15] It does not follow, of course, that because justification is not by coherence alone, reality or the law is not a coherent whole. They may be coherent wholes even if considerations about the coherence of one's beliefs are irrelevant to their justification.

[16] To simplify, I will concentrate on law, and will make no special mention of adjudication except when the arguments bear differently on law and on adjudication.

notion of mutual support is inappropriate to the new context.[17] For one thing, we are now concerned not with coherence of beliefs but with the coherence of legal norms, rules, standards, doctrines, and principles.[18] Furthermore, epistemic coherence is relative to each person. The justification of each person's beliefs is relative to that person's totality of beliefs. This makes it possible for each of two people to be justified in holding beliefs that contradict those of the other. As justified beliefs may be false, there is no problem about that. A constitutive account of law cannot enjoy the same luxury. It cannot be person-relative. What is or is not the law in the United States today is one thing, and what people believe it to be is another. If two people hold contradictory views about American law, then at least one of them is wrong. So if coherence is to play a role in an account of the nature of law (or of correct adjudication), it cannot be understood in a person-relative way.

This draws attention to the fact that to make coherence play a role in an account of the law (or of justified belief), that account must consist of another consideration beside a preference for coherence. It must include a principle providing what I will call 'a base', that is, something which is to be made coherent. Epistemic accounts take the base to be a person's belief set. Each of a person's beliefs is justified if and only if it stands in a certain relation to that person's belief-set. Constitutive coherence accounts of the law cannot have the same base. They cannot take as their base each person's beliefs, nor that person's legal beliefs which correspond to (a potential) legal principle. That would make them person-relative, and we have just seen that they cannot be person-relative. Their base must be, practically speaking, the same for all believers, so that the coherence imposed on it will yield one legal system per state, however much people may disagree about its content.[19]

The introduction of the base may sound like a betrayal of coherence in favour of a form of (a constitutive version of) foundationalism. Why should we not say that all legal propositions, let us say all the propositions starting with 'according to law . . .', should be submitted to the test of coherence?

---

[17] I do not mean that it is logically impossible to apply the epistemic notion of mutual support here. I suggest only that we need a more abstract formulation of coherence, not committed from the outset to its epistemic understanding. That formulation, broadly of a system whose principles are unified, will leave open what form of unity is relevant. It may turn out that epistemic support provides the answer to this question.

[18] For every standard there is a corresponding belief. To the principle *pacta sunt servanda* corresponds the belief that they should be. But not every belief corresponds to a legal standard. Neither the belief that oaks blossom in the spring nor the belief that Jenny made a valid contract with Jane corresponds to any legal principle. Constitutive coherence is not even the coherence of all legal propositions, only of those which correspond to legal principles.

[19] In principle, if a transitory base is admitted, each person may have a different transitory base from which he or she is led, by considerations of coherence, to converge on everyone else's conclusions.

On this view, the law is as stated by the most coherent subset of all legal propositions. Only in this way—you may say—can coherence be the sole judge of truth in the law. And I agree. So the first lesson we learn is that, even according to coherence accounts, coherence is but one of at least two components in any theory of law. The other components provides the base to which the coherence account applies.

This is the first lesson we learn, for clearly the suggestion we just envisioned, that the coherence test be applied to all legal propositions, is a non-starter. Think of it: among possible legal propositions are the propositions, 'According to law one should act to maximize the happiness of the greatest number' and 'According to law one should always act in accordance with the categorical imperative'. That is, if we take all possible legal propositions as the base, we may end up with a morally perfect set of propositions as allegedly being the law, but this moral perfection will be purchased at the cost of losing contact with reality. What will be baptized as law by the pure coherence account of the law will bear no relation to the law.

This first lesson has far-reaching ramifications. It suggests a division of labour between the two components of a theory of law. The base assures it contact with the concrete reality of the law; the coherence test provides the rationalizing element which enables us to view the law as a rational system governing the conduct of affairs in a country. This characterization is not precise, but its intuitive force is sound. It is strengthened by the second lesson which has already been pointed out above: the base cannot be subjective. It must be the same for all persons. In particular, theories of law cannot take as their base each person's beliefs, nor each person's legal beliefs. The law is not subjective in that way. It is not the case that there are many legal systems in the United States because different people have different beliefs about what American law is. Because the law is one, the base to which the coherence test must apply is one. Were the coherence test to apply to people's beliefs about the law, one would end with different legal systems for different believers. The need to find a common base to which the coherence test applies emphasizes the importance of that part of the theory and its connectedness to the concrete realities of the country concerned.

It is true that the base itself is not immune to coherence considerations. It provides the starting-point, the material to which one applies the coherence test. In the process of applying the test, the base may be modified. Elements may be added while others are rejected. One possibility for a coherence theory is to have a transitory base, that is, one which provides a starting-point on which some coherence-maximizing procedure is applied, leading eventually to a discarding of the base. Rawls's writings on reflective equilibrium illustrate the possibility of a base which can, in principle, be transitory. To achieve reflective equilibrium, one starts a process of deliberation leading toward it from one's existing normative beliefs, against the background of all other beliefs. During the deliberation one is led to accept principles which increase the coherence of the totality of one's normative beliefs at the time (again, given the rest of one's beliefs). In this process one also may discard some of one's original beliefs or beliefs which one has reached at that stage. Deliberation continues until one is content with the beliefs one has at that time. While in practice one is likely to reach that point while continuing to hold many of one's original beliefs, in principle they all may have been replaced by other beliefs.[20]

While a transitory base is logically consistent with a coherence account of law and adjudication, we can dismiss that possibility from our deliberation. Nobody has ever suggested a view of law which allows for it. All coherence accounts of law admit an additional consideration, one which provides the base from which only modest deviation is allowed. Thus, all coherence accounts of the law are mixed accounts. In due course I will raise the question of what that additional consideration could be. For now, it is enough to understand coherence theories of law as those which take a certain base, say, court decisions and legislative and regulatory acts, and hold the law to be the set of principles that makes the most coherent[21] sense of it. The more unified the set of principles, the more coherent it is. If all the principles follow from one of their number, then we have strong monistic coherence. If they all follow from a small group of principles which display a unified spirit or approach, they are less coherent but more so than if the principles derive from a plurality of distinct and irreducible principles which do not display a unified spirit or approach.[22] Similarly, if the law is derivable from a set of distinct principles which are completely ranked, then it is more coherent than if they are only partially ranked, and so on. Other forms of unity displaying coherence are possible as well. One can imagine unity through circular interdependency of a set of propositions such that giving up one principle requires the abandonment of all the others. If coherence takes this form, then no proposition enjoys priority over any other.

It is not possible to determine in advance precisely what coherence means, and how precisely different accounts of the law compare in the degree of coherence they show the law to have. These questions are among those which are at issue between competing accounts of the law, and can only be determined concretely in the face of the competing accounts. Only the

---

[20] See Raz, 'The Claims of Reflective Equilibrium'. As is clear from this schematic and not very accurate description, reflective equilibrium need not be committed to coherence. But consideration of this point need not detain us here.

[21] But resist the natural inclination to understand 'coherence' as 'intelligible' in this sentence.

[22] I am assuming here that distinct principles can display a similar approach, or one spirit, without being derivable from one more abstract principle. Different jokes can evince the same attitude, or express the same outlook, without being derivable from a statement of that point or attitude. I am assuming that the same is true for moral, political, or legal principles.

very broad characterization of coherence as the degree of unity in the legal system can be stated in advance. The more united the law is made to be the more coherent it is. The more pluralistic the law, the less coherent it is. Coherence theories claim that a greater degree of coherence is one of the considerations which make an account of the law true.[23]

III. IS THERE AN ARGUMENT FROM RADICAL INTERPRETATION?

The existence of law depends on social practices, and this makes coherence theories tempting. There are two arguments to be considered. The first can be dismissed fairly quickly. The second, however, will occupy much of what follows. The first argument suggests that law is dependent on social practices, i.e. dependent on human actions, desires, and beliefs. If so, then to identify the law one needs to identify the relevant social practices, and the actions, desires, and beliefs which constitute them. Familiar arguments establish that the attribution of actions, desires, and beliefs to people is interdependent. What a person does depends on what he believes and wants, what he wants depends on what he does and believes, what he believes depends on what he wants and does. There is no need to rehearse these arguments here.[24] An example will make their point clear. The Metropolitan Police in London used a photograph by Don McCullin in its drive to recruit more minority police officers. In it a young black man is running, followed by a white police officer. The caption read something as follows: 'Do you see a policeman chasing a black youth? If so you are prejudiced not us.' The photo is of a uniformed constable assisting a black plain-clothes police officer in pursuing a suspect. You see the point: while one knows neither the beliefs nor the desires nor the goals of the agents, one cannot know what actions to attribute to them. Once one knows their beliefs and goals, one knows what they are doing. Conversely, once one knows the agents' actions and desires, one can easily determine their beliefs. (The agent wants to eat, he opens the cupboard, so he must believe that there is food in the cupboard.) Similarly, once one knows their beliefs and actions one knows what they want. (The agent takes a book off the shelf, believing it to be a biography of Jean Rhys, so he wants to find out something about Jean Rhys.)

These examples are simplified. They overlook the possibilities of alternative

[23] The Appendix includes a discussion of some other ways in which 'coherence' is sometimes used.

[24] A crisp statement of them may be found in Anthony Kenny, *The Metaphysics of Mind* (Oxford: Oxford Univ. Press, 1989).

explanations and other nuances. They do illustrate, however, the general point we need: that we attribute beliefs, goals, and actions to people, not singly but in interdependent clumps. This interdependence means nothing other than a presumption of coherence. That is, the attributions determine each other on an assumption that the agent has coherent sets of beliefs, goals, and actions; that the agent acts rationally as one would given that one has these beliefs and goals; that one has the goals appropriate to someone with these beliefs who performs these actions; that one has the beliefs appropriate to someone who, having the goals one has, performs these actions. Given that actions, beliefs and goals are attributed on an assumption of coherence, and that the law depends on social practices, i.e. on actions, beliefs, and goals that people have, does it not follow that the law forms a coherent whole?

Clearly, to conclude so would be to commit a gross *non sequitur*. The argument merely establishes that to have beliefs and goals and actions one must have clumps of coherent sets of the three. Cases in which the coherence fails do exist, but they are—must be—the exception rather than the rule. It is a far cry from here, however, to an assumption of global coherence in any agent's overall set of beliefs, goals, and actions. Conceding that local coherence is necessary for rational agency is consistent with recognizing that people are all too often quirky, inconsistent, wayward, and even incoherent overall. It is certainly consistent with thinking of them as having consistent but murtually independent sets of goals and desires, displaying very little unity.

Some philosophers, notably Davidson,[25] have generalized the argument in an attempt to establish that to understand any creature as a person, i.e. as an agent who has goals and beliefs, presupposes an assumption that for the most part his beliefs are true and his goals and beliefs cohere. That argument depends for its plausibility on the supposition that we understand our parents and closest friends, indeed that we understand ourselves, in the same way in which we might inquire whether a newly encountered creature of an unknown species on Mars is a person, and what beliefs and goals he has. The soundness of that argument need not detain us here. Even if it is sound, it does not establish that the law is coherent. What the law is is the result of the activities of a multitude of people, and the interactions among them, over many years, sometimes over centuries. One cannot infer, in a Davidsonian-style argument about radical interpretation, the coherence of the activities, beliefs, or goals of all those whose activities make the law what it is.

Given the previous remarks, I will proceed on the basis of two propositions.

---

[25] See e.g. Donald Davidson, 'Radical Interpretation', in *Inquiries into Truth and Interpretation*, (Oxford: Oxford Univ. Press, 1984), 125, and other of the essays in that volume.

First, that the law is a function of human acts and social practices (though not necessarily exclusively so). Second, that one can identify the acts, beliefs, and goals of people without presupposing that they form, collectively, a coherent set. When discussing the law we are often concerned with the promulgation of statutes or statutory instruments, and with judicial decisions stating reasons for reaching a certain outcome to litigation. Such acts have a content: the statute, the judicial reasons. Coherence theories offer a solution to the problem of the relation between human action and the law.

To show how coherence theories deal with this relation, I will look at the two steps of another simple alternative—what I call the intention thesis. First, statutes and judicial decisions have the content that their makers intended them to have. Second, the law is the sum total of all the statutes and those judicial decisions which have the force of precedent.

The intention view is widely ridiculed today. But it is not without its appeal. After all, legislators promulgate statutes with the content they intend to become law; courts advance those reasons which they intend to be understood as the justification of their decisions. If the intentions of legislators and judges are not made into law, it is not clear why they are chosen to legislate or adjudicate. This explains why we care so much who is elected or appointed to the legislature and to the courts. We know that those people will try to affect the content of our law, and given the power to legislate or decide cases they will do so. They will be able to translate their intentions into law. But for this, why do we care whether a Democrat or a Republican is elected to the Senate? Why care whether a pro-choice or an anti-abortion person is appointed to the Supreme Court? It is not enough to say that we care because the court and the legislature affect the law. If they do not affect it by translating their intentions into law, then there is no need to care about their intentions. So the intention thesis has a core of good sense. Many dismiss it because legislatures and courts consist of many people, and no single person's intention can be decisive. The problem of institutional intention is a serious one, and not only for supporters of the intention thesis, but it cannot be discussed here. The burden of the earlier discussion is that we can identify intentions without presupposing any degree of collective coherence. So there is no way from the intention thesis to any coherence account of the law. Quite the opposite. It is unlikely that the intentions of all law-makers cohere, and, therefore, one would not expect the law to display a high degree of coherence.

Given all that, can one resist the intention thesis? Is it not the inevitable consequence of the fact that the law is a function of human acts and social practices? Not at all. The answer depends on what sort of a function it is. We share a concept of law which assigns a special status to rules and other standards which stand in a certain relation to, are a certain function of, human activities. But what is this function? The intention thesis suggests that it is one of identity with all the principles representing the content of the intention with which law-making acts and court decisions are undertaken. This is but one possibility. Another might be that the law consists of the valid moral principles which are closest (i.e. most similar) to the propositions representing the intentions of law-makers and courts. On this thesis, which we may call the moral approximation thesis, one acts as if each law-making act points to a valid moral principle. Sometimes it identifies the principle correctly. In these cases, the result of the moral approximation thesis is the same as that of the intention thesis. At other times, the law-maker's or the court's intention, while aiming at a valid principle, misses it. The law-maker or the court wants to identify correctly the principle of respect for freedom of contract, or of just, progressive taxation on income, but the rule they establish falls short of the morally sound rule. In this case the law is not as is stated by the intention thesis; rather, it is the valid principle nearest to the legislator's or court's intention.

I do not suggest that the moral approximation thesis be taken seriously. I mention it only because it shows how the law can be a function of legislative acts and judicial decisions without being as stated by the intention thesis. Moreover, the moral approximation thesis is sensitive to the intentions of the legislator. It therefore can claim to explain why it makes sense to care who the legislator is. It shows that the intention thesis is not the only one which can capture the basic sound sense which lies at its core. Nor is the moral approximation thesis the only alternative to it which is sensitive to the intentions of courts and legislators.

It all depends on the concept of law, by which I mean the way we conceive of the social institution known as the law.[26] The exploration of that understanding is a theoretical enterprise aimed at improving our understanding of human society. On the one hand, it must be true to the basic features of the institution, which in its basic elements and manifestations is known to all. On the other hand, it is not an attempt at an exhaustive description of the law. Rather, it is an attempt to highlight the law's most significant features, those which contribute most to our understanding of the functioning of the institution in our lives and its relations to other institutions and social practices. The intention thesis is one suggested, partial answer to this theoretical quest. It captures some elements correctly, and any adequate explanation of the law will have to succeed in doing justice to these elements. The moral approximation and the coherence views of the law offer rival ways of understanding the law. It remains to be seen how successful coherence accounts are.

---

[26] I have discussed the methodology of the inquiry into the nature of law elsewhere. See e.g. *Authority, Law and Morality*; Ch. 8 above.

IV. THE EXTREME PARADIGM: LAW AS COHERENCE

Following my method so far, I will formulate a pure version of a coherence-based account of the nature of law:

The law of a certain country consists of the most coherent set of normative principles which, had they been accepted as valid by a perfectly rational and well-informed person would have led him, given the opportunity to do so, to promulgate all the legislation and render all the decisions which were in fact promulgated and rendered in that country.[27]

Before we consider the thesis, the examination of one possible objection to it will help clarify its nature. The thesis, one may say, presupposes that we know what legal decisions, legislative or judicial, are, but that we do not know their content without the coherence exercise. This, the objector concludes, is unwarranted. If we know what the decisions are, we also can know their content, and have no need for the coherence thesis. The objector claims that having to introduce a base to which the coherence test applies undermines coherence. The base provides all we need for a theory of law without help from coherence. But in this form the objector misunderstands the thesis. It is perfectly capable of accommodating the objection, by incorporating the very identification of the legal acts of promulgating legislation and rendering of judicial decisions within the coherence test itself. After all, the content of the law which the test identifies includes the rules establishing courts, their rules of jurisdiction, and their procedures, as well as rules for the constitution, election, appointment, and procedures of legislative institutions. The identification of the legal acts which the test uses to establish the law is itself secured by the law which the test identifies. This is a totally innocuous circularity. Of course, the thesis assumes some base. It assumes a rough identification of the relevant legal acts with which to start, an identification that can be confined to the totally uncontroversial acts of the legal institutions of the country concerned. But the thesis does

---

[27] Many accounts of law emphasize the importance of coherence. Many of them bear no resemblance to the thesis formulated here. An example of such an unrelated accounts is to be found in Ernest J. Weinrib, 'Legal Formalism: On the Immanent Rationality of Law', *Yale Law Journal*, 97 (1988). I have discussed Weinrib's ideas in 'Formalism and the Rule of Law', in Robert George (ed.), *Natural Law Theory* (Oxford: Oxford Univ. Press, 1992). Other theorists who assign importance to coherence include Rolf E. Sartorius, 'The Justification of the Judicial Decision', *Ethics*, 78 (1968); *Individual Conduct and Social Norms* (Encino, Calif.: Dickenson, 1975), 181–210; S. Hurley, *Natural Realism*; Robert Alexy and Aleksander Peczenik, 'The Concept of Coherence and Its Significance for Discursive Rationality', *Ratio Juris*, 3 (1990). Ronald Dworkin's work also has affinities with coherence theses, and will be considered below. My aim here, however, is not to address any theorist's specific views but rather to address a generic position. Given the difference in the understanding of the relations between the law and coherence, my arguments do not apply directly to all these coherence-oriented accounts. But they do bear on the general merits of coherence, and to that extent they have implications for all coherence-oriented accounts.

not remain bound by this initial identification. It expands the range of legal activities assigned to its rational legislator-cum-court as the legal doctrine it identifies requires, and it may even, within limits, conflict with the initial consensus and delete certain institutions from its list if that seems necessary to improve the coherence of the main body of legal propositions.[28]

Think of this thesis what you like. It clearly offers various hostages to fortune, for example in its fictional would-be single legislator-cum-judge, acting on the basis of a set of principles, and outside the constraints of any political process. Nevertheless, two features stand out as potentially great advantages of the coherence over the intention thesis. First, it regards the law as contemporaneous, and as free from the dead hand of age-old intentions which shackles the intention thesis. Second, it presents the law as a rational, meaningful whole, rather than as the higgledy-piggledy assemblage of the remains of contradictory past political ambitions and beliefs, as does the intention thesis.[29] I describe these as potential advantages because, as they stand, they are suspect of wishful thinking. It would be nice if the law were a coherent rational system, free from the dead hand of past intentions and from the debris of past political struggles. But we all know that this is not so, that the law suffers precisely from all these disadvantages, and that so long as it remains, as it must, the main vehicle of politics, it will remain so marred.

Are these suspicions justified? Defenders of the coherence thesis will protest that they are as aware as anyone of the vagaries of politics. The question, as we saw, is what is the relation between these facts and the law. It is common ground to most writers on the nature of law today that the law

[28] A similar objection has been raised against H. L. A. Hart's doctrine of the Rule of Recognition. According to it, the law of a legal system consists in those laws which the courts and other institutions of that country are under a customary duty to apply. This presupposes an independent way of identifying which are the relevant institutions, it has been objected. See Neil MacCormick, *H. L. A. Hart* (London, Arnold, 1981); see also Mathew H. Kramer, *Legal Theory, Political Theory, and Deconstruction* (Bloomington: Indiana Univ. Press, 1991), 120. Not so. The Rule of Recognition itself identifies certain institutions as the relevant ones. Potential Rules of Recognition are represented by any proposition of the right form, e.g. a proposition identifying certain bodies and imposing on them a duty to apply a set of doctrines and rules. That proposition is the Rule of Recognition of a country which meets the following two conditions. (1) The institutions it refers to do exist. (2) They actually follow a rule whose content is that proposition, i.e. they have a practice whose content is as stated by the proposition. Hart's Rule of Recognition escapes from the circularity even without assuming an external starting-point, which seems necessary for coherence thesis. But if his theory is to be a theory of law, rather than of some other institutionalized normative system, Hart needs to rely on a similar device to identify the undoubted legal institutions as the starting-point for the process.

[29] The coherence thesis also gets around the problem of attributing intentions to institutions. But, as I have indicated, there is no reason to take this problem too seriously, except as against rather silly versions of the intention thesis. The problem may be sufficient, however, to reject the views sometimes known as 'originalist'. Cf. their discussion in Michael J. Perry, *Morality, Politics, and Law* (New York: Oxford Univ. Press, 1988).

is meant to be taken as a standard for conduct and for judgment by its subjects, and that typically they do take it so. That fact must be at the centre of any explanation of law. An explanation must show how the law can be taken as a standard for conduct and for judgment, and how it is typically so taken by its subjects. Further, the explanation must make these facts central to our understanding of the law.[30] the acceptance of the law as a standard is sometimes regarded as the reason for embracing the coherence thesis. The reason is plain to see. An outsider observing a foreign legal system can see it as a hodgepodge of norms derived from the conflicting ideologies and the pragmatic necessities which prevailed from time to time over the many years of its evolution. Someone who adopts the internal point of view cannot possibly do this. Adopting the internal point of view means that he regards the norms as valid for him, as guides for his behaviour and judgment. It makes no sense to accept an assemblage of norms as one's own norms unless one regards them as valid and justified, and one cannot regard them as justified unless they form a coherent body.[31]

There are several decisive objections to this argument, but before I address them let me discard one failed objection. It is no objection that we do not always view the law from the internal point of view. True, most people have this attitude toward the law of their country only, and some do not share it even there. All people are perfectly capable of understanding that states have legal systems and of finding out what the law is. Therefore, the law must be comprehensible from the point of view of an observer. And it was acknowledged that, for an observer, it need not be coherent. All this is true, but none of it is an objection to the argument. Given the admitted priority of the participant's point of view, even the observer, in order to acquire a sound understanding of the law, must understand it as it would be seen by a participant. If it must be coherent to a participant, then coherent it is.

The most fundamental objection to the argument I am considering

---

[30] This point has been more or less explicitly denied by Oliver Wendell Holmes in *The Common Law* (Boston, Mass.: Little, Brown, 1881) and implicitly by Marxist and economic theories of the law. It has been made central to his theory by H. L. A. Hart, in developing his thesis about the centrality of the internal point of view; see *The Concept of Law* (Oxford: Oxford Univ. Press, 1961). Among other works which further developed this idea (in ways which go beyond Hart's conception of it) are: R. A. Duff, 'Legal Obligations and the Moral Nature of Law', *Juridical Review*, 25 (1980); Raz, *Practical Reason and Norms*, 2nd edn.; *The Authority of Law*, ch. 2; John M. Finnis, *Natural Law and Natural Rights*, ch. 1 (Oxford: Oxford Univ. Press, 1980); Ronald Dworkin, *Law's Empire* (Cambridge, Mass: Harvard Univ. Press, 1986) (the theme has, of course, been central to Dworkin's work from the beginning); Philip Soper, *A Theory of Law* (Cambridge, Mass: Harvard Univ. Press, 1984). On Hart's distinctive position, see *Essays on Bentham*, ch. 5 (Oxford: Oxford Univ. Press, 1982). See my comments on it in 'Hart on Moral Rights and Legal Duties', 4 *Oxford Journal of Legal Studies*, 4 (1984).

[31] This argument does not vindicate the coherence thesis as articulated above, nor any other specific coherence thesis. All it does, if anything, is argue for coherence as an element in any explanation of the nature of law.

amounts to a rejection of its premiss that it is unintelligible for people to accept a less coherent body of principles over a more coherent alternative. The clearest counter-instance is the case of morality. Some moral theories enjoy great coherence, perhaps even the greatest coherence possible. Utilitarianism might be such an example, but any monistic morality, i.e. one which derives all its precepts from one fundamental precept, is an illustration of a coherent moral system. All of them, however, are misguided. In fact, morality is not a system or a coherent body of principles. It contains, to be sure, pockets of coherence, and it is consistent. But it consists of a large number of principles which neither derive from a common source nor are capable of fitting into a uniform system or a system whose principles are mutually supportive and interdependent. Unfortunately, though sound and interesting, this objection cannot be pursued here, as this is not the occasion to explore the nature of morality. Instead, we can resort to a second argument, of a more limited scope but pertinent to law. The argument for coherence we are considering proceeds from the assumption that, to be acceptable, a set of principles must be coherent. Let us assume that to be cogent and valid in themselves, directly, that is, due to considerations which are of the primary, most basic kind in establishing validity and cogency, principles must be coherent. This is consistent with the possibility that they are valid even though they do not form a coherent body of principles, for their validity may derive from indirect considerations. For example, if the set of principles one is considering represents the dictates of authority, they may fail to cohere and yet be valid because the authority is a legitimate one with power to bind its subjects.[32]

An authority may be justified, for example, because it is capable of achieving social co-ordination without which the level of personal security, social facilities, and economic prosperity enjoyed by the population would be much lower. Granting for the sake of argument that an ideal authority would have promulgated and sustained a coherent set of principles, an authority may be legitimate and its directives may be binding on its subjects, even if it is far from ideal and its directives a far from coherent body of rules. Even so, it is entirely possible that those rules secure the social co-operation necessary for the realization of goals which could not have been secured any other way, and whose importance is sufficient to overcome the shortcomings resulting from the fact that the authority is less than ideal.

To put the point more directly, it is possible, indeed I would argue that it is the case, that many existing governments and legal systems fit the description of the previous paragraph. That is, their law is the result of the rough-and-tumble of politics, which does not exclude the judiciary from

---

[32] The comments on authority and the law which follow draw on my discussions of authority in Ch. 9 above and *The Morality of Freedom*, pt. I.

its ambit, and reflects the vagaries of pragmatic compromises, or changing fortunes of political forces, and the like. Their law, therefore, does not form a coherent body of principle and doctrine. But it makes sense to accept it and regard it as binding. Sometimes citizens are duty-bound to do so because of the benefits of maintaining its authority in spite of all its defects. At other times, it may be morally wrong to acknowledge the legitimacy of legal authorities. Most of the time, however, it is intelligible that people take it to be binding, regardless of its degree of coherence. None of this assumes that the law is not necessarily coherent. I merely point out that sets of principles can be sensibly embraced even when not coherent. Therefore, the fact that the law is typically embraced by many of its subjects is no argument that it is necessarily coherent.

This second argument, the argument from authority, applies only to the special cases where principles are valid for indirect (content-independent) reasons.[33] But that the law is such a special case is not disputed. The coherence thesis takes as its base the activities of legal authorities. It regards the law as the most coherent set of principles which could lead one who believes in them to act as the legal authorities in the country concerned have acted. The existence of legal authorities is fundamental to the law: on this, coherence theorists agree with their opponents. Hence we come to the third argument against the coherence thesis, which establishes that it fails to make sense of the existence of legal authorities. The third argument is simple. This much is common ground: (1) the law is to be explained in a way that illuminates how those who are subject to it are meant to view it;[34] (2) those subject to the law are meant to take it as a set of valid standards for the guidance of their conduct and judgment; (3) those standards are, moreover, standards which emerge from the activities of authoritative institutions, and are to be taken as justified in the way which is appropriate to the justification of authority; (4) legal authorities are required to act with deliberation and for good reasons. Judicial authorities are often required to state their reasons, or some of them. Legislative bodies are not as commonly required to state their reasons, but they are subject to a requirement of acting with deliberation, in good faith, and for cogent reasons.

As we saw, the third point means that, if the law reflects the intentions of its makers, we need not expect a high degree of coherence in the law. Together with the fourth point, it also means that we must assign considerable importance to the intentions of legal authorities and to their reasons for acting as they do when we interpret the law and establish its content.

---

[33] Ibid. Ch. 2.

[34] I have here gone beyond the vaguer, more open formulation of the primacy of the internal point of view given above, in order to render it in the way which I believe is most appropriate. While this formulation will be disputed by some, most theorists agree on the primacy of the internal point of view, and that is all that is required here.

Otherwise, it would be a mystery why legal institutions are invested with authority in the first place, and why they are required to exercise it on the basis of reasons. If the way we determine the content of the law does not reflect the intentions and the reasons of legal authorities, then—barring the existence of a yet-to-be-discovered invisible-hand mechanism—nothing is gained by their acting for reasons rather than arbitrarily.

This point is so simple that I feel I ought to apologize for making it. My excuse is, of course, that it shows that the coherence thesis is wrong. It establishes that because the law is meant to be taken as a system based on authority its content is to be determined by reference to the intention of legal authorities and their reasons, and, therefore, that, given the vagaries of politics, including, let me repeat, judicial involvement in politics, there is no reason to expect the law to be coherent. By and large, one would expect it to be coherent in bits—in areas relatively unaffected by continuous political struggles—and incoherent in others. Perhaps coherent regarding the mental conditions of criminal liability, but not on the rights and wrongs of abortion.

I suspect that one reason, perhaps the main reason, why this lesson is often overlooked is that people think that it drives them back into the bosom of the intention thesis, which we all know to be wrong. But it does not. It points to the importance of the intentions and reasons of legal authorities, not necessarily to those of the legislator. This is a large theme and cannot be fully addressed here. Briefly, the intention thesis errs in isolating each act of law-making and regarding the law made by it as determined by that episode in isolation, once and for all. This is an unsustainable view. What we need is a way of regarding the law as the function of the activities of legal authorities in general, that is, a way of seeing how its content is a function of various activities, and layers of activities, in continuous interaction, rather than as a function of a single act, fixed once and for all. This authority-based view of the law will avoid the pitfalls of the intention thesis, while preserving its ability to explain the institutional nature of the law, something the coherence thesis fails to do.[35]

---

[35] It may be of interest to reflect on the methodological assumption underlying this argument by comparing it with Ronald Dworkin's views on method, a subject to which he has contributed more than any other legal philosopher in recent years. Dworkin would regard the considerations raised here as legitimate (though not necessarily convincing), but would place them further down the deliberative process. For him, explaining the nature of law (the main task of jurisprudence) is one of many questions about American law. For example, can corporations be guilty of intentional crimes? It is a legal question like any other, except at a higher level of abstraction. As such, it is to be understood as an attempt to interpret the legal practices of the USA, an attempt which is subject to the fundamental principle of (constructive) interpretation: that interpretation is correct which shows the law to be the best item of its kind. The criteria for assessing which explanation of the nature of law is correct are essentially moral criteria. The conclusion that the law is to be understood as authority-based and, therefore, that its content is a function of the intentions and reasons of legal authorities, if correct, is to be

The failure of the coherence thesis which I have been tracing can be viewed as a failure to take due notice of the base to which the coherence thesis applies. The coherence thesis seeks the most coherent set of principles which would have led to the promulgation of all the legislation and the rendering of all the judicial decisions which have been promulgated and rendered in a country. But why pay such attention to these acts of legislation and adjudication? One reason is that we have to do so because we are concerned with the law, and whatever a coherence theory which has a different base may be a theory of, it is not a theory of law. Our common understanding of the law, that is, of 'the law' when used in the relevant sense, is that it is intimately concerned with acts of legislation and adjudication. This is true, but it fails to answer the question. When I asked why we take these acts as the base, I did not mean to question that they are to be taken as the base. I asked about the significance of this fact. We take legislation as the base because of its centrality to the understanding of law and of the governance of human affairs by deliberate decisions of human institutions appointed to control and give direction to human conduct and to social change. An account of the law must explain the main features of the working of those institutions, for example, that they tend to generate a plurality of directives which cannot be readily fitted into a neat system. It must explain why they have these features. Coherence accounts take the base because it is too absurd to disregard it; then they strive to ignore it, and to explain the law in a way which transcends the inherent limitations of the workings of human institutions, and by transcending them they misunderstand them.

V. COHERENCE IN ADJUDICATION

Some may feel that, so far, I have refrained from mentioning the most powerful case for coherence: that courts have no alternative but to rely on coherence in deciding cases. The case is, one may say, a variant of the argument from the priority of the internal point of view. It says that, even

---

regarded as based on the view that seeing the law in this way makes it morally better than alternative ways of seeing it. By contrast, I am regarding the question of the nature of the law as different in kind from questions about the content of American law, different even e.g. from questions of the constitutional conditions of validity of legislation in the USA. In addition, while the argument, like Dworkin's, relies both on familiar and uncontroversial facts about the law and on evaluation, the evaluation involved is not a moral one, nor is it concerned with showing American law to best (moral) advantage. Rather, the evaluation concerns structural aspects of practical reasoning, and not its content (authority-related, content-independent justification of principles versus their direct, content-dependent justification). The evaluation is of what is important to our understanding of the processes shaping our social environment, e.g. that the existence of social authorities is important, rather than of anything which shows them to be morally worthy.

if ordinary citizens can have the internal point of view without seeing in the law a coherent whole, judges cannot do so. Their job requires them to apply a coherent body of principles. The argument about adjudication, however, cannot undermine our conclusions so far. I have argued not only that the advocates of the coherence thesis have failed to produce convincing arguments for their thesis, but also that it is false because it is inconsistent with the authority-based character of law. This argument establishes that the existence and content of statutes and binding precedents must be identified in relation to the intentions and reasons of legal institutions. The argument from adjudication must, and can, accommodate this conclusion. I will take the argument as advanced to support the adjudicative coherence thesis which claims:

> Given the law's settled rules and doctrines, a court ought to adopt that solution to the case before it which is favoured by the most coherent of the theories (i.e. set of propositions) which, were the settled rules of the system justified, would justify them.[36]

The difference between the adjudicative coherence thesis and the extreme paradigm considered in the previous part is that the adjudicative coherence thesis assumes a way of establishing, free of coherence considerations, the content of the prima-facie rights, duties, and powers created by law. Coherence comes into play at a later stage. Given that the law consists of many prima-facie reasons, arising out of myriad pieces of legislation, rules, and doctrines, including the common law and constitutional doctrines, the different prima-facie legal reasons may, and often do, conflict. Coherence is invoked by the adjudicative coherence thesis to establish the relative ranking of the different prima-facie reasons. By allowing for a coherence-independent identification of the settled law, the thesis is consistent with the argument from authority, which led to the rejection of the extreme paradigm. Considerations of authority are given their due in the first stage, in establishing what is the settled law. The resolution of the conflict among the prima-facie reasons established by settled law is the province of coherence.

Some advocates of this thesis distinguish between a doctrine of law and a doctrine of adjudication. The law, they would say, consists of what I called the settled rules and doctrines.[37] The adjudicative coherence thesis is about how courts should decide cases. Its import is that they should follow

---

[36] It may have been simpler to say 'statutes and binding precedents' instead of 'settled rules and doctrines'. But in order to accommodate legal systems which admit other sources of law, let us use the wider expression, understanding it to mean all those rules and doctrines to which the argument from authority applies.

[37] They include much more than what David Lyons called the explicit law; see 'Moral Aspects of Legal Theory', in Peter A. French *et al.* (eds.), *Midwest Studies in Philosophy*, 2 (Minneapolis: Minnesota Univ. Press, 1982).

the law where it applies, and should extend it according to its 'spirit', as articulated by the most coherent theory which would justify the law were it justified. Others regard the thesis as being about the nature of law, on the ground, perhaps, that if it is true then courts never have discretion. They are always duty-bound to decide cases according to what the most coherent theory which justifies settled law requires. If the adjudicative coherence thesis is sound, then this latter view has much to recommend it. I will, however, refrain from engaging in this argument, as I suspect that the thesis is not sound.

How strong is the thesis meant to be? It can be read to state a necessary and sufficient condition for a judicial decision being correct. It can be seen as a comprehensive and complete theory of adjudication. Alternatively, it can be seen as advancing one desirable feature of judicial decisions only. It is possible to hold that, while it is desirable that judicial dicisions should accord with the most coherent theory, they are to be judged by other criteria as well. Given a multiplicity of criteria, it is possible that sometimes coherence has to be sacrificed for some other good. There is one powerful argument favouring the latter view. It appears that the relation 'a more coherent theory than' is not connected, that is, various theories are neither more nor less coherent than each other. Various theories can equally account for the settled law without any of them being the most coherent one. If so, then it is reasonable to invoke other criteria for the guidance of courts, and to hold that coherence is but one of various considerations which make one outcome better or more correct, legally speaking, than any other. A natural suggestion is to add that of the theories among which coherence does not decide, that theory is to be preferred which is morally best.[38] But natural as this suggestion is, it is eminently resistible on reflection: must moral merit be confined to being a tie-breaker? It may be thought more plausible to make it another desired feature of the best theory of adjudication, so that one may prefer the morally better theory over the more coherent one, up to a limit. Given my doubts about the importance of coherence, I share the sympathies of those who prefer that option. Once this further step is taken, the problem of underdetermination reappears: there is no way of deciding which mix of coherence and other values is best.[39] I will

[38] It is possible that all the solutions recommended by all the theories which account for settled law, and are not less coherent than any other theory which does so, are acceptable, and it is a toss-up between them. But it is more plausible to expect that, while quite possibly some cases may have various outcomes, all of which are acceptable with nothing to choose between them, some of the time there are other considerations which may break ties.

[39] For a criticism of Dworkin's theory which points out that it is caught in an analogous problem, see John M. Finnis, 'On Reason and Authority in *Law's Empire'*, *Law and Philosophy*, 6 (1987). Of course, the problem is not necessarily overwhelming for anyone who is willing to allow for underdetermination and for gaps in the law. But the matter requires further consideration which cannot be undertaken here, as we are not specifically concerned with problems of underdetermination.

consider the weaker of these interpretations of the adjudicative coherence thesis. That is, I will take it merely to indicate one desideratum in good judicial dicisions. If this weaker theory is vindicated, one will have to consider the stronger thesis, giving it lexical priority over all other values, or even excluding all other values.

A number of arguments in support of this thesis can be culled from writings on coherence.[40] To consider them, we have to understand clearly what it is they must show. The adjudicative coherence thesis applies to all judicial decisions. It applies to cases to which settled law provides a definite solution, and it instructs the court to adopt that solution. It also applies to cases to which settled law fails to provide a definite answer. Plainly, the reason courts should follow settled law when it provides a definite solution has nothing to do with the merits of coherence. The adjudicative coherence thesis presupposes that settled law is to be followed, and extrapolates from this to other cases. The answer to the binding force of settled law derives from the doctrine of authority.[41] The adjudicative coherence thesis comes into its own where settled law does not provide a definite answer.[42] These are the cases on which we should concentrate.

Recall that we are assuming, for the sake of argument only, that sound moral and political principles form a strongly coherent theory. It follows that, if the law is all that it should be, the adjudicative coherence thesis leads to the same results that the courts would reach if they were to disregard it and successfully follow sound moral and political principles, because those principles form a coherent set of which settled law is a part. Were we faced with such an ideal law, it would be difficult to determine whether the courts ought to decide according to the morally best outcome or to follow the adjudicative coherence thesis. Forunately, no legal system

---

[40] See e.g. Neil MacCormick, *Legal Reasoning and Legal Theory* (Oxford: Oxford Univ. Press, 1978), chs. 7, 8; 'Coherence in Legal Justification', in Aleksander Peczenik *et al.* (eds.), *Theory of Legal Science* (Norwell, Mass; Kluwer Academic, 1984), 235–51; Robert Alexy, *A Theory of Legal Argumentation*, trans. Ruth Adler and Neil MacCormick (Oxford: Oxford Univ. Press 1989); S. Hurley, *Natural Realism*, chs. 4, 10, 12; 'Coherence, Hypothetical Cases, and Precedent', *Oxford Journal of Legal Studies*, 10 (1990), 222–6. As has been noted at the outset, the most influential writer on coherence in the law has been Ronald Dworkin, who has developed a rich legal theory which is generally taken to be based on coherence. See *Law's Empire*. I will adapt some of his arguments in considering the adjudicative coherence thesis in this section, and consider his own use of these arguments in the Appendix

[41] I have argued elsewhere that it is wrong to think that judges should always follow the law where its effect is definite. Their power may vary from one country to another, and their desirable power depends on complex factual issues such as the legal culture of the country concerned, the traditions of advocacy, and the qualifications of judges. But in all common-law countries courts, both judges and juries, have a legally recognized discretion to refuse to enforce a clear law on grounds of equity, or because it violates fundamental constitutional doctrines. While this refutes the adjudicative coherence thesis, I will not pursue this matter here.

[42] Such cases are sometimes known as 'hard cases', though they need not be hard at all. The best outcome in them may be evident to any right-minded person upon a moment's reflection.

is that perfect. Therefore, among other alternatives, the courts are faced with the question, 'Should we adopt what would have been morally the best outcome had settled law not been imperfect, or should we follow the adjudicative coherence thesis, which may lead to an otherwise less than ideal solution in view of the imperfections of settled law?' The arguments I will canvass all support the second alternative.

The Argument from the Nature of Theory

The Argument: No argument for the adjudicative coherence thesis is needed. It is simply an application to the law of the general maxim of rationality. Rational conflict resolution is simply the construction of the most coherent theory incorporating the settled cases.

Refutation: If anything hangs on the idea of constructing 'a theory', then the argument begs the question. Perhaps the right way for courts to adjudicate does not involve any theory construction.[43] If the argument is that there is no method of rational reasoning other than maximizing coherence, it begs the question in another way. It assumes that there is a general method of rational argument, or of rational thought. But there is no general method of rationlity in the sciences or in daily reasoning. We use whole congeries of methods and rules of reasoning and inference, almost entirely unawares. Nor are they constant fixtures of rationality. We learn to discard some, and we acquire others. And so do science and other areas of human endeavour through their history. If, given the state of our knowledge, legal adjudication should be governed by the one method of adjudicative coherence, there must be specific reasons to explain why this is so.

The Argument from Analogy

The Argument: This is exactly what adjudication is like. It requires no argument, looking only at the facts. The facts are that courts always rely on analogies, and analogies are an informal way of describing the process of establishing coherence between previous decisions and the current one.

Refutation (or perhaps I should call it a deflection): The view of analogy presupposed in the argument is correct.[44] But the conclusion does not follow from the very reliance on analogy. First, while use of analogy is a common feature of common-law jurisdictions, there is no evidence that it is universal, let alone necessary, in all legal systems. Second, reliance on analogy in common law countries is too unsystematic and unreliable in effect. The apparently random effects of resort to analogy have often been

[43] This indeed is my view.
[44] On the analysis of analogies, see MacCormick, *Legal Reasoning,* and Raz, *The Authority of Law*, ch. 10.

used as evidence that courts do what they like, and use arguments from analogy as a fig-leaf, because one can use analogy of one kind or another to vindicate any possibly supportable conclusion.[45] None of this shows that reliance on analogy is humbug. But it does mean that the apparent facts do not speak for themselves. One needs an account of the rationale of argument by analogy. Although coherence accounts offer one such rationale, it is not the only one available.[46] Moreover, analogies are always partial and local. The adjudicative coherence thesis is global and speaks of coherence with the totality of settled law. No direct support for any such practice can be gleaned from simply noticing the facts of judicial practice. One needs a theoretical argument to support one understanding of them or another, and we are yet to find one leading to the adjudicative coherence thesis.

The Argument from Fairness

The Argument: A principle of formal justice requires treating like cases alike and different cases differently. Treating certain people one way, under settled law, and others, in like situations, in some other way is unjust to them. The adjudicative coherence thesis establishes a baseline of similarity, so that treating people who are alike, in its terms, differently is unjust.

Refutation: The weakness of the argument is evident. The question is why should the adjudicative coherence thesis provide the baseline for the application of the principle of formal justice (if there is such a principle)? Surely there could be some other baseline, and what we need is a reason to prefer this one to others. That the argument does not provide. Instead, it betrays a misunderstanding of the nature of formal justice. Given that it can be satisfied by any baseline, and that the choice of the correct baseline requires independent justification, formal justice itself cannot help in justifying any principle of action. Its effect is confined to condemning arbitrary deviations from principles which are otherwise justified.[47]

The Argument from Authority

The Argument: In a way, the duty to follow (an imperfect) settled law is itself an example of justified deviation from doing what would be right had settled law not been imperfect. Following the most coherent theory which leads to all the same decisions as settled law leads to is no more a deviation

---

[45] See e.g. Julius Stone, *Legal System and Lawyers' Reasoning* (Stanford, Calif: Stanford Univ. Press, 1964).

[46] I will discuss several alternatives below.

[47] The argument from fairness is supported by MacCormick. Dworkin introduces it as an independent argument only to relegate it to a consequence of his argument from integrity, which will be considered below. See *Law's Empire*, 165–7.

than that. It requires no more than following the spirit of the law, or the implicit law, just as the duty to follow settled law requires following the letter of the law, or explicit law. Both flow from the duty of obedience to legitimate authority.

Refutation: Could the argument be based on a misunderstanding of the nature of authority? Authoritative directives bind because they are actually promulgated by authority. A principle cannot be authoritatively binding because of abstract arguments. It must arise out of actual human or institutional actions. Of course, one can direct implicitly as well as explicitly. But one has to direct for there to be directives to obey. Because settled law includes all the law issued by authority, implicitly and explicitly, the adjudicative coherence thesis cannot apply outside settled law on grounds of obeying authority.

But there is another way of reading the argument. It can be seen as a denial that there is anything which falls outside settled law, if settled law is understood broadly to include implicit law. For it can be seen to argue that implicit law always includes all that is required by the adjudicative coherence thesis. The thesis is simply a way of working out the (implied) meaning of authoritative actions. But if so, then the argument is misguided. Different legal institutions at different times pursue different goals; the implications of their activities are as numerous, diverse, and lacking in coherence as their explicit directives. There is no spirit to the law, only different spirits to different laws or bodies of law. Working out the implications of the law on the assumption that all of it was promulgated in pursuit of one set of principles is to be false to the spirit of all of the bodies which enjoy legal authority, and cannot be justified as an obligation of obedience to their authority.

The Argument from Loyalty to the Community

The Argument: Perhaps I should have called it the argument from integrity, for I have in mind Dworkin's argument.[48] But, as I am using it to support the adjudicative coherence thesis rather than Dworkin's own view of adjudication, it is best to give it a different name.[49] The demise of the argument from authority makes the justification of the adjudicative coherence thesis much more difficult. The problem we face is how the existence of a less than perfect settled law justifies deviating from what is otherwise morally

---

[48] Ibid. chs. 6, 7.

[49] One may also doubt whether Dworkin's argument has anything to do with integrity. Dworkin's integrity comes into play when people or communities fall short of the requirements of justice and fairness. It is the virtue of sticking by principles which 'justify' one's past actions, however misguided they were, even though such principles fall short in justice and fairness; see ibid. 176–7. It is doubtful whether any of this is true of the virtue of personal or institutional integrity.

best. The authority argument amounts to saying that we are not really deviating from the best that we can do. Rather, our limitations and the limitations of political practices make following the authority the best approximation of doing the best which is open to us.[50] Barring this justification, however, how can the existence of less than perfect settled law justify (even if prima facie only) doing less than the best in cases to which settled law provides no definite solution? The answer must be that such deviations from what would otherwise be best are justified, because they manifest a distinct virtue which is brought into play precisely by the existence of a less than perfect settled law.

This is precisely what Dworkin claims to have established. He argues that, in all but degenerate legal systems, one has an obligation to obey the law. Legal systems, he implies, are constitutive elements of political communities. Therefore, membership in a political community entails an obligation to obey the law. Moreover, he argues that the features which make communities genuine political communities ensure them a character which makes membership in them intrinsically valuable. Those features entail the doctrine of law as integrity. Here, I am not concerned with all aspects of Dworkin's views on law as integrity. Instead, I will consider the claim that genuine political communities have a character which yields the adjudicative coherence thesis (a thesis which is, arguably, an aspect of the law-as-integrity doctrine). Naturally, this consideration cannot be regarded as an examination of Dworkin's own views, though my conclusions may be transferable to a consideration of his writings.

'Political association, like family and friendship and other forms of association more local and intimate, is in itself pregnant of obligation.'[51] Membership in a society is a good in itself, and the duty to obey the law is part and parcel of membership. There can be no doubt that membership in decent political communities is valuable, both instrumentally and intrinsically.[52] The

---

[50] For a detailed argument that authority is justified only when this is so, see Raz, *The Authority of Law*, and Ch. 11 above.

[51] Dworkin, *Law's Empire*, 206. At times Dworkin appears to say that the existence of such a duty as an element of membership in what he calls 'political communities' is clear and beyond dispute (see e.g. p. 208). But as it is in fact very much disputed by philosophers and non-philosophers alike, and as he offers no arguments in support of his position, I will disregard these claims.

[52] On the notion of a decent society, see Avishai Margalit, *The Decent Society* (forthcoming). We need not consider here whether Dworkin's description of what makes a community a genuine moral one is adequate to what I called a decent society. More relevant to our purpose is the question whether only degenerate societies fail to be decent societies, or at least approximately decent ones. If, as some would argue, most human societies to date fail this test, if most of them are such that their members (ought to) feel shame in their societies and guilt by association for their character and actions, then there is little we can learn about the law in general from the notion of an approximately decent society. For law exists in all political societies, decent or otherwise, and those which fail the test of decency cannot be dismissed as occasional deviations from the norm.

question is what this tells us about the law. The argument from loyalty makes four claims: First, membership in a genuine political community carries with it an obligation to obey the law, because the law is the organized voice of the community. Second, this presupposes personifying the law, regarding it as a separate person, which means, of course, that the law does not speak for any of the institutions which create it and administer it, nor for the social groups which dominate and direct them; rather, the law speaks in its own voice, which differs from theirs. Third, this independent voice is an extrapolation from actual decisions. Fourth, this extrapolation is the one described by the adjudicative coherence thesis. All four stages are necessary to the argument, for it is people's relation with their community which explains the obligation to obey the law, and it is the fact that the law is an aspect of the community which forces one to accept its personification. The personification in turn leads to the need to disregard, to transcend, as one may say, the political vagaries reflected in the law. This is achieved, and here I turn Dworkin's argument away from its original target and toward ours, by embracing the adjudicative coherence thesis.

Refutation: The argument touches on more issues than can be adequately handled here. I will comment briefly on each of the points. First, we should beware of a tendency to over-intellectualize the implications of membership in national groups. It is primarily a matter of socialization, which is a major factor giving content to and setting the limits of one's options and capabilities on the one hand, and of one's imagination, affection, tastes, and ambitions on the other hand. National groups vary in character. Most of them are non-ideological in the sense that membership in them does not require adherence to any religion or morality.[53] Some, however, are ideological. One cannot be a member of those (assuming membership to be morally permissible) without being bound by the duties their ideology imposes. It is less clear whether membership in other societies imposes any additional moral duties. To be sure, living in one's own country concretizes many universal duties in ways which direct one toward one's society: one should contribute to its services, to the support of its members (though not only to them) who require assistance, and so on. When one is visiting a different country, however, those duties are directed toward that society and its members.

Does membership impose duties which are not so contingent, i.e. which are really essential to membership in national communities?[54] I believe that

---

[53] For a more extensive discussion of membership, see Ch. 5 above.

[54] The question is not whether such duties will or will not be universalizable. I take it for granted that they all are. The question is whether they are such as to be undetachable from membership in a national society, rather than those which are addressed toward one's national community simply because one happens to reside there at the time, or due to other contingencies which can change without change of membership.

there are such duties. They appear to me to derive from one's own identification with certain groups and communities.[55] It does not follow, however, that membership in a community carries a special obligation to obey
the law. Dworkin bases his claim to the contrary on his view that the law
is a constitutive aspect of the community. The view is difficult to assess.
Communities are constituted by social practices, and there is no reason to
think that they are all constituted by similar practices. It is clear that the
relations between the polity and the law vary from place to place and from
time to time. Today, in many countries, we are used to associating the law
with the state, though some believe, and many hope, that the development
of supernational organizations portends a decline in that identification in
the future. In Britain, for example, where there are several legal systems
(notably the English and the Scottish) in one country, the association has
never been very strong. Perhaps for the Scots their law is an important
aspect of their Scottish identity (though not of their British identity). For the
English, things are very different. Many in the middle classes regard the
common law and its judicial institutions as part of the English genius. Statutory law and Parliament, however, are a different matter. Moreover, work-
ing-class English people have traditionally felt that the law is not theirs but
that of the upper classes.

More generally, in many subcultures a fierce sense of national pride and
loyalty (not always expressing itself in admirable forms: football hooligans
tend to be fiercely nationalistic) accompanies a lack of any sense of obligation to obey the law, and often a high degree of lawlessness without guilt
feelings. While these are empirical observations, the claim about what
accompanies membership in certain communities should be regarded as
subject to empirical examination.[56] As a general claim about political communities, however, it is mistaken.

The second limb of the argument, that the law should not be regarded as
a simple function of the aims and actions of the people engaged in shaping
it, is clearly true. It is true simply because the law is the product of such
complex interactions between so many individuals that, as we were taught
by students of collective action, it is idle to think that its content can correspond to the beliefs or goals of any of the people who contribute to its
creation and administration. Notice, however, that this argument for the
personification of law has nothing to do with any moral value that it, or the
society of which it is the law, possesses. There is no moral argument for

---

[55] Identification does not mean willing endorsement. It means one's self-understanding of
who one is. People can see themselves as Jews, or Muslims, or as academic types, and so on,
while hating themselves and/or Judaism or Islam or academic types generally, and that hate
may be fuelled precisely because their identification with the group, or type, is hateful for
them.
[56] Dworkin regards it, I assume, as an interpretive claim. But that leaves it subject to the sort
of empirical considerations I adduced.

personification. Dworkin rests his claim to the contrary on the fact that integrity presupposes personification, and that there is a (partially moral) argument for integrity.[57] Before turning to this point, however, let me pause to agree with the third proposition in the argument from loyalty—that the independent voice is an extrapolation from previous decisions. As I argued in the previous part, the fact that the law claims authority requires regarding its content as a function of the activities, aims, and beliefs of the legal institutions with authority to fashion it. The question is, why should its content be extrapolated from their activities in accordance with the adjudicative coherence thesis?

The answer is that we recognize, as a distinct virtue of communities, that the government is required 'to speak with one voice, to act in a principled and coherent manner toward all its citizens'.[58] This involves two principles: 'a legislative principle, which asks lawmakers to try to make the total set of laws morally coherent, and an adjudicative principle, which instructs that the law be seen as coherent in that way, so far as possible'.[59] It is this second principle which is our concern, as it is the one which governs adjudication, and (partially) determines the content of the law (it determines the 'grounds of law' as Dworkin says[60]).

The notion of 'speaking with one voice' is taken by Dworkin to require coherence. But why should it? We can readily see that a person who is contradicting himself, saying and unsaying the same thing, is not 'speaking with one voice'. Is there anything more to 'speaking with one voice' than consistency? It seems that one speaks with one voice if one is saying, or promulgating as law, what could be said or made into law by a single person who does not act randomly and who does not change his mind. 'Speaking with one voice' can be understood as a metaphor for these two conditions. It can also be understood to include a third condition, the 'no-compromise' condition. I speak or legislate with one voice if I say or enact what I think is in its content best, given the conditions of the society to which my legislation applies. I do not speak with one voice if, in order to secure a majority in the legislature, or to avoid a presidential veto, or to secure re-election, or for other similar reasons, I compromise what I say or enact in order to secure the agreement or lessen the opposition of people whose views I regard as mistaken. Unless otherwise indicated, I will use 'speaking with one voice' to express all three conditions. Should adjudication be guided by the ideal of speaking with one voice, thus understood? And, if so, does this vindicate the requirement of coherence in adjudication?

---

[57] See Dworkin, *Law's Empire*, 187–8: 'We must not say that integrity is a special virtue of politics because the state or community is a distinct entity, but that community should be seen as a distinct moral agent because the social and intellectual practices that treat community in this way should be protected.'

[58] Ibid. 165. [59] Ibid. 176. [60] Ibid. 110.

This last question will be taken up in the Appendix. Let us now confront the first, more fundamental issue. Should adjudication be conducted on the assumption that the law speaks with one voice? Ideally, the law should speak with one voice. That much follows from the fact that it should be just and fair and, in general, morally ideal. It cannot be morally ideal if it is random, or reflects changes of mind or compromises with people whose views are wrong. This does not entail, of course, that speaking with one voice is something desirable in itself. It may be simply the by-product of what is correct and sound. But possibly being random is a distinctive way of going wrong. We need not adjudicate such questions here.[61] The problem is that we know that it is in fact unlikely, to engage in hyperbolic understatement, that the law is just and fair and morally correct in all respects. Given that the law falls short of the mark, should the courts decide cases as would be right were it up to the mark? Should they decide cases as if the law were morally correct, even though it is not? In the politics of this imperfect world we know that imposing one voice on the law can be achieved—if at all—only through the imposition of a regime with an inherent tendency to sacrifice justice and fairness, restrict civil rights, and curtail individual freedom. We therefore design constitutional processes to foster compromises in a way which we hope will approximate the ideal.

Compromises take various forms. On the one hand, we accept as normal the persistence of laws passed by the previous government, even when a new, more morally sound government comes into power. There is a strong body of opinion, both lay and academic, in Britain, for example, which regards it as highly objectionable for either Conservative or Labour governments to overturn all the principled legislative innovations introduced by their predecessors in government. Another way in which we regard compromise as acceptable is in passing legislation which does not answer to the principles of any particular section of the population, but meets various of them half-way. To give examples of a similar, yet not exactly the same, kind let me confess that I do not believe that mothers have a right to maternity leave. I believe that, aside from what is required by the pregnant woman/mother for health reasons, either parent (at their discretion) or both should have it. But I am willing to accept existing arrangements as the best that can be expected at present. I believe that the right to marry should not be confined to marrying a person of the opposite sex, and that gay men and lesbians should not be denied the opportunity to adopt and to foster children. Again, while I regard present arrangements as unsound in principle, I accept them as the best that can be hoped for for the time being.

In all these cases we accept the nearest approximation to morally sound

---

[61] I suspect, however, that reaching a compromise with people with wrong views or changing one's mind are not in themselves distinctive ways of going wrong.

solutions that we can obtain, even though by doing so we may reduce the coherence of the law. We make no concession to any alleged principle about speaking with one voice. Nobody who cannot have a whole loaf refuses, on principle, half of one.[62] This is precisely what the adjudicative coherence thesis asks one to do with respect to adjudication. I do not mean to suggest that courts should themselves engage in direct political compromises. The question cannot be answered in the abstract because the role of the judiciary varies from country to country, and from time to time. In general, I would simply say that courts should adopt the most morally sound outcome. The question remains, however, whether they should deviate from what is otherwise the morally preferable solution on the ground that, in the past, less than satisfactory rules have been adopted, even though those rules do not apply to the case before them. In other words, should they deviate from what is otherwise the best solution in order to make the law speak with one voice? We must bear in mind the following important point: so that the law might speak with one voice, the thesis requires a court, say the High Court in Britain, to extend a precedent which it regards as misguided in principle, but cannot overturn in the instant case (either because the precedent has the authority of the House of Lords or because, given the cause of action before it, the court has no jurisdiction to overrule those principles to which it objects), even though the doctrine of precedent does not bind the court to follow the objectionable precedent. Of course, sometimes it would be unjust to treat some people worse than others are treated, even if those others do not deserve the relatively favourable treatment they receive. Hence, if an unsatisfactory rule benefits some people this may be a reason for extending the benefit to other people, even though neither group deserves it. Sometimes, therefore, such considerations will weigh against replacing the unsatisfactory rule with a better one. But this is so only where special circumstances exist. Such circumstances are unlikely to exist, for example, when specified individuals will have to suffer in order to secure a benefit to those not entitled to it.[63]

In sum, no principle of speaking with one voice has any validity as a general principle of law or of adjudication.[64] It is not necessary in order to

---

[62] They may do so on tactical grounds, e.g. as a means of forcing the rest of the population to concede their full case.

[63] *McLoughlin* v. *O'Brian*, 1 App. Cas. 410 (1983) is a case in point. In this case, the defendants objected to the payment of compensation to a woman who suffered nervous shock. Those who object to compensation for nervous shock would be happy to leave an anomalous exception allowing compensation for a shock caused at the scene of accident at the time or immediately after it. Ideally, they would like to overturn that rule. But if they cannot, they would not regard its existence as a reason for extending it further to shock caused away from the accident. To extend it you must believe in its soundness, rather than in the need for the law to speak with one voice.

[64] It could be argued that in some countries, given their constitutional arrangement, the best implementation of a separation of powers doctrine requires judges to act on the adjudicative

regard the national society or membership in it as valuable, nor is it necessary in order to regard the national society as a distinct entity, not reducible
to its members. Speaking with one voice is a by-product of an ideal situation. In an ideal world, because morality is properly applied and morality
speaks with one voice, so does the law. But it is not an independent ideal
with the moral force to lead us to endorse solutions less just than they need
be. Without it, we are left with no reason to support the adjudicative coherence thesis.

VI. THE RELEVANCE OF COHERENCE

The critical character of the discussion so far should not be seen as a
sign that I do not see a role for coherence in the law. In conclusion I will
mention three reasons for valuing coherence in the law. The coherence I
will speak in favour of is local coherence: coherence of doctrine in specific
fields.[65] The coherence-based explanations to which I objected are global
coherence accounts. They impose coherence on the whole of the law. They
seem to me to err in two important ways, and these considerations underlie
the discussion in the preceding parts. First, and this point must remain in
the background for it cannot be explored here, global coherence accounts
underestimate the degree and implications of value pluralism, the degree to
which morality itself is not a system but a plurality of irreducibly independent principles. Second, and this has been the main lesson of the arguments
above, they are attempts to idealize the law out of the concreteness of
politics. The reality of politics leaves the law untidy. Coherence is an attempt to prettify it and minimize the effect of politics. But in countries with
decent constitutions, the untidiness of politics is morally sanctioned. It is

coherence thesis. It could be said e.g. that in the conditions of that country courts will forfeit
their legitimacy if they attempt to apply considerations of justice and fairness. Therefore, it will
be suggested, they should follow coherence simply because doing so keeps them away from
attempting to follow moral and political considerations. While the structure of the argument
is sound and the need to minimize reliance on moral and political considerations by the courts
may be important in some countries, it seems to me unlikely to lead to coherence doctrines
because coherence does not provide courts with determinate guidance, as this argument
requires. Due to pervasive incommensurabilities among values, many incompatible lines of
reasoning are equally coherent with the rest of the law. This makes coherence an unsatisfactory guide to courts if the problem is finding a determinate and value-free guide. For a discussion of this problem, see John M. Finnis, 'Natural Law and Legal Reasoning', 38 . Clev. St. L.
Rev. 1, 7 (1990), and 'On Reason and Authority in *Law's Empire*'. On incommensurability in
general, see Raz, *The Morality of Freedom*, ch. 13. It is also worth noting that coherence is in
fact very difficult to establish. It requires intellectual capacities, formal training, and a command of information about the law generally that is in excess of what is needed to reach
decent decisions on most moral issues facing the courts.

[65] For an instructive account giving coherence a limited role in reasoning, see Barbara B.
Levenbook, 'The Role of Coherence in Legal Reasoning', *Law and Philosophy*, 3 (1984).

sanctioned by the morality of authoritative institutions. There is no reason to minimize its effects, nor to impose on the courts duties which lead them to be less just than they can be.[66]

Where does coherence come in? The first point to bear in mind is that value pluralism does not mean incoherence. Sound moral principles are consistent, and should be consistently applied in the law. The coherence to which value pluralism is hostile is the felt need, to which moral philosophers seem to be professionally prone, to subsume the plurality of values under as few as possible supreme principles. While these attempts ought to be resisted, we must recognize that the application of each of the distinct values ought to be consistently pursued, and this generates pockets of coherence which exist, or should exist, where the law should reflect one overriding moral or evaluative concern. Two examples of such cases are the doctrines concerning the mental conditions of criminal responsibility and those which establish fault in private law, where fault is a condition of a duty of reparation. Morality recognizes mental conditions for responsible agency and also separates conditions which render the agent guilty from those which make him liable to a duty of reparation (in some circumstances I ought to apologize and help someone I hurt by accident, even though I am not guilty and do not deserve punishment). The law ought to incorporate these precepts in its doctrines of criminal and civil liability, and we can expect it to develop a coherent body of doctrine deriving from the consistent application of the moral doctrines to the complex factual situations which confront the courts, taking into account the institutional setting of their application.

Three features distinguish this type of case from the other two to which coherence is also relevant and which are discussed below. First, coherence is not here an independent consideration, not something to be pursued for its own sake. It is a mere by-product of the consistent application of a sound moral doctrine. Second, I am tempted to say that the moral doctrine of responsibility is a pure one: it does not reflect the outcome of a conflict of competing values and rival concerns. This may be an exaggeration, but it is true if qualified somewhat by saying 'in the main' or 'as applied under normal circumstances', or some other moderating qualification. In the main, the moral doctrines of the personal conditions of responsibility do not involve settling conflicts between competing values, or other legitimate concerns. This is a type of case to which value pluralism is largely irrelevant.

---

[66] While I am not advocating courts which are fully involved in political decisions on the same footing as legislatures, the nature of their task requires them to be somewhat political (in the wider meaning of the word). The form and manner of their political involvement, however, should be sensitive to the methods of recruitment to the courts, the qualifications and terms of tenure of judges, the nature of other political institutions, and—most importantly—the political culture of the country at the time. There is little of general principle that can be said. What was true of the USA in the mid-19th c. is not true of the USA today.

Finally, this type of case illustrates coherence as applying equally to legislation and adjudication.

Perhaps in this last respect the contrast between my first type of case, where coherence is relevant in the law, and the others is only a matter of degree. In the first case, in common-law countries, doctrines of responsibility are primarily developed by the courts, legislation having a subsidiary role. The other two cases also apply to legislation as well as to adjudication, differing only in their special pertinence in common-law adjudication. Both, however, are cases in which coherence becomes an independent (though not ultimate) consideration, and is no mere by-product. Each of them arises out of one of the two types of value and moral pluralism: pluralism in the sense in which a society is pluralistic when there is wide divergence of views in it regarding value and moral issues (at most one of which is true or sound, the others being mistaken); and pluralism in the sense that morality is pluralistic if it (truly or correctly) asserts the validity of a plurality of irreducibly distinctive and competing values.

Social pluralism, that is, the existence of a plurality of inconsistent views on moral, religious, social, and political issues in democratic (and in many other) societies, is likely to be reflected in a society's law. That is, it is likely to lead to legal rules and principles being in force reflecting the different outlooks of the people who fashioned them. This may lead the courts (and legislatures) to a dilemma. A court may be faced with a case in which it can, in principle, embrace a ruling which is morally best. Because the law on related matters was developed by people with misguided ideas, however, embracing the morally best rule may lead to bad consequences. That is, it may lead to the existence of different rules pushing in different directions, encouraging conflicting social and economic conditions. Thus, the actual consequences of embracing the (otherwise) morally best ruling may be far from ideal. Indeed, there may be a less than ideal alternative ruling which, if adopted, would have better social and economic consequences for as long as the other misguided rules remain in force.

When a problem of this kind faces the legislature it can simply revoke the bad rules, replacing them with better ones. The legislature can, in principle, opt for a comprehensive reform. The courts have fewer opportunities to do so. Given the cause of action in the instant case, for example, protected tenancy, they may be unable to revise other laws (e.g. tax laws) which promote opposing social consequences. Even the legislature, empowered though it is to adopt comprehensive reform, may find it politically inexpedient to do so. In such cases, both courts and legislatures are faced by what I term 'the dilemma of partial reform'.[67] They have to decide whether compromising and choosing the morally second-best rule which has better consequences is best in the circumstances, or whether it is more important

---

[67] See Raz, *The Authority of Law*, 200–1.

to let the law speak clearly and soundly on a moral issue, and hope that an occasion to extend the correct ruling to other cases will arise and be followed before long. This conflict is a conflict between coherence of purpose[68] and uncompromising pursuit of the morally correct line. Depending on the circumstances, it will be best to go one way on some occasions and the other way on others. In such circumstances we see pluralism[69] generating the dilemma of partial reform, and giving a local and limited value to coherence.

Finally, the third reason for local coherence. It derives from the way moral pluralism gives coherence (non-ultimate) value. Moral pluralism means that various irreducibly distinct and competing values are valid. It leads to conflict as a permanent moral state, arising not because of moral disagreement and mistakes but as an inescapable aspect of sound morality. Moral pluralism means that conflict is not a result of any imperfection but is the normal state for human beings. Furthermore, most of the time 'the correct way of balancing the competing values' does not exist. More precisely, on many occasions there is a whole range of ways of mixing the different values, none of which is superior to the others.[70] In such situations there is no moral objection to adopting any of the mixes which are not ruled out as inferior. People simply do what they like, choosing in accordance with their personal taste. Where many people are involved, the ability to achieve any of the not-ruled-out possibilities may depend on social co-ordination, that is, on its adoption as a rule for this society. Hence the permanent state of conflict between opera-lovers and sport-lovers, puritans and hedonists, and so on, over collective decisions.

Legislatures may be required to strive toward some equitable resolution of such disputes, allowing those who share each taste opportunities to satisfy it. That means legislatures should give weight to numbers, and decide on equitable distribution, through zoning or other measures. Even after such considerations are exhausted, there still remain many mixes of values which are not inferior to any alternative. It comes down to choice. Courts may reach situations of choice even more quickly than legislatures, because their institutional ability to reach sensible judgments on equitable distributions and their jurisdiction to put them into effect are much more limited. Either way, moral pluralism leads to the permanence of conflict and to occasions in which social policies are adopted by choice rather than reason.[71] In these instances, it is important to adhere to a policy once it is

---

[68] Ibid. 200–6.

[69] I highlight the role of social pluralism here, but the same problems can arise because of previous mistakes of like-minded judges or legislatures.

[70] See Raz, *The Morality of Freedom*, ch. 13; 'Mixing Values', *The Aristotelian Society*, 65 (suppl. 1991).

[71] This does not mean that these choices are either arbitrary or unreasoned. They are not unreasoned because they are taken for the reasons which support that policy. Reason only fails to provide sufficient argument to prefer this policy over all alternatives. That is where choice

chosen.[72] There are two reasons for this. First, adhering to the chosen solution is necessary for it to work in all cases where its benefits depend on
social co-ordination. It is often also necessary for the efficient operation of
bureaucratic institutions. Where a person can decide one way one day and
the opposite way the following day (in matters in which there is no overriding reason to decide one way or the other), an institution may well be
thrown into considerable confusion and chaos if it is allowed to do so.
Second, ordinary rule-of-law considerations come into play. Only by adhering to one coherent policy can the law be made widely known and its
application predictable.

Thus, this is another context in which coherence comes into its own,
another context in which precedent acquires a natural force, where there is
reason to follow it even in countries which do not have a formal doctrine
of precedent.[73] Coherence, as we saw in the previous part, forces one to
decide in a certain way because past decisions are of a certain character.
Coherence gives weight to the actual past, to the concrete history of the
law. The burden of the argument of the previous part is that there is no
general reason of coherence which applies to the settlement of all cases.
The consideration of moral pluralism shows, however, that local coherence
is, because of moral pluralism, of great importance. I call it local coherence
because there are many isolated decisions which amount to an unconstrained
choice between different possible compromises between conflicting values.
There is no reason to lump all these compromises together as one decision
covering all cases, and I suspect that the very attempt is incoherent. Societies are faced with numerous discrete issues of conflict, and decide on
solutions to them as they arise. Each solution gives rise to considerations of
coherence within its scope, based on the need to secure co-ordination and
on rule of law values.

In this schematic discussion it is impossible to analyse conflict cases in
detail. It is important, however, to note in conclusion how pervasive they
are. They include issues of the allocation of resources to public amenities;
regulation of the character of the natural and human environment (noise as

comes in. They are not arbitrary, for it is only arbitrary to disregard reason; i.e. where reason
dominates one can be arbitrary; where there is none, it is not arbitrary to choose in accordance
with one's wish or taste (is it arbitrary to choose a peach rather than an apricot when offered
one or the other?).

[72] I do not mean that it should never change, only that it should not be changed too
frequently.

[73] Formal rules of precedent, like the English rule that all the courts (other than the House
of Lords itself) are bound by the *ratio decidendi* of the House of Lords, give precedent a force
similar to that of legislation, i.e. within the scope of the rule laid down in the ratio of the binding decision. The natural force of precedent which does not depend on any formal doctrine
is not so limited. It works through considerations of coherence of purpose, and applies outside
the scope of the rule enunciated in the precedent-setting decision, so long as coherence considerations require that.

well as river pollution); constitutional rights adjudication, such as the balance between the interest of people in being able to express their views and being heard and the interest of the same or other people in being able not to listen and not being made to hear unless they want to; and the allocation of liability to risk and its imposition on others, as in rules which determine what forms of conduct are negligent and what standards of care people are required to observe. These are but a few examples of the pervasiveness of choice-demanding conflicts. Therefore, they are also examples of the pervasiveness of the force of localized coherence considerations.

Coherence, one might say, is everywhere. But it is local rather than global coherence, and it comes into its own mostly once questions of principle (including questions of resolving conflicts of value where they are resolvable by reason) are resolved on other grounds.

Appendix

Speaking with One Voice: On Dworkinian Integrity and Coherence

It is impossible to miss the ambivalent interpretation of Ronald Dworkin's work in this chapter. On the one hand, it is regarded as one of the mainsprings of the interest in coherence theories in the law, and the argument from integrity has been examined as the most promising argument for a coherence account of the law. On the other hand, I dissociated Dworkin from this use of the argument, and warned the reader not to assume too hastily that Dworkin does see coherence as important. My ambivalent attitude stems from Dworkin's less than clear discussion of these subjects. In this appendix, I will examine his attitude toward coherence as revealed by the central chapters of *Law's Empire*. The interest in doing so is not merely an interest in understanding Dworkin. Part IV above included a refutation of the suggestion that there is a distinct virtue of coherence through loyalty to the past which justifies deviating from the precepts of justice and fairness. I will suggest below that Dworkin's view of law as integrity is subject to the same criticism independently of whether it does favour coherence. This shows that the argument deployed in the text catches theories other than coherence theories. It applies to any idealizations of the law which diminish the importance of the doctrine of authority and the role of politics in its explanation. It is an objection of principle to any doctrine which requires the courts to adjudicate disputes on the assumption that the law speaks with one voice, regardless of whether this univocality expresses itself through a doctrine of coherence or in some other way.

For Dworkin, explaining the nature of law is offering an interpretation of the law. This is not the place to assess his view of the nature and role of interpretation. I merely want to discover the way it does or does not interact with considerations of coherence. The ambivalence begins at the beginning. At the most basic level, Dworkin explains interpretation as follows: 'constructive interpretation [of which the interpretation of the law is an instance] is a matter of imposing purpose on an object or practice in order to make of it the best possible example of the form or genre to which it is taken to belong.'[74] Here, interpretation is defined in terms of strong monistic coherence. Coherence, as we know, means close systematic interdependence of all the parts. Seemingly, Dworkinian interpretation is conceived from the start as committed to strong monism, for it is committed to finding *one* purpose which unites and dominates all the parts of the interpreted object or practice (dominates, for in the post-interpretive stage,[75] what the practice requires is adjusted to suit the imposed purpose).

But is it right to attribute to Dworkin this commitment (which is never justified even by a shadow of an argument) to strong coherence? Perhaps his reference to one purpose is simply a *façon de parler*, perhaps Dworkin is willing to contemplate a plurality of unrelated purposes imposed by the interpretation, which shows whatever is interpreted as being the best of its kind. In the more detailed general description of interpretation, he writes of 'some general justification' for the practice.[76] A general justification can be monistic, exhibiting a high degree of coherence, but it need not be. It may be of any degree of coherence down to pluralistic justifications by a plurality of unrelated elements. The evidence is ambiguous, tending on balance to support an unargued-for endorsement of monistic coherence when the interpretation of social practices is concerned.[77]

The tendency toward strong coherence seems to reappear when Dworkin introduces integrity:

It will be useful to divide the claims of integrity into two more practical principles. The first is the principle of integrity in legislation, which asks those who create law by legislation to keep that law coherent in principle. The second is the principle of integrity in adjudication: it asks those responsible for deciding what the law is to see and enforce it as coherent in that way.[78]

---

[74] *Law's Empire*, 52.   [75] Ibid. 66.   [76] Ibid.

[77] For several additional references to one purpose in *Law's Empire*, see ibid. 67, 87, 94, 98. Other locutions, however, are more open to pluralistic justifications.

[78] Ibid. 167.

Dworkin's first principle is to guide legislators in making law. My concern is with the second principle, which determines both how cases are to be decided and what the law is, because, according to Dworkin, these two question are one and the same. How the courts should determine the law is far from clear from this statement. What stands out is the duty to see the law as coherent. But does the principle as stated really express an endorsement of coherence? It seems to do so because the word appears in its formulation. We know, however, that coherence is often used to indicate no more than the cogency or even the intelligibility of a principle or an idea. Which way does Dworkin mean to use it? Dworkin's earlier discussion of interpretation, which, to be any good, must be understood to lead to a strongly, monistically coherent view of interpretation, suggests that he means something similar here.

But does he? A few pages later he states (discussing integrity in legislation): 'Integrity is flouted . . . whenever a community enacts and enforces different laws each of which is coherent in itself, but which cannot be defended together as expressing a coherent ranking of different principles of justice or fairness or procedural due process.'[79] There is no trace of one point or purpose here. The degree of coherence is much less; it is merely that of ranking a plurality of irreducibly distinct principles of justice and fairness. This is still a commitment to a greater degree of coherence than exists, given that, in fact, such principles are not rankable. My purpose is simply to point out the difficulty in attributing any definite view on coherence to Dworkin.

When Dworkin turns from integrity in legislation to his explanation of law as based on integrity, coherence simply drops, quietly and without comment, out of the picture: 'According to law as integrity, propositions of law are true if they figure in or follow from the principles of justice, fairness, and procedural due process that provide the best constructive interpretation of the community's legal practice.'[80] It is inconceivable that Dworkin would have allowed coherence to disappear without explanation had he been genuinely committed to it. It is especially important to remember that there is nothing in *Law's Empire* to suggest that the principles of justice are not themselves irreducibly plural, and the same is true of fairness and procedural due process.

I suggest, therefore, that his is not a coherence explanation of either law or integrity. His position is as explained in the previous quotation: the law consists of those principles of justice and fairness and procedural due process which provide the best (i.e. morally best) set of sound principles capable of explaining the legal decisions taken throughout the history of the polity in question. Whether or not such principles display any degree of

---

[79] Ibid. 184.   [80] Ibid. 225.

coherence, in the sense of interdependence, is an open question. Thus, while coherence may be a by-product of the best theory of law, a preference for coherence is not part of the desiderata by which the best theory is determined. The reason for thinking that Dworkin is not at all committed to the desirability of coherence is that his text is ambivalent and that, while Dworkin argues at length that interpretations are necessarily evaluative, and that they try to show their object as the best of its kind, and that the interpretation of the law is committed to integrity, he never provides any reason whatsoever to suggest that coherence is a desideratum in correct interpretations.

Three objections may be raised to the conclusion that Dworkin's theory of law contains no commitment to any degree of coherence. First, in the quotation above, while coherence is not specifically mentioned, it is implied in the reference to 'constructive interpretation', for, as we saw above, interpretation must, according to Dworkin, be not only coherent but monistic. This would be a decisive argument but for the fact that Dworkin's commitment to a monistic view of interpretation must itself be questionable, partly on textual grounds, partly because it is so unlikely that he would have committed himself to such an initially implausible view without even a shadow of an argument to support it.

Second, it may be argued that while integrity (in adjudication) itself is not committed to coherence, this does not show that either the law or adjudication need not be based on a set of principles displaying tight coherence, because integrity is only one element in law and adjudication. This is a matter of some delicacy. Clearly, integrity is not a conclusive ground for good legislation. While legislators should value integrity for its own sake, they may find that other considerations prevail and thus may compromise it.[81] The adjudicative principle of integrity has, however, a different status from that of the legislative principle. On the one hand, it is a principle about how courts should decide cases. On the other hand, it is a principle identifying the grounds of law[82] and, as such, is the touchstone distinguishing what is the law from what is not.[83] As a principle about how courts should decide cases it is merely prima facie,[84] and there may be cases in which the courts ought not to compromise justice and fairness for the sake of integrity. But in its second capacity it is definitive. Rules which do not pass the test of integrity are not part of the law.

The two aspects of the principle are consistent. It merely means that sometimes courts ought not to decide cases on the basis of the law, but that they should overturn it and lay down a different rule. Less clear, however, is whether this imperative—the requirement that judges go against the law

---

[81] Ibid. 181, 217.   [82] Ibid. 218.
[83] Ibid. 225.   [84] Ibid. 218.

when it calls for too great a sacrifice of justice for the sake of integrity—is a legal or a non-legal one. That is, does *Law's Empire* recognize a legal duty on the courts to decide cases on appropriate occasions by transcending the law, or does the book hold that legally the courts ought always to apply the law, but morally they sometimes should not do so? Most theorists agree that the latter is sometimes the case. Many legal theorists believe that the former is always the case, though not normally for the reasons indicated in *Law's Empire*. When courts are legally required to apply non-legal consider-ations they are commonly said to have discretion.[85] Dworkin has first dis-tinguished himself as a legal theorist who denies that courts are ever legally required or permitted to do anything other than apply the law (to the facts). It therefore would seem that, while he holds that courts always have and sometimes should exercise moral discretion to transcend the law, they are never legally allowed to do so. This position indicates a major develop-ment in Dworkin's views. In the past he had no independent theory of law. Unlike theorists like Hart, Kelsen, and others who distinguish between (1) 'what is the law?' and (2) 'what considerations should guide courts in deciding cases?' and hold that the answer to the second includes more than the law, Dworkin has always identified the two questions. His theory of adjudication was his theory of law. The answer to the question what con-siderations should guide courts in deciding cases answers the question of what is the law. Given that assumption,[86] courts have no discretion and must always obey the law. In *Law's Empire*, a new position emerges. We have a concept of law which is totally independent of any reference to adjudi-cation.[87] This leaves room for the possibility of discretion. As we saw, Dworkin allows that such discretion exists. He still seems to differ from other theorists, however, in thinking that in exercising discretion courts violate the law. But that is a moot point. First, he does not explicitly say this. Second, because according to *Law's Empire* the reasons to deviate from the law are open moral reasons which guide the action of the courts in appro-priate circumstances, it is not clear why the law should not be understood

[85] The term does not mean that they can do what they like. Its meaning in the debates in legal theory is that courts are entrusted with more than applying the law. Their task, their legally appointed task, includes power to revise and develop the law, which they do with guidance from legal standards which direct them to step beyond the bounds of the law and apply moral considerations.

[86] I call it an assumption as Dworkin has never argued for it. It may seem that he has not realized, at least not at the beginning, that it is at this point that he disputes the work of Hart and others; i.e he may not have realized that once this assumption is granted the question whether courts enjoy discretion is settled. Of course, if everything they can take into account is the law, they do not have (so-called strong) discretion to go outside the law. See Raz, postscript to 'Legal Principles and the Limits of Law', in M. Cohen (ed.), *Dworkin and Con-temporary Jurisprudence* (Towota, NJ: Rowman and Allanheld, 1984); Ch. 8 above.

[87] Dworkin states: 'The law of a community . . . is the scheme of rights and responsibilities that meet that complex standard: they license coercion because they flow from past decisions of the right sort'; *Law's Empire*, 93.

to sanction them. Even writers like myself and others whose understanding of the law allows room for the role of extralegal considerations in adjudication hold that the law recognizes the practice of resorting to them, a recognition which is expressed in the very fact that courts do so openly and without any legislation or directive to stop them. In the past, Dworkin has suggested that there be no resort to extralegal considerations in adjudication. There was never a strong argument to justify this, and he does not repeat this claim in *Law's Empire*. It is now moot whether and why Dworkin does not accept judicial discretion as legal practice. Be that as it may, given that the requirement to go against integrity is a requirement to go against the law, there is nothing we can learn from it about the degree of coherence in the law.

I have to admit that there are further unclarities in the position advocated in *Law's Empire*. In the course of Dworkin's extensive discussion of the *McLoughlin* case,[88] he says 'but here . . . questions of fit surface again, because an interpretation is *pro tanto* more satisfactory if it shows less damage to integrity than its rival. [The judge] will therefore consider whether interpretation (5) fits the expanded legal record better than (6).'[89] This seems to imply that integrity is a matter of achieving the greatest possible fit with past legal record. We know from the general discussion that fit is but one of two dimensions which identify the law. The other is value. If so, then integrity is but one, and not—according to *Law's Empire*—a lexically prior consideration in determining the content of the law and what the courts may legally be required to do. Hence, it may well be that Dworkin regards the law as much more coherent than his commitment to integrity would suggest, for it may be that the combination of the two dimensions will make it so. But this line of thinking gives undue weight to the one text in which Dworkin equates integrity with fit. It seems best to disregard it.

Third, the final objection to my earlier conclusion that *Law's Empire* assigns no importance to coherence in the law is that my arguments turn on close textual analysis. This, according to the objection, is the wrong attitude toward the understanding of a book which does not carefully formulate the views it advocates. The general feel of the book suggests that coherence is to be striven for. Perhaps it is impossible to say in advance what degree of coherence is to be achieved. But the drift of the argument suggests that coherence is a distinctive advantage, and that therefore one should strive to end up with a view of the law which regards it as coherent as possible, provided not too much violence is done to other values.

There is something to this point. The position it assigns to *Law's Empire* is explicitly advocated by Hurley,[90] who seems to think that she is following Dworkin with regard to the law. The difficulty is that Dworkin provides no

---

[88] *McLoughlin* v. *O'Brian*, 1 App. Cas. 410 (1983).
[89] *Law's Empire*, 246–7.   [90] *Natural Reasons*, 262.

argument to support that position, unless the suggestion is made that the arguments for integrity are also meant to be arguments for coherence.[91] If so, then they have been dealt with above. My feeling that Dworkin does not regard coherence, as understood here, as a virtue at all is strengthened by his use of the term at times to convey other ideas, and by his belief in the virtue of coherence when understood in some of those other ways. He believes that the law is coherent = inteligible, he believes that the law is coherent = holistic, and, more distinctively, he believes that the law speaks with one voice (on the strength of the argument canvassed in Part V). In Part V, I took that requirement to imply at least a preference for coherence = unity. But there is no sign that Dworkin does so, nor is there any reason to do so. Speaking with one voice may mean no more than that the law is not arbitrary nor reflects changes of mind or policy. For Dworkin, 'speaking with one voice' means also that the law does not reflect compromises among people or factions. Whatever 'speaking with one voice' means in Dworkin's writings, it can be represented as 'coherence', and it is a way of employing 'coherence' unrelated to the concerns explored here. Finally, 'coherence' is sometimes used by him to indicate fitting the historical record.[92] This again has nothing to do with coherence as explored here. None of this shoes that Dworkin does not regard coherence as unity as desirable. The degree to which, and the reasons for which, *Law's Empire* is committed to coherence must remain moot.

But if I am right in the main conclusion above, namely that there is nothing in the book's advocacy of what Dworkin calls interpretation and integrity to require an endorsement of, or any presumption in favour of, coherence, does this not undermine my own criticism of the value of Dworkinian integrity offered above? Not so. My criticism of integrity is valid even if integrity is not taken to support coherence. It relies on one feature of integrity only: that it advocates acting on principles which may never have been considered or approved, either explicitly or implicitly, by any legal authority, and which are inferior to some alternatives in justice and fairness. The objections I raised were to this as groundless in morality and as deriving from a desire to see the law, and judicial activities, as based to a larger degree than they are in fact, or should be in morality, on an inner legal logic which is separate from ordinary moral and political considerations of the kind that govern normal government, in all its branches.

---

[91] This is indeed Hurley's view; ibid. 262–3.
[92] See discussion in n. 89 above and accompanying text.

14

On the Autonomy of Legal Reasoning

Is legal reasoning *sui generis*? Or is it just ordinary reasoning applied to law? Some have alleged that ordinary logic does not apply to legal reasoning; that it obeys the rules of a special logic. Others have suggested that there is a special legal logic which applies to legal reasoning in addition to ordinary logic. These suggestions have been rebutted often before. Logic is universal and encapsulates (some of) the presuppositions of thought and communication. What is special to the law is its subject-matter, not its logic. When I ask whether legal reasoning is *sui generis*, I do not mean to doubt that it is subject to the same rules of reasoning as other areas of thought and discourse. The question as here understood is about the autonomy of legal reasoning in its use of its specific material. Legal reasoning is a species of normative reasoning. It concerns norms, reasons for action, rights and duties, and their application to general or specific situations. Does the fact that legal standards, legal rules, legal rights and duties feature large in legal reasoning mean that they and no other normative or evaluative considerations feature in it? In particular the question is: if legal reasoning turns on legal reasons, is there room in it for moral reasons? The question is central to our understanding of the relation between legal doctrine and doctrinal reasoning, and morality and moral reasoning. Is doctrinal reasoning—reasoning based on 'the inner logic' of legal doctrines—an alternative to moral reasoning? Or is it an instance of moral reasoning? Can moral and doctrinal considerations conflict? And if they do, which shall prevail?

I

Legal reasoning is reasoning about the law, or reasoning concerning legal matters. A humble enough activity in which most people regularly engage as part of the conduct of their normal affairs. People buy commodities, they worry about manufacturers' and stores' guarantees. They are concerned about their pension rights and other legal rights at work, or in their relations with their landlords, or neighbours. People—at least many of us—also reflect occasionally about the working of Parliament and the courts. Writers about legal reasoning often write as if legal reasoning is special to judges

This essay was first published in *Ratio Juris*, 6/1 (Mar, 1993). It was read as a paper at CIRFID, the Centre for Research into Philosophy of Law and Legal Computer Science of Bologna University, on the occasion of the first *Ratio Juris* Seminar, held in Bologna on 18 Mar. 1992.

and the courts. In what follows I will often adopt the same convention. So it is important to emphasize at the outset that it is not my view that legal reasoning is exclusive to the courts, or that it has a special character when undertaken by the courts. This last point is particularly pertinent.

It is sometimes thought that the special position of the courts implies that there is a special form of judicial reasoning all their own. This is not so. Courts' decisions are legally binding; the decisions of ordinary people are not, at least not normally. But it does not follow that courts reason in a special way. We may—people sometimes do—think of problems which arise before the courts. In reasoning about the merits of the case for plaintiff or defendant we reason—if we reason well—as the courts do, if they reason well. You may say that this is so only because ordinary people imitate the reasoning of the courts. They try to find out what the courts will conclude and they do so by mimicking judicial reasoning. If this is one's aim—and sometimes it is—then clearly one should be taking whatever steps are reasonable to discover how the courts will reason, and on occasion this will include mimicking the reasoning one anticipates the courts will engage in—mimicking them with all their fallacies and mistakes, where anticipated, carefully included.

But that is not legal reasoning. Legal reasoning is reasoning either about what the law is or about how legal disputes should be settled according to law. In engaging in legal reasoning one is reasoning as a court does, but one is not imitating the court. One may just as well—and just as wrongly—say that the courts imitate ordinary people's reasoning about the law. The truth is that no imitation takes place. People and courts alike attempt to establish the law, or to establish how—according to law—cases should be settled. Talk of imitation might have been in place had the law been what ideal judges declare it to be. Given such a constructivist approach to law, both courts and others imitate what ideal judges would do, or at least try to do so. In the absence of legal constructivism we should conclude that legal reasoning is merely reasoning about the law, and about how courts should decide cases in accordance with law.

II

A simple argument suggests that legal reasoning is moral reasoning about the law. Surely the question how courts should decide cases is a moral issue. Some people see it as a moral issue because the very question 'how should one act?' is moral. But one need not take this view in order to regard the question 'how should courts act?' as moral. Clearly, courts' decisions affect both defendants or accused and plaintiffs in substantial ways, and every decision by one person which significantly affects the fortunes of others is, whatever else it may be, a moral decision. A body which is duty-bound to take such decisions only after careful deliberation clearly ought to reason morally.

The simple argument is, however, somewhat too simple. In saying that legal reasoning includes reasoning about how, according to law, courts should decide cases, I mean to indicate a task which should not be confused with that of deciding what courts should do about the case before them. Sometimes courts ought to decide cases not according to law but against it. Civil disobedience, for example, may be the only morally acceptable course of action for the courts. From the fact that the question 'how, all things considered, should the courts decide the case?' is a moral question it does not follow that the question 'how, according to law, should cases be decided?' is a moral question.[1]

III

I want to put on one side with little consideration one argument for declaring the autonomy of legal reasoning from moral reasoning. It arises out of the view of morality as a specialized perspective, comparable to the perspective associated with special roles. A headmaster may say to one of his teachers: 'I am now talking not as a headmaster but as a friend', or vice versa. He could say to his child, 'As a parent I am fully with you, but as a headmaster I have to discipline you.' For good or ill, we assume that certain offices carry with them certain responsibilities, and that these establish what counts as 'thinking as a [. . .]'. The distinctiveness of that perspective is not, of course, in the application of a special logic or method of reasoning. It is in the dominance, perhaps even the exclusivity, of certain concerns. Certain values and reasons predominantly or alone govern one's thought.

Some people think of morality in a similar way. They regard it as a system of thought governed by the exclusivity of impartial concern for all human beings. We can think and act morally, i.e. from the moral perspective, or not. There could be a question whether we should think and act morally on certain issues, just as there is a question whether one should think and act as a headmaster when dealing with children at one's school outside school hours, or whether one should imagine oneself to be an eighteenth-century barrister and spend the evening thinking of whatever happens to one, as he

---

[1] Nor should one commit the opposite mistake and assume that reasoning about how cases should be decided according to law is merely reasoning aiming to establish what is the law regarding the case. The courts may have legal discretion to modify the law, supplement it, or to use equitable jurisdiction to deviate from it, or to supplement it where it is unsettled. The question 'how should a case be decided according to law?' should therefore be distinguished both from the question 'how should be case be decided, all things considered?' and from the question 'what is existing law on the issue in the case?'

might have done. If so, then morality and law are two separate systems of thought each with its own autonomy. Of course they can interact. One can ask whether morality approves of the law. But one could also ask whether the law approves of morality. Perhaps the answer to the first question has some greater significance than the answer to the second. Be that as it may, the ability of one system to pass judgment on the other does not violate their respective autonomy. When reasoning legally one is reasoning within one system of thought, whereas when reasoning morally one is engaged in a different system of thought, and one is free to engage or not with either system.

I think that the view of morality assumed in this picture of the relations between law and morality is mistaken. I cannot explain here why, but I can say a little to explain how I think morality should be understood.

Let me call 'a point of view' any such perspective which we can assume and reason from, or turn away from and shun. I'll say that we can occupy or refrain from occupying a point of view, with its constitutive values, reasons, and the rest.[2] The question naturally arises whether there are considerations which should guide us in deciding which point of view to occupy, from which point of view to reason and act at any given time. To deny that such considerations exist is to make all values and reasons, whichever point of view they belong to, depend on an arbitrary fiat. If there are no considerations which are not themselves optional in the way that points of view were imagined and which determine, if not always then at least some of the time, when it is right to reason and act from various points of view, then all values and reasons, whichever point of view they belong to, are based on nothing but arbitrary fiat.[3]

I will assume that there are reasons which are not themselves part of any point of view and which determine when it is appropriate to resort to points of view. Now morality, I think, must be part of those background considerations which we resort to in virtue of being rational animals. i.e. reasoning animals. Put it a different way: there are values and reasons

---

[2] The expression 'a point of view' has of course been used in several other ways as well. My use of it is a matter of convenience and is not meant to rival its other uses.

[3] I am here simplifying. If there are other values and reasons which neither determine which point of view should be occupied nor are themselves mere points of view, then the above should be modified to allow for their effects. If points of view are seen as nested such that some determine the use of others, then the point made in the text above holds good but in a more roundabout way. Some points of view may determine when to resort to some other points of view. But given that they themselves, being points of view, are optional, the question arises when should they be relied upon. To say that that is determined by further points of view is to be committed to an infinite regress, or to circularity. The only way to escape both is to admit that at some level that reasons determining whether or not to engage in one or another of the possible points of view is governed by reasons which are not part of any point of view, reasons which are not optional—as those in points of view are—but part of one's essence and a necessary condition of rationality.

which unconditionally govern our thought. We call some of them moral. Which are moral and which are not seems to me to be a matter of classificatory convenience, and not anything of any great moment. The thought that that is not so, in particular the thought that morality constitutes a point of view such that the proper occasions to resort to it are determined by non-moral considerations, seems to run counter to central features in our understanding of the role and importance of morality.

IV

Given this view of morality, a new thesis about the relations between law and morality seems attractive. Legal reasoning is a specialized type of technical reasoning obeying its own rules, like economic reasoning or reasoning about plumbing. Moral reasoning can establish whether the law in general or the law of a particular country is morally binding, and whether or not it is in need of reform to make it as it should morally be. In virtue of this, the art of legislation, and more generally of law-making, is that of moral reasoning. But legal reasoning is reasoning about the law as it is. As such it is free from any infection by moral reasoning. One can reason morally about legal reasoning but not in it, not as part of it.

I will call this the formalist doctrine.[4] It is a hard doctrine to sustain. First, there is the question whether the resources of the law are sufficient to provide the resources necessary for the courts both to obey the law and to follow the formalist doctrine. Second, there is the difficulty of reconciling the doctrine with legal practice. Finally, there is the moral issue: is the formalist doctrine morally acceptable? Let me explain.

Whatever the differences between different theories of law, for the most part they agree that the law is intimately related to legal institutions, legislative, administrative, and adjudicative, and their activities. The law directs those institutions to act within their powers as if their intentions, expressed in the legally stipulated ways, will be made law. Arguably not all the intentions of legal institutions are transformed into law, and not all those which do affect the law have exactly their intended effects. Arguably the law is not exhausted by the scope of the intentions of law-making and law-applying institutions. But beyond doubt they form (at least part of) the core of the law. So let us consider for a minute this core.

Given that the law—in its core—is the product of the activities of human institutions intended to affect the law, it is only natural that it reflects the multiplicity of aims and beliefs held by various people manning those

---

[4] There is no agreed meaning to this term in legal theory. See e.g. F. Schauer, 'Formalism', *Yale Law Journal*, 97 (1988), 509; E. Weinrib, 'Legal Formalism: On the Immanent Rationality of Law', *Yale Low Journal*, 97 (1989), 949.

institutions from time to time. It is natural to find reflected in the law conflicting values, goals, and aims.[5] Notoriously, if our sole concern is to work out what ought to be done in order to obey the intentions, purposes, or goals of the law-makers, we will often find ourselves faced with conflicting directives. These conflicts cannot be resolved merely by resort to rules of conflict resolution which themselves derive solely from the will of law-makers. There are two aspects to this point.

First, suppose one relies on rules such as *lex posterior derogat lex anterior*, or *lex specialis derogat lex generalis*, because they are incorporated in one's country's statute of interpretation. The question arises: why give priority to the will of the legislator of that statute over the will of the rule of law which will be displaced by it? That question has good and easy answers. But they do not derive—not exclusively at any rate—from any claim that the law-makers intended their legislation to be governed by the statute of interpretation.[6]

Second, no rules of this kind can provide resolution for all conflicts. There will always be conflicts which escape the remit of conflict rules, however carefully and exhaustively formulated. This follows from the standard arguments for the open texture and vagueness of language and intention.[7] Besides, no actual legal system provides as comprehensive and exhaustively formulated rules for conflict resolution as is logically possible. This is not because law-makers are not as clever as logicians. It is because absolute determinacy of application is not their only, often not their top, priority. Aware of the possible impact of the law on the life of its subjects, they are wary of advancing rules which will apply in circumstances where their impact on people's lives is uncertain.

It follows that, both as a matter of necessity and as a matter of sound practice, insofar as the law is based exclusively on acts of law-makers and their intentions it makes formalism inconsistent with obedience to law. Obedience to law requires deciding each case for either plaintiff or defendant, for the prosecution or for the accused.[8] On the other hand, if the law

---

[5] Plurality of sometimes conflicting values is the mark not only of the law but of morality as well. But for the purpose of the present discussion I disregard the conflicts which pertain to morality itself and focus attention on those causes of the competitive plurality of values in the law which are due to the fact that law is a product of human activity.

[6] Given the existence of interpretative standards, it is reasonable to assume that careful law-makers intend their activities to be understood in the ways provided for by those standards. But this argument assumes that the standards are valid for other reasons, even if those reasons may be—at least in part—the desire to generate a situation in which law-makers will know how their actions will be interpreted.

[7] See e.g. the discussion of this topic in Raz, *The Authority of Law*, ch. 4.

[8] Strictly speaking this is not true. On occasion the court can dismiss the case on procedural or other grounds in ways which, in law, and sometimes in substance as well, do not amount to settling the dispute between the parties. For example, it can find itself without jurisdiction to adjudicate. But these cases are sufficiently specialized not to affect my argument; i.e. the argument can be restated in a way which allows for the existence of such cases. This is

is based exclusively on the acts of law-makers it is undetermined in ways which occasionally—some would say quite frequently—make it impossible for the courts to find for either party on the basis of the law alone.

Of course this argument does not refute formalism. You may just as well say that it refutes the suggestion that the law derives exclusively from, or is dependent exclusively on, the activities and intentions of law-makers. I will call this last suggestion the sources thesis.[9] The point is that, even if one rejects the sources thesis, one has to reject formalism alongside it. The reason is plain. If the law is determined by the considerations indicated by the sources thesis, then it is prima facie arguable that the application of law can be free from moral considerations. According to the sources thesis, reasoning about what is the law is autonomous. This is, of course, no help to the formalist position, for it follows from the sources thesis—as we have just seen—that there is much more to legal reasoning than applying the law, and the rest, which I will call as I did all along reasoning according to law, is—arguably—applying moral considerations. If—on the other hand—one attempts to save formalism by claiming that legal reasoning is exhausted by the answer to the question 'what is the law on this issue?', one has to admit non-source-based considerations into the determination of the law. The questions then arise: What do they derive from? Why should courts be bound by them?

These questions confront the sources thesis as well. But there they can be answered in ways which are at least prima facie consistent with formalism. Within the range of considerations sanctioned by the sources thesis, legal reasoning is about the implications of the actions, goals, and intentions of legal institutions, and the courts should obey them because, and to the degree that, the doctrine of authority establishes that these legal institutions enjoy legitimate authority.[10] When we step outside the reach of the sources thesis to considerations which feature in legal reasoning but which are not provided in accord with the sources thesis, the doctrine of authority is of no avail. The doctrine of authority can only apply to source-based standards, as they are the only ones which are the product of the activities of institutions which in principle can have authority.

I have divided legal reasoning into reasoning about the law and reasoning according to law. The first is governed by the sources thesis, the second

---

because the fact that the law on the matter before the court is undetermined is hardly ever a ground entitling the court to refuse to consider the matter.

[9] This is only a rough and ready identification of the sources thesis. I have discussed it at various places. See e.g. *The Authority of Law*, ch. 3.

[10] See Raz, *The Morality of Freedom*, chs. 3 and 4. The fact that the doctrine of legitimate authority is itself a moral doctrine is prima facie consistent with the autonomy of legal reasoning. The argument for autonomy I am currently considering provides for a two-stage procedure. First the law is morally justifiable by moral reasoning, then it is applied by autonomous legal reasoning.

I believe to be quite commonly straightforward moral reasoning. Commitment to the sources thesis does not commit one to formalism or to the autonomy of legal reasoning.

The difficulty the formalist encounters is clear. He has to produce a body of grounds for decisions which can be reasonably believed to be morally better than any alternative, in particular one which will be reasonably believed to lead to morally better legal decisions than instructing the courts to reason morally directly, and which is capable of being applied without invoking moral considerations in its application. Barring considerations of authority, I do not know of any body of grounds for decisions which meets this dual condition.

Two misplaced objections to this line of reasoning should be noticed and dismissed here. First, it may be thought that, in assuming that legal reasoning may involve more than establishing what is the law and applying it to a particular case or class of cases, I am going back on the distinction I drew earlier between what ought to be done according to law and what ought to be done all things considered. Is not that the distinction between establishing the law and going beyond it? Not so. The law itself quite commonly directs the courts to apply extralegal considerations. Italian law may direct the courts to apply European Community law, or International law, or Chinese law to a case. It may direct the court to settle a dispute by reference to the rules and regulations of a corporation, or an unincorporated association, or by reference to commercial practices or moral norms. In all these cases legal reasoning, understood to mean reasoning according to law, involves much more than merely establishing the law. This still leaves the possibility that the law gives morally unacceptable directions to the court, and in those cases what ought to be done all things considered may well be contrary to what ought to be done according to law.

Second, it may be thought that, given my assumption that the law could be contrary to morality, I have no right to assume that the formalist must 'produce a body of grounds for decisions which can be reasonably believed to be morally better than any alternative', as I have put it. This assumption, it may be objected, presupposes a necessary connection between law and morality of the kind that I am rejecting. Not so. I am assuming no necessary connection between law and morality. I am taking it to be a necessary truth, however, that whatever people do they do because they believe it to be good or valuable, however misguided and even reckless their beliefs may be.[11] Given that the courts are manned by people who will act only in ways they perceive to be valuable, principles of adjudication will not be viable,

---

[11] Even *akratic* actions are undertaken because of the good perceived in them. They are akratic because the agent believes that on balance it is against reason to engage in them, not because they are done for no reason at all. Still, the principle is overstated in the text and has to be modified to allow for pathological cases. This, however, need not detain us here.

will not be followed by the courts, unless they can reasonably be thought to be morally acceptable, even though the thought may be misguided. So let us return to the main argument.

So far I have argued that the courts cannot be formalists and obey the law which requires them to decide between the parties in all cases in non-arbitrary ways. Given that legal decisions have a significant impact on people's lives, the argument ran, they must at least appear to be morally acceptable. This means that legal reasoning can be autonomous only on the basis of the two-stage argument, i.e. only if there is a body of considerations which can be applied without using moral considerations, which is such that its application by the courts appears to be morally acceptable. The doctrine of authority provides such sanction for the application of source-based considerations. But legal reasoning must, due to the indeterminacy of the law which derives entirely in accordance with the sources thesis, go beyond source-based material. The other considerations will be moral considerations, for there is no other moral justification for the use of an autonomous body of considerations by the courts.

Observation of judicial practice, at least in the countries that I am familiar with, does more than confirm this argument. It provides strong grounds for the additional contention that it is sound moral practice, which is followed in many legal systems, to require the courts to engage in moral reasoning to a degree much greater than the minimum made necessary by the argument I have just advanced. A clear case in point is constitutional adjudication of the interpretation and application of bills of rights. Rights of freedom of expression, assembly, the free exercise of religion, freedom of movement, privacy, non-discrimination, and others are typically declared in broad terms, and the courts are left free to develop legal doctrines giving these rights concrete content in light of sound moral considerations. How else than through considering the moral requirements of non-discrimination can a court apply the anti-discrimination provisions in a way which will indeed be an application of a right against discrimination, rather than something else masquerading under that name?

We must reject the argument for the autonomy of legal reasoning which we have been examining. It is based on an analogy between legal reasoning and reasoning about practical engineering problems, or more generally between legal reasoning and reasoning about matters which Kant identified as the realm of the useful and the Greeks called *techne*. Working out how to mend the plumbing is autonomous of morality in the way the argument assumes. Barring special circumstances, the activities involved are in themselves morally neutral. Knowledge of plumbing, or of navigation, or of electrical engineering have their own internal purposes, which can be achieved by the exercise of a skill, an exercise with its own internal 'logic'. Morality comes only at the preliminary stage, when the question is whether the use of the skill for the purpose at hand is justified. Legal reasoning is not like that. It is not a specialized skill to do with the pursuit of a specific, limited good. It has to do with many aspects of social and interpersonal relations, and while part of it has to do with mastering highly specialized rules (like the rules of takeover and mergers), much of it is not more technical and specialized than morality itself. Does it follow that legal reasoning is just a species of moral reasoning? Yes and no. There is certainly nothing in our conclusions so far to deny the existence of a technical body of legal rules and doctrines which require special knowledge and skill for their use. The conclusions I was driven to were merely that (1) there is more to legal reasoning than just the application of that special knowledge and the exercise of that special skill; (2) quite commonly courts have the discretion to modify legal rules, or to make exceptions to their applications, and where they have such discretion they ought to resort to moral reasoning to decide whether to use it and how. It follows that legal expertise and moral understanding and sensitivity are thoroughly intermeshed in legal reasoning, though at times, for partial stretches, the one or the other predominates.

V

There is another argument for the relative autonomy of legal reasoning. It differs in kind from the others. It does not deny that legal reasoning is a species of moral reasoning. It denies that there are moral considerations which determine how legal cases should be decided. It denies that, not because morality should be excluded from legal reasoning, but because there is nothing to exclude: morality—it claims—runs out. Our normal understanding when thinking of moral reasoning in the law (or anywhere else) is of reasoning which appeals at suitable points to moral considerations (e.g. 'never torture the innocent', 'deceit is prima facie wrong') or to tests of moral principles (e.g. 'act only on universalizable maxims'). But suppose that the return from morality, when asked for its contribution to the issue at hand, is that it has no guidance to give, or that its guidance is very partial and insufficient to establish the moral advantage of one course of action over all other options open to us. Suppose further that the return from morality is that whatever we decide to do becomes, in virtue of our decision, the right thing to do. Is our reasoning moral reasoning? If it is, then this is in a different sense of the term. Our reasoning, or rather the decisions it leads to, determine what is morally right.

This suggestion is not, of course, surprising. Whenever we make promises or undertake commitments of any sort we create duties. Similarly, we think of the law as creating duties even when none existed before. The fact that courts' decisions impose duties where none existed does not in itself entail that they are not guided by moral considerations in the way I have just described. But the supposition I want to explore is precisely this. Within certain limits, courts' decisions change moral duties, without themselves being dictated by moral considerations. Once the courts have rendered their decisions, new duties which are binding both in law and in morality come into being. But morality does not provide considerations which make one decision better than its alternatives. For reasons of space, however, I will confine myself to a few remarks on one of the two aspects of the question. I will say nothing on the ways in which legal decisions can change moral duties. I will comment exclusively on the way judicial decisions according to law can be under-determined by morality.

If the state is the soul writ large, then the view I am exploring is not in the least surprising. We commonly assume that, in deciding whether to spend the evening at home or go to a concert, whether to take one's summer holidays in Greece or in Norway, whether to have another child or not, whether to emigrate to Australia, or merely to change jobs in one's home town, etc., moral considerations, while not irrelevant, are not decisive. They are unlikely to form the main substance of one's reflections on these issues. Moreover, we commonly assume that in matters such as these at some stage in one's deliberations reason gives out altogether. Ultimately, we would say, one should do what one likes or wants most.[12]

It is less common to think that the same applies to legal decisions. But think of ordinary governmental decisions, such as whether to spend money on improving health services, or the transport system; on protecting coasts from land erosion or on the development of national parks. Should we not say that here too the question in the last resort is what the people really want? Four obvious (at least partial) differences between the case of the individual and that of the state should be noted. First, the political issue may not be choosing between health services and the transport system, but rather what priority to give each. This difference between the individual and the state is, however, most superficial. An individual too may distribute his resources and time between options, spending his summer in Greece one year and in Norway the next. On the other hand, the state may find that having a bit of all options is not feasible; some, or all but one, have to be sacrificed.

Second, what the people want is not, of course, a question of the wants

---

[12] I am assuming here that one's likes and wants are not reasons for one's action (though they may be reasons for others). This is Aristotle's position, powerfully revived by G. E. M. Anscombe, *Intention* (Oxford: Blackwell, 1957). See my discussion of the same issue in *The Morality of Freedom*. Given that assumption, it is relatively easy to show that such options are ultimately incommensurate. (See ibid. ch. 13.)

of a superhuman person; it is a matter of what many different people want. The decision what to do has to be based on an attempt to give all of them as much of what they want as possible. This—the question of satisfying as many individuals as much as possible within the limited resourses available—is a moral question with no parallel in the individual case. Here we have a real difference between the political and the individual case, a difference which points to the greater role moral considerations play in the political case.

Third, what people want can often be secured only, or best, through co-ordinating the activities of many people. This requires promulgating schemes of action and expecting all to co-operate in their implementation on the assumption that all, or most, others do. Such schemes have to be fair to the participants. They should not require some to contribute more than their fair share while others are allowed to get away with less. Here too we see morality inhabiting public decisions in ways more pervasive than pertains to private actions.

Fourth, and finally, once legal schemes are in place people are entitled to expect them to be followed and enforced by legal institutions. This arises because of the fact that the law is put in place to foster expectations, and to encourage people to plan on the assumption that it will be followed and enforced by legal institutions. In large measure this is the way law achieves its intended social effects. This does not mean that people have a right that the law should remain the same and not be changed in ways adverse to their interests. But it means that changes in the law have to answer to considerations of fairness regarding existing expectations.

These four considerations, especially the last three, show that there is no simple route from the soul to the state, that just because individual decisions are often not, nor can be, guided by morality or reason it does not follow that the same is true of the state. But do they show that all legal decisions are morally guided? Is it not possible that at least some of the time both morality and reason run out in political, just as they do in individual, decisions?

Were moral decisions to be entirely determined by the right way to satisfy existing preferences, it might well be the case that moral considerations about the right way to do so would exclusively dominate the merits of every political decision. But in fact issues of political morality are not at all like this. They are predominantly about securing the environment, i.e. the social, economic, and cultural conditions in which people can best develop valuable tastes and character traits, and in which they can enjoy rewarding and fulfilling lives. Political morality is primarily about creating the conditions which tend to favour the development of desirable tastes and character and provide the wherewithal for good lives. It is about the moulding of, not the satisfying of, tastes and preferences. It follows from this and from value pluralism that there are many different conditions which are valuable and incommensurate, i.e. that there is no moral reason, nor indeed any other reason, to favour one of them over the others. Hence in deciding whether to spend public resources on museums or sport facilities, whether to concentrate them in a few regional centres or disperse them among many towns, whether to favour conservation of the countryside and of farming communities or to encourage urbanization based on service industries, or indeed whether to generate more public resources through taxation or to leave more resources with individuals to do with what they like, in these and many other questions there may be no solution which is best, only a range of incompatible solutions to choose from which are all good.

This view relates to one aspect of morality and rationality. It concerns those aspects of morality and rationality whereby they contribute to the morality of an action by its being guided by reasons, moral ones where they pertain. An action can be moral not because of the reasons for which it is done but because of what it expresses. A political decision can be rational because it expresses 'the will of the people', i.e. it was reached in ways which realize the value of participation in public affairs, regardless of its consequences or the reasons which motivated it. The fact that within a certain range reasons are silent on which decision ought to be taken has important consequences for the evaluation of political institutions, partly because of its implications regarding the relative role of expressive and guiding reasons in their evaluations.

All this—you may say—is very important for our understanding of legislative and executive political institutions. But what has it to do with judicial decisions? Surely they are very different in character. Surely morality and reason never run out in matters which can be adjudicated before the courts. Here I beg to differ. Leaving out of account for the moment the effect of moral under-determination on judicial reasoning, litigated issues differ from other political issues in two respects. First, they tend to fall under existing legal schemes rather than to call for new legal schemes to be put into place. Second, and largely as a result of this, often court cases concern matters regarding which people have formed expectations about their legal rights and relied on them in their actions. These points will tend to give a special character to the considerations affecting judicial reasoning, and mark them apart from other political decisions. But the difference is only a matter of by and large. Quite often courts are called upon to fill in gaps in the law, and regularly they are called upon to continue developing the law, an activity which includes changing and revising existing legal arrangements. Consequently, quite often people do not have expectations regarding their legal rights—at least not justifiable ones—since they know, or should know, that the law is gappy or that it is liable to change on the issue in dispute.

So I conclude that judicial decisions, just like other political decisions, can encounter choices between various options which are good, but none of which is better than the others. These are cases where we say that some reasonably clear and publicized rule is needed or advisable, but that within certain limits it does not matter which is adopted. This would apply to problems such as the setting of standards of care in order to fix liability in negligence, setting standards of liability for nuisance, deciding the details, procedural or substantive, of legal transactions, and many others.

Does this reflection help the argument we have been exploring? The argument sought to establish the autonomy of legal reasoning, its autonomy from moral reasoning. If that is meant to be a thoroughgoing thesis, then the argument is unequal to the task. It may show that some judicial decisions cannot be based on moral reasoning. But it does not show that legal reasoning is impervious to moral reasons. Still, the fact that morality is possible quite often exhausted before legal decisions are done is itself of great importance, and it is a much neglected fact. Its implications are far-reaching for our understanding of morality and rationality, as well as for our understanding of politics and the law. But these are large matters which must remain unexplored here.

Does this argument establish at least a partial autonomy of legal reasoning? Not so. At least, not yet. All that I have suggested was that morality can run out without justifying why one decision rather than another should be reached. It does not follow that some other form of reasoning, a *sui generis* form of legal reasoning, takes over at the point. If we revert once more to the case of individual agents and their decisions, what takes over is choice, a determination of the will not itself determined by reason. Such choice is not necessarily beyond being judged as rational or irrational. It can possess, or fail to possess, expressive rationality. Is the same true of judicial decisions? Perhaps it is. But judicial decisions need not resemble private decisions in all respects. The fact that they are decisions taken by bureaucratic institutions, by people not acting for themselves but fulfilling a role of trust, gives rise to certain additional considerations. It may be unacceptable that people when acting as judges should simply express their will, their inclination or taste favouring one solution over another. This is fine when they act as private agents deciding where to live, where to go on holidays, or even which policy or party to vote for. But it may be unacceptable that their private tastes should determine rules about duties of disclosure of information in contract formation, or standards of care in negligence. If so, we need an artificial system of reasoning which could help determine cases where natural reason runs out, thus assuring the public that the decisions are no mere expression of personal preference on the part of the judges. This, I would submit, is one important and neglected reason for the relative autonomy of doctrine in law. Doctrinal reasons, reasons of system, local simplicity and local coherence, should always give way to moral considerations when they conflict with them. But they have a role to play when natural reason runs out.

VI

We can now gather together the threads of the argument into two conclusions regarding the relations between doctrinal and moral reasoning. I have rejected the strong thesis of the autonomy of legal reasoning. Legal reasoning is an instance of moral reasoning. Legal doctrines are justified only if they are morally justified, and they should be followed only if it is morally right to follow them. The legal systems of different countries, with their doctrines of balancing the powers of the different organs of government, make varying claims, and have differing principles, as to when the courts are morally justified or even required to deviate from legal doctrine when it conflicts with morality and when the courts should leave the reform of doctrine to other bodies of government. These separation-of-power principles determine the official view of the right, i.e. morally right, balance between morality and doctrine, when they conflict. In reasoning according to law the courts ought to follow those principles, which are moral principles, though they may be mistaken moral principles. Thus legal reasoning is an instance of moral reasoning, though sometimes it is morally incorrect, or based on morally deficient legal principles.

When morality runs out, however, the requirements of proper institutional conduct bar reliance by the courts on their personal tastes and preferences. To avoid that, they have to rely on artificial reasons. In those cases legal doctrine takes on a life of its own. There it is quite properly independent of—rather than having to reflect—moral considerations. Within these bounds legal reasoning is autonomous. How extensive this autonomy is depends on the extent to which morality runs out and leaves the courts faced with incommensurate options.

15

The Obligation to Obey: Revision and Tradition

The turbulent 1960s, years of the civil-rights movement and of the Vietnam War, brought, as a by-product of civil strife and widespread discontent, renewed interest in the question of the duties an individual owes his society. It was soon to give way to a preoccupation with what society owes to its members, that is, to the swelling of interest in theories of justice and individual rights. But before it did so, a good deal of common ground seemed to have been established among many of the political and moral theorists who did and still do attend to the issue. It is summed up by the view that every citizen has a prima-facie moral obligation to obey the law of a reasonably just state. Its core intuition is the belief that denying an obligation to obey its laws is a denial of the justice of the state. This is believed to be so either on instrumentalist grounds or on grounds of fairness. The instrumentalist contends that the state will not be able to function if its citizens are not obligated to obey its laws and respect that obligation for the most part. The fairness argument has it that anyone who denies an obligation to obey in a just state take unfair advantage of others who submit to such an obligation.

I have joined several theorists who challenge this consensus.[1] There have, of course, always been those who deny the existence of an obligation to obey the law on the ground that no state can be just. Their most powerful philosophical spokesman in recent years has been Robert Paul Wolff.[2] The challenge posed by the arguments referred to is that they claim that even in a just state, if there can be such, there is no general obligation to obey the law. Not even all those who deny the existence of a general obligation to obey the law have realized its full implications. If there is no general obligation to obey, then the law does not have general authority, for to have authority is to have a right to rule those who are subject to it. And a right to rule entails a duty to obey. I shall contend below that in a very real sense this conclusion returns to the main line of thought of the founders of modern political theory. However, it appears to be a novel position and not

First published in *Notre Dame Journal of Law, Ethics and Public Policy*, 1 (1984).

[1] See M. B. E. Smith, 'Is There a Prima Facie Obligation to Obey the Law?', *Yale Law Journal*, 82 (1973); A. Woozley, *Law and Obedience* (London: Duckunth, 1979); Raz, *The Authority of Law*; R. Sartorius, 'Political Authority and Political Obligation', *Virginia Law Review*, 67 (1981).

[2] *In Defense of Anarchism* (New York: Harper and Row, 1970).

surprisingly has led to a number of misunderstandings as typified in Dr Finnis's article.[3] This essay aims to help dispel some of the misunderstandings.

I. GOVERNMENT WITHOUT AUTHORITY

Let us start by considering the (apparent) paradox of the just government. Most political theorists acknowledge that there is no general obligation to obey the law of an unjust state. But, it is contended, there is an obligation to obey the law of a reasonably just state, and the greater its justice the stricter, or at any rate the clearer, the obligation. But is this so? Isn't the reverse the case? The morality of a government's laws measures, in part, its justice. Its laws are moral only if there is a moral obligation to perform the actions which they impose a legal obligation to perform. That moral obligation cannot be due to the existence of an obligation to obey the law. To establish an obligation to obey the law one has to establish that it is relatively just. It is relatively just only if there is a moral obligation to do that which it imposes legal obligations to do. So the moral obligations on which the claim that the law is just is founded are prior to and independent of the moral obligation to obey the law. The alleged moral obligation to obey arises from these independent obligations to act as the law requires.

Since the obligation to obey the law derives from these other moral obligations, its weight or strictness reflects their weight. The stricter they are the stricter is the obligation to obey. But if so, then the obligation to obey the law is at best redundant. It may make a moral difference if it exists in an unjust state, for there it imposes a moral obligation where none exists. But in a just state, it is at best a mere shadow of other moral duties. It adds nothing to them. Since the obligation to obey exists only in a just state, it is at best redundant.

Consider the question whether there is a legal obligation to obey the law. The obligation exists, but it is hardly ever mentioned, for it is the shadow of all the specific legal obligations. The law requires one to pay tax, refrain from murder, assault, theft, libel, breach of contract, etc. Hence, tautologically, one has a legal obligation to pay tax, refrain from murder, assault, theft, libel, breach of contract, etc. A short, though empty and uninformative, way of describing one's legal duties is to say that one has a legal duty to obey the law. One has a legal duty to obey the law because one has a legal duty to obey this law and that, and so on, until one exhausts their list. It is likewise, the paradox can be interpreted as alleging, with the moral duty to obey the law. It exists only to the extent that there are other,

---

[3] J. M. Finnis, 'The Authority of Law in the Predicament of Contemporary Social Theory', *Notre Dame Journal of Law, Ethics and Public Policy*, 1 (1984).

independent moral duties to obey each of the laws of the system. It is merely their shadow.

In fact the paradox is even worse. The obligation to obey the law is no mere shadow. It would be, were it to exist, a moral perversion. Consider legal duties such as the duty not to commit murder and not to rape. Clearly there are moral duties to refrain from murder and from rape. Equally clearly we approve, if we do, of the laws prohibiting such acts, because the acts they forbid are morally forbidden.[4] Moreover, we expect morally conscientious people to comply with these laws because the acts they forbid are immoral. I would feel insulted if it were suggested that I refrain from murder and rape because I recognize a moral obligation to obey the law. We expect people to avoid such actions whether or not they are legally forbidden, and for reasons which have nothing to do with the law. If it turns out that those reasons fail, that it is only respect for the law which restrains them from such acts, then those people lose much of our respect.

But if the obligation to obey the law is not a morally correct reason by which the morally conscientious person should guide his action, at least not in such elementary and fundamental areas of the law as those mentioned, then can there be such an obligation? Can there be a moral obligation to perform an action if to take the existence of the obligation as one's reason for the action it enjoins would be wrong, or ill-fitting?

So much for the apparent paradox of the just law. The more just and valuable the law is, it says, the more reason one has *to conform to it*, and the less *to obey it*. Since it is just, those considerations which establish its justice should be one's reasons for conforming with it, i.e. for acting as it requires. But in acting for these reasons one would not be obeying the law, one would not be conforming because that is what the law requires. Rather, one would be acting on the doctrine of justice to which the law itself conforms.

I called the paradox merely 'apparent' because it is overstated. For reasons we will examine in the next section, sometimes the law makes a moral difference. In particular, sometimes the law is just, although no independent obligation attaches to what it requires. In these cases it is morally obligatory to act as the law requires because it so requires. But even though overstated, the alleged paradox is instructive. It challenges the existence of a general obligation to obey the law. To succeed, it need only establish that in some fairly central cases there is no such obligation. From this point of view it matters not that some laws are not like the laws against murder and rape. If a legal prohibition of murder neither imposes an independent moral obligation nor makes the duty not to murder stricter or weightier than it was

---

[4] Here, as elsewhere in this essay, I am assuming that the immorality of an action, even if a necessary condition of the justice of a law prohibiting it, is never a sufficient condition.

without the law, then the case is made. The prohibitions of murder, rape, enslavement, imprisonment, and similar legal prohibitions are central to the laws of all just legal systems. Their existence cannot be dismissed as marginal or controversial. If these laws do not make a difference to our moral obligations, then there is no *general* obligation to obey the law. There may be a moral obligation to obey some laws, but this was never in contention.

The argument so far depends on two assumptions, both of which are open to challenge. First, the argument assumes that to refrain from murder or any other moral perversion solely because the law proscribes it is morally distorted and undesirable. It may be objected that while this is not the best motive for refraining from murder it is not the worst either. It is better, for example, than sparing a person's life because he will then suffer a more painful death. Second, it assumes that the reasons for obeying the law, when such can be found, must derive from the reasons for having laws with that particular content. It may be objected that the reasons for obedience normally thought of as constituting the obligation to obey have nothing to do with the desirability of any particular law but with the desirability of the existence of a legal system and a structure of government by law as a whole.

The argument of the following pages will help rebut these objections and will bolster the assumptions, especially the second one.[5] My present purpose is more modest. Even if the alleged paradox fails to disprove the existence of an obligation to obey, it succeeds in making us re-examine some of our assumptions about the functions of law in society. It reveals that much of the good that the law can do does not presuppose any obligation to obey.

Once more, a simplified picture will help bring out the point more clearly. Let us assume that in its sole proper function, the law prohibits murder, neglect of children by their parents, and other similar immoralities. On this assumption it is plausible to claim that the law's direct function is to motivate those who fail to be sufficiently moved by sound moral considerations. The conscientious, knowledgeable person will do what the law requires of him regardless of whether the law exists or not. The law is not for him. It is for those who deny their moral duties. It forces them to act as they should by threatening sanctions if they fail to do so. By addressing the self-interest of those who fail to be properly moved by moral considerations, the law reassures the morally conscientious. It assures him that he will not be taken advantage of, will not be exploited by the unscrupulous.

This oversimplified picture demonstrates the good a government without

---

[5] The first objection is indecisive. The fact that some motives for action according to law are worse than the desire to obey may be nothing more than the ranking of evils. It may show merely that we normally regard intellectual confusion (the belief in an obligation to obey and action for it) as a lesser evil than cruelty, hatred, etc.

authority can do.[6] One can threaten and penalize people without having authority over them. One can also have an organization to issue and carry out threats without authority over them either. We can imagine the law-enforcement functions we have in mind being carried out by people who are paid salaries, or given other incentives to enforce and to administer the laws. The personnel in charge of the implementation of the law need not necessarily be subject to the authority or the government or its law; they may be doing a job under a contract. Their actions are morally permissible for reasons independent of the law. Even when they encroach on the personal liberty of the offender, they need not invoke the law in justification. They treat offenders in ways morally appropriate for those who renege on their moral duties.

The picture is oversimplified. But it is so in what it leaves out, not in what it says. Governments fulfil the functions we described, but they do much else besides. Some of their other functions do not presuppose the recognition of authority either. It is an important fact about the modern state that to an ever greater extent it affects our fortunes by means other than exercising, or claiming to exercise, authority over us. In many states the government, or public authorities generally, are the largest employer in the country, control much of the infrastructure through a state monopoly on the provision of mail, telephone, airport and seaport services, and the like. The armed forces are the largest clients for many high-technology industries, and so on. The details vary from state to state, but the overall picture is rather similar.

The effects of this concentration of economic power are evident in the state's growing use of its economic muscle to achieve aims which in previous times would have required legislation or administrative actions. Governments attempt to affect the direction of industrial development, the level of economic activity, the rate of inflation, the level of unemployment, the regional distribution of wealth in the country, and other objectives through their economic power alone. Even non-economic objectives such as racial equality in employment are sometimes pursued by the use of economic power, rather than by the exercise of authority. It is often argued that the awarding go governmental contracts only to equal-opportunity employers is the best way of pursuing such objectives.

Many of these developments are relatively recent, and raise difficult questions about the adequacy of the existing machinery for controlling

---

[6] My analysis here is loose and informal. It runs parallel to the ingenious discussion of the pre-state existence of voluntary protection associations in R. Nozick's *Anarchy, State ad Utopia* (New York: Basic Books, 1974). I do not share his picture of the working of the invisible hand, nor his understanding of people's moral rights and duties. But my argument parallels his in the emphasis on the extent to which governments do or can carry out functions which do not presuppose possession of authority.

governmental powers. The machinery evolved primarily as a check on the government's exercise of legislative and administrative power. It is ill-suited today to supervise the economic activities of public authorities. Nevertheless, it is clear that only the degree to which governments affect their populations by non-governmental means is new, for governments have always affected individuals by changing their physical or economic environment by means which do not invoke its authority. Governments have built roads, dug canals, constructed state buildings and monuments, employed people, and the like for as long as political society has existed.

II. ON THE FOUNDATION OF POLITICAL AUTHORITY

Governments affect us through their intervention in the market by changing the physical environment, and by providing the morally unscrupulous or misguided with self-interested reasons to do that which they ought to do, but which moral reasons fail to make them do. Focusing on these aspects of governmental activity helps dispel the myth that denying the existence of an obligation to obey the law amounts to denying the possibility of a just government. This myth is based on a misperception of the aims and means of governmental action. If in principle governments can discharge all the mentioned functions without authority, then they can do so justly as well as unjustly. From our perspective it does not matter if the same ends can be achieved by other means, ones which do not involve the existence of governments. I am not challenging the justice of alternative modes of social organization, nor comparing their precise merits. I only seek to establish that those who favour the continued exercise of many of the existing functions of governments cannot argue from that to the existence of a general obligation to obey the law. For those functions can be discharged by governments independently of such an obligation.

One objection may be that the argument overlooks that at least government officials must accept governmental authority for government to function as described. If the officials do not obey the law, then the morally unscrupulous, for example, will have no fear that legal sanctions may be applied to them. The contract model answered this objection, because officials would serve the government by consent rather than because they recognize its authority. This may not be a very practical arrangement in some cases. A more important objection may be that, where governments do not exercise any authority, not even over their officials, one may well doubt whether they are governments at all rather than corporations who voluntarily undertake some good social services. Be that as it may, the functions described which are normally carried out by governments can in principle be carried out without authority. Furthermore, let us remind ourselves that the argument does not require that nobody is under the authority of government. It only claims there is no general obligation to obey the law, i.e. that not everyone is under an obligation to obey all the laws, not even in a relatively just society.

My basic position is not that no one has any moral reason ever to take account of the existence of the law. I argue that the extent of the obligation to obey varies from person to person. In no case is the moral obligation as extensive as the legal obligation. Consider three typical situations in which ordinary citizens do find themselves under an obligation to obey.

First, imagine that I use in the course of my employment tools which may create a safety hazard to passers-by. The government has issued safety regulations detailing the equipment which may be used and the safety measures that I must take to make their use safe. The government experts who laid down these safety regulations are experts in their field. Their judgment is much more reliable than mine. I am therefore duty-bound to obey the regulations which they have adopted.

Second, we all have reason to preserve the countryside. In areas visited by many people, this goal would be enhanced if no one had barbecues. In fact everyone had barbecues in those areas. The damage is done, and my refraining from a barbecue will not help. The situation is so bad that my having a barbecue will not make even a small difference. At long last the government steps in any forbids having barbecues except in a few designated locations. Because the regulation might reverse the trend, I have an obligation to obey this law.

Third, I disagree with the government's policy of allowing the construction of nuclear-power plants. I can try to block the roads leading to the construction sites to stop building material and machinery from reaching the workers. Doing so will be against the law. It will also, if successful to any degree, encourage other people to take the law into their own hands when they think they can force the government to change its policies. This will undermine the ability of the government to discharge its functions. Despite this lapse on the government's part, I still regard it as a relatively just and moral government. I have an obligation to obey the law and avoid breaking it in the way described.

In one respect the last case differs from the first two. Though I am obligated to obey the law, the obligation does not show that the law or government had authority over me regarding the issue in question. In the first two cases my obligation to obey results from the law's authority. It knows best, or it can best arrange matters. Hence, I had better accept its instructions and obey. In the last case there are no such assumptions. It is merely that I will undermine the government's ability to do good. That reason can, and often does, apply to people not subject to the authority of the government. A foreign state may restrain its action in order not to undermine the ability of my government to fulfil its useful functions. But a foreign state is not subject to the authority of the government.[7]

More important are the features the three cases have in common. 1. They are typical cases. Much of planning law, laws concerning safety at work, regulations regarding standards of manufactured goods such as cars, pharmaceuticals, and the like, rules concerning the safe maintenance of cars, or concerning standards of safe driving, qualifications required for engaging in certain occupations, and many more, all belong to the first category. Standards for the preservation of the environment, for the protection of scarce resources, for the raising of revenue through taxation to finance public projects, welfare services, or other valuable projects, and many more belong in most cases to the second category. Any act aimed at forcing public authorities to change their policies or actions by unlawful means belongs to the third category. Some laws are more likely to be broken for these reasons than others, but the violation of any law can, on occasion, be used for such a purpose.

2. In all the examples, the law makes a difference to one's moral obligations. The moral obligation is a prima-facie one; it may be overridden by contrary considerations. But for the law, I might well have adopted different safety precautions. I accept the superior reliability of the law on such issues, and defer to its judgment. I would not have had any reason to avoid having barbecues in the beauty spots of the second example, but for the introduction of the law which gives rise to the expectation that the widespread but damaging practice will come to an end, or at least that it will be sufficiently reduced so that my self-restraint will make a difference, however little. Finally, had the blockade of the nuclear-power plant site not been against the law, it would not have been an act tending to undermine the ability of the government to carry out its proper functions. That is why it is proper to talk in all these cases of my obligation to obey some laws.

3. None of the cases separately nor all of them together offer an argument capable of being generalized to point to a general obligation to obey. The contrary is the case. They highlight the degree to which the obligation is limited and varies in accordance with circumstances. The first case depends on the law's superior knowledge. But if I am the greatest living expert on pharmaceuticals, then the law has no authority over me regarding the safety of pharmaceuticals. Sometimes I have the option of investing time, money, and mental effort in a problem to solve it myself, or to go to a knowledgeable friend and follow his advice. The law, in cases of the first type, is like a knowledgeable friend and the same range of options are available. So that in such matters the range of the law's authority over individuals varies from one person to another.

---

[7] In other words, I agree with R. P. Wolff's contention that sometimes one has reason to obey someone who claims authority for reasons which do not amount to submission to his authority. See *In Defense of Anarchism*, 15–16.

The second example concerns not the law's superior knowledge but its ability to achieve goals which individuals have reason to pursue, but cannot do so effectively on their own, because their realization requires co-ordinating the actions of large numbers of people. Although central to the normal functioning of the law, such cases cannot be generalized to generate an obligation to obey the law of a relatively just state. First, not all laws purport to fulfil such a function. Laws of the kind involved in the first class of cases, as well as laws like the prohibition of rape and murder, differ from laws which co-ordinate the efforts of large groups. In the former cases, the reasons for acting in accord with the law apply with the same stringency in each case regardless of the degree of general conformity with the law. Every time someone murders or recklessly engages in a risky activity he acts wrongly, harming or risking others. Not so in our second example. Here the existence of reasons for the action, and their weight, depend on general conformity, or the likelihood of it. Some laws are of this character, others are not. The reasons which lead one to acknowledge the law's authority in cases of co-ordination do not apply elsewhere. Second, laws striving to achieve co-ordination address masses of people, and are designed to be enforced and regulated through the activities of judicial and administrative institutions. They are drafted not merely to state most accurately the actions required if co-ordination is to be achieved, but also to be easily comprehended, and to avoid giving rise to administrative corruption, the harassment of individuals, and other undesirable by-products of the operation of the legal machine. A person who understands the situation will often have reason to go beyond the law, and to do more than the law requires in pursuit of the same co-ordinating goal. Alternatively, he may find that on occasion he has no reason to follow certain aspects of the law. They may be the inevitable simplifications the law has to embrace to be reasonably understood and efficiently enforced. There is no reason for an individual not faced with the same considerations to conform to the law on such occasions.

The third type of example is often invoked to supplement the previous two and plug the remaining holes. It is argued that, if the law is reasonably just, cases like those of the first two types exist in large numbers. In other cases one ought to obey the law, for otherwise one would undermine its ability to function effectively. The argument is based on a false premiss. Law breaking is liable to undermine the effectiveness of the government in many cases. In others, violations of law have no such effect. Offences never known to anyone or violating the interests of one private individual only, as with many torts and breaches of contract, generally do not diminish the government's effectiveness. There may be other reasons for conforming with the law in some of these cases, but the threat to the effectiveness of government and the law is not among them.

These three types of argument illustrated by our examples are not the only ones which lead to obligations to obey some laws or others. I have discussed them because, other than consent and voluntary commitments, they most commonly give rise to an obligation to obey. They usefully illustrate the main points which need emphasizing. First, that the extent of the duty to obey the law in a relatively just country varies from person to person and from one range of cases to another. There is probably a common core of cases regarding which the obligation exists and applies equally to all. Some duties based on the co-ordinative argument (e.g. duty to pay tax) and on the bad-example argument (e.g. avoiding political terrorism) are likely to apply equally to all citizens. Beyond this core, the extent of the obligation to obey will vary greatly. Second, the extent of the obligation depends on factors other than whether the law is just and sensible. It may depend on the expertise of the individual citizen, as in cases of the first kind, or on the circumstances of the occasion for the violation, as often in cases of the third kind.

III. REVISIONISM IS TRADITIONALISM

Dr Finnis's article[8] exemplifies some of the confusions which pervade our reflections on the obligation to obey. His central claim is that the law presents itself as a seamless web: its subjects are not allowed to pick and choose.[9] This is certainly the case. But Finnis does not even pause to indicate that he draws from this the conclusion that we are not allowed to pick and choose, let alone present any reason in support of it. For him, if this is how the law presents itself, then this is how we ought to take it. To be sure, if we have an obligation to obey the law, then the conclusion does indeed follow. But one cannot presuppose that we have such an obligation in order to provide the reason ('the law is a seamless web') for claiming that we have an obligation to obey. This would be a most vicious circle indeed. Does he perchance imply that we cannot pick and choose, for if we do the whole system of law and order will be undermined and will eventually collapse? He certainly does not argue to that effect, nor does he consider the case to the contrary which I have presented above and previously.[10] Under these circumstances one hesitates to foist and particular interpretation on Finnis's statement.

Dr Finnis's intriguing article contains similar throwaway points which leave the reader wondering how they are meant to be taken. Does he really believe that 'apart from the law' a person 'could reasonably be relatively

---

[8] 'The Authority of Law in the Predicament of Contemporary Social Theory'.
[9] Ibid. 120.   [10] *The Authority of Law*, ch. 12.

indifferent to the concerns and interests of persons whose activities . . . do not affect him or at least do not benefit him'?[11] There are no doubt people who do hold that we have no moral obligations to people who do not benefit us. But such a broad statement has no hope of carrying conviction without any word in its defence. Moreover, most of those people will take the point as militating against there being an obligation to obey the law, at least to the extent that it requires us to benefit strangers. Finnis regards it as a further reason to believe in an obligation to obey.

Finnis tells us that, even if farmers have a duty not to pollute the river, they may misguidedly dispute this, and that therefore the way to get them to do their moral duty is to have a moral obligation to obey the law. They will then refrain from pollution, because the law requires them to do so. But that will be the case only if they will not make a mistake about their obligation to obey the law, and only if the law makers will not make a mistake about the obligation not to pollute the rivers. Even if these conditions are met, they constitute an argument for the existence of an obligation to obey the law only if the law-makers are not likely to make fewer mistakes than the farmers on other issues as well. For the obligation to obey is general, and what is won in the absence of pollution can easily be lost in the maltreatment of old-age pensioners or of the mentally ill.

Those who emphasize the danger of every person deciding for himself whether the case for the law's authority over any range of questions is good or not often overlook this last point. Human judgment errs. It falls prey to temptations and bias distorts it. This fact must affect one's considerations. But which way should it incline one? The only general answer which I find persuasive is that it depends on the circumstances. In some areas and regarding some people, caution requires submission to authority. In others it leads to denial of authority. There are risks, moral and other, in uncritical acceptance of authority. Too often in the past, the fallibility of human judgment has led to submission to authority from a misguided sense of duty where this was a morally reprehensible attitude.

Finnis's elegant discussion of the river-pollution case illustrates one way in which the law can do good, and when it does it should certainly be obeyed.[12] It is a good illustration of an occasion on which the existence of the law makes a difference. While some laws make a difference, I doubt that all do. Some of the examples used above show how greatly many legal rules, all equally central to the law, differ from the river-pollution example. One should not be so captivated by one paradigm that others go unnoticed. Consider the river-pollution case itself. Finnis quite reasonably directs our attention to a time when co-ordination, though desirable, does not obtain and the law steps in to secure it. But travel ten years on. By now (let us

[11] *The Authority of Law.*   [12] Ibid. 134–7.

simplify), either the scheme introduced by the law has taken root and is the general practice or it has long since been forgotten and is honoured only in the breach. In the second case, my conforming with the law will serve no useful purpose unless it happens to protect me from penalties, or to stop my behaviour being misunderstood by others. There is then no point in obeying the law. There is reason to conform with it if the scheme is in general effective. But, as is evident by comparing this case with the previous one, where the law is the same but the practice of conformity is missing, that reason is not the law but the actual practice.

All the questions I raise can be answered. I have stated my answers in previous publications and supplemented them above. Finnis seems to disagree, but he fails to tell us why. He properly explains why the law is a way of achieving co-ordination,[13] but he never even attempts to show that co-ordination requires general obedience to law.[14]

I should make clear my agreement with Finnis in his doubts about the value of social choice and game theory as guides to moral decisions. This is not the occasion to go into such issues. But we should remember that all the arguments concerning an obligation to obey which have been canvassed so far were essentially instrumental arguments. They assumed that we have reason to promote or protect certain states of affairs, and examined whether recognition of an obligation to obey the law, or obedience to law, is a way of doing so. But are there not non-instrumental reasons for obeying the law?

Non-instrumental reasoning is central to a distinguished tradition in political philosophy. Today one of the most common arguments, often repeated in different forms, is based on alleged considerations of fairness. It is unfair, it is claimed, to enjoy benefits derived from the law without contributing one's share to the production of those benefits. As has been pointed out many times before, this argument is of dubious validity when one has no choice but to accept the benefits, or even more generally, when the benefits are given to one who does not request them, and in circumstances which do not imply an understanding concerning the conditions attached to their donation and receipt. Besides, even where it is unfair not to reciprocate for services received, or not to contribute one's share to the production of a good of general public value, it cannot be unfair to perform innocuous acts which neither harm any one nor impede the provision of any public good. Many violations of law are such innocuous acts. Therefore, appeals to fairness can raise no general obligation to obey the law.

The more traditional, non-instrumental justification of the obligation to obey the law relies on contract and consent. Not all consent theorists base

---

[13] Ibid. 134–5.

[14] Throughout I am using 'co-ordination' in its ordinary signification, rather than in the narrow and artificial sense it has been given in some recent writings in game theory.

either the validity of the consent or the reasons for giving it on non-instrumental reasons. Hobbes wished to derive it all from enlightened self-interest. Locke allowed moral reasons to enter the argument, but they are instrumental reasons. Consent to obey is designed to bring greater conformity with the natural law and greater respect for the natural rights of men than is likely to be achieved in a state of nature. Rousseau was the most important eighteenth-century thinker to highlight the intrinsic value of the social contract as the act which constitutes civil society, as well as the personality of those who belong to it.

Consent to obey the law of a relatively just government indeed establishes an obligation to obey the law.[15] The well-known difficulty with consent as the foundation of political authority is that too few have given their consent. This argument in its customary form can be right and wrong at the same time. Consent or agreement requires a deliberate, performative action, and to be binding it has to be voluntarily undertaken. Many people, however, have never performed anything remotely like such an action. The only time I did was during my national military service, in circumstances where failure to take the oath would have led to being court-martialled. I would not have made the oath but for these circumstances, and I do not think I was ever bound to observe this coerced undertaking.

Nevertheless, this objection is also misguided. There are other ways of incurring voluntary or semi-voluntary obligations. Consider a family or a friendship. There are obligations which friends owe each other, and which are in a sense voluntary obligations, as it is obligatory neither to form friendships nor to continue with them once formed. Yet we do not undertake these obligations by an act of promise or consent. As does friendship, these obligations arise from the developing relations between people. Loyalty is an essential duty arising from any personal relationship. The content of this duty helps us to identify the character of the relationship. If the duty precludes your having sex with another person, then your relations are of one character; and if it precludes publicizing disagreements between you, then you have relations of another kind, and so on. In other words, duties of loyalty are semi-voluntary, because the relationship itself is not obligatory. Moreover, they are non-instrumentally justified because they are part of what makes the relationship into the kind of relationship it is. (I am assuming that having the particular relationship, friendship, is itself of intrinsic value.)

What has this excursion into the normative aspect of personal relations to do with the obligation to obey the law? It demonstrates the possibility of one kind of obligation to obey which arises out of a sense of identifying

---

[15] I discuss the issue at some length in my 'Authority and Consent', *Virginia Law Review*, 67 (1981).

with or belonging to the community. Such an attitude, if directed to a community which deserves it, is intrinsically valuable. It is not, however, obligatory. One does not have a moral duty to feel a sense of belonging in a community; certainly there is no obligation to feel that one belongs to a country (rather than one's village, or some other community). I talk of a feeling that one belongs, but this feeling is nothing other than a complex attitude comprising emotional, cognitive, and normative elements. Feeling a sense of loyalty and a duty of loyalty constitutes, here too, an element of such an attitude.

The government and the law are official or formal organs of the community. If they represent the community or express its will justly and accurately, then an entirely natural indication of a member's sense of belonging is one's attitude toward the community's organization and laws. I call such an attitude respect for law. It is a belief that one is under an obligation to obey because the law is one's law, and the law of one's country. Obeying it is a way of expressing confidence and trust in its justice. As such, it expresses one's identification with the community. Respect for law does not derive from consent. It grows, as friendships do; it develops, as does one's sense of membership in a community. Nevertheless, respect for law grounds a quasi-voluntary obligation. An obligation to obey the law is in such cases part and parcel of one's attitude toward the community. One feels that one betrays the community if one breaks the law to gain advantage, or out of convenience, or thoughtlessness, and this regardless of whether the violation actually harms anyone, just as one can be disloyal to a friend without harming him or any of his interests, without even offending him.

An obligation to obey which is part of a duty of loyalty to the community is a semi-voluntary obligation, because one has no moral duty to identify with this community. It is founded on non-instrumental considerations, for it constitutes an attitude of belonging which has intrinsic value, if addressed to an appropriate object. Vindicating its existence does not, therefore, establish the existence of a general obligation to obey the law. For good or ill, there are many who do not feel this way about their country, and many more who do not feel like this about its formal legal organization. It is sometimes said that the denial of a general obligation to obey is of recent vintage. It is in many ways the opposite. At the birth of modern political theory in the seventeenth and eighteenth centuries, there was one clear orthodoxy: if there is a general obligation to obey the law, it exists because it was voluntarily undertaken. That is the view defended here. The fathers of modern political theory also believed that such obligations were indeed voluntarily undertaken. If this view is no longer true today, it is because the societies we live in are less homogeneous, more troubled about their own identity and about the role of government and the law in the social fabric. Society has changed, not political theory.

16

Government by Consent

The idea that the legitimacy of government rests on consent is deeply embedded in Western thought. The role of consent in the legitimation of government is the topic of this chapter, and its theme is that this role is only marginal and secondary.

The first section explains the nature of the problem within the context of the wider issues of the justification of government. The argument begins in the second section with one of the familiar paradoxes of authority, the conflict between authority and autonomy. The attempt to escape from the paradox by basing authority on consent leads to a consideration of the ability of consent to form the foundation of any political authority.

I. AUTHORITY AND DOMINION

It is common among philosophers to regard the problem of the justification and limit of governmental power as identical with the legitimation and limits of governmental authority. Governments exercise authority by giving binding instructions. But their power is not bounded by their authority. Governments, like everyone else, have rights under private law which enable them to own property and make contracts. In contemporary industrial societies, two processes go hand in hand. Governmental economic power continues to increase. In many countries they are the largest employers, the biggest customers of advanced technology, and so on. At the same time, governments have a growing tendency to use their economic power to achieve goals that used to be regarded as requiring governmental authoritative action, legislative or executive. Partly they do so in order to evade the complex machinery for controlling governmental action, which in many countries is stricter and more efficient regarding their activities as public authorities using authoritative powers. Partly they do so because use of economic muscle enables governments to achieve many objectives more efficiently than the use of their authority, with its often inevitable reliance on the inefficient and not infrequently counterproductive criminal penalties.

A theory of the justification of government should encompass both aspects of governmental power. A just government is one that conducts itself justly in both its capacities. It is tempting to say that in their use of

First published in *Nomos*, 29 (1987).

economic power governments are just like any other person, that only their public authority is subject to the principles of justice that apply to states. But this would be a formalistic view, assigning too much importance to the means by which power is exercised. What matters is the power governments have over people, their actions in exercising these powers, and the goals that inform those actions. In all these respects, since governments tend to regard the choice of methods they employ—i.e. the invocation of public authority on the one hand or action as a private agent in the market on the other hand—by and large as a matter of expediency, it is plain that both methods, both kinds of power should be subjected to the same principles of justice.

This is not meant to deny that each aspect of governmental power raises unique moral issues. In particular, I do not wish to obscure the fact that exercise of authority involves a claim that those subject to it have a duty to obey it. This raises the special problem of the legitimacy of authority, which is but one aspect of the wider issue of the justification of government. Explaining the conditions under which, and the ways in which, governments may operate as property-owners involves setting principles defining the goals they may pursue and the ways in which they may manipulate the environment in which we live in order to achieve them. Both questions are pertinent to the justification of authority as well. But here a new question arises: What can justify holding some people to be duty-bound to obey others? Under what conditions can some have a right to rule others?

Consent theories are those that find the answer to these questions in the consent of the subjects to the authority of the rulers. Consent theories are not and cannot be complete accounts of the justification of government. They are addressed to the question of the legitimacy of its authority, not to the issue of the justification of its dominion. Their dominance, at times, in writings on the justification of government is evidence of the narrow perspective through which theorists often see the problem of government.

Having said that, I will concentrate on the role of consent in legitimizing authoritative power. Consent may enter the theory of legitimacy in three ways. It may be a condition, or the condition of holding legitimate authority. Or, though not a condition of legitimacy itself, those conditions may be such that only a government based on the consent of the governed meets them. Finally, legitimate government may deserve the consent of its subjects. They may have a duty to give it their consent. In popular political thought, government by consent often means a government whose constitution and policies enjoy the support of the majority of the population. This is not the sense of consent in traditional consent theories of authority. They are concerned with the conditions for holding binding authority, and with whether having the consent of a person is either a necessary or a sufficient condition of having authority over him. This is the problem to which we must now turn.

II. AUTHORITY AND AUTONOMY

One may start by recalling one of the familiar paradoxes of authority, the conflict between authority and autonomy. Authorities, argue some philosophical anarchists, are there in order to decide for their subjects. Therefore to admit that an authority is legitimate, which entails that its directives are binding, is to hold that those subject to its authority must surrender their judgment to that of the authority. This is inconsistent with their autonomy. Therefore one cannot have legitimate authority over autonomous persons.[1]

Many of the attempted refutations of this argument miss its point. They argue that all that follows from the fact that an authority is legitimate is that its subjects ought to give its directives some weight in their deliberations. The directives of a legitimate authority are valid reasons for action. But that, so the attempted refutations proceed, does not mean that one surrenders one's judgment to the authority. There is nothing more problematic in giving authoritative directives weight on one's deliberations than in giving similar weight to the needs or desires of other people. In both cases one's action should be affected by the way other people are or behave. But in both cases it is up to one to decide for oneself how to act. Autonomy implies an independent exercise of judgment in determining one's conduct in the light of right reason. It does not imply that what is right for one is unaffected by the conduct of others. The anarchist confuses the issue of who decides with the question of what are the valid reasons that the decision should take into account.

Appealing as this response sounds, it fails to meet the anarchist challenge, for it ignores its source. It ignores the fact that authority is justified only if its directives make it more likely that those subject to them will, if they acknowledge the legitimacy of the authority, better conform to reasons which apply to them anyway, i.e. reasons which should guide the action of the subjects if the directives are not issued.[2] If this is so, then authorities

---

[1] The best defence of philosophical anarchism is in R. P. Wolff, *In Defense of Anarchy* (New York: Harper and Row, 1970), though my discussion does not attempt to follow the details of his argument. Cf. my 'Authority and Justification', *Philosophy and Public Affairs,* 14 (1985), and pt. I of my *The Morality of Freedom* for a more extensive discussion of the issues involved in the justification of authority. I there support the anarchist argument against attempts to claim that an authority can be legitimate even if its directives are not binding.

[2] I shall assume throughout this discussion that authority comes with a claim of legitimacy. Governmental authorities do not merely command their subjects, they also claim the right to do so. To acknowledge the legitimacy of an authority is to agree that it has that right. By normal usage mere *de facto* authorities, authorities who rule over their subjects but do not have a right to rule, are included among authorities. Many have seen this as proof that an authority cannot be distinguished from a gunman by reference to a right to rule, for both may lack it. This is a *non sequitur.* While both may lack it, *de facto* authorities are characterized by their claim to have it, a claim that is typically acknowledged, sometimes unjustifiedly acknowledged, by at least some of the population they govern. Only those who claim authority can have it, one might say, remembering that it is the claim of legitimacy that is a condition of the possession of *de facto* authority.

function by displacing their subjects' judgments. They function, and can only legitimately function, by substituting their own judgment for that of their subjects. I will not argue for these conclusions here.[3] But it may be worth noting that they are strongly supported by the common belief that it is the duty of governments to govern in the interest of the governed, and that a degree of success in doing so is an important element in any justification of political authority.

If these premises are accepted, it follows that authoritative directives ought to be such that, in conforming to them, their subjects will be acting as they should act in virtue of reasons that apply to them independently of the authority's action. Similarly, it follows that an authority is legitimate and its directives are binding only if they meet this condition to such a degree that its subjects will better conform with reasons that apply to them if they try to follow the authority's directives than if they do not. I shall therefore refer to it as the condition of legitimacy. Finally, it follows that normally authorities should issue directives after considering how their subjects ought to act and what would be best for them, in order to judge which directives might conform most closely with the above condition.

There is only one respect in which these conclusions diverge from the premiss that government is legitimate only if it is in the interest of the governed. This common premiss excludes the right of governments to pursue moral objectives when these are not in the interest of the governed, or perhaps only when they conflict with it. On this conception it would appear that, if an active anti-apartheid policy is not in the interest of Americans, not even in their long-term interest, then the US government should not pursue anti-apartheid policies. This result is paradoxical, at least if one assumes that each American ought to contribute his share to the struggle against apartheid. If the most effective means of doing so is by the government taking action in the name of its citizens, why should it be barred from doing so by endorsing anti-apartheid policies that will help its citizens do their moral duty? One can avoid the paradox by claiming that, though the US government's duty to its subjects is to look after their interests and nothing more, it has another duty to protect human dignity wherever it is infringed, and that is why it ought, within bounds, to adopt anti-apartheid measures.

I find this an unsatisfactory conception, for it assumes that the duty to protect human dignity conflicts, in the apartheid case, with the government's duty to its citizens. It seems to me more plausible that if individual Americans need not contribute to the protection of human dignity outside their country their government has no reason to do so either. That is, it seems plausible to regard the government, in this as in other matters, as acting for its people. Individual Americans contribute their share to the

---

[3] See the references in n. 1 above for the detailed argument.

protection of human dignity throughout the world in part by getting their government to act in a way consistent with that aim and by supporting it when it does so. This point does not, however, make any difference to the argument below. Those who disagree could still accept the argument of this chapter once they replace the above condition that authoritative directives should be such (that in acting on them their subjects would be pursuing reasons which apply to them anyway) by the narrower condition that the directives should be such that by conforming to them their subjects will be serving their interests better than if they do not.

As was noted above, in normal circumstances this condition of legitimacy can be best satisfied, can indeed be satisfied at all, only by authorities that act having done their best to establish what is the right or the best way for their subjects to behave. There are exceptions to this rule. Sometimes the best way to achieve a certain result is not to aim at it, just as in order to hit a moving target one should aim not at it but in front of it. Advocates of the virtues of the market often argue that one of them is that by aiming at one's own good one does, in a free market, serve the interests of the community better than in any other way. They typically contrast the market with attempts to achieve the same goals through the actions of authorities that specifically aim at them. Be that as it may, it is common ground that authorities try to establish what is the best course for them to pursue. And since that is the issuing of directives which, if followed, will enable their subjects to conform to reasons that apply to them better than they otherwise can, authorities typically engage in trying to establish what those reasons are.

This fact, which is at the heart of our understanding of authority, gives the lie to the claim that valid authoritative directives are just ordinary reasons with (prima facie) force to be added to the balance of reasons when considering what is to be done. Governments decide what is best for their subjects and present them with the results as binding conclusions that they are bound to follow. A government does not merely say to its subjects: 'Here are our laws. Give them some weight in your considerations. But of course you may well be justified in deciding that on balance they should be disobeyed.' It says: 'We are better able to decide how you should act. Our decision is in these laws. You are bound by them and should follow them whether or not you agree with them.' Take taxation, for example. Let us assume that its justification is in the moral reasons individuals have to contribute to the provision of certain communal services. The government assesses the just rate of contributions and demands that each of us should pay as assessed. It does not say: 'We think that that is the just rate, but we will understand if you refuse to pay, provided you did so after giving careful consideration to the balance of reasons, our demand included.' They say: 'It is for us to decide what is the just rate of pay. You must pay the sum we prescribed unless you fall into one of the exceptions we allowed for.'

We all know that the claim I have just described is not the expression of one government's excessive zeal. It is part of the notion of government, part of the way in which, by their very nature, all governments operate. Whatever else they are, they claim the right to rule us by right reason, i.e. to take over from us the job of deciding what we should do, on certain matters. Does it follow that the anarchist is right and that there cannot be a legitimate government over autonomous people? Yes, if one assumes that autonomy requires that one does not hand over to anyone the right to decide for one. But if so, then one abandons one's autonomy when one authorizes an agent to represent one in a sale or in some complex commercial negotiations. One surrenders one's status as a moral agent when joining a trade union which has the power to reach binding agreements concerning one's wages and conditions of employment. And one cannot appoint an attorney to conduct a lawsuit without losing one's status as an autonomous moral person. For all these are just a few of the innumerable occasions on which people find it reasonable to give up their right to decide for themselves on certain matters, in certain circumstances. True, in none of them is one put under an authority that claims such an extensive right to rule as do governments. We shall return to this point below. But it does not bear on the argument against the anarchist.

The anarchist claimed that submission to authority is inconsistent with autonomy. We saw that his argument is not guilty of the confusion with which it is often charged. The anarchist regards an authoritative directive not as a consideration to be added to the balance of reasons but as a decision by another that displaces his right to act on his own judgment on the merits of the case. In this he finds the disturbing and problematic aspect of authority. And in this he is right. He further claims that autonomy implies always deciding every issue for oneself on the merits of each case. This is an unargued-for misconception. One way of wisely exercising one's autonomy is to realize that in certain matters one would do best to abide by the authority of another.

III. GOVERNMENT BY CONSENT

The argument above may give the impression that the conciliation between autonomy and authority is to be found through consent. This is a popular mistake. But it derives from a powerful picture, whose force must be acknowledged. Autonomy is a notoriously slippery notion. But whatever else one may say of it, it has to do with controlling one's life by one's own decisions. To consent is to take a decision for oneself. Therefore, whereas duties appear problematic from the autonomy perspective, for having a duty to perform an act denies one's freedom to act as one wishes, obligation assumed through consent appears to point to the only source of obligation that is consistent with autonomy.[4]

The flaw in this view is familiar. It presupposes that consent is a valid source of obligations but does not explain why. One requires an explanation why one's decision now should bind one later. One cannot dispose of the point by saying that whatever one does structures one's future options, and that many of one's actions or inactions restrict future options. This shows that if consent is a valid source of obligation then it is not the only case by which a person's present actions limit his future options. But this is no way to explain why consent is a source of obligations.

The need for an explanation finds no parallel in ordinary acts. There is no special need to explain why, if I lock myself in a room and throw the key out of the window, my options for the immediate future are rather limited. But there is a need to explain why consent to stay in a room restricts my options. For it does so only if it is a valid source of obligations. And what is and what is not a valid source of obligations is not a brute fact. It is an intelligible fact that can be explained, and which is what it is because of the availability of the explanation.

Many explanations have, of course, been offered for the binding force of obligations undertaken through voluntary consent. If consent is binding, then those who can so bind themselves have an additional asset that is a marketable commodity. They can undertake obligations in exchange for some other benefits. It is in their interest to have that asset, and rules that serve people's interests are valid rules. Therefore, consent is binding. Another explanation emphasizes that consent is a way of incurring special obligations, i.e. a way of incurring obligations over and above the common duties that every person owes anyone else, or which he owes all other members of his community. In that sense voluntary obligations help in the formation of special bonds between people. Since it is desirable that people should form special ties, consent is a binding way of creating obligations.

Both explanations are good ones, or rather they point to the way sound, complete explanations can be developed. There are other good explanations for the validity of consent. There was never a problem in finding good explanations. The problems lay elsewhere. One was the tendency of many to assume that there can be only one true explanation. Those who fall into this trap assume that they have refuted all other accounts of the binding force of consent by producing an account of their own. They then proceed to argue that consent does not have certain features or consequences because it does not have them in virtue of their account of it.

Another surprisingly common fallacy is the assumption that consent, i.e.

---

[4] I will concentrate exclusively on consent as a source of voluntary obligations. For an analysis of other aspects of consent and its relations to promising, see *The Morality of Freedom,* ch. 4.

truly voluntary and informed consent, either does not bind at all or can bind one to anything one consents to. In fact, each justification of consent validates certain categories of acts of consent but not others. And while by multiplying justifications one can extend the binding categories, there is plenty of reason to believe that not all kinds of consent are binding. Take consent to perform a moral atrocity. It can be used to foment or express a special bond between people, or to gain benefits for the agent. But it is not the sort of relation that people should have, nor is it desirable that they should gain advantages by such means. As it seems unlikely that any other justification of consent will extend to this type of case, it is not a case of valid consent. Those who consent to perform atrocities are not bound by their consent.

Doubts about the range of valid consent are particularly pressing when considering the question of authority by consent. A voluntary undertaking to obey a government, which is the major part of consent to its authority, is evidently unlike the common or garden variety of voluntary undertakings, such as agreeing to babysit for a neighbour, to prepare the first course for a party organized by a friend, or to go on a three days' march in support of a campaign calling for a nuclear freeze. The nearest common undertaking is that of the marriage vows. It is a lasting commitment, encompassing many aspects of one's life. But marriages are closely regulated by law and by custom. The many uncertainties that the future holds notwithstanding, one's commitment in marriage is bounded by law and custom in a way in which consent to a government is not. It is considerably more comprehensive and more open-ended.

Governments typically claim authority to govern any and all aspects of their subjects' lives. They do in fact interfere with their education, their relations with their parents, with their children and spouses. They decide which sexual activities are allowed and when and where. They decide how many children one may have, how many spouses, and of what age and race. They decide whom one can visit and befriend, and where and how much, which religion one may follow and where, and in what form, which ideas one may propagate and by what means. One can go on forever with horrendous illustrations of the range of powers that governments claim the right to, and which they in fact exercise over people's lives. You may say: but my government does not control me in these ways, mine is a liberal and enlightened government. I think that most people who are tempted by this response will discover, if they take trouble to study the matter, that their government interferes with the life of its subjects in much more far-reaching ways than they imagine. But be that as it may. It is true that my list of examples is drawn from the activities of many states, some of them in faraway parts. But it is equally true that all of them are matters that each of our governments claims the right to decide. Whatever activity or pursuit you may think of, whether or not it is now forbidden by your law, your government claims the right to forbid it. In just about all states there are legal means to change any law, and to pass any conceivable or inconceivable law.

If consent to authority is consent to respect the claim the authority makes for itself, then it is hard to see what justification there can be for the binding force of consent to the authority of governments, given the extremely extensive powers modern governments claim to have. At this point some may feel that consideration of a long-overdue objection to my train of thought can no longer be postponed. I have dismissed the idea that consent is the only way in which authority and autonomy can be reconciled on the ground that the fact that obligations created by the agent's own consent are consistent with his autonomy is no explanation of why consent is binding. This is true, but it should not obscure the fact that autonomy provides a straightforward additional account of the validity of consent as a source of obligations.

The two justifications of consent sketched above consist in pointing out (*a*) that if consent is valid it increases the opportunities available to people, and (*b*) that the addition is likely to be to their advantage, i.e. to enhance their well-being. An autonomy-based explanation of consent also proceeds from (*a*), but it does not depend on (*b*). Instead it argues that increasing people's opportunities enhances their autonomy, for it gives them greater control over the course of their lives. Here, as before, we are not concerned with the precise shape of the notion of autonomy at work. It may well be that the present argument is based on an understanding of autonomy considerably at odds with that which underlies some of the other claims in the name of autonomy that were mentioned above. None of this matters to us, as it does not affect the validity of the present argument. Its distinctiveness is in being rooted in autonomy and not in personal well-being. Even if people's use of consent is likely to detract from their well-being it is, according to this account, valid, for it enhances their autonomy. Autonomy is intrinsically valuable. One can use it in a way detrimental to one's interest, or in a way contrary to reason. This is no reason to invade or restrict one's autonomy. It is no mere means to rational action or to personal prosperity. Hence the autonomy-based account of consent shows that it is valid even in cases to which the previously delineated accounts do not apply.

This seems to vindicate the belief that autonomy and authority can be reconciled if, and only if, authority rests on consent. Authority, then, derives its legitimacy through an exercise of the autonomous power of its subjects and is therefore not in conflict with autonomy. That submission to authority is not in the interest of the subjects is irrelevant to the validity of their consent in so far as it rests on considerations of the value of autonomy. The last point should indeed be conceded, but the argument is flawed none the less, and for very familiar reasons. Consenting to be ruled by a government, when understood as the granting to it of the powers it claims to have, is not only an exercise of autonomy, it is also a submission to a power that may at any time take away all one's autonomy.

This is not the anarchist argument that was refuted in the first part of the chapter. I am not resting the claim on an alleged incompatibility of autonomy with authority as such. I am relying on the claim to unbounded power that authorities of one particular type, i.e. governments, make. My argument is that, to the extent that the validity of consent rests on the intrinsic value of autonomy, it cannot extend to acts of consent that authorize another person to deprive people of their autonomy. Whatever else one may gain by such submission to authority, no autonomy-based reason is served by allowing another to violate one's autonomy.[5]

IV. QUALIFIED CONSENT

But is not the argument against the possibility of regarding consent as conferring authority on a government based on an unjustified all-or-nothing approach? Let it be assumed that there is a government that rules in a liberal and enlightened spirit. Let it further be assumed that all its subjects consented to its authority. Does not the autonomy account of consent justify holding their consent to be effective for as long as the government continues to rule in the same liberal and enlightened way?

I have not considered that possibility so far, for it is often assumed that consent to authority is an all-or-nothing affair. Either one consents to the claims that an authority makes for itself or one rejects them. No half-way house exists. If so, I argued, consent cannot be regarded as the foundation of the authority of governments at all. It cannot even be the foundation of the authority of governments that are behaving in the most just way, for they all claim the power to rule in all respects. It is now time to examine the suggestion that a qualified and hedged consent to the authority of governments may be valid.[6]

The first question to arise is what qualifications are required to render the consent valid. A ready answer is offered by the condition of legitimacy

[5] It is generally agreed that the intrinsic value of autonomy is the value of an autonomous life, and not the value of one autonomous act throwing away one's autonomy once and for all. Whether or not a person reaching the end of his life may surrender the autonomy of the rest of it, and other similar questions, cannot be considered on this occasion.

[6] A qualified consent (e.g. I will abide by whatever you say unless it adversely affects my interests) differs from an unqualified consent, valid only if certain conditions obtain, e.g. only if the authority's directive does not conflict with the subject's interest. But I will disregard this difference and will avoid considering which is the better view of the matter.

explained in the first section: authoritative directives ought to be such that their subjects will be acting as they should act in virtue of reasons that apply to them independently of the authority's action, and an authority is legitimate and its directives are binding only if, by and large, they meet this condition to such a high degree that its subjects will better conform to reason if they try to follow the authority's directives than if they do not. It was argued that, when this condition is met, submission to authority is not inconsistent with autonomy. Does it not follow that any consent to authority that is subject to the qualification that it is valid only if the condition of legitimacy is met is consistent with autonomy, and is therefore binding in virtue of the autonomy account of consent?

At this point the anarchist is likely to protest. It is far from clear that the condition of legitimacy that refuted the philosophical anarchist's challenge to the possibility of any authority is able to resolve the doubt about the legitimacy of any political authority. The reason should by now be clear. The condition of legitimacy is concerned with one's success in following right reason. An authority is legitimate, it says, only if by following it one is reasonably successful in following right reason. What is left out is what the believer in autonomy cares about most, i.e. that one should decide for oneself. In Section I we rejected the philosophical anarchist's claim that to be autonomous one must decide everything for oneself. Autonomy, we said, is consistent with authorizing your lawyer to decide how to handle your suit against your landlord, and authorizing your doctor to decide upon examination whether mastectomy or radiation therapy is most advisable, and to proceed to remove the breast if he so decides, without further authorization. The doubt remains whether autonomy is consistent with handing over to the government the right to decide everything for us, even if giving it this right will improve our conformity with reason.

Every government, as we saw, claims unbounded power to decree whatever it decides. The condition of legitimacy only says that it cannot have that power unless its use of it leads its subjects to conform to reason. This condition protects against one kind of danger. But does it protect our interest in autonomy? Is it enough that we can decide how to conform with the law, even if the law never tells us to do anything that we would have decided not to do had we decided how to act by ourselves, and had we been successful in following reason? Clearly, sometimes it is more important that we should decide for ourselves than that we should decide correctly. It is, for example, generally thought that, at least within limits, it is more important that we should choose our friends and conduct our relations with them ourselves than that we should do so wisely or successfully. So our first condition of legitimacy has to be supplemented with a second, to the effect that governments can have legitimate authority only over matters regarding which acting according to right reason is more important than deciding for oneself how to act.[7] Since we saw that such matters exist, the anarchist's challenge is met. Government within the bounds set by the two conditions of legitimacy is consistent with the autonomy of its subjects.

But rebutting the anarchist's objection only leads to another objection. Is not the fact that an authority meets the conditions of legitimacy sufficient to establish its legitimacy? If so, what room is there for consent? It appears that one can validly consent only to an authority that is legitimate anyway, on independent grounds. It is important to see that the objection is not repeatable against consent generally. It is peculiar to the case of consent to authority. The reason is that such consent, if valid without qualification, surrenders one's autonomy. This is not the case with ordinary consent. It means that consent to be governed can be binding only if limited so as to be consistent with autonomy. That entails that it must be consistent with the two conditions of legitimacy. But it seems that the two conditions are in themselves sufficient to show both that the governments that meet them are consistent with autonomy and that they are legitimate. There seems to be nothing that consenting to be governed can do. It imposes no duty and confers no right except those that exist independently anyway.

In common political discourse, government by consent often means no more than democratic government. That is, the expression is used to refer to any structure of political authority with legal arrangements ensuring that the composition and decisions of the government are sensitive to the wishes of the adult population. It is arguable that in some countries some democratic constitution or another is better than any non-democratic alternative in the sense of satisfying the two conditions of legitimacy to a higher degree. The doubts just raised about the place of consent are not doubts about the advantages of democratic constitutions. We assume that some system of government, whether democratic or not, meets the two conditions of legitimacy. The question arises whether the fact that one or all its subjects consent to be governed under that system of government adds to its legitimacy.

V. CONSENT AND TRUST

At the very least consent cannot be denied one modest role. Those who consent to be governed by an authority that is anyway legitimate have

---

[7] This brief discussion of autonomy shows that conformity to reason is not everything: how we decide what to do is, sometimes, of independent value. The value of autonomy comes to saying that sometimes there is intrinsic value in a person deciding for himself. But other considerations may make it desirable that others will decide for him, even though this will not improve his conformity with reason. This may free him to attend to other things, or it may relieve him of the anxiety that the need to decide for oneself imposes on many people. Such considerations show, as was pointed out to me by Prof. Donald Regan, that the first condition of legitimacy is not strictly speaking a necessary condition. I suspect that its satisfaction is in

strengthened their obligation, which now rests on two sources even if the one is a precondition for the existence of the other. In this way consent strengthens the bond between subject and government. But can consent do more? Can it make the difference to the legitimacy of an authority so that an authority that is not otherwise legitimate is so if its subjects consent to be ruled by it? The question boils down to this. The two conditions of legitimacy concern the value or otherwise of being subject to authority. What if consent to be governed is itself valuable? Would it not then be binding because of its own value, thus, indirectly as it were, lending legitimacy to the government one consented to?

This strategy seems impeccable.[8] But one may doubt whether it will ever yield the desired result. After all, we are considering consent to an authority that does not meet the two conditions of legitimacy. Consenting to its claim to unbounded rule has such far-reaching consequences that conflict both with one's welfare and with one's autonomy interests that it is hardly imaginable that it can have some other independent value which will compensate for these drawbacks. This observation seems to me right in general. But what if the authority concerned, though not meeting the two conditions of legitimacy, nearly does so? Here, you may say, consent sacrifices very little. It is possible that consent itself will be valuable to a degree that will justify holding it to be valid and thus conferring authority on a government that would lack legitimacy without it.

It is perhaps a trivial conclusion that if but a trivial gap blocks the argument for the legitimacy of an authority any trivial advantage in consenting will tip the balance. But I would like to mention one intrinsic value of consent to be governed that is not trivial, and is, to my mind, at the heart of the connection between consent and authority. Consenting to be ruled by someone expresses confidence in that person's ability to rule well. It is easier to see this if we think of personal relations. Think of a person putting his affairs in the hands of a friend when he goes abroad, or while he is ill in the hospital, or a person entrusting his children to the care of a friend. Consenting to be ruled by a friend is an expression of great trust, and as such is often greatly cherished. One may be deeply touched that one was so chosen. That very fact can help to cement the relation and to deepen it. As an expressive act, consent has here an intrinsic value. People are aware of this, and may entrust themselves or their affairs to the care of another

fact necessary for the legitimacy of any political authority, since the other reasons to abandon deciding for oneself generally in a whole class of cases are unlikely to apply in the relation of a subject and his government.

[8] It would not seem so to someone who thinks that autonomy is a matter of all or nothing, and that its preservation has lexical priority over all else. I am assuming, however, that autonomy, in the sense relevant to this part of the argument, is a matter of degree, and that other gains can justify compromising it to some degree.

because he is the one toward whom such a gesture of trust is most becoming, even though they know of another who is willing to take charge and will do so more successfully.

The same is true, and is recognized to be true, in our relations with our governments. It is seen in some of the attitudes people have to related actions, such as naturalizing in a country they emigrated to, or giving up the citizenship of a country they left. Naturalization normally involves an oath of loyalty. Given that consent to be governed is not a common event, it is one of the ways in which people come close to it in the course of ordinary life. Another is an oath of obedience and loyalty which one has to take upon assuming certain offices, such as judicial offices or membership of the legislature of a country. In all these cases the oath is an expression of confidence and trust. And in being such an expression it strengthens the trust that it expresses. It is no arbitrary legalism that one way in which in many countries a duty of loyalty to the state, and a right to protection by the state, are created is the taking of an oath of allegiance.[9]

If one believes, as I do, that loyalty and trust should mark the relations of a citizen to his government, in part because one's attitude to one's government is an aspect of one's attitude to one's society, then consent to be governed is intrinsically valuable as an expression of such an attitude and a way of strengthening it. Indeed, the expressive value of consent may be considered to be of such importance as to refute the earlier suggestion that it can make a difference only when the conditions of legitimacy fail by no more than a small margin to establish the legitimacy of the government in any case. This would be a mistake. It overlooks the fact that trust is valuable only where it is deserved. There is no value in people trusting their fate to an immoral government, and such trust speaks poorly of the discrimination and the moral character of those who so misplace it. In these circumstances the expression of trust cannot be regarded as valuable either, and consent is not binding. Therefore, consent has an expressive value only where the conditions of legitimacy are satisfied or are nearly satisfied.

This point alerts us yet again to the dual nature of the argument from trust. On the one hand, trust is owed to a just and humane government that has legitimate authority in virtue of the conditions of authority in any case. Since it is owed, acts that express and foment the attitude of trust are valuable. They are acts that one has reason to perform because of their intrinsic value.[10] Since they are intrinsically valuable, there is reason to perform them even where no other reasons justify their performance, i.e. even

---

[9] It is not part of my claim that this is the only way in which trust and loyalty can be expressed or forged.

[10] The argument of the text depends on regarding the relation between a valuable attitude and the actions that express it as an internal one. They are part of the attitude, constitutive of it, and not merely causal consequences of its existence, nor causes of it.

when the conditions of legitimacy are insufficient in themselves to endow an authority with legitimacy. That is why such acts of consent are binding and why they can give legitimacy to an authority that does not have it for other reasons. On the other hand, since the value of such consent is due to the fact that it expresses and cements a relation of trust, and since trust is valuable only if it is not misplaced, the consent is binding, at least in so far as these considerations are concerned, only if the authority substantially meets the conditions of legitimacy in any case. Hence consent has an independent, but auxiliary and derivative, place as a source of legitimacy.

One final consideration: inasmuch as the validity of consent to authority rests on its contribution to an attitude of trust to the authority, consent must be regarded as a marginal special case, since that attitude does not depend on consent and is only exceptionally formed by it or expressed through it. It is arguable, and I have argued the point elsewhere,[11] that the very existence of an attitude of trust in the government includes as a constituent element an acceptance of an obligation to obey the government. And this can endow it with authority over the people who have that attitude, under the conditions we examined above. Such attitudes of trust and respect are normally formed, not through deliberate decisions, let alone formal acts of consent, but through the normal habit-forming processes of education and habituation. They are none the worse for that. Such habit-forming processes can but need not be blind to reason. They can be responsive to right reason. In any case, where the attitude they give rise to is morally valuable, it is so even if not acquired as a product of deliberate choice.

Consent represents merely one end of the spectrum in the myriad of processes and actions that lead to the formation of and that express this attitude of trust in one's government. It represents the deliberate and relatively formal end of that spectrum. This makes it particularly suitable for some circumstances, such as a public attestation of loyalty by officials. But inevitably it can have no more than a marginal ceremonial, as well as an auxiliary and derivative, role. So Hume understood the matter better than Locke.

[11] See pt. IV of my *The Authority of Law*. I there refer to the attitude as one of practical respect, but its analysis makes clear that it is the same attitude that is under discussion here.

17

The Politics of the Rule of Law

I

From a narrow legal point of view the rule of law consists of a number of principles such as *nulla poena sine lege*, that new laws should be publicly promulgated, reasonably clear, and prospective, that judicial decisions should be in accordance with law, issued after a fair and public hearing by an independent and impartial court, and that they should be reasoned and available to the public; and a few others. When we turn from these principles to their institutional and ethical presuppositions the picture becomes less clear. Both the detailed ways in which the principles are understood and implemented and their actual effects vary from country to country. Therefore their moral justification and political significance vary as well. As this essay will make plain, I do not regard the rule of law as a universal moral imperative. Rather it is a doctrine which is valid or good for certain types of society provided they meet the cultural and institutional presuppositions for the rule of law, i.e. those on which the rule of law depends for its success. This should not be understood to mean that the doctrine can be justified in only one way, and that it is valid only for one narrowly circumscribed political culture. Like many other political doctrines (such as that of democratic government) the rule of law, precisely because it varies in details and thrives in a variety of political and cultural environments, can have different meanings and moral justifications in different countries.

This essay is about the political significance and the moral justification of the rule of law in one country, Britain.[1] Its conclusions apply to other countries in proportion to the degree to which their political culture is similar to the British one.

I find two traditions, two contemporary approaches to the justification of the rule of law. The first regards it as a requirement of formal justice. I will call it the 'justice on a bureaucratic model argument for the rule of law'. The second is the tradition-oriented approach. It emphasizes the aspects of the rule of law which depend on a strong, independent judiciary which is entrusted with the major responsibility for controlling and shaping the development of the law. According to it the common law, i.e. the law as a

First published in *Ratio Juris*, 3 (1990).

[1] In *The Authority of Law*, ch. 7, I concentrated mostly on the content of the doctrine and on the more universal aspects of its value.

set of judicial practices which has evolved over time and withstood the test of time, is the purest manifestation of the rule of law.

My own understanding of the doctrine differs from both these approaches, though it incorporates elements of both. You may think that it is a wishy-washy compromise, especially since it does not avoid all the criticism that can be levelled at the other approaches. This kind of imperfect compromise seems to me inevitable when dealing with relatively concrete political doctrines and their attendant institutions. But before explaining and defending my view, I need to say something more about the other approaches.

II

The argument for the rule of law as an aspect of bureaucratic justice regards compliance with the doctrine as a requirement of fairness. The law should be clearly and publicly laid down for all to see, so that people should be aware of it and will be able to plan their lives accordingly. When any dispute arises they should be able to present their point of view in open court before impartial judges, who come to the case with an open mind and judge by the evidence presented, and give public reasons for their decisions. The emphasis is on predictability, and an ability to conduct one's life without being frustrated by governmental arbitrariness or unpredictability. This view of justice is bureaucratic because it concerns the conduct of bureaucratic institutions in their relations with isolated individuals. So understood, the doctrine concerns law-making and dispute resolution by anonymous strangers inhibiting impersonal institutions based on abstract principles and elaborate procedures. It does more than presuppose this bureaucratic context. It positively requires it. It argues for an implementation of the rule of law in a way which requires elaborate bureaucratic machinery with meticulously observed and policed procedures, which can be relied upon to be fair even when used by anonymous officials, and which require for their success anonymous impartial institutions, inhabited by impartial strangers. This approach contrasts sharply with a view of the law as the common way, the common tradition of the people. This is the ideal of *community law*. According to it, the need to promulgate the law is no more than a requirement of clarifying its details. The law should be applied by people who rely not only on skills acquired by formal training but on sharing the traditions of the community. They belong to the same community, come from the same background as the litigants, and rely on local knowledge which cannot be proved in court and cannot even be fully articulated in a reasoned judgment.

The ideal of community law is upheld by some critics of the rule of law, who point out that on the bureaucratic model the rule of law creates a gulf between the law and the people. Its insistence on reasoned principles and meticulously observed and elaborate procedures requires the growth of a powerful and specially trained legal profession. This has two major drawbacks. First, it makes justice expensive. The complexity of the legal process required by the rule of law means that to litigate one has to obtain the services of a highly qualified and highly trained professional. Second, as a result of the growth of a legal profession and a highly articulated legal culture, legal issues are formulated in technical terms, caught in legal categories which are far removed from the way ordinary people understand their conduct and interactions with others. The law becomes financially inaccessible and conceptually remote and alienating. It serves the business community, but is unresponsive and unavailable to serve the people.

These criticisms should be taken seriously. They do more than point to remediable aspects of our law. They refute any claim that the rule of law is a universal standard of justice. The ideal of community law is a valid ideal for some societies. In those societies the rule of law, far from being a requirement of justice, does more harm than good.

The only question is: is the ideal of community law relevant to our societies? The answer is negative. For good or ill, we live in modern industrialized societies which are characterized by high mobility of labour, as people move about in search of jobs, and by a high rate of technological change, fuelled by the needs of capitalism for continuous innovation to make continuous growth possible. In such societies too many people are outside the social support network of stable neighbourhoods and stable customs. Very often they are isolated individuals who will be crushed unless they can rely on the fairness of dealings with strangers under conditions of anonymity. In such conditions the bureaucratic justice of the rule of law is essential. Add to this that we also live in pluralistic societies and the case for the rule of law strengthens. I will address this point later. First let us return to the question: can one avoid the distortions revealed by the criticism of the rule of law? They are real enough.

Here the second approach to the rule of law claims to have the answer. It regards the common law as better than communal law. According to it, the common law embodies the legally relevant customs and practices of the country, as tested and refined by the judiciary. On this view, an essential condition of the rule of law is that the law should not express the will or decision of any individual or group. This applies both at the level of the administration and at the level of legislation. There should be no unfettered discretion. All discretion should be guided. All decisions should be merely the concretizing, refining, and developing of established practices and traditions which have proved themselves by withstanding the test of time. On this view, the bearers and protectors of the rule of law are the common-law courts. Legislators and administrators should be kept within narrow bounds, which unfortunately they do not observe.

I find this version of the ideal of the rule of law deeply unsatisfactory. It too may be an ideal for a homogeneous society undergoing little social change. But it is totally inadequate for societies which are in a process of fast social change, including a high rate of social and geographical mobility, and a continuous emergence of new forms of occupational and social organization, with their attendant moral consequences. The evolution of social and judicial practices is too slow a process to respond adequately to such trends. I am not saying that judicial practices are totally unresponsive to such changes, only that their response, welcome as it is, is necessarily inadequate.

These difficulties are compounded when the society concerned is pluralistic rather than homogeneous. In homogeneous societies everyone, the judiciary and the people, shares, broadly speaking, the same culture and the same values. In pluralistic societies, broken up into ethnic, religious, or economic groups, this is often not the case. Different sections of the population have different cultures and value systems. Usually there is also an overlap. But while the overlap may be enough to sustain a civil society united in its rejection of treason and the major crimes of violence and crimes against property, it is usually insufficient to provide a common understanding of the justice of various ways of organizing family life and other personal relations, of the justice of the economic structure of the state or its civil liberties.

Therefore pluralistic societies fail to have enough shared practices to sustain the rule of law understood according to the second approach. All they have are divergent practices for their different constituent, sometimes overlapping, but sometimes segregated, groupings. In pluralistic societies the law is often required to adjudicate between subcultures, to set a limit to their autonomy, to the measure of toleration they are entitled to from other subcultures, and to the measure of common standards to which all subcultures in a society should conform. Reliance on common or judicial practices in such societies is likely to lead to evil and oppression. It is likely to favour élite groupings at the expense of others. The reason is that social processes inevitably lead to an over-identification of the judiciary with the (or part of the) élite group in society. Given that sensitivity to the point of view of a certain group or culture cannot be reliably secured except by its members, or people who closely interact with them, the second approach of the rule of law is not an ideal in a pluralistic society.

III

So we finally come to the third view of the rule of law, which finds its core idea as principled faithful application of the law. Its major features are its insistence on an open, public administration of justice, with reasoned decisions by an independent judiciary, based on publicly promulgated, prospective, principled legislation. On this understanding, the principle of the rule of law is directed primarily at the judiciary and other subordinate legal institutions such as the police, prosecution service, and administrative authorities. It directs them to apply statutory and common law faithfully, openly, and in a principled way. The principle of the rule of law also applies to the legislature, and directs it (and the courts to the extent that they develop and change the law) to make laws which could be faithfully applied, i.e. to make them reasonably clear in formulation, and coherent and transparent in purpose. It also directs them to establish and maintain a system of courts, and other legal institutions, which are capable of observing the requirements of the rule of law.

The difference between this view of the rule of law and the second approach is its greater emphasis on the role of legislation. The precise constitutional contribution of the doctrine of the rule of law to the political culture of a society depends on its political organization. In the following remarks I will be assuming a democratic, non-federal constitution. The reason for the importance of legislation in modern societies is that democratic legislation seems essential for the adequate government of a pluralistic society in a continuous process of social and economic change. I am referring here, of course, to my earlier observation about the results of pluralism and change. Only democratic politics can be sufficiently sensitive to the results of change, and only democratic politics can respond adequately to the different interests and perspectives of different subcultures.

You may think that, on my understanding, the rule of law has a simple relationship to democratic government. It makes the legislature supreme. But this is far too simple a view. Mine is not the theory that courts should have no share in making and developing the law. I am an advocate, not an opponent, of both judicial discretion and judicial power to set precedents, which between them give the courts considerable law-making power. There are two ways in which this view of the rule of law reinforces democracy. On the one hand it requires legal institutions to be loyal to legislation emerging from a democratic legislature, thus enhancing its power. But the rule of law also sets limits to majoritarian democracy, represented in the legislature. It requires principled, as well as faithful, adjudication.

This point requires a little amplification. Principled decisions are reasoned and public. As such they become known, feed expectations, and breed a common understanding of the legal culture of the country, to which in turn they are responsive and responsible. The courts are not formally accountable to anyone, but they are the most public of governmental institutions. They are constantly in the public gaze, and subject to public criticism. Thus their decisions both mould the public culture by which they are judged and are responsive to it. The requirement of public, principled justification is not a demand for great philosophical sophistication. On the whole, judges who become philosophically ambitious are bad judges. The requirement is for justification in terms of the common legal culture of the country concerned. It is a requirement for justification by reference to the common values and shared practices of the legal culture.

Do I now contradict my earlier criticism of an exclusive reliance on judicial practices in a changing pluralistic society? I do not think so. The common legal culture I am now referring to is shaped by legislation as much as by judicial practices. It is a legal culture responsive to the democratic impulse. But it is a culture created over time, and evolving very slowly. In insisting that judicial decisions should be not only faithful but also principled, I am suggesting that the function of the rule of law is to facilitate the integration of particular pieces of legislation with the underlying doctrines of the legal system. A particular piece of consumer-protection legislation, let us say, should be applied faithfully, to give effect to the legislative purpose, and in a principled way, that is, in a way consistent with the underlying doctrine of contract law. A particular reform of police powers to search for prohibited drugs, to take another example, should be applied in a manner which is both faithful to the legislative purpose and principled in integrating it with traditional doctrines of the liberties of the citizen.

Since not infrequently integration in the existing legal culture will conflict with the interpretation which is most faithful to the legislature's intent, this view of the rule of law assigns the courts an active role in interpreting the law, and a role which may appear to be undemocratic. The courts are required to tame the democratic legislature in the light of existing legal doctrine. In fact, far from being undemocratic, it encapsulates the second way in which the rule of law underpins democracy.

The authority of the courts to harness legislation to legal doctrine arises neither from their superior wisdom nor from any superior law of which they are the custodians. Rather it arises out of two considerations.

1. In bringing legislation into line with doctrine, the courts ensure coherence of purpose in the law, ensuring that its different parts do not fight each other.[2] A law which is incoherent in purpose serves none of its inconsistent purposes very well. In saying this I distinguish between conflicting and inconsistent purposes. Purposes conflict if, owing to the contingencies of life, serving one will in some cases retard the other. Purposes are inconsistent if their conflict is logical. Pluralistic societies always espouse conflicting values. But no rational society should entertain inconsistent ones. The desire to enable women to pursue independent careers conflicts with the need to preserve the family bond, and calls for compromises. But the desires to allow divorce on demand and ensure the indissolubility of marriage are

---

[2] See *ibid.* ch. 10.

inconsistent. The courts continuously interpret statutes and refashion doctrine to avoid incoherencies, and to turn them into conflicting values which are amenable to compromise.

2. The second basis for the authority of the courts to integrate legislation with doctrine is the need to mix the fruits of long-established traditions with the urgencies of short-term exigencies. Legislatures, because of their preoccupation with current problems, and their felt need to secure re-election by a public all too susceptible to the influences of the short term, are only too liable to violent swings and panic measures. Those effects are mitigated by the courts as guardians of the tradition.

There is no denying that both these justifications are anti-majoritarian. But then, no cogent political theory has ever found much merit in majoritarianism. The two justifications are, however, democratic in a deeper sense. In ensuring the coherence of the law they ensure the effectiveness of democratic rule. In giving weight to the preservation of long-established doctrines (= traditions), they protect the long-term interests of the people from being swamped by the short term. In doing whatever they do in a reasoned and public way, they make themselves susceptible to public criticism, and therefore to indirect public influences, and this, together with their being ultimately subject to the power of the legislature, guarantees their ultimate accountability.

There is one apparent omission from this account of the rule of law which may surprise some readers. I have said nothing about the importance of the protection of basic civil rights to the rule of law. This is not because the rule of law can flourish while basic civil rights are violated. It is because their protection is partly presupposed and partly implied by the points made above. Since my discussion of the moral and political significance of the rule of law is confined to its function in democratic societies, those political and civil rights without which no democracy can prosper are here presupposed. Since the rule of law assures individuals of bureaucratic justice, it implies conformity with many civil rights which guarantee the fair process of the law. Finally, and most importantly, in insisting on the integration of legislation and other current measures with legal tradition enshrined in doctrine, the rule of law respects those civil rights which are part of the backbone of the legal culture, part of its fundamental traditions.

I would not deny that this way of breaking up the application of the rule of law to civil rights is itself significant. It attests to a reluctance to give them pride of place in the legal culture, and its morality. It implies a claim that they should be seen as historically conditioned, and as fulfilling a variety of roles, the most important of which may be as an element in the fundamental legal tradition of a country, an element among others.[3]

---

[3] *The Morality of Freedom*, ch. 10.

We now see that my picture of the rule of law is not altogether unrelated to the second approach which I criticized above. The rule of law functions in modern democracies to ensure a fine balance between the power of a democratic legislature and the force of tradition-based doctrine. In guaranteeing this balance lies its value as an element in the doctrine of good government. In curtailing arbitrary power, and in securing a well-ordered society, subject to accountable, principled government, lies the value of the rule of law.

IV

As was indicated at the outset, formally speaking the rule of law is observed whenever a small number of principles is respected, like public promulgation, no punishment without law, no retroactivity (generally speaking), clarity of law, avoiding free discretion in favour of guided discretion, by the administration and the courts. I have emphasized the political significance of these principles in (some) contemporary democracies. I have argued that in such societies the rule of law encapsulated in the idea of principled decision-making is essentially a device for the separation of powers. On the one hand it requires judicial faithfulness to legislature, reigning in the forces of the court and the executive. On the other hand it calls on the courts to act to integrate legislation and doctrine, a task which requires independence and ability to withstand political pressures. It should be clear that these benefits of the rule of law are valuable, and obtainable only in countries with certain practices and traditions.

The first and most important is that the country must be suitable for democratic government. This demands above all a culture of restraint and willingness to compromise. It requires a spirit of restraint and compromise on the part of the current minority, which has to submit to policies which go against its interests and beliefs, and it requires a spirit of restraint and compromise by the majority, which has to avoid taking advantage of its current dominance in a way which disregards the interests and beliefs of the current minorities. But this is obviously not the occasion to elaborate on the cultural presuppositions of democracy.

So let me turn to the second presupposition, which is the existence of a strong and independent judiciary, legal profession, and civil service. We often emphasize the importance of an independent judiciary. But it is crucial to remember that it can be independent only if it is supported by a strong and independent legal profession. A politically manipulable legal profession can subvert the rule of law just as much as weak and politically manipulable courts. In addition one requires an independent civil service, owing allegiance first to the law and only under the law to the government of the day. Again, the ways in which a corrupt police force or civil service can undermine the rule of law are too numerous and too obvious to require elaboration.

Finally, to sustain the independence of the courts, police, legal profession, and civil service, one requires a pervasive common culture, bridging the differences between the subcultures of the country. One requires a culture of legality, of respect for the law, and a willingness to abide by it even when one loses by it. To be viable, this means a culture in which people are accustomed to measure their situation, and their relations to others, in legal terms. They may think of their needs, and of their rights, in the light of the norms of their subculture, or of their own moral views, but they accept that when disagreements arise, and have to be settled by public authorities, the law provides the common measure of right and wrong in the country.

V

My remarks were meant to show the value of the rule of law in a fast changing pluralistic society. I emphasized two virtues: Bureaucratic justice, the protection of the individual in anonymous social surroundings; Democratic continuity. I also argued that these virtues can only be achieved in a country with a democratic culture, and a culture of legality with a tradition of independence for the courts, the legal profession, the police, and the civil service. It is not an ideal which can be secured by passing a few statutes.

It is also not an ideal free from blemish. It brings in its wake the problems of denial of effective access to the courts, and of alienation from the law. To some extent there is no escape from these blemishes. We have to be chastened by an awareness of their existence, do our best to minimize them, and be modest in our pride in the rule of law.

INDEX OF NAMES